Best wishes

Maclaren

A Derbyshire Armory

Compiled by
Maxwell Craven

Illustrated by
Elizabeth Forrest

Derbyshire Record Society
Volume XVII, 1991

Published by the Derbyshire Record Society
9 Caernarvon Close, Chesterfield S40 3DY

First published 1991

ISBN 0 946324 13 1

Typeset at Oxford University Computing Centre

Printed by Technical Print Services Ltd
Brentcliffe Avenue, Carlton Road
Nottingham NG3 7AG

CONTENTS

NOTE BY GENERAL EDITOR

The Derbyshire Record Society wishes to expresses its profound gratitiude to the Marc Fitch Fund for a generous benefaction in support of this publication, which has enabled the Society to include 80 line drawings of shields in the text and, for the first time ever, to use full-colour printing for the dust-jacket.

Members will be aware that some five years have elapsed since Mr Craven's work was provisionally accepted for publication by the Society and the committee is grateful for the forbearance of both members and the Marc Fitch Fund during this period. Much of this time has been spent in revising the text with the aim, as far as this is possible in a work of this sort, of achieving consistency in the inclusion or exclusion of material and in the presentation of information, including references to authorities. Although there has been considerable progress in this direction, Mr Craven's work remains a pioneer attempt to catalogue a very large amount of detail in a field in which little has previously been published for Derbyshire. He would be grateful, therefore, if readers who notice errors or omissions would send them to him for inclusion in a supplementary publication.

Special difficulty has been experienced in deciding which families resident in Derbyshire since 1945 should be included, in view of the more rapid changes in professional and social mobility which have obtained over the last half-century. The committee hopes that anyone living in the county today who feels that his or her arms have been omitted will overlook the inadvertent discourtesy and will send details to Mr Craven.

Finally, the Society's best thanks are due to its Assistant Editor, Dr David Edwards, who has not only assisted in the unusually onerous task of reading the proofs of this book but is entirely responsible for compiling the index of place-names. This has involved far more than merely preparing slips for typesetting, since, as far as possible, the parish and county in which every place is situated has been identified in the hope of eliminating errors. The entire text was also read in proof by Mr Gladwyn Turbutt and Mr Dudley Fowkes.

ACKNOWLEDGEMENTS

I owe a considerable debt of gratitude to a great many people in the gestation of this volume. One or two, however, are pre-eminent: my wife, Carole, whose entire acquaintanceship with me and marriage has been interwoven around eruptions of Derbyshire heraldry, deserves gratitude enough for such forbearance. My indebtedness must go further than that, however, for she has read proofs, checked references, annotated MSS, compiled tables and driven great distances to enable me to see achievements, mainly in churches and private residences. My late and much missed friend, Prince Michael Grousinski, who originally suggested writing this book, also put in many hours of sterling work as my 'agent' in London, checking MSS in the British Library and elsewhere. Thirdly, I must record my thanks to my friend Robert Innes-Smith – himself a distinguished heraldic writer – who read proofs, suggested alterations and emendations and contributed information and ideas, to the lasting benefit of this work.

Others, too, have been constantly plagued by my quest for information, especially Sylvia Bown and her colleagues at Derby Local Studies Library, and her predecessor Ann Mellors. Their colleagues at the Derbyshire Record Office have also rendered indispensable advice and assistance, especially Miss Joan Sinar, formerly the County Archivist, and Mrs Miriam Wood. I must also express my special thanks to Anthony Hoyte, who has, over the years, so zealously and assiduously sought to encourage and promote this work.

I also extend my thanks to all the following: Judy Anderson, P. Bander van Duren, the late E.J. Barber, the Very Revd R.A. Beddoes, Mark Bence-Jones, Martin Biddle, Peter Billson, Michael Bishop, J. Blackwall, T. Boden, H. Bodkin, Messrs Brigden of Derby, J.T. Brighton, C. Carr, R.H.C. Carr-Gregg, Major J.W. Chandos-Pole, Roy Christian, David Coke-Steele, Prof. Anthony Cox, Richard Craven-Smith-Milnes, Mrs O.A. Dale, James Darwin, the Derbyshire Family History Society, G. Dethick, P. Dethick, Anne Donnelly, the late George Dow, the Revd J.O. Drackley, W.M. Draycott, David Durant, J. Eardley-Simpson, the East Midlands Heraldry Society, D.G. Edwards, the late Sir John Every Bt, the late Claude

Fitzherbert, John Freeman, Dudley Fowkes, Major A.J. Francis, David Fraser, the late Humphrey Gladwin-Errington, R. Goodall, Clifford Harpur, J.L. Harpur, the late Charles Harpur-Crewe, Anne Haslam, C.E. Heather, Jack Henderson, A.J.M. Henniker, Mark Higginson, Col. and Mrs Peter Hilton, J. Holden, D. Hopkin, P.R. Huey, R.G. Hughes, Vivienne Irish, Pamela Kettle, Mr and Mrs M.A.B. Mallender, the late Rosemary Meynell, Canon P.W. Miller, A.F. Minshull, the late Patrick Montague-Smith, Ambrose Moor, the Ven. R.D. Ninis, Prof. Richard Osborne, Robin Payne, J.R. Pierrepont, Princess Judith Rhodocanakis-Dukas, Mary Rose Rogers, Chris Rose, Edward Saunders, G.M. du Sautoy, Michael J. Sayer, Viscount Scarsdale, the Earl of Shrewsbury, Sir Reresby Sitwell Bt, Mr and Mrs C. Smith, Lord Stafford, Mr and Mrs M.F. Stanley, Mrs M.A. Steel, Jane Steer, D. Swinscoe, the late Lord Teignmouth, Peter Townend, Gladwyn Turbutt, Howard Usher, W.J.C. Waddingham, Sir Charles Wolseley Bt, Pamela Lady Wolseley, Margaret Ward, David Wilson and the late Tom Wrigley.

Finally, I would like to express my thanks to the Derbyshire Record Society for agreeing to publish the work and, most especially, to Sir Colin Cole, Garter King of Arms, for allowing his officers and staff to assist me so unstintingly.

INTRODUCTION

Despite its value as historical evidence, heraldry has suffered some neglect as a subject worthy of serious study. This, however, is to misunderstand a living, thriving phenomenon. Heraldry is some 850 years old and is still in use throughout much of the world. A perusal of the twentieth-century grants of arms in this book alone demonstrates the vitality of the tradition, although the emphasis has swung from personal arms to those of institutions, such as local authorities, public utilities and some larger companies. The main value of heraldry to the historian, however, is the information which can be gleaned from the correct identification of arms, which often provides a vital short cut in the interpretation of other material.

It is not the function of this volume to serve as a manual of heraldry, of which several can be found in any reference library. All provide a simple guide to the complex terminology which is as old as heraldry itself, and is based on the Norman French used by the first heralds. Without it, the blazon, or description, of coats of arms would be impossibly long-winded. Without an understanding of these terms this book will not make much sense, but once the reader has mastered the essentials, few of the terms will present any difficulty, especially as an effort has been made here to render the blazons into a standard format, rather than quote the original wording in every case.

The inventory of Derbyshire arms presented here includes not only all arms authorised by the College of Arms for use by those entitled to bear the, but those mistakenly or deliberately assumed by individuals and found in local sources. The latter category comprises nearly half the entries, since various kinds of unauthorised arms are constantly met with, and to have catalogued merely those arms of unquestionable legitimacy would have rendered this work seriously inadequate. The scope of the book is limited to arms borne by individuals belonging to families long domiciled in the county since the introduction of heraldry in the twelfth century, or by their descendants.

Heraldry was taken up first by the higher nobility in the second quarter of the twelfth century. From there it spread to the knights and, ultimately, to other landed families. Even at this stage, there were instances of this misuse of arms, which henceforth constituted a growing problem. The College of Arms came into being in 1415. Prior to this grants of arms, where such things could be said to have existed, were made by the sovereign, princes and great nobles to their followers, as for example the grant to Mackworth of Mackworth by Lord Audley in 1404. This gave rise to anomalies, while the lack of a general registry of arms allowed a man to claim arms to which he was not entitled, knowing that a check would be well-nigh impossible. From 1415, however, the sovereign arrogated solely to himself the right to grant arms and appointed the officers who made up the College under Garter Principal King of Arms and, ultimately, the Earl Marshal. This did not in itself eliminate the abuses, but it helped to contain them, gave men desirous of bearing arms a channel through which their wishes might be met, and set up machinery, including the Court of Chivalry, to redress abuse.

From 1530 the heralds instituted their 'Visitations' of the counties of England. In their fully developed form the visitations were preceded by notices published locally through the sheriff that all pretending to arms and the estate of gentleman in a particular county should present themselves at a certain place over a certain period of days. Those summoned had to show what arms they bore and by what authority, and have their pedigrees recorded. From 1570, evidence from original documents and dates were added to the basic information previously recorded.

The bearing of arms is by hereditary right from the grantee, sometimes extending further by remainders added to grants, more frequently so from the later seventeenth century. Thus, at the visitations, the gentry had to prove their right to arms by a grant, patent or similar document, and provide a pedigree accompanied by sufficient proofs to demonstrate their entitlement. Some families entered pedigrees but 'disclaimed' any right to arms: in other words, they claimed to have no pretensions to such things. Sometimes, such people had been using arms without authority and merely wished to disguise the fact. Others exhibited arms to the heralds but these were shown to have been falsely assumed. Such people were branded 'usurpers' and their heraldic ensigns regarded as illegal. Others again exhibited arms but for some reason had either lost their entitlement or their ancestors had been bearing them from a period before the regulation of arms. Or they were simply 'trying it on' in the hope of convincing the heralds that their achievement was genuine. In all such cases, the heralds could not, for their part, prove that the arms were the subject of usurpation from another family or had been invented. Sometimes it was merely lack of genealogical evidence of descent from the grantee that was the problem, as with Sir Francis Rodes of Barlborough Hall. These cases were usually marked 'sans proof' or 'respited for proof': that is, claimants were allowed further time to produce better evidence. On other occasions, arms falling between two stools in this way were entered in the herald's notes 'with a dubit'. Sometimes such notes include expressions like 'Promised to come to London'. In this case, the idea was for the claimant, having failed to provide proof, to come to the College of Arms, and arrange for a grant, exemplification or confirmation of arms. There are numerous examples of these reservations in this volume, many never subsequently resolved, including quite grand families, with long armigerous traditions. Others simply 'did not appear'.

In Derbyshire, heralds made visitations in 1569, 1611, 1634 and 1662. Another was planned for 1688 but the revolution of that year put paid to the whole concept. The last visitation to be completed was that of Northamptonshire in 1687. Nevertheless, a set of notes, combining on-the-spot assessments by local agents and comments drawn up by the heralds from previous visitations, was compiled as a preliminary, which provides a great deal of information, especially about disclaimers, usurpers and 'dubited' arms. These notes include grants made between 1662 and 1686, mainly to previous disclaimers and those respited for proof, and lists of likely candidates for future grants.

The end of the visitations led to an upsurge in the use of unauthorised arms: the number of eighteenth- and early nineteenth-century examples in the text tell their own story. The number seems to increase during the nineteenth century, as the examples published here show.

THE PRIMARY SOURCES FOR DERBYSHIRE HERALDRY

A definite attempt has been made in this volume to differentiate between authorised arms and those assumed without authority, although precision in this matter is by no means easy. All (or nearly all) grants of arms, with dates and the names of the officers of arms responsible, have been published, mainly without blazons, by the Harleian Society, including those made under royal licence but not those allowed in visitations which were not covered by previous grants. In both cases the originals are in the College of Arms but the visitations were widely copied and many versions exist in national and local collections. The problem is that information regarding usurpers, dubits, unproved and similar entries in the visitations are in the notes prepared at the time by the heralds and now at the College of Arms. In the case of Derbyshire, this lack is remedied by the notes prepared by the heralds with a view to conducting a visitation in 1688. The main problem is to identify the arms displayed by the usurpers and others from elsewhere, which has been attempted as necessary in the main text. Another problem is that many of the copies of visitations disagree, making consultation of the originals highly desirable. The difficulty here, as with uncertain grants, is that to consult the College of Arms – which supports itself mainly from fees – would be prohibitively expensive. Nevertheless, thanks to the kindness of Sir Colin Cole, Garter King of Arms, details of a number of unpublished grants have been made available. With regard to the numerous discrepancies in visitation manuscripts, I have sought to mention all substantial variations but not ventured to say which is correct without corroborative evidence.

For arms in use before the establishment of the College, the best evidence is that found in the medieval rolls of arms, of which there are fifty or so in all, both in the College of Arms and elsewhere. Most are lists of sovereigns, princes, noblemen, knights and, occasionally, gentlemen, named (often without a locale to identify them firmly) with their arms; some take the form of ordinaries laid out thematically in accordance with the main charges and tinctures; others are heraldically illuminated manuscripts or lists of knights and nobles present at certain events – sieges, treaties, tournaments and the like – with their arms. The earliest of these date from the time of Henry III (1216–72), the latest from the early sixteenth century. Quite a few are sixteenth- or seventeenth-century copies of lost originals, with mistakes in copying adding to the problem of interpretation, quite apart from inaccuracies present in the originals. A further difficulty is that some rolls were retrospective compilations, which leads to speculative attributions, errors and inventions.

Apart from the rolls, seals are a valuable source. For example, Challoner's manuscript copy of the Derbyshire visitations of 1569 and 1611 contain copies of many seals, as do some other manuscripts, as well as medieval church glass, much of which was destroyed by the Puritans or Victorians. Monumental inscriptions constitute another source for both authorised and unauthorised arms right up to the present. Many of those in Derbyshire were recorded *c.* 1710 by Francis Bassano, whose notes are now at the College of Arms. Other sources include church plate and hatchments.

THE SCOPE OF THIS VOLUME

Quite apart from efforts to decide what arms are and are not authorised, an attempt has to be made to define the scope of a volume such as this. All arms found in Derbyshire used by families resident or owning substantial landed property in the county, or originating in Derbyshire, are included.

Excluded are professional people whose careers brought them into the county and took them out of it, such as most clergy. Exceptionally, such people have been included, such as the Revd William Mompesson, the hero of the Eyam plague. Excluded also are doctors, justices in eyre, castellans, constables of castles and MP's not of local origin. The expansion of the population of the county from 160,000 in 1801 to about 890,000 in 1977 implies that the representatives of many more armigerous families must have come to reside in Derbyshire, especially over the last fifty years. There may thus be many who consider themselves or their kin slighted through omission. Nevertheless, an earlier cut-off date would have been out of the question, simply because grants and grants under royal licence have been obtained by representatives of families long established in Derbyshire up to the present, and without their being recorded this work would have been incomplete. Information on less prominent armigerous families who have come into the county since 1900 has also been harder to come by, so that the entries here may be less complete for the twentieth century than for earlier periods.

Under each entry, in which personal names have, as far as possible, been modernised, are given the places in Derbyshire with which the family in question has been associated. Where these places are not themselves parishes, the parish has been given in brackets after each name. Then comes the blazon of the arms: first the shield, followed by the crest and, where applicable, the supporters and motto. If the blazon includes only shield and motto, then it may be assumed there is no crest (or none known). Where an entry refers to a peer, supporters are included where known. Where an entry refers to a person descended from a peer (but not himself holding the title), or other person entitled to supporters, or an ancestor of a peer, then the suporters, dates of creation (and, where applicable, extinction) and additional grants are given. In brackets after the blazon will be found a reference, generally abbreviated according to the conventions listed below. The blazons have been modernised in accordance with standard usage; no tinctures are given for chapeaux unless those in the grant differ from *gules turned up ermine*. If a date of grant is known, then the reference following the grant is merely to an illustration of the arms, e.g. in Fox-Davies or one of Burke's publications. Dates are all new style. If the only authenticating source is a visitation or a medieval roll of arms, this is stated. If the arms are of unknown authenticity or unauthorised, then the reference is to the source of the information. Also included are entries for visitation 'disclaimers' and others whose arms are not known.

In the explanatory text which follows the blazon is recorded (where known) the date of the grant, the earliest date the arms were allowed at a visitation, or the earliest date attributable to the bearer of the arms in a medieval roll. Also included is the name of the person to whom the grant was made but not the responsible officer of arms. If the grantee is not of Derbyshire descent or did not belong to the county in one of the ways already defined, the first bearer of the arms *in Derbyshire* is usually given. Arms used (rather than borne) without authority prior to a grant are also noticed where applicable. Thereafter remarks are confined to variations in the arms; to subsequent grants to descendants (even if no longer resident in Derbyshire); and to hereditary titles and life peerages. These are arranged thus: date of creation, title, remainders (except where the grant is only to heir male of the body of the grantee lawfully begotten), and date of extinction. The method of creation of a title is mentioned only where it is not by letters patent. The fate of baronies created by writ of summons has not been discussed, since this difficult question is well covered by the *Complete Peerage*. Where a family has more than one armigerous branch in Derbyshire with significantly different arms, a separate entry has been included.

Finally, there are cases of families bearing, or claiming to bear, arms granted to people of the same name where it has proved impossible to establish a connection between them. Here the name of the person to whom the arms apply is given with the expression 'borne or used by'. Sometimes there is no specific name discoverable at all, in which case this is stated in the text. Another pitfall is where the arms of early families are known only as quarterings of their successors. Often there is a strong possibility, in the absence of other evidence, that these are later inventions by the family themselves or the heralds. Constant repetition has established these arms as entities and they thus deserve attention, although where the text only cites a quartering as evidence for particular arms, the achievement should be treated with caution.

THE SECONDARY LITERATURE

Much of the value of the secondary sources for Derbyshire heraldry lies in the wealth of unauthorised material therein. Foremost amongst such sources is Burke's *General Armory* (1884), referred to in the text simply as Burke. This claimed to contain, in a single alphabetical sequence, all the arms in use in the United Kingdom and is based on Berry's earlier but similar *Encyclopaedia Heraldica*. Unfortunately, Burke included unauthorised arms without any form of differentiation and gave very few references. Almost all the entries require corroboration from other sources. To some extent, the same also applies to other publications by the same family.

The heraldry is most reliable in *Authorized Arms* (1863); the various editions of the *Peerage* also contain a majority of reliable entries, although some of the genealogy was highly speculative in earlier editions and not all had been revised by the time the last full edition appeared in 1970. The same is true for the *Landed Gentry* and *Irish Landed Gentry* series, where there is also much unsound heraldry. Again, the last edition of each (1965–72 and 1976 respectively) was greatly improved. Indeed, in the latter the grants of arms were dated where possible, something which Burke's publications have never done before, except incidentally.

Far more reliable is A.C. Fox-Davies's *Armorial Families*, where, especially in the later editions, most grants are dated. Fox-Davies was a careful compiler, who did not allow entries in return for a fee, as one suspects was the case with *Authorized Arms*, where the selection is so eclectic as to admit of no other likely explanation.

G.E. Cokayne's *Complete Peerage* does not particularly concern itself with heraldry but where the subject does occur the references are careful and useful. Other similiar compilations have been used selectively, notably that of Joseph Foster, a careful antiquary. His work is generally reliable for heraldry, although the usual drawbacks – the lack of dates of grants or references to authorities – are prevalent. His publication was taken over by Lodge, who preserved Foster's pedigrees and delightful heraldic illustrations by Fr Anselm. Other *Peerages* are cited here merely because they provide a reference to the arms of long departed grandees. Collins (1779) has the best illustrations: some of the others require a magnifying glass and a dash of imagination.

Amongst local sources, Daniel and Samuel Lysons, in Volume V (1817) of their unfinished project, *Magna Britannia*, include over a hundred pages of arms, including visitation references and some dates of grants but no evidence for the medieval coats. They were careful compilers and their sources can mostly be identified. Stephen Glover's two-volume *History and Gazetteer of Derbyshire* (1829; 2nd ed. 1833), the topographical portion of which proceeded no further through the alphabet than 'Derby', includes a wealth of unathorised arms and speculative genealogy. Glover's notes and correspondence, now in Derby Local Studies Library, together with a draft of the remaining parochial histories, make clear that he wished to flatter patrons and prospective subscribers, sparing little effort to endow them with impressive pedigrees. The Coxes, Derby lead merchants descended from a Brailsford schoolmaster, he provides with Leicestershire landed ancestors with a Holy Roman Empire barony, and includes their quite spurious arms with a something of a flourish. Glover is valuable as a source for unauthorised heraldry but is not to be relied upon.

Another local antiquary who proceeded more in hope than expectation was Joseph Tilley, whose *Old Halls, Manors, and Families of Derbyshire* (1892–1902) contains a wealth of unsubstantiated heraldry, much of it culled from the *General Armory* and attributed on a congruence of names only. Nevertheless, as with his remarks on some of the buildings, there are nuggets of useful information. Several of the arms he noted were apparently culled from private papers and are unique references to unauthorised arms, some pertaining to families whose forebears had usurped or disclaimed at visitations. A source containing much the same sort of information is the 'Derbyshire Armorial' of John Sleigh of Leek (Staffs.) and Thornbridge Hall, near Ashford, who published the work in instalments in three volumes of *The Reliquary* (1865, 1866 and 1872). Unfortunately, Sleigh's work is merely a list of names and blazons, with no reference to authorities and no annotation. Nonetheless, it contains much unique material and the compiler claims that he had extracted all the arms from primary sources, enumerating seals from local family papers, bookplates (of which his own collection is now Derby Local Studies Library, MS 7769), Samuel Pegge's Derbyshire Collections at the College of Arms and the collections of Adam Wolley of Matlock at the British Library. Some of Sleigh's entries plainly do not belong to Derbyshire but all have been listed here simply because his is the only previous attempt at a dictionary of Derbyshire arms and has been much quoted (often without attribution) in later publications. Sleigh's *History of Leek* also contains much material relating to unauthorised Derbyshire arms, especially for the Dove Valley parishes on the Staffordshire border.

Adjacent counties have fared rather better than Derbyshire with projects for large-scale histories, all of which have proved of value in this study. Leicestershire had the redoubtable John Nichols and, much earlier, Burton (1622); Staffordshire had Robert Plot and the incomplete Stebbing Shaw; Nottinghamshire had Robert Thoroton and south Yorkshire had Joseph Hunter, who gave us not only his monumental *Hallamshire* but also *Familiae Minorum Gentium*, which includes numerous yeoman and gentry families of Derbyshire origin, and the arms (often unauthorised) of some.

A good deal of unauthorised heraldry (and some quite legitimate) has been culled from local collections of objects. Derby plates at both the Crown Derby Museum and City Museum enshrine one or two oddities, such as the crest of Castlyn over two hundred years after the family fades from record. A large collection of servants' livery and other buttons was discovered in a Derby draper's shop a few years ago. Although subsequently dispersed, this yielded a crop of late nineteenth- and early twentieth-century usurpers (mainly of crests – the accompanying shields are by no means certain, even if such were ever in use by the families concerned), including the Derby solicitors Whiston and Woolley. It also showed that Mr Catt of Breadsall was armigerous, which had not previously even been suspected.

This kind of research was one of the reasons why, in 1976, my late friend and relative, Michael Grousinski, encouraged me to begin work on this compilation. It was also the growing number of livery buttons coming into Derby Museum as a result of the increasing use of metal detectors which began to underscore the desirability of a book along these lines, coupled with the need for heraldic identifications of the devices on Derby porcelain plates by my then colleague, Rosemary Blake, and her successor, Judith Anderson. Had the dimensions of the task then been apparent, however, it might never have been started. The work of compiling an ordinary and a list like Sleigh's was simple enough, but for publication details of the right of families, insitutions and individuals to bear or use arms were needed. Every effort has been made to ensure that the entries presented here are as accurate as possible but undoubtedly errors and omissions will come to light. I would be much obliged if these could be sent to me, with a view to the publication in due course of a 'Supplement' to the volume.

Derby Museum & Art Gallery   Maxwell Craven
April 1991

BIBLIOGRAPHICAL
AND OTHER ABBREVIATIONS

Ald.	Alderman
MS Ashmole	Bodleian Library, Oxford, Ashmole Manuscripts.
ASP	A.R. Wagner and others, *Aspilogia. I. A Catalogue of English Medieval Rolls of Arms; II. Rolls of Arms, Henry III* (Harleian Society and Society of Antiquaries, 1950, 1967).
b.	born
Ballard's Book	College of Arms, MS M3 (*c.* 1465–90).
Berry	W. Berry, *Encyclopaedia Heraldica* (n.d., *c.* 1830).
Birch	W. de G. Birch, *Catalogue of Seals in the Department of Manuscripts of the British Museum* (1887–1900).
Boroughbridge Roll	Bodleian Library, MS Ashmole 831, ff. 100–106 (*temp.* Edward III); cf. *Genealogist*, new series, I and II (1884–5).
Box 57	Derby Local Studies Library, Collection of genealogical notes by Ll. Jewitt and others.
BL Add.MS	British Library, Additional Manuscripts.
BLG	*Burke's Landed Gentry* (18 editions, 1833–1972).
BP	*Burke's Peerage and Baronetage* (105 editions, 1826–1975).
Briggs	G. Briggs, *Civic and Corporate Heraldry* (1971).
bt, btcy	baronet, baronetcy.
bur.	buried.
Burke	J.B. Burke, *General Armory* (1884).
Burke, AA	J.B. Burke, *Authorized Arms* (1863).
Burke, CG	J.B. Burke, *Colonial Gentry* (1891–5).
Burke, DFUSA	L.G. Pine, *Distinguished Families of the United States of America* (1939).
Burke, DEB	J.B. Burke, *Extinct and Dormant Baronetcies* (1838).
Burke, DEP	J.B. Burke, *Extinct, Dormant and Abeyant Peerages* (1883).
Burke, FR	A.P. Burke, *Family Records* (n.d. [1897]).
Burke, IFR	H. Montgomery-Massingberd, *Burke's Irish Family Records* (1976).
Burke, LGI	A.P. Burke and others, *Landed Gentry of Ireland* (4 editions, 1898, 1904, 1912, 1958).

c.	*circa* (around).
c	century.
Caerlaverock Roll	N.H. Nicholas (ed.), *The Caerlaverock Roll* (1828).
Calais Roll	British Library, Harl.MSS 246, 3968, 6589, 6595, and Cotton Tib.E IX; Bodleian Library, MS Ashmole 1120.
Camden Roll	British Library, Cotton Roll XV.8; cf. J. Greenstreet, 'The original Camden Roll of Arms', *Journal of the British Archaeological Association*, XXXVIII (1882), 309–28.
Charles Roll	Society of Antiquaries, MS 517: copy of lost original of *c.* 1300; cf. C.S. Percival, 'Two rolls of arms of the reign of King Edward the first', *Archaeologia*, XXXIX (1863), 389–446.
Clay	J.W. Clay, *Extinct and Dormant Peerages of the Northern Counties of England* (1913).
conf.	confirmed.
Corder	J. Corder, *A Dictionary of Suffolk Arms* (Suffolk Record Society, 7, 1965).
Cotgrave's Ordinary	N.H. Nicholas (ed.), *A Roll of Arms compiled in the Reign of Edward III* (1828).
CP	G.E. Cokayne, *The Complete Peerage* (2nd ed., 1910–59).
cr.	created.
Cox	J.C. Cox, *Notes on the Churches of Derbyshire* (Derby and London, 1875–9).
Cox & Hope	J.C. Cox and W.H. St J. Hope, *The Chronicles of the Collegiate Church of All Saints', Derby* (1881).
d.	died.
D369	DRO, Derbyshire Archaeological Society's MS copies of Derbyshire Visitations: see Appendix I.
DAJ	Derbyshire Archaeological Journal (1879–).
dau.	daughter.
Dering Roll	*The Reliquary*, XVI–XVII (1876–8).
DM	*Derbyshire Miscellany* (Derbyshire Arch. Soc. Local History Section, 1957–).
Dow	G. Dow, *Railway Heraldry* (1973).
DRO	Derbyshire Record Office, Matlock.
dsp	*decessit sine prole* (died childless).
Dunstable Roll	*Collectanea Topographica et Genealogica*, IV (1837), 135.
(E)	Peerage of England.
Egerton MS	British Library, Egerton Manuscripts.
ext.	extinct.
f.	*filius* (son of).

Fairbairn	J. Fairbairn, *Book of Crests* (4th ed., 1905).
FD	A.C. Fox-Davies, *Armorial Families* (7 editions, 1895–1929).
FitzWilliam Roll	Fitzwilliam Museum, Cambridge, MS 297.
FMG	J. Hunter, *Familiae Minorum Gentium* (Harleian Society, 38–40, 1894–6).
Ford	*A History of Chesterfield* (Published by Thomas Ford, 1839).
(GB)	Peerage of Great Britain.
gent.	gentleman.
Glover	S. Glover, *History and Gazetteer of Derbyshire* (Derby, 1829–31; 2nd ed. 1831–33).
Glover, *Notes*	S. Glover, *Notes on the History of Derby* (Derby, 1840).
Glover's Ordinary	British Library, Cotton MS, Tib. D X; Harl.MSS 1392 and 1459.
Glover's Roll	N.H. Nicholas, *A Roll of Arms compiled in the Reign of Henry III* (1829).
gr.	granted.
Grantees of Arms	*Grantees of arms named in doquets and patents ...*, Ed. W.H. Rylands (Harleian Society, 66–68, 1915–17).
Grimaldi Roll	John Rylands Library, Manchester University, MS 88, published in *Collectanea Topographica et Genealogica*, II (1834), 320.
Harl.MS	British Library, Harleian Manuscripts.
Heathcote	E.D. Heathcote, *An Account of some of the Families bearing the name of Heathcote which have descended out of the County of Derby* (Winchester, 1899).
Heralds' Roll	College of Arms, MS B.29, pp. 20–27.
Howard	M. Howard, *Chinese Armorial Porcelain* (London, 1974).
Humphery-Smith	C. Humphery-Smith, *Anglo-Norman Armory* (Canterbury, 1978).
Huxford	J.C. Huxford, *Arms of Sussex Families* (Chichester, 1982).
(I)	Peerage of Ireland.
J.	I.H. Jeayes, *Descriptive Catalogue of Derbyshire Charters in Public and Private Muniment Rooms* (1906): documents cited by number.
Jeavons	S.A. Jeavons, *The Church Plate of Derbyshire* (Derby, 1906).
Jenyns' Ordinary	BL Add.MS 40851.
Jenyns' Roll	British Library, Harl.MS 6589; cf. *Antiquary* (1880, I.205 and II.97, 238).

King	G. King, *Staffordshire Pedigrees*, Ed. G.J. Armytage and W.H. Rylands (Harleian Society, 63, 1912).
kt	knight.
kt bt	knight banneret.
Le Neve	P. Le Neve, *Pedigrees of the Knights Created between the years 1660 and 1714* (Harleian Society, 8, 1873).
LO	Lyon Office, Scotland.
Local Deed	Derby Local Studies Library, Collection of Local Deeds.
Local MS	Derby Local Studies Library, Collection of Local Manuscripts. In addition to copies of heralds' visitations discussed in Appendix I, the following are also cited in the text:
3525	Francis Bassano's account book of *c.* 1725, in which he recorded his commissions to paint hatchments etc, plus his payments, during the early C18.
4556	An anonymous collection of Derbyshire shields from various dates, containing much unauthorised material and no references to sources.
7769	Large collection of bookplates and letterheads, mainly C19, amassed by John Sleigh.
8627	William Beckwith's MS collection of Derbyshire pedigrees and arms.
9555	Volume of sketches, tricks and bookplates, used as a working record of commissions for Holmes & Co., Derby coachbuilders, from early C19 to *c.* 1910.
Lodge	*Lodge's Peerage* (1852, 1911 and 1912 editions).
Lysons	D. and S. Lysons, *Derbyshire* (Magna Britannia, 5, 1817).
marr.	married.
Matthew Paris Shields	British Library, Royal MS 14 C VII.
Military Roll	British Library, Harl.MS 4205.
MI	monumental inscription.
Nichols, *Leics.*	J. Nichols, *The History and Antiquities of the County of Leicester* (1795–1815).
Nobility Roll	British Library, Add.MS 29505.
Papworth	J.W. Papworth, *An Ordinary of British Armorials* (1874).
Parliament Roll	N.H. Nicholas (ed.), *A Roll of Arms of the Reign of Edward II* (1829).
Pierrepont	J.R. Pierrepont, 'Derbyshire Hatchments' in P. Summers and J.E. Titterton (ed.), *Hatchments in Britain*, 8 (Chichester, 1988).
Pine	L.G. Pine, *A New Extinct Peerage* (1972).

Planché Roll	British Library, Harl.MS 1068; cf. *Genealogist*, old series, III–IV (1879–80).
Powell Roll	British Library, Add.MS 26677; Bodleian Library, MS Ashmole 804.
PRO, P.	R.H. Ellis, *Catalogue of Seals in the Public Record Office. Personal Seals* (1978, 1981); seals cited by number.
RBC	J. Blair and P. Riden (ed.), *Records of the Borough of Chesterfield and related documents, 1204–1835* (Chesterfield Borough Council, 1980).
Rel.	*The Reliquary*, 1st series, 1860–86.
RL	Royal Licence.
RSM	Royal Sign Manual.
(S)	Peerage of Scotland.
St George Roll	C.S. Percival, 'Two rolls of arms of the reign of King Edward the first', *Archaeologia*, XXXIX (1863), 389–446.
Scott-Giles	C.W. Scott-Giles, *Civic Heraldry* (2nd ed., 1953).
Shirley	E.P. Shirley, *The Noble and Gentle Men of England* (2nd ed., 1860).
Simpson	R. Simpson, *A Collection of Fragments illustrative of the History and Antiquities of Derby, compiled from authentic sources* (Derby, 1826).
Sleigh, *Leek*	J. Sleigh, *A History of the Ancient Parish of Leek* (2nd ed., Derby, 1883).
Thompson	G. Thompson, Unpublished antiquarian notes in Derby Local Studies Library.
Thoroton, *Notts.*	R. Thoroton, *The Antiquities of Nottinghamshire* (1677; 2nd ed., revised and enlarged by J. Throsby, 1790).
Tilley	J. Tilley, *The Old Halls, Manors and Families of Derbyshire* (Derby, 1892–1902).
(UK)	Peerage of the United Kingdom.
UO	Ulster Office.
V., Vv.	Heralds' Visitation(s): cited by date and county or date alone in the case of Derbyshire. See Appendices I and II.
VCH	*Victoria History of the County of Derby* (1905– 07).
Wagner 1939	A.R. Wagner, *Historic Heraldry of Britain* (1939).
Walford	*Walford's County Families of the United Kingdom* (1863, 1871 and 1909 editions).
Willement Roll	T. Willement (ed.), *A Roll of Arms of the Reign of Richard II* (1834).
Woolley	C. Glover and P. Riden (ed.), *William Woolley's History of Derbyshire* (Derbyshire Record Society, 6, 1981).
yr	younger.

Appendix I

THE HERALDS' VISITATIONS
OF DERBYSHIRE

WILLIAM FLOWER'S VISITATION OF 1569

Manuscripts

Harl.MS 886. Includes V. Staffs. 1563 and V. Notts. 1569.

Harl.MS 1093. Continues with copy of V. 1611.

Harl.MS 1484, f. 23. Includes a V. Norfolk, said to be of 1581, and some continuations of pedigrees.

Harl.MS 2113, f. 34. Part copy in narrative, rather than tabular form.

Harl.MS 2134, f. 99. Copy.

Add.MS 6675. From Collections of Adam Wolley for a history of Derbyshire.

Queen's College, Oxford, MSS 91 and 97.

Derby Local Studies Library, Local MS 6341. Compiled by J. Chaloner; also contains V. 1661, plus additions, church notes copies of seals etc.

Derby Local Studies Library, Local MS 8627. Partial copy, with some additional material dating from c18.

Derbyshire Record Office, D369 G/Z. Amongst the collections of the Derbyshire Archaeological Society (additional deposit, as yet lacking piece-numbers) are two MS volumes of Visitation material acquired by the society about 1910. See the articles by H. Lawrance cited below.

Publications

'Pedigrees contained in the Visitations of Derbyshire, 1569 and 1611', *Genealogist,* new series, VII–VIII (1891–2).

Derbyshire Visitation Pedigrees, 1569 and 1611(1895).

H. Lawrance, 'The arms of the gentlemen of Derbyshire in 1569', *DAJ,* 35 (1913), 269–82 and 36 (1914), 45–86.

RICHARD ST GEORGE'S VISITATION OF 1611

Manuscripts

Harl.MS 1093. See above.

Harl.MS 1153, f. 93. A narrative copy.

Harl.MS 1486, f. 23. Includes substantial elements of V. 1569, also extracts from deeds, church notes and seals.

Harl.MS 1537. Copy with additions.

Egerton MS 996. Copy.

Queen's College, Oxford, MS 91. Extended from V. 1569.

Derby Local Studies Library, Local MS. 6341. See above.
Derbyshire Record Office, D369 G/Z. See above.

Publications

See above under 1569.

RICHARD ST GEORGE'S VISITATION OF 1634

College of Arms, MS C 33. Unpublished but cited by Lysons.
Derbyshire Record Office, D369 G/Z. See above.

WILLIAM DUGDALE'S VISITATION OF 1662

Manuscripts

Harl.MS 1082, f. 81. Part only.
Harl.MS 6104. Includes V. Staffs 1663; most of the arms contain minor errors.
Derby Local Studies Library, Local MS 6606. A poor copy from the Phillipps MSS,
    providing minimal new material.
Derbyshire Record Office, D369 G/Z. See above.

Publications

J. Rogers (ed.), *The Visitation of Derbyshire taken in 1662* (1854).
'Visitation of Derbyshire taken in anno domini 1662 and reviewed in anno 1663. By
    William Dugdale, esq., Norroy King at Armes', *The Genealogist*, old series,
    II–III (1878–9).
Sir W. Dugdale, *The Visitation of Derbyshire, taken in 1662, and reviewed in 1663*
    (1879; reprinted from the *The Genealogist*).
H. Lawrance, 'The heraldry of Dugdale's Visitation of Derbyshire, 1662–3', *DAJ*, 42
    (1920).
G. Ireland and G.D. Squibb (ed.), *Dugdale's Nottinghamshire and Derbyshire Visit-
    ation Papers* (Harleian Society, new series, 6, 1987).
G.D. Squibb (ed.), *The Visitation of Derbyshire begun in 1662 and finished in 1664
    made by William Dugdale Norroy King of Arms* (Harleian Society, new series, 8,
    1989).

THE PROPOSED VISITATION OF 1687–88

H. Lawrance, 'A Derbyshire Visitation Manuscript', *DAJ*, 32 (1910), 33–72. An MS
    owned in 1910 by the Revd C.V. Collier, containing copies of the Visitations of
    1569, 1611 and 1662, with notes compiled between January and June 1687
    giving details of families included in 1662 and others who had come to pro-
    minence in the intervening years. Also contains a list of grants to Derbyshire
    families in the same period.

Appendix II

VISITATIONS OF OTHER COUNTIES

The following published editions have been consulted in the preparation of this volume and are cited in the text by the name of the county and date. All the titles listed below are published by the Harleian Society except where stated.

Bedfordshire: 1566, 1582 and 1634 (Harl. Soc. 19, 1884).
Berkshire: 1532, 1566, 1623, 1665–6 (Harl. Soc. 56 and 57, 1907–08).
Buckinghamshire: 1566 and 1634 (Harl. Soc. 58, 1909).
Cambridgeshire: 1575, 1619 (Harl. Soc. 41, 1897).
Cheshire: 1580, 1613 and 1663 (Harl. Soc. 18, 1882; 59, 1909; 93, 1941).
Cornwall: 1620 (Harl. Soc. 9, 1874).
Dorset: 1623 and 1677 (Harl. Soc. 20, 1885, and new series 3, 1977).
Essex: 1552, 1558, 1570, 1612 and 1634 (Harl. Soc. 13–14, 1878–9).
Gloucestershire: 1623 (Harl. Soc. 21, 1885).
Hampshire: 1530, 1575, 1622, 1634 (Harl. Soc. 64, 1913).
Hertfordshire: 1572 and 1634 (Harl. Soc. 22, 1886).
Kent: 1530–1, 1574 and 1592 (Harl Soc. 74–75, 1923–4), 1619–21 (Harl. Soc. 42, 1898) and 1663–8 (Harl. Soc. 54, 1906).
Lancashire: 1533 (Chetham Soc. 98 and 110, 1876 and 1882); 1567 (Chetham Soc. 81, 1870).
London: 1568 (Harl. Soc. 109, 1957–8); 1633–5 (Harl. Soc. 15 and 17, 1880 and 1883); 1664 (Harl. Soc. 92, 1940).
Norfolk: 1563, 1589 and 1613 (Harl. Soc. 32, 1891); 1664 (Harl. Soc. 85–86, 1933–4).
The North: 1552–8 (Surtees Soc. 122, 1912).
Northamptonshire: 1681 (Harl. Soc. 87, 1935).
Nottinghamshire: 1662–4 (Thoroton Soc. Record Series 13, 1950).
Rutland: 1681–2 (Harl. Soc. 73, 1922).
Somerset: 1623 (Harl. Soc. 11, 1876).
Suffolk: 1561 (Harl. Soc. new series 2, 1981); 1664–8 (Harl. Soc. 61, 1910).
Surrey: 1530, 1572 and 1623 (Harl. Soc. 43, 1899); 1662–8 (Harl. Soc. 60, 1910).
Sussex: 1530 and 1633–4 (Harl. Soc. 53, 1905); 1662 (Harl. Soc. 89, 1937).
Warwickshire: 1619 (Harl. Soc. 12, 1877); 1682–3 (Harl. Soc. 62, 1911).
Wiltshire: 1623 (Harl. Soc. 105–106, 1954).
Worcestershire: 1569 (Harl. Soc. 27, 1888); 1634 (Harl. Soc. 90, 1938).

Related Material:

East Anglian Pedigrees (Harl. Soc. 91 and 97, 1939 and 1945).
Lincolnshire Pedigrees (Harl. Soc. 50–52 and 55, 1902–04 and 1906).
Middlesex Pedigrees (Harl. Soc. 65, 1914).
Staffordshire Pedigrees (Harl. Soc. 62, 1912).
Yorkshire Pedigrees (Harl. Soc. 94–96, 1942–4).

A DERBYSHIRE ARMORY

Abell. Upper Hall (Hartshorne); Stapenhill; Ticknall. *Argent on a saltire engrailed azure nine fleurs-de-lys of the field* (V. 1611). Allowed 1611 to Ralph Abell of Stapenhill. In V. 1569 these arms were entered to the family 'with a dubit'.

Abercromby. Stubbing Court (Wingerworth). *Argent a fesse embattled gules between in chief issuant a dexter arm embowed in armour proper garnished or the forearm encircled by a wreath of laurel the hand grasping a representation of the French Republican military flag in bend sinister proper in base a chevron indented of the second between three boars heads erased azure;* crest: *a bee volant proper;* supporters: *on either side a greyhound per fesse argent and or lined and pendent from the collar gules an escutcheon azure charged with a representation of the House of Commons Mace erect of the second and each charged below the escutcheon with a sprig of thistle proper,* mottoes: (over) *'Vive ut vivas'* and (below) *'Industria'* (BP (1862) 354). Gr. (LO) to Speaker Abercromby, later (1839) 1st Lord Dunfermline (Fife). Supporters gr. 1839, and augmentation 1801 to his father, Gen. Sir Ralph Abercromby. 1st Lord Dunfermline was of Stubbing Court; title ext. 1868.

Abney. Willesley Hall; Measham Hall. *Or on a chief gules a demi-lion rampant argent;* crest: *a demi-lion rampant or between the paws a pellet;* Motto: *'Fortiter et honeste'* (Vv. 1569, 1611, 1662). Arms assumed by William Abney of Willesley *c.* 1420 *jure uxoris,* having previously been borne by his father-in-law William Ingwardby of Willesley. The previous coat of the Abneys (then claiming to be 'of Abney') was: *Argent on a cross sable five bezants* (Lysons, cxii). The crest and motto were conf. to the cadet (Measham) line in 1569.

Adderley. Breadsall; Radbourne; Beeley; Heage. *Gules on a chevron or three crosses botonnée sable* (Thompson II.84; Local MS 4556). Borne by William de Adderley, MP (Derbys.) 1384–5, and father, Henry, a patron of Breadsall Priory. Sister and heiress marr. William Dethick of Breadsall.

Adderley. Derby. *Argent on a bend azure three lozenges of the field on each a pheon gules* (V. 1634). Borne by George Adderley ('Atherley' in V. 1634) whose son paid tax on 13 hearths in Derby, 1662. They were cadets of the Adderleys of Staffs., one of whom later inherited the Snitterton estate. Another, John, of Bramshall, Staffs., was a Derby attorney. Both also bore crest: *on a chapeau a stork argent gorged with a chain or therefrom an escutcheon azure charged with a mascle of the first;* motto: *'Addere legi justitiam decus'* (conf. to 1st Lord Norton 1878). The coat *argent on a bend three mascles of the field* often attributed (e.g. Burke) to Adderley of Heage is an early coat of the Staffs. family (V. Staffs. 1583).

Adlington. Calow; Tibshelf. *Argent a cross flory sable;* crest: *a goat's head erased argent* (Harl.MS 891.100). If *Rel.* V (1865) p. 228 is to be believed, the Major Adlington who was a comrade-in-arms of Anthony Browne (of Lings, N. Wingfield) after Marston Moor and who settled at Calow was a cadet of Adlington, Lancs., and bore these arms. William Adlington was of Tibshelf after the Civil War.

Agard. 'Allaston'; Alvaston; Foston; Scropton; Parwich; Chatsworth. *Argent on a chevron engrailed gules between three boars' heads couped sable langued of the second a fleur-de-lys or;* crest: *a buglehorn argent garnished or stringed sable* (Vv. 1569 (Foston), 1611 ('Allaston', Foston, Parwich), 1662). Gr. to Francis Agard, 1 Aug. 1566, who had previously used the arms of Agard of Lancs. (as above, omitting the fleur-de-lys, and so recorded for this branch in V. 1662), with whom he may have been anciently connected. This earlier coat was also that of the Sapertons (qv) who might well have shared a common ancestor and who held land at Foston.

I

Also borne or used by the Derby and Ockbrook Agards (descended from those of Markeaton C15) on the evidence of a Chinese armorial plate of *c.* 1790 (Howard, 802).

Agard. Sudbury; Chatsworth; Cromford. *Argent a chevron gules between three boars' heads couped sable (langued of the second)* (V. 1569, Local MS 6341). Allowed to Nicholas Agard of Sudbury 1569. On an escutcheon on a monument at Scropton church to his possible yr brother Humphrey is: *a buglehorn quartering three boars' heads and three cocks* (1627).

Aincurt: see d'Eyncourt.

Airmine: see Armine.

Aket: see Hacket.

Alcock. Ravenstone. *Sable a fesse between three cocks' heads erased argent combed and wattled or;* crest: *a cock argent combed and wattled gules spurred azure;* motto: *'Vigilananter'* (Burke, LGI (1898) 422–3). Registered UO to William St Leger Alcock-Stawell of Kilbrittain Castle, co. Cork, as quartered by Stawell, 1908. He was grandson of William Alcock of Ravenstone (1723–64), himself a cadet of Alcock of Sibbertoft, Northants., gr. arms 8 June 1616 but with the crest *ermine*.

Alderley: see Adderley.

Alfreton. Alfreton. *Azure two chevronels or* (Fitzwilliam Roll, 532). Arms of Robert f. Ra(nu)lph lord of Alfreton and sheriff of Notts. and Derbys., 1165–70. Thomas Chaworth, son of the heiress of this family, also bore this coat; his successors merely quartered it (cf. Chaworth).

Alfreton Urban District Council. *Azure two chevronels and on a chief or as many croziers in saltire of the field between two further cressets sable fired proper;* crest: *out of a mural crown sable charged with three trefoils slipped argent a mount vert thereon issuant an oak tree proper fructed of five acorns or between two lozenges of the first;* motto: *'Ex terra vires'.* Gr. 1963, authority abolished 1974. Previously *England ancient* had been used.

Allcard. Burton Closes (Bakewell). *Quarterly argent and or on a bend nebulée azure three swans' heads erased of the first beaked gules;* crest: *a swan rising argent semée d'estoiles sable.* Gr. 1849 to William Allcard JP of Warrington, Lancs., and Burton Closes, the house built for his father John a few years before.

Allestrey. Alvaston; Derby. *Per chief gules and argent on a bend azure three escutcheons of the first each charged with a chief or;* crest: *an ostrich or, tail feathers azure, or, gules* (V. 1662). Also on the MI to William Allestree, recorder of Derby (d. 1555), but crest *a peacock or* and at present restored with incorrect tinctures. Harl.MS 6104 gives for this family the tinctures of the related Turnditch branch (qv).

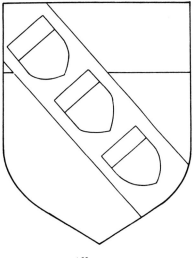

Allestrey

Allestrey. Turnditch Hall. *Argent a chief gules over all a bend azure charged with three escutcheons of the field on each a chief of the second;* crest: *an ostrich or holding in his beak a horseshoe* (V. 1662). This is believed to be the senior branch of the family.

Allestrey. Allestree. *Per chief azure and argent on a bend gules three escutcheons per fesse* (intended for *per chief?*) *vert and of the second;* crest: *a demi-lion azure brandishing a scimitar argent hilt or.* Used by 'Mr Allestree', 'an usurper', V. 1611.

Alleyne. Caldwell; Derby; Wheston. *Argent a cross moline sable* (FMG III.1032; *Rel.* XIV (1874) 64; XX (1880) 256; XXIII (1883) 108–12). Used by Revd Thomas Alleyne (1699–1761) rector of Loughborough, Leics., grandson of John, of Derby, descended from Alleyne of Wheston Hall.

Alleyne. Chevin House (Milford). *Per chevron gules and ermine in chief two lions' heads erased or*; crest: *out of ducal coronet a horse's head argent*; motto: *'Non tua te (moveant) sed publica vota'*. Gr., presumably when a btcy was conferred on 6 April 1769 on Sir John Gay Alleyne of Four Hills, Barbados, but in use on Chinese armorial porcelain as early as 1726 (Howard, D2, P16). The 3rd bt settled in Derbys.

Alleyne. Gresley Hall. *Sable a cross potent or*; crest: *a demi-lion rampant sable grasping a rudder or* (V. 1662). The crest is given as *issuant sable* in Harl.MS 6104. Borne by the descendants of Sir Christopher Alleyne, 1st of Gresley, who usually quartered the family's previous arms: *or three ogresses on each a talbot passant of the field on a chief gules a lion passant guardant also of the field*, e.g. on MIS in Gresley Church. This coat was borne by Sir John Alleyne of Ightham, Kent, Lord Mayor of London in 1525 and 1535, father of Sir Christopher, and by the consanguineous Alleynes of Hatfield Peverel, Essex.

Alleyne

Alleyne. Stanton in Peak; Stanton Lees Hall. *Or a fesse gules between three oak leaves vert* (Harl.MS 1537). Conf. 1586 to George son of Thomas Alleyne of Stanton.

Allport. Duffield; Littleover. *Barry wavy of six argent and azure on a bend or three mullets gules*; crest: *a demi-lion rampant erminois gorged with a mural coronet gules*. Gr. 1884 when Sir James Joseph Allport of Littleover House was knighted for services to the Midland Railway; his 3rd son, Charles, of Duffield, also bore these arms (Jewitt, Notes Box 57; cf. BLG 1894, p. 2198).

Alsop. Alsop en le Dale etc. *Sable three doves rising argent beaked and legged gules*; crest: *a dove close argent beak and legs gules* (Vv. 1611, 1662). Crest appears only in Harl. MS 6104. Shield blank in V. 1569 for no obvious reason, as these arms appear consistently on seals from C14. In some MSS the doves in these arms all hold *an ear of wheat or* in their beaks. Ancient arms, borne allegedly by the Templar and Crusader, Sir Hugh de Alsop: *argent a fesse gules between six falcons heads erased sable* (cf. Glover, II.20). Several descendants of this family had varied grants: Alsop of Markfield, Leics: *Sable on a chevron between three rooks or a mullet of the field* (V. Leics. 1619). John Alsop of London, gr. Aug. 1597: *Sable on a bend argent between six doves wings expanded of the second beaked and legged gules in the beaks an ear of wheat proper and in base three pheons or*; crest: *a dove as in the arms between two ostrich plumes* (D369). Ald. Robert Alsop, sheriff of London, gr. 29 March 1738: *azure three doves proper on a canton or a key erect sable*; crest: *a dove holding in its beak an ear of corn all proper in the dexter claw a key erect sable*. A kinsman of the previous, gr. 1752; as above, but *doves or, canton argent, key gules*.

Alsop. Derby. *Per fesse or and ermine a pale counterchanged and three mullets (pierced) sable*; crest: *a dove with an olive branch in its beak proper.* (Cox, III.19; Thompson, II. 19). Used by Thomas Alsopp of Derby, 3rd son of Robert of Atlow (Ince's MS, Local 8022).

Allsopp. Alsop en le Dale; Bladon House (Newton Solney) etc. *Sable three pheons chevronwise or between as many doves rising argent each holding in the beak an ear of wheat of the second*; crest: *on a pheon point downwards a dove close holding an ear of wheat all or*; supporters: *on either side a foxhound gorged with* a pair of couples all proper; motto: 'Festina Lente'. Gr. to Henry Allsopp and Elizabeth (Tongue), his wife in 1880, the year he was made bt (on 7 May); supporters gr. 1886 on his elevation to the peerage as Lord Hindlip of Hindlip, Worcs., and Alsop. Previously, this family had used: *sable three plovers rising argent beaked and legged gules*; crest: *a plover wings expanded or beak and legs gules in the former an ear of wheat of the first*; same motto. (Giover, II.20).

Alsop. Durrant Hall (Chesterfield). V. 1611: respited for proof: 'promised to come to London' (no grant known).

Angell. Chaddesden. *Azure two garbs in saltire or* (Tilley, II.197). Used by Thomas Angell of Chaddesden *c.* 1640, whose sister and heiress marr. Cockayne (qv).

Amber Valley District Council. *Vert a pale wavy or and a bordure argent five horseshoes sable on a chief of the second a beacon fired proper between two lozenges of the fourth; crest: out of a tower embattled and masoned proper between two shepherds' crooks respectively in bend and in bend sinister, crooks outwards, an oak tree issuant fructed also proper and crowned with an ancient crown or;* supporters: *dexter a unicorn argent armed crined and unguled or collared gules pendent therefrom a cross fleury of the second, sinister a panther proper similarly gorged pendent therefrom a fleur-de-lys also or;* motto: 'Per Laborem Progredimur' (as printed in colour on a local handbook, 1990, but not blazoned therein). Gr. 1989.

Ann. Derby. *Per chevron or and sable a roundel ermine between in chief two bucks' heads caboshed of the second and in base a like head of the first;* crest: *a buck's head caboshed or resting on the scalp and between the attires an escutcheon per chevron or and sable charged with a roundel as in the arms* (FD (1910) 33). Gr. 1908 to Ald. Sir Edwin Ann, of Parkfields House, Derby, mayor there 1906, knighted 1907.

Anson. Catton Hall. *Argent three bendlets engrailed and in sinister chief a crescent gules;* crest: *out of a ducal coronet or a spear staff purpure headed proper.* Gr. to George Anson of Orgreave Hall, Staffs., on adoption of surname and arms of Anson in lieu of Adams 1773. Crest gr. 1804. Conf. to Henry Anson-Horton who in 1899 assumed by RL the surname and arms of Horton in addition to his

Ann

own. (FD (1929) I.42): thereafter quartered by Horton (qv).

Appleby. Appleby Manor; Newton Solney. *Azure six martlets or;* crest: *an apple or stalked and leaved vert* (Vv. 1569, 1611; V. Leics. 1619). Tilley (IV.155) gives the crest of this family (although on what authority is unclear): *a long cap hatched with feathers thereon a martlet's head or.*

Apsley. Palterton; Scarcliffe. *Barry of six argent and gules a canton ermine;* crest: *a fleur-de-lys or between two wings erect and conjoined argent.* (V. Sussex 1633; Le Neve 372). Borne by Sir Peter Apsley who purchased his Derbys. estates 1690.

Arbalaster: see Trusley.

Archer. Abney; Great Hucklow; Highlow. *Ermine a cross sable* (Lysons, xcix). Borne, apparently, by Ralph Archer of Great Hucklow, and his son, of Highlow; the latter d. 1340. Note that William, grandson of Robert Eyre of Highlow assumed by RL the surname and very similar arms of Archer of Coopersale, Essex.

Arkwright. Willersley (Matlock); Sutton Scarsdale etc. *Argent on a mount vert a cotton tree fructed proper on a chief sable between*

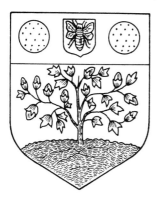

Arkwright

two bezants on an escutcheon of the field a bee volant proper; crest: *an eagle rising or holding in its beak pendent by a ribbon gules an escutcheon azure thereon an hank of cotton proper*; motto: *'Multa tuli fecique'*. Gr. 29 Jan. 1787 to Sir Richard Arkwright, to include several charges reflecting the manner in which he made his fortune.

Armine. Brushfield; Cromford. *Ermine a saltire engrailed gules on a chief of the second a lion passant or*; crest: *on a mount vert an ermine proper*. Ancient coat borne by Sir William Armine of Osgodby, Lincs., who held the above estates in 1627: the *ermine* field and crest are allusive of the surname. He was cr. a bt 28 Nov. 1619, ext. 1688.

Armitage. Holme Hall (Bakewell); Longstone Grange (Great Longstone). *Gules a lion's head erased within an orle argent between three crosses potent or*; crest: *in front of a dexter arm embowed vested gules cuffed argent the hand grasping the blade of a sword in bend sinister point downwards proper hilt and pommel or an escutcheon of the last thereon a cross potent gules* (FD (1910) 40). Gr. 1849 to Sir Elkanah Armitage, of Hope Hall, Lancs., whose grandson, Benjamin (son of Benjamin)

was of Holme Hall early C20 and whose son was of Longstone Grange.

Arthur. Church Broughton. *Or on a chevron azure between two clarions in chief gules and a kangaroo sejant in base two swords point upwards all proper hilts and pommels or on a chief of the third a horse courant argent*; crest: *in front of two swords saltirewise proper hilts and pommels or a pelican in its piety sable, nest or*; motto: *'Stet fortuna domus'*. (BP (1970) 111). Gr. 1838 to Lt.Gen. Sir George Arthur KCH, cr. a bt 1841, whose descendant in the fourth generation was Dr L.J.H. Arthur (1926–83) of Church Broughton.

Ash. Caus Hall (Brampton). *A fesse overall a saltire* (seal on charter, Add.MS 6668 f. 36). Used, without authority in all probability, by John Ash of Chesterfield and Caus Hall *(jure uxoris)* impaling Cauz, 1464. A similar device was recorded by Bassano *c.* 1710 on an alabaster slab to Philip (son of John Ashe) of Brampton (d. 1517) then in the church there.

Ashbourne. Ashbourne; Wirksworth etc. *Argent a fesse between three crescents gules.* Only known as a quartering of Bagshawe of The Ridge (Chapel en le Frith) and Cockayne (Vv. 1569, 1611 and Local MS 6341). Arms, almost certainly, of Sir Robert de Ashbourne, d. without issue sometime after 1253; the heiress must, from the invariable disposition of the quarterings, have marr. Geoffrey son of Sir Geoffrey Savage of Tissington (d. 1230), although no deed or pedigree records this. She was presumably a sister of Sir Robert, from the date, thus further implying that these arms were borne by Sir Robert's father, Robert lord and seneschal of the Honour of Tutbury. The Lowes of Denby quartered the above arms but with the *fesse engrailed* (V. 1569). This could be a mistake for the above arms, for they made two Cokayne marriages, but neither with an heiress. However, Local MS 6341 gives the wife of Humphrey Lowe (1527) as 'Margaret, dau. & heiress of Lymster de Ashbourne'. This MS also (uniquely) places *three mullets or* on the fesse.

Ashbourne. Ashbourne; Clifton; Brampton. *Argent on a fesse between three crescents gules as many mullets of the field* (Burke). Plainly cadets of preceding; Burke probably got the reference from a seal, not subsequently noted. The Lowe quartering (noted above) combines two versions of the arms.

Ashby. Chellaston. *Azure a chevron ermine*

between three leopards' faces or; crest: out of a mural crown argent a leopard's face or; motto: 'Be just and fear not' (Harl.MS 6592; Local MS 4556). Borne, apparently, by William Ashby of Chellaston (d. 1499), whose son's heiress marr. Hastings.

Ashenhurst. Beard Hall (New Mills); Glossop Dale (Glossop). *Or a cockatrice tail nowed with a serpent's head sable combed wattled and headed gules in the beak a trefoil vert*; crest: *a cockatrice as in the arms*. (V. 1662 (Harl.MS 6104 omits the details of the tail), V. Staffs. 1583). Allowed to this family V. Staffs. 1583, conf. 12 Feb. 1603 and formally gr. all over again to James Ashenhurst of Derby, and Park Hall, Church Leigh, Staffs. (where the crest can still be seen on a gate by Robert Bakewell), son of Francis, Archdeacon of Derby (1643–1704), and second cousin of the last Ashenhurst of Beard.

Ashton. Castleton; Stony Middleton. *Argent a mullet sable*; *a boar's head couped argent* (V. 1662, 'arms sans proof: did not appear'). Recorded nevertheless 28 June 1667 but with crest as Ashton of Killamarsh (qv), and *a crescent for difference*). Used by Robert Ashton of Castleton (1610–87), perhaps with good cause, for the difference mark may imply a genuine tradition of descent (as claimed) from Ashton of Shepley in Ashton under Lyne, Lancs. His father, however, was described as 'yeoman' in other sources (*DAJ* VI (1884) 52f.)

Ashton. Killamarsh. *Argent a mullet sable debruised by a baton sinister gules*; crest: *a mower with his scythe face and hands proper cap and habit quarterly argent and sable handle or blade argent, as in action* (Local MS 6341); on most MSS of V. 1569 the shield is shown blank; the notes for prospective V. 1687 say 'supposes to be entered in the office: see the arms Ao. 1567 but with a dubit'. Borne by James Ashton of Killamarsh, son of Alexander, of Barlborough, son of Sir John, alleged natural son of Sir John, of Ashton, Lancs.

Aston. Burnaston; Risley etc. *Per chevron sable and argent*; crest: *an ass's head proper*; motto: *'Prest d'Accomplir'* (V. Cheshire 1580, Harl.MS 1424, f. 55). Sir Willoughby Aston, 2nd bt, inherited the estates of Willoughby of Risley; his father was cr. a bt 25 July 1628 (ext. 1815).

Aswall. Ticknall. *Per pale argent and sable*

three leopards' heads in pale counterchanged; crest: *on a chapeau a garb proper* (Burke). William de Aswell (sic) has left us a fragmentary heraldic seal of 1328 which resembles the above (*DAJ* LIII (1932) 76); from whence Burke supplied the details and crest is unclear. The family emerge *c.* 1260 and flourish to 1429.

Atherley: see Adderley.

Athorpe: see Middleton.

Atlow. Atlow; Bradley. *Per pale indented argent and sable* (as a quartering of Okeover, Vv. 1569, 1611). Borne by Engelhard de Atlow of Atlow, dead by 1341, whose dau. and heiress marr. Sir Roger de Okeover, and, no doubt, by at least one preceding generation.

Auden. The Laurels (Etwall); Repton. *Argent on a cross gules a lion passant or between four increscents of the field*; crest: *a caduceus in bend sinister surmounted of a scimitar in bend all proper hilt and pommel or*; motto: *'Cresco et Spero'* (BLG (1952) 77). Gr. C19 (with remainder) to a medical member of this Staffs. family. Borne by the late W.H. Auden, whose father was of Repton, and by Maj. J.L.

Auden

Auden of the Laurels, whose son lives at Repton. Another member of the family was recently patron of Boyleston.

Audley. Ashbourne. *Gules fretty or a canton ermine* (in glass at Ashbourne church, Glover, II.34). Borne by Thomas Audley, natural son of John Touchet, Lord Audley, living at Ashbourne *c.* 1450. Ancestor of Audley of co. Lincs. (cf. V. Lincs. 1564).

Aula: see Willington.

Avenell. Haddon; Baslow. *Gules six annulets argent* (known from quarterings of Kniveton of Mercaston and Vernon of Haddon, V. 1569 and Local MS 6341). Borne by William de Avenell of Nether Haddon and Baslow, *c.* 1220, who left two daus. and heiresses marr. to the ancestor of Vernon of Haddon and Basset of Haddon and Baslow.

Avenell. Haddon. *Argent a fesse between six annulets gules* (known from a quartering of Rollesley of Rowsley, V. 1569 cf. Cox II.164 and on a seal in the Belvoir MSS (BL Add.MS 6696, f. 54)). Borne by William son of Robert Avenell, whose heiress marr. John de Rollesley *c.* 1230. They also had a small estate in Haddon.

Avranches: see Chester, Earls of

Order of St John, Grand Prior of Ireland and sometime commander of the Preceptories of Yeaveley, Barrow upon Trent and Rothley (Leics.) – at which last a branch of the family settled after the Dissolution – bore *ex officio: argent ten torteaux and on a chief gules a cross argent* (Dethick church tower frieze, Cox. I.42)

Bache. Stanton Hall (Stanton in Peak). *Or a lion rampant guardant pean within a bordure sable bezantée*; crest: *a demi-lion rampant guardant pean holding a bezant* (Vv. 1634, 1662). Gr. 10 Dec. 1634 to Raphael Bache of Stanton. Most MSS fail to give the tincture of the *bordure*. It is supplied by D369. The Lysons (p. cxv) give the lion in arms and crest as *reguardant*.

Bagnold. Hilton; Exeter House (Derby). *Barry of six or and ermine a lion rampant azure* (MI in All Saints', Derby, impaled by Chambers). Used by John Bagnold of Derby MP (1643–98), of a Marston on Dove family and subsequently by his cousin, William ('sub-mayor of Derby', 1710: Poll Book in Derby Library, p. 1) and his sons. Slightly altered from the arms of Bagnold of Newcastle under Lyme, Staffs. Bagnold was listed as a

Babington. Dethick; Lea; Normanton by Derby; Litchurch (Derby); Bradbourne etc. *Argent ten torteaux four three two and one and a label azure*; crest: *a dragon's head between two dragons' wings gules and out of the mouth an escroll*; motto: *'Foy est tout'* (MI at Ashover church, Cox I.21; Glover's Ordinary; V. 1569 (Dethick and Normanton); V. London 1634; V. Staffs. 1583). Sir Anthony Babington of Dethick was typical of the family in bearing the above arms. He also used supporters which at the same time were rebuses: *on either side a baboon statant upon a tun proper* (see carvings on wainscot at Babington Hall, Glover, II.522). An earlier member of the family bore for supporters, *dexter a griffin and sinister, an unicorn* (S. side of frieze on steeple of Dethick church: arms of Sir John Babington, d. 1485). Another crest borne by the family (especially the numerous Normanton branch) in some MSS was a *a demi-bat displayed gules,* which plainly started out as a straightforward misinterpretation of the crest given above. Sir John Babington (d. 1533), Bailiff of Aquila and Turcopolier of the

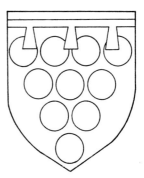

Babington

7

'person for a grant' in 1687, but does not seem to have had one.

Bagshawe. Abney. *Or a buglehorn sable between three roses proper;* crest: *an arm couped at the elbow and erect proper grasping a buglehorn sable stringed vert* (V. 1569; Lysons, lxxvi). Borne by Nicholas Bagshawe of Abney and Great Hucklow in 1569, and by his ancestors 'through eleven generations'. However at the V. 1662 the representative of the family (whose grandfather had sold out to some kinsmen in 1593) had his arms 'respited for proof; entered in the former books being a branch of Bagshawe of Ridge 1569'; the families actually divided in 1317!

Bagshawe

Bagshawe. Ford (Chapel en le Frith). *Or a buglehorn sable garnished argent stringed vert between three roses gules.* (Local MS 4556; Burke). Borne by Col. Samuel Bagshawe MP (1713–62) of Ford. The heiress marr. Greaves. The arms were conf., with crest, *a dexter cubit arm couped proper the hand grasping a buglehorn argent garnished or,* and motto, *'Forma flos, fama flatus',* by RL 27 Feb. 1914 to Ernest Bagshawe, formerly Carver, who marr. the Greaves-Bagshawe heiress in 1886.

Bagshawe. Ridge Hall (Chapel en le Frith). *Or a buglehorn stringed sable between three roses gules (pierced of the field);* crest: *a cubit arm erect proper holding a buglehorn sable enguichy or* (Vv. 1569, 1611, 1662; only Harl.MS 6104 of the latter supplies the tinctureless crest). This is the oldest and senior branch of the Bagshawes, recorded as early as 1141.

Bagshawe. Wormhill; Goosehill Hall (Castleton); The Oaks (Norton). *Or a buglehorn sable garnished argent between three roses gules* crest: *a dexter cubit arm couped proper the hand grasping a buglehorn argent stringed and garnished or;* motto: *'Forma flos, fama flatus'* (Glover, II.214). Used by Adam Bagshawe of Wormhill from *c.* 1707, although he was entitled to bear the arms of the Abney branch (if their V. 1569 entry holds good) with due difference. The heiress marr. William Chambers of Derby, and his heiress marr. Ralph Darling. Sir William Chambers Darling, the son, assumed the surname and arms of Bagshawe by RL 1801, and received a grant of arms in 1815: *per pale ermine and gules a buglehorn stringed between three roses all counterchanged barbed and seeded proper;* crest: *a dexter cubit arm issuant out of clouds hand proper holding a buglehorn or handle sable within the strings a rose gules;* motto: *'Forma flos, fama flatus'.*

Baillie: see Bass.

Bainbrigge. Derby; Ashbourne; Alvaston. *Argent a fesse embattled between three battleaxes sable;* crest: *on a mount vert a goat passant sable horned unguled and collared argent* (V. 1611: Ashmole MS 844, ff. 237–8). Arms conf. and crest gr. 14 Feb. 1584 to William Bainbrigge of Derby and Lockington (Leics.) and borne later by his descendants of Rocester Priory (Staffs.) and Derby. The arms were re-conf. by RL of 1832 (to Peter Bainbrigge of Ashbourne, additional surname and arms of Le Hunte) and 1845 (to William Bainbrigge of Uttoxeter and Derby, additional surname and arms of Arnold). Glover (II.552) gives a variant of these arms as used by some members of this family: *argent a chevron embattled between three battleaxes sable.*

Bainbrigge. The Friary (Derby). *Argent a chevron ermine between three battleaxes sable;* crest: *a demi-arm armoured gauntlet or grasping a battleaxe sable* (*Rel.* XXI (1881)

240). Gr. 20 Nov. 1582 to Ald. William Bainbrigge of the Friary, bailiff of Derby 1555, 1563, 1575, who died without issue. Ashmole MS 844, f. 566, gives a different crest for this grant: *a bloodhound passant or gorged with a collar vert 'tierets' or* (perhaps for *tierced*).

Bainbrigge. Snitterton; Wormhill. *Argent on a chevron between three Cornish choughs proper beaked and membered of the field as many stags' heads caboshed also of the field an escallop for difference* (V. Yorks. 1584). Borne by Richard Bainbridge of Snitterton living *c.* 1463 and three generations of his successors, along with a junior branch briefly at Wormhill; the senior line were at Wheatley Hill, Yorks. (V. Yorks. 1584, wherein Flower remarks, 'filius junior Baynbriggorum de Snotterton'). The Lockington and Derby Bainbrigges all claimed descent from this family (Nichols, *Leics.*, III(2), pp. 632, 875, 882–3).

Bakepuize. Alkmonton; Barton Blount; Hungry Bentley; S. Wingfield. *Gules two bars argent in chief three horseshoes or* (Lysons, xcix, and in glass Sutton on the Hill church, recorded by Wyrley 1596, Cox III.331). In use before 1166 by Robert Bakepuize of Barton etc, by virtue of the bearing of these arms by descendants of two of his sons (quartered by Longford of Longford–Barton line, and Bonnington of Bearwardcote–Alkmanton line). Note Ferrers motif – the *horseshoes in chief.*

Baker. Derby. *Or three piles one issuant from chief and two from base azure on each a swan's head erased argent*; crest: *a dexter arm embowed in armour grasping a caduceus in bend surmounting the truncheon of a tilting spear in bend sinister splintered all proper*; motto: *'Dum spiro spero'.* Gr. 1854 to Dr William Baker of Friar Gate, Derby (Burke, AA, 22).

Bakewell. Bakewell; Eyam; S. Wingfield; Dunston (Newbold); Newbold. *Or three magpies proper* (as a quartering of Eyre, V. 1569 etc). Borne by Henry Bakewell of Dunston and Newbold, and presumably, his grandfather, as the arms were transmitted via his cousin and heir, Robert Whittington, whose dau. and heiress carried the quartering to the Eyres. The occurrence of the coat in glass in various Derby. churches (all noted 1596 and 1710 but now vanished) confirms the general use of the arms by this family.

Bakewell. Wilne. *Two bars gules* (MI at

Baker

Wilne church). Borne by Robert Bakewell of Wilne, living C16. The escutcheon reveals two wives, one a Clifton of Clifton (Notts.) the other unidentifiable from her arms: *on a bend three anchors gules.*

Bakewell. Stanton by Dale. *Argent three magpies proper* (formerly in glass at Staveley church, recorded by Wyrley 1596). John Bakewell of Stanton marr. Catherine, dau. of Anker Frecheville of Staveley, and this glass commemorated a descendant, John Bakewell, chaplain at Stanton, C16. The field of this coat was recorded as *sable* in Local MS 6341. Also borne by Revd Thomas Bakewell, rector of Rolleston, Staffs., son of Augustus, of Stanton, living 1651–72.

Baléan. Ashbourne Green Hall (Offcote & Underwood). *Gules a fesse between three crosses patée in chief issuant from the fesse a demi-lion or*; crest: *out of a circlet of eight lilies argent a tower proper*; motto: *'A vous entier'* (BLG I (1965) 35). A C20 grant borne by Wing Cmdr Peter Bradford Baléan who sold Ashbourne Green Hall in 1965. The arms are largely similar to those borne by his ancestor Guillaume Baléan (d. 1810), who fled to England during the French Revolution.

Balguy. Aston; Derby; Derwent Hall; Duffield Park; Spondon; Swanwick (Alfreton). *Or three lozenges azure*; crest: *a bear passant proper collared and chained or*; motto: *'Bear and forbear'* (arms: Vv. 1569, 1611, 1662; crest: *DAJ* VI (1884) 15 and n.; motto: Local MS 9555, 142). One of the longest running sagas of the use of unauthorized arms; even discounting the 'long fictitious pedigree' (notes for projected V. 1687), these arms were in use by the family from at least C15, and are recorded in various editions of BLG up until 1952; two representatives of the family survived in 1985. All Visitations agree: 'Non probavit arma' (V. Lincs 1634, Stamford); V. 1611 'an usurper'; V. 1662 'Pretend to have arms; respit for proof given', and so on. Fictitious quarterings of Brailsford and Leigh occur, e.g. in glass at Hassop Hall (Cox II.264 and n.).

Ball. Ambaston (Elvaston); Horsley. *Argent a lion rampant sable*; crest: *a demi-lion rampant guardant sable.* (V. Norf. 1589, Harl.MS 1552). Gr. 1589 to Robert Ball of Scottow, Norfolk, 3rd in descent from a Henry Ball 'of co. Derby', said to be the same as Henry Ball of Horsley 1488. In C17 the family were of Norfolk (V. Norf. 1612).

Ballidon. Derby; Stanley Hall. *Argent two bars vert on each three crosses crosslet or*; crest: *a demi-lion rampant vert ducally crowned and holding a cross crosslet or* (MI in All Saints', Derby, V. 1662). Gr. 4 Dec. 1663 to Paul son of Paul Ballidon of Derby, merchant. The heiress marr. Coke of Trusley.

Bamford. Bamford. *Argent a fesse wavy gules*; crest: *on a chapeau a serpent nowed proper* (V. Yorks. 1612 and Berry, who supplies crest). Borne by 3rd cousins, John Bamford of Pule Hill (Halifax), Yorks., and Lionel, both descendants in the 4th degree from John Bamford of Bamford, and to whom was gr. the crest, and the arms conf. 28 May 1625. D369 gives as crest: *an arm embowed in armour argent holding in bend a lance sable with a flag thereon a torteau.*

Bamforth. 'High House, co. Derby.' *Argent a fesse engrailed gules* (Local MS 7769). Borne or used by Margaret, heiress of this family (it is unclear where 'High House' was), who marr. William Burton of Royds Mill (Huddersfield), Yorks., c. 1730. Arms quartered by the descendants of Sir Montague Roger Burgoyne, 8th bt, of Sutton, Beds., who marr. the heiress of John Burton of Owlerton, Yorks., 1794 (bookplate, c. 1840–50).

Bancroft: see Unidentified.

Banke, De: see Debanke.

Banks. Overton Hall (Ashover). *Sable a cross or between four fleurs-de-lys argent*; crest: *on the stump of a tree couped proper a stork close argent beaked or ducally gorged gules*; motto: *'Nullius in verba'.* Conf. to Rt.Hon. Sir Joseph Banks in 1781 on his receiving a btcy; previously his family (Banks of Beck Hall, Giggleswick, Yorks.) had borne *sable a cross between four fleur-de-lys argent* (Banke, V. Yorks. 1612). Sir Joseph's father assumed for a time the surname and arms of Hodgkinson (qv).

Barber. Castleton; Derby; Mam (Castleton); Woodseats (Castleton). *Or on a chevron gules between three moles sable as many fleur-de-lys of the field*; crest: *issuant out of a coronet composed of four crosses botonnée set on a rim or a bull's head sable armed and charged on the neck with a water bouget of the first*; motto: *'Veritas omnia vincit'.* Gr. 17 Oct. 1932 to Ivan Graham Mitford-Barberton of Castleton, Cape Province, South Africa, 8th in descent from Roger Barber of Woodseats and Mam, a cadet of Barber of Castleton. His father assumed the surname of Mitford-Barberton in 1916. Col. Maurice Hilton-Barber of Durban, 3rd cousin of the above grantee, was allowed: *Or on a chevron gules between three horses' heads erased sable as many fleurs-de-lys of the field*; crest: as above, but *charged on the neck with a horseshoe or*, in lieu of the *bouget*; motto: as above (ibid.). Gr. or allowed c. 1952 by the Bureau of Heraldry, Pretoria, S.A.

Barber. Chesterfield. *A chevron between three fleur-de-lys* (Tilley, IV.155). Used by John and his brother Adam Barber of Chesterfield in C18.

Barber. Derby. *Ermine two chevronels between three fleurs-de-lys and a bordure embattled gules*; crest: *in front of two swords in saltire points upward proper hilts and pommels or a bull's head erased also proper*; motto: *'In Deo Spes'.* (BP (1970) 175). Gr. to Sir Thomas Philip Barber of Greasley, Notts., on being cr. a bt 25 July 1960, who was 5th in descent from Francis Barber of Derby, attorney.

Barber. Derby. *Ermine two chevronels between three fleurs-de-lys in chief and one in* *base all within a bordure gules* (as quartered by Cooper of Culland (Brailsford), BLG (1937) 478). Gr. as a quartering to A.F.T. Cooper of Culland (qv) when he received a grant *c*. 1910–18, and represents the arms of Robert Hartshorne Barber of Hayton Castle, Notts., son of John, of Stainsby House (Horsley Woodhouse), and grandson of the Francis Barber of Derby mentioned in the preceding entry.

Barber. Whitemoor Hall (Belper); Darley. *Argent a bend engrailed vair between six storks sable*; crest: *a stork argent semée of estoiles azure motto: 'Homo proponit, Deus disponit'* (BLG (1937) 2129). Gr. 1873 when William Joseph Barber of Darley Dale assumed by RL the additional surname of Starkey, and the arms alone. The family were previously of Whitemoor Hall.

Barber-Starkey: see previous entry.

Barberton: see Barber.

Bardolf. Elton; Bradwell; Ockbrook. *Azure three cinquefoils or*; crest: *out of a ducal coronet a dragon's head or wings expanded gules* (FitzWilliam Roll, 130; crest: Berry). Borne by William Bardolph of Wormegay (Norfolk), also of the above and governor of Nottingham Castle, d. 1275. His son was summoned to parliament 1299 as a baron. The ultimate heiress's husband sold the Derbys. estates *c*. 1420.

Bardolph. 'Co. Derby'. *Azure a mascle between three cinquefoils or*; crest: *out of a mural coronet a dragon's head between two wings gules on each a mascle or* (Burke) Attributed to Simon Bardolph of London, Merchant Tailor, son of William of Blithfield, Staffs., 'descended out of co. Derby' (*Rel*. VII (1867) 19). Plainly differenced from preceding and perhaps connected therewith.

Barker. Bakewell; Darley. *Sable a saltire engrailed argent* (Local MS 4556). Used by John Barker of Castle Hill House, Bakewell (d. 1795) his descendants, and their kinsmen, George Barker of Darley Hall (1753–1822) and his children.

Barker. Bolsover; Norton Lees. *Per chevron engrailed or and sable a lion rampant counterchanged on a canton azure a fleur-de-lys of the first.* (V. 1634; canton *azure* on MI at Bolsover Church). Borne by Francis, elder son of Edward Barker of Dore, who marr. an heiress of Parker of Norton Lees, which arms are quartered with those of Barker and Gotham

on the MI. In the V. 1611 (Local MS 6341) and V. 1662 (but with the qualification, 'Sans proof') the arms are those of the Dore branch with *a label of three points* and the crest of Parker (qv).

Barker. Dore; Glapwell. *Per chevron engrailed or and sable a lion rampant counterchanged a canton azure thereon a fleur-de-lys of the first*; crest: *a demi-lion wings expanded vert holding a sword erect proper* (V. 1611, Local MS 6341 version; crest: D369 for V. 1662). Entered by Edward Barker of Dore V. 1611 but shield blank in most MSS, with the word 'usurper' added. 'Promised to come to London' added on Harl.MS 6104 of V. 1662. No record of an official grant of arms, even when the last of the family, Sir Robert Barker MP of Bushridge (Godalming), Surrey, was made a bt 24 March 1781. Yet members of this family were sealing with similar arms late C14 and so could easily have regularised their position.

Barlow (Barley). Barlow; Eckington; Stoke. *Argent three bars wavy sable a chief per pale ermine and gules*; crest: *a demi-stag salient argent charged on the body with three bars wavy sable* (Vv. 1569, 1611). Represented by Thomas Barlow of Stoke and George Barlow of Barlow Lees 1569, whose common ancestor was Robert, of Barlow, whose greatgrandfather, another Robert, used the names Barlow and d'Abitot indiscriminately. The arms of the d'Abitots of Barlow were *Per pale or and gules three roundels counterchanged* (quartered by Barlow, Vv, 1569, 1611).

Barnes. Brizlincote (Bretby); Derby; Stanton (Newhall). *Quarterly or and vert in the first quarter a cinquefoil gules* (hatchment on N. wall of St Werburgh's church, Derby, quartering D'Arcy and impaling (?)Chatterton, recorded by Simpson (1828) I.423). Achievement used by William Barnes gent. of Stanton Manor and the Wardwick, Derby, who marr. at St Werburgh's 8 Jan. 1708 Mrs Elizabeth Greenes (née Chatterton), and by their sons, Philip of Brizlincote and William.

Barn(e)sley. Alkmonton; Youlgreave. *Sable a cross between four roses argent*; crest: *a man's head affrontée couped at the shoulders proper* (V. 1662; V. Staffs. 1663–4). D369 has the note, 'Attested by the Kings of Armes Ao. 1597', therefore to William Barnesley of Alkmonton (cf. V. Worcs. 1568).

Barrow. Matlock; Ringwood Hall (Staveley); Spondon; Sydnope Hall (Darley). *Per pale indented sable and azure two swords in saltire proper hilts and pommels or between four fleurs-de-lys two in pale of the last two in fesse argent*; crest: *on a perch proper a squirrel sejant or collared and chained azure cracking a nut also proper*; motto: *'Non frustra'*. Gr. 1815 to Revd Richard Barrow of Howgill, Yorks., ancestor of all the Derbys. branches of this family.

Basford. The Grange (Killamarsh). *Azure three eagles displayed in bend between two cotises argent* (Harl.MS 6592; Thompson IV.65). George Basford's forebear inherited a small estate at Killamarsh C17; his heiress marr. a Sitwell. Authority for the arms unknown.

Bass. Bladon (Newton Solney); Derby; West Hallam Hall. *Gules on a chevron cotised argent between three plates on each a fleur-de-lys azure a demi-lion couped of the field*; crest: *a demi-lion rampant gules resting the dexter gamb on a plate thereon a fleur-de-lys azure and charged on the shoulder with three annulets two and one argent;* motto: *'Basis virtutum constantia'*. Gr. to Michael Bass 17 May 1882 when cr. a bt and replaced unauthorised arms used by his father M.T. Bass MP and his nephew, Roger Bass of West Hallam: *gules a chevron argent between three plates*; crest: *a demi-lion gules resting the dexter gamb on a cartouche or thereon a fleur-de-lys azure* (in window glass of 1879 at Derby Museum). In 1887 Sir Michael was cr. Lord Burton of Rangemore and of Burton on Trent, Staffs., and obtained a grant of supporters: *on either side a lion reguardant sable each resting the inner gamb on a stag's head proper and charged on the body with a plate thereon a fleur-de-lys azure*. A further barony (Burton of Burton on Trent and Rangemore, Staffs.) with remainder to his dau. Nellie Liza and her heirs male was obtained 1897 and is now enjoyed by the Baillie family. The present peer thus bears: *Azure nine estoiles argent within a bordure engrailed or*; crest: *a boar's head couped argent armed or langued gules*; supporters: (as 1st Lord Burton); motto: *'Quid claribus nostris'*.

Bassano. Derby. *Per chevron vert and argent in chief three silkworm moths and in base a laurel bush counterchanged*; crest: *a silkworm moth volant proper*; motto: *'Grace me guide'*. (Glover, II.575). Gr. 1604 to (Arturo)

Bassano 'musition to Q. Eliz'. His descendant in the 4th generation was Christopher Bassano (1679–1745), first of a dynasty of Derby attorneys; his brother, Francis, was the famous heraldic artist.

Basset. Baslow; Haddon. *Or three piles gules and a canton vair* (as a quartering of Pole of Langley, V. 1569; Local MS 6341). Of a moiety of Haddon and of Baslow through an heiress of Avenell (qv). Their close kin, the Bassets of Sapcote, Leics., bore the piles *wavy*.

Basset. Brailsford; Kirk Langley. *Or three piles in point gules on a canton argent a griffin segreant of the second*; crest: *out of a ducal coronet or a boar's head gules* (V. 1569; V. Staffs. 1583). The same branch of Basset as were of Blore and Cheadle, Staffs.; the Derbys. estates passed to cadets, quartering respectively Brailsford and Dethick. Heiresses marr. Shirley, Curzon, Howard and Cavendish.

Basset. Bassett Hall (Scarcliffe). *Or three piles in point gules and a canton ermine* (as quartered by Chaworth, Local MS 6341). A branch of the Bassets of Sapcote (*DAJ*, LVII (1936) 19).

Bassano

Bate. Foston. *Sable a fesse engrailed between three dexter hands bendwise palms upwards argent*; crest: *a stag's head transfixed through the neck with an arrow.* (Lysons, cxvii; seal of *c.* 1686 quoted in Harleian Soc. New Series, VII (1987), 57). Richard Bate of Foston was a 'person for a grant' in the notes for a prospective V. 1687, wherein his 'title [was] suspected'. The hands are sometimes given as *or* (Local MS 3525).

Bate. Little Chester (Derby); West Broughton (Doveridge). *Sable a fesse argent between three dexter hands bendwise palms upwards or*; crest: *a cross patée* (V. 1662, without tinctures, supplied by the Lysons). Nathaniel Bate of Little Chester, despite being nominated as a knight of the Royal Oak in 1660, exhibited his arms 'sans proof', and his grandfather Robert was branded 'an usurper' in 1611. One MS of V. 1662 blazons the hands as *sinister couped* (Harl.MS 6104) and the crest as *a cross formée.* Thomas Bate of Ashby de la Zouch, a great nephew of Nathaniel, used as crest: *a dexter hand apaumée* (Nichols, *Leics.*, III(2), 636).

Bateman. Middleton Hall; Lomberdale Hall (Youlgreave). *Or three crescents each surmounted of an estoile of six points gules*; crest: *a crescent surmounted of an estoile of six points gules between two eagles' wings expanded or*; motto: *'Sidus adsit amicum'* (bookplate of Thomas Bateman *c.* 1850, Local MS 7769). Supposedly Gr. 1613 to Thomas Bateman of Wolfscote (Hartington) and Hartington, ancestor of the antiquary. The cadet Batemans of Hartington and Derby (qv) and their close kin, the Batemans of London and Howe, Norfolk, bts (cr. 31 Aug. 1664, ext. 1679) used the same before their grant.

Bateman. Breadsall Mount; Derby; Hartington; Morley; Wheathills (Kirk Langley). *Or three crescents each surmounted of an estoile of six points gules and a canton azure*; crest: *an estoile of six points issuant from a crescent gules between two eagles' wings expanded or*; motto: *'Sidus adsit amicum'* (V. 1662; hatchments in Derby, All Saints'). Allowed thus to Hugh Bateman of Derby and Hartington at V. 1662 with a *canton.* His descendant, another Hugh, was cr. a bt 15 Dec. 1806 with an unusual remainder to his daus. and their heirs male in default of his male issue. Originally gr. 16 April 1613 (V. London 1633).

Bathurst. Derby; Scarcliffe. *Sable two bars ermine in chief three crosses patée or*; crest: *an arm embowed habited in mail holding in the hand all proper a spiked club or*; motto: *'Tien ta foy'* (Le Neve, 360). Gr. June 1616 and borne by Sir Benjamin Bathurst, whose wife brought him the Derbys. estates of the Apsleys. His son Alan was cr. Lord Bathurst of Battlesden, Beds., Jan. 1712, being allowed supporters the same year: *on either side a stag argent each gorged with a collar gemel ermines.* These were conf. 1771 when an earldom was conferred. The first earl's nephew, Henry, was of Derby.

Bayley: see Paget.

Beard. Beard Hall (New Mills). *Argent three men's faces affrontée bearded sable within a bordure azure* (V. 1569). Conf. to William Beard of Beard 1569, thought to be of the same ultimate stock as the Birds (qv). The heiress marr. Ashenhurst. Heard's pedigree of the Blackwalls at Blackwall Hall gives for this family: *azure a chevron argent between three trefoils slipped or.*

Beardsley. Derby; Hartington; Wirksworth. *Or two bars and a canton gules* (Bassano's MS, Local 3525). Used by the wife of John Cooper of Thurgarton Hall, Notts., 1734, heiress of the Beardsleys of Wirksworth and Cockpit Hill House (Derby), claiming descent from Hartington.

Beauchamp. Chellaston; Melbourne; Normanton by Derby. *Gules fretty argent* (Glover's Roll, 1st version, 96). Hugh de Beauchamp of Eaton Socon, Beds., was also of the above and thus can be attributed these arms: he d. 1187. The arms were borne by his successor, Roger (seal, ASP II.133), and adopted, with his name, by his nephew and heir, William de Mandeville, who dsp 1259.

Beauchamp. Coton in the Elms. *Or a lion rampant sable crowned gules* (Berry). Arms of the Beauchamps of Lamarsh, Essex, who held Coton c13. See also Pyndar.

Beauchief Abbey. *Semée of mullets of six points a dexter arm couped at the elbow issuant from the sinister holding a crozier in chief a crescent* (Tilley III.267). A Praemonstratensian house, founded *c.* 1172, suppressed 1536.

Beaufei (Beaufoy). Park Hall (Denby); Trusley. *Argent on a chevron sable three crosses patée or* (as quartered by Frecheville, V. 1569). Borne by Sir Richard and his son Sir John Beaufoy of Park Hall c13; the latter's heiress marr. Ralph Frecheville. The same arms were borne by Robert son of Robert de Beaufei of Trusley, living 1229, and by John de Beaufoy MP (Derbys.) 1316, probably of the same family (Local MS 4556). See also Trusley.

Beaumont

Beaumont. Barrow upon Trent; Derby. *Azure semée-de-lys and a lion rampant or a crescent for difference*; crest: *on a chapeau a lion statant or with difference*. (V. 1611, Harl.MSS 2113, 1537). Cadets of Coleorton, and Gracedieu, Leics., and ultimate descendants of Lords Beaumont of Folkingham, Lincs. (cr. by writ of summons, 1309), whose arms are given in Jenyns' Ordinary with the lion *armed and langued gules*. As usual, Harl.MS 6104 of V. 1662 differs in detail: *azure a lion rampant within an orle of fleurs-de-lys or*; crest: *on a wreath a lion passant or*.

Bec. Pleasley etc. *Gules a cross moline argent* (Lysons, c note a; *DAJ* XLVIII (1926) 24). Borne by Henry Bec of Pleasley and his descendants. Differences occur amongst his numerous clerical kinsmen: *Gules a cross moline argent:* Thomas Bec, Bishop of St Davids 1280–93 (once in glass at Chesterfield church, Local MS 6341); *Gules a cross moline ermins:* Anthony Bec, Bishop of Durham, 1283–1310; *Argent a cross moline and a bordure engrailed gules:* Anthony Bec (Loseby, Leics. branch), Bishop of Norwich 1337–43 (*DAJ* loc.cit.); *Argent a cross moline gules a bordure azure charged with eight crosses crosslet of the field:* Thomas Bec, Bishop of Lincoln 1342–46 (ibid.). The heiresses marr. Willoughby (qv) and Harcourt.

Bee. Stapenhill. Henry Bee of Stapenhill disclaimed 1662. Possibly an error for Mee (qv).

Beeley. Beeley. *Argent a chevron sable between three pellets* (Papworth 464). Normally these arms are listed under 'Beverly', a name which does not occur in Derbys. It seems highly likely that this is due to an early misreading of Beel(e)y.

Beighton. Wirksworth; Hazelwood. *Sable on a bend between two stags' heads caboshed argent a greyhound courant of the field*; crest: *a demi-greyhound courant ermines collared or issuant from a mural crown of the second*. Gr. 1 June 1675 to Thomas Beighton of Wirksworth who had disclaimed at V. 1662. Lysons (cxvii) blazon the crest inaccurately: the *greyhound* is whole, and the *crown* ducal.

Beighton. Beighton. *Ermine a fesse and a chief indented sable* (*Rel.* VII (1867) 183). The heiress of John Beighton of Beighton marr. Henry Ince of Spinkhill c. 1452, and T.N. Ince (Local MS 8022) attributes these arms to him; on what authority is unclear.

Belers. Crich. *Per pale gules and sable a lion rampant argent crowned or* (formerly in glass at Crich church, V. 1569: Cox IV.62). Sir Roger Belers of Crich d. 1380 and his heiress marr. Swillington.

Belfield. Unstone. *Ermine a chief sable* (Burke; cf. Tilley II.268). A Lincs. family, of which Adam de Belf(i)eld was *jure uxoris* of Unstone and was succeeded in his moiety by his son Christopher, c. 1433. The heiress marr. Chederton.

Belper, Town of. *Azure semée-de-lys or quartering gules three lions passant guardant in pale of the second overall a label ermine* (Scott-Giles, 99). Device on common seal, representing that of John of Gaunt, Duke of Lancaster, whose hunting lodge stood at Belper.

Belper Rural District Council. *Per pale vert and sable a pale wavy argent surmounted of another wavy azure on a chief dancettée or a Tudor rose barbed and seeded between two oak* *trees couped proper fructed of the 5th*; crest: *issuant from the battlements of a tower gules a mount vert thereon a popinjay or gorged with a collar gules pendant therefrom a horseshoe sable resting the dexter claw on an ancient lamp of the third, inflamed proper*; motto: *'Beau repyr'* (Briggs, 54). Gr. 31 Aug. 1953, authority abolished 1974; arms used by the successor authority, Amber Valley District Council until at least 1988 (pers.comm., Clerk & Chief Executive) but without authority. Position currently being rectified.

Bemrose. Derby; Duffield; Idridgehay; Littleover; Milford. *Paly of six gules and or on a chevron of the last a lion rampant between two roses of the first barbed and seeded proper on a chief ermine a lion passant guardant also of the first between two spearheads erect of the second*; crest: *a lamb holding in the sinister forepaw a staff proper flowing therefrom a pennon or thereon a chaplet of roses barbed and seeded proper between two like roses*; motto: *'Semper paratus'* (FD (1910) 121). Gr. 1894 to Sir Henry Howe Bemrose of Derby, with remainders to issue male of father, William.

Bemrose

Bennet. Derby; Littleover; Snelston Hall. *Argent on a cross between four demi-lions rampant gules each holding between the paws a bezant, a like bezant*; crest: *a demi-lion rampant (gules) holding a bezant* (V. 1662, cf. *DAJ* XLII (1920) 20). Harl.MS 6104 of V. 1662 uniquely adds the crest, omits the *bezants* between the lion's paws and adds 'no proof'. In the Visitation papers, Dugdale recorded for Gervase Bennet of Derby (mayor 1645) and Snelston Hall *or on a cross between four demi-lions rampant gules a bezant*.

Bennet. Bennetston Hall (Chapel en le Frith). *Vert three demi-lions rampant or* (*Rel.* XII (1872) 93). Used by William Bennet of Well Close (Hartington Nether Quarter), whose 4th son, Dr R.O.G. Bennet, built Bennetston Hall.

Bennett. Derby; Hathersage. *Gules on a pale or a leopard's face jessant-de-lys in base between two like leopards' faces in chief of the second overall as many chevronels engrailed ermine*; crest: *a buglehorn sable stringed gules surrounding a leopard's face jessant-de-lys or*; motto: *'Per aspera surgo'* (BLG (1952) 157). Gr. to Edward Osbourne Bennett of Llanvihangel Court (Llanvihangel Crucorney), Mon., early C20, great-grandson of Joseph Bennett of the Lead Hill, Derwent: Joseph's son was an exciseman of Derby, later C18.

Benskin. Derby; Hartshorne. Did not appear, V. 1662; arms if used not known.

Bent. Ashbourne; Derby. *Azure on a fesse or between six bezants three torteaux*; crest: *a demi-lion azure holding between the paws a bezant*; motto: *'Nec temere nec timide'* (BLG (1833–5) II.408). Used by Dr Thomas Bent, 3rd son of J.J. Bent of Basford House, Staffs., living in Friar Gate, Derby, early C19, and by his kinsman, Sir John Bent (d. 1857), who lived at Ashbourne Hall.

Benthall. Overton Hall (Ashover). *Or a lion rampant queue fourché azure crowned gules*; crest: *on a ducal coronet or a leopard statant argent pelletée*; motto: *'Tende bene et alta pete'* (BLG III (1972) 63): see Vv. Salop 1584, 1623 etc for this family. Maj. John Lawrence Benthall (1868–1947) settled at Overton Hall.

Bentinck. Bolsover Castle etc. *Azure a cross moline argent*; crest: *out of a ducal coronet or two arms embowed vested gules gauntlets of the first each holding aloft an ostrich feather argent*; supporters: *on either side a lion double queued the dexter or the sinister sable*; motto:

'Craignez honte'. Gr. by the Holy Roman Emperor; supporters to Count Bentinck, 1st Earl of Portland, Viscount Woodstock and Lord Cirencester 3 July 1689; the 3rd Duke of Portland assumed the additional surname and quartered the arms of Cavendish (as of Dukes of Newcastle) by RSM 5 Oct. 1801. The family acquired their Derbys. estates as heirs of the Dukes of Newcastle. The dukedom and the Marquessate of Tichbourne were cr. by elevation of the 2nd Earl, 6 July 1716 and became ext. 1990; the 1689 creations continue. In 1880 Gen. Lord Arthur Cavendish-Bentinck was honoured by the elevation of his widow as Baroness Bolsover of Bolsover Castle.

Bentley. Hungry Bentley; Breadsall; Horsley. *Or three bendlets sable*; crest: *a curre dog passant argent* (V. 1611). Arms gr. 16 April 1589 to John Bentley of Breadsall, son of Humphrey of Derby. Cadets of Holbrook added *in sinister chief a cross crosslet sable* (Local MS 6341). The crest (a 'curre dog') is surely intended for a greyhound, but is usually drawn as a spaniel (V. 1611) and is misquoted by the Lysons (cxviii) as *a lion statant argent*.

Beresford. Alsop en le Dale; Broadlowash (Thorpe); Brampton; Fenny Bentley; Wirksworth etc. *Argent a bear rampant sable muzzled collared and chained or*; crest: *a dragon's head erased sable pierced through the neck with a broken spear or and holding in the mouth the spear's head and upper shaft also or headed argent* (Vv. 1569, 1611). This family, originally from Staffs., anciently seem to have borne *argent three bears rampant sable muzzled or* (Sampson Beresford of Beresford, V. Staffs. 1583). The crest seems to have been *a bear's gamb erect* (seal of 1593, Harl.MS 1485, f. 23); they occur on an MI at Fenny Bentley of 1607 and at this period in Derbys. the family seem to have quartered the coats.

Beresford. Newton Grange. *Argent three fleurs-de-lys between nine crosses crosslet fitchée and a bordure engrailed sable* (V. 1662, Harl.MS 6104). In addition to the better known Beresford coat (above) this branch bore the coat given here, somehow appropriated from the medieval knightly family of Bereford of Northants (Sir William Bereford, Parliamentary Roll, *argent crusilly and three fleurs-de-lys sable*). Of this branch, Tristram, 3rd son of Michael Beresford of Otford,

Kent, went to Ireland and his son, on being made a bt 5 May 1665, was gr. arms (UO) as above with a crest as Beresford of Fenny Bentley, and motto: *'Nil Nisi Cruce'*. It was his descendant who was cr. Marquess of Waterford (1789) with grant of supporters: *on either side an angel proper vested argent crined and winged or holding in the exterior hand a sword erect also proper* (UO, 1720). Also cr. (all in the Irish peerage) Lord Beresford, Viscount Tyrone (1720) and Earl of Tyrone (1746), and in the peerage of GB Lord Tyrone (1786).

Beresford. Hartington etc. *Argent crusilly fitchée three fleurs-de-lys sable and a bordure pean*; crest: as previous, but *out of a mural coronet or,* the head *per fesse wavy azure and gules*; supporters: as Marquess of Waterford, but each *charged on the breast with three fleurs-de-lys azure*; same motto. Arms of Gen. William Carr Beresford, natural son of 1st Marquess of Waterford, cr. 1814 (when the grant was made) Lord Beresford of Albuera and Dungarvan, Co. Waterford, raised 1823 to the Viscountcy of Beresford of Beresford, Staffs. He was also Duke of Elvas, Marquis of Campo Major (Spain 1815) and Count Trancoso in the Kingdom of Portugal (1811), and purchased much of the old Beresford Hall estate in Staffs. and Derbys. but dsp 1854, when all the honours became ext.

Berkeley. Bretby; Ible. *Gules crusilly patée and a chevron argent*; crest: *a mitre gules labelled and garnished or charged with the arms as above*; supporters: *on either side a lion argent, that on the sinister ducally crowned gules collared and chained or*; motto: *'Dieu avec nous'* (arms: Lord Berkeley: ASP II.147; remainder, J. Foster, *Peerage* (1881) 70). Thomas, 1st Lord Berkeley, of Berkeley, Gloucs., adopted these arms; his father had borne *gules a chevron argent* (Glover's Roll, 1st version, 167). His descendant Sir William, 7th Lord Berkeley, (cr. by writ 1295) later 1st Viscount (1481), Earl of Nottingham (1483), Earl Marshal and Marquess (1488) was gr. the Mowbray estates in Derbys. in the later c15. His mother was the Mowbray heiress. Sold 1585 by his heirs. Another branch of the family held Chilcote c13. Titles (except barony) ext. 1492. A seal (PRO, P.74) of James, Lord Berkeley (1422) shows the supporters as *two mermaids*.

Bernake. Beighton; Upper Padley (Hathersage); Stony Middleton. *Argent three horse*

barnacles sable (as quartered by Eyre and Fitzherbert of Padley, and by Cromwell, V. 1569). Borne by Sir William Barnake of Beighton who marr. the heiress of Tatteshall; his ultimate heir marr. Ralph, Lord Cromwell (qv). These canting arms were also borne by a cadet branch, who inherited Padley from the family of that name (Lysons, c), which they then assumed, although retaining these arms. The heiress marr. Eyre.

Beverl(e)y: see Beeley.

Bill. Norbury. *Ermine two billhooks in saltire on a chief azure a pallet or charged with a rose gules between two pelicans heads erased argent*; crest: *a pelican's head erased argent*; motto: *'Omne solum patria'* (BLG (1898) I.115). The arms were used by the Bills early C19; crest and motto were presumably added later, before 1898. They were settled, as yeomen, at Norbury some generations before 1607, when Richard Bill inherited Farley Hall, Staffs.

Billesby. Derbys. *Argent a chevron between three stonebills sable*; crest: *a demi-cat affrontée argent charged on the breast with a mullet* (D369). Inserted in the MS without names, locale or explanations. Early C17. Allowed at V. Lincs, 1564.

Bingham. Staveley. *Or on a fesse gules three water bougets ermine overall a bendlet azure* (in a glass at Staveley church, noted in V. 1611). The *bend* is given in the visitation as *sable*, but Cox, IV.479, corrects to *azure*. Borne by Thomas Bingham of Staveley, *c.* 1471; the family, if, as one assumes, a root of the Binghams of Bingham, Notts., were co-descended from the Bugges with the Willoughbys.

Bingham. Chesterfield; Derby. *Or on a fesse gules three water bougets argent*; crest: *a lion's head erased proper*; motto: *'Spes mea Christus'* (Local MS 9555). Painted on the carriage of and used by Henry Corless Bingham esq., and impaled with the arms of Frances Belcher, his wife, mid C19. His kinsman, John Edward Bingham, of Sheffield, Yorks., was cr. a bt 12 Dec. 1903; gr. arms 20 April 1904: *per pale azure and sable a bend between six crosses patée within two flaunches or on each a garb vert*; crest: *a falcon rising proper resting the dexter claw on a garb fessewise vert and charged on each wing with a cross patée or*; motto: *'Spes mea Christus'* (FD (1929) I.155). Title ext. 1945. Corless

Bingham was a son of Revd Thomas Bingham, rector of Norbury, descended of a family of Derby mercers, who used: *Azure a bend cotised between six crosses patée or*. The family are found in the town from at least 1540. The arms are those of the ancient Binghams of Melcombe Bingham, Dorset, and of the Earls of Lucan, Co. Dublin; we have Tilley's authority for their use (II.26).

Bird. Bakewell; Derby; Nether Locko (Spondon); Stanton in Peak. *Gules a chevron embattled argent*; crest: *on a mount vert a stump of a tree couped and erased thereon a falcon volant all proper* (Vv. 1569, 1611). Borne by William Bird of Nether Locko, 4th in descent from John Bird of Derby, esq., MP. Local MS 6341 gives the field as *sable*. On an MI to a member of the family at Spondon church, the arms are shown as *a chevron between three birds*. (Cox, III.299: C15); were these arms used or borne before the Visitation?

Bird. Over Locko (Spondon). *Sable a chevron embattled counter-embattled argent* (Rel. V (1865) 229). Borne (or used) by Thomas Bird of Over Locko, *c.* 1600, 4th in descent from John Bird of Derby. The similarity in these arms to those above implies that the Derby MP must have borne something similar; the Spondon MI, on the other hand, suggests that this may not have been the case.

Birkin. Belper. *Argent a cross raguly couped vert in the 1st and 4th quarters a bee volant in the 2nd and 3rd birch tree eradicated proper*; crest: *a scorpion erect proper*; motto: *'Pace et bello paratus'* (BP (1956) 214). Gr. 25 July 1905 to Thomas Birkin, cr. a bt the same year; his grandfather, Richard, was of Belper 1805.

Birmingham & Derby Junction Railway. Derby. *Per fesse indented azure and or quartering gules a bend sinister lozengy or*. Amalgamated with the Midland Railway (qv) 1844. Another device was the placing of the arms of Birmingham (as represented above) and Derby (qv) on separate cartouches encircled by a garter. See examples of both at Derby Industrial Museum.

Birom. Ashbourne Green Hall (Offcote & Underwood); Hulland. *Argent on a chevron between three urchins sable as many plates*; crest: *an urchin sable.* (Lysons, clv; MIS at Bradley 1674, 1714). Borne by George Birom of Ashbourne Green, and by William and

Thomas, of Byrom Hall (Clayton, Manchester), Lancs., buried at Bradley, but without *plates*. The D369 MS of V. 1662 gives: *argent three bendlets enhanced gules quartering argent on a bend azure three bezants and a cross crosslet for difference all within a bordure argent:* this, with its Colwick quartering, must represent a much earlier branch of Byron of Lancs. and Notts. Most V. 1662 MSS give this family's arms *sans proof* and *bezants* for *plates*.

Biron: see Burun; Byron.

Bishop Lonsdale College: see Derby Diocesan Training College.

Blackwall. Blackwall Hall (Kirk Ireton); Steeple Grange (Wirksworth). *Argent a greyhound courant sable collared or on a chief indented of the second three bezants;* crest: *two arms in mail holding a greyhound's head couped and erect sable collared chequy or and gules* (Lysons, cxix). Borne at V. 1569 by William son of John Blackwall, conf. 1764 to John Blackwall. They were again gr. 1871 quarterly with Evans as a result of an RL due to an heiress marrying Evans

Blackwall. Blackwell (High Peak); Calke; Wensley. *Argent a greyhound courant sable collared chequy or and gules on a chief indented of the second three bezants;* crest: *two arms embowed habited in mail proper hands argent holding by the nose and ear a greyhound's head couped sable collared chequy or and gules.* Arms conf. and crest gr. 8 Aug. 1494 to Richard Blackwall of Blackwell whose family are frequently alleged to be unrelated to the Blackwalls of Kirk Ireton. The evidence (such as it is) points to their consanguineity. These Blackwalls were, at least before the Civil War, more numerous and opulent than the others (Vv. 1569, 1611).

Blackwell Rural District Council. *Argent a spade and pick in saltire hafts upwards proper within an orle of pellets on a chief sable three stags' heads caboshed argent;* crest: *an arm embowed holding in the hand a Davy lamp all proper;* motto: *'Lux et humanitas'.* (Scott-Giles, 100).These unsubtly allusive arms were gr. 24 Sept. 1942 to an authority abolished in 1974.

Blake. Castle Hill House (Bakewell). *Per chevron argent and gules fretty or in chief two garbs sable and in base a rose of the first barbed and seeded proper;* crest: *on a billet fesswise gules fretty argent a martlet of the*

last; motto: *'Dum vivimus vivamus'.* (FD (1929) I.168). Gr. 22 April 1920 to Robert Greaves Blake of Sheffield and Castle Hill, whose son William was of Mylnhurst (Ecclesall), Yorks.

Blake. Chesterfield. *Argent a cat-à-mountain passant proper between three frets couped gules;* crest: *a demi-cat-à-mountain proper resting its sinister paw on a fret as in the arms;* motto: *'Nec temere nec timide'* (FD (1929) I.169). Gr. 1920 to Sir Arthur Ernest Blake of Nottingham KBE, JP, b. Chesterfield 1866, son of Henry Blake of the same place.

Blakiston. Sandybrook Hall (Offcote and Underwood). *Argent two bars and in chief three cocks gules;* crest: *a cock gules;* motto: *'Fac bene nec dubitans'.* (J. Foster, *Baronetage* (1882), 49). Used (for Foster averred that no authority could be found) by Sir Matthew Blakiston, 4th bt, of Sandybrook, who succ. his father, who had purchased the estate in 1812. They finally sold in 1946. BP (1970, 278) gives the motto in English: *'Doe well and doubt not'.*

Blane. The Pastures (Mickleover). *Argent on a fesse sable a mullet between two crescents of the field in base a rose gules and in chief an anchor erect entwined by a serpent proper;* crest: *a sword erected proper;* motto: *'Paritur pax bello'.* (J. Foster, *Baronetage* (1882), 50). Borne by Sir Hugh Blane, 2nd bt, of the Pastures, to whose father, Sir Gilbert, MD, the *anchor* had been gr. as an augmentation in 1811; he was cr. a bt a year later. The crest comes only from Local MS 9555.44, and would seem to lack authority. The arms were originally gr. to the Blanes of Blanefield, Stirlingshire (LO); title ext. 1916.

Blood. Makeney (Milford). *Argent a fesse indented gules between six martlets sable;* crest: *issuant from waves of the sea a demi-figure of Neptune all proper;* motto *'Honor virtutis praemium'* (Burke, IFR (1976) 152). Gr. (quartering Bindon), to Gen. Sir Bindon Blood in 1899 by Ulster. He was a descendant of Capt. Edmund Blood of Makeney (son of another Edmund who died there 1588), who went to Ireland *c.* 1615.

Bloodworth. Derby. *Argent three bars sable in chief as many torteaux all within a bordure ermine;* crest: *a naked arm embowed proper goutée-de-sang holding a wreath of laurel vert* (Tilley, IV.155). Used by Joseph Bloodworth, mayor of Derby 1702.

Blore. Derby. *Or on a chevron between three pommes a crescent of the field* (Local MS 4556). Used by Thomas Blore of Derby, historian, and his son Edward, born in Derby 1787, later architect to William IV and Queen Victoria. The arms were those of an old family called 'Blower', i.e. the Blores of Blore, Staffs.

Blount. Barton Blount. *Barry nebulée of six or and sable*; crest: *a sun in splendour or*; motto: *'Lux Tua, via mea'*. (V. 1569 Harl.MSS 2113, 1093 only). Borne by Walter Blount of Barton *c.* 1395 (Willement's Roll) where it is blazoned *undée (of 8) or and sable*. These arms are often found quartering *or a tower triple towered azure* (for Ayala, a Navarre heiress who marr. into the family), e.g. formerly in glass at Ashbourne church (*DAJ* III (1881) 91). Sir Walter Blount was cr. (by patent) 1st Lord Mountjoy of Thurvaston 1465 and the 8th Lord Mountjoy was further elevated (1603) as Earl of Devonshire (to which county the family had migrated): the supporters for both were: *on either side two wolves sable* (Burke). Lord Devonshire's marriage with Lady Penelope Devereux was declared void, and their children illegitimate. The eldest was cr. Lord Mountjoy of Fort in Ireland (1618), Lord Mountjoy of Thurvaston, Derbys. (1627) and Earl of Newport, Isle of Wight (1628); all ext. 1681. The arms were: *Barry nebulée of six or and sable within a bordure compony argent and gules*; crest: *out of a ducal coronet or a wolf passant sable between two feathers of the first*; supporters: *on either side a knight in complete armour proper collared, belted, hilt and pommels of swords all or* (Burke). There were numerous cadet branches, some of great eminence, of the Blounts of Barton; only those which remained in Derbys. follow.

Blount. Arleston. *Barry nebulée or and sable on a fesse gules three martlets argent* (V. 1611). Borne by Edward Blount of Arleston 1611, a cadet of Blount of Burton on Trent, Staffs., themselves cadets of Blount of Barton Blount. The Burton Blounts bore, however, *barry nebulée of six or and sable and a bordure compony of the first and second* (Local MS 6341).

Blount. Eckington. *Barry nebulée of eight or and sable on a fesse gules three crowns of the first* (V. 1611, D369). Borne by George

Blount 1611, apparently a cadet of Blount of Barton Blount. His arms were, however, respited for proof.

Blundeville: see Chester, Earls of.

Blythe. Birchitt (Coal Aston); Norton. *Ermine three roebucks trippant proper*; crest: *a roebuck's head erased gules attired or gorged with a chaplet vert* (V. 1569, Norton; V. 1662, Burchet). Gr. *temp.* Henry VII to William son of William Blythe of Norton, conf. and (?) crest gr. 11 Dec. 1566 to Jerome Blythe of Norton. In V. 1662 the roebucks in the arms are blazoned *stags gules ungorged* and the crest *or collared azure*. Local MS 6341 blazons the arms: *ermine three goats' heads erased gules wreathed about the neck and attired or* which is so radically different from the above that it is hard not to think that they represent a totally different family: Papworth offers Gatesford.

Blythe. Derby. *Ermine on a fesse gules three lions rampant or*; crest: *a lion sejant gules.* (V. 1662, D369). Arms conf. and crest gr. 19 April 1575 to George Blythe of Lincoln's Inn, son of John son of Gregory of (Co.) Derby; the V. gives Derby as the locale.

Blount

Boam. Derby. *Argent on a bend azure three fleurs-de-lys or* (*Rel.* V (1865) 229). Used by Henry and Cornelius Boam, aldermen of Derby, successively mayors in 1895 and 1903, of a Derby family.

Boden. Ednaston (Brailsford); The Friary (Derby); S. Wingfield. *Argent a chevron sable between three teazles proper within a bordure of the second*; crest: *in front of a swan rousant proper a staff reguly fessewise sable*; motto: *'Contra a*u*dentior'* (BLG (1937) 189). Gr. *c.* 1900 to Henry Boden of The Friary (1836–1908); previously the family had used the above arms without *bordure*, with crest: *a swan sejant proper*, both visible in the Friary Hotel, Derby.

Boissier. Repton; Idridgehay. Crest: *a demi-greyhound rampant collared and lined the line reflexed over the back* (in current use). Borne or used by Roger Boissier of Easton House, Repton, yr son of E.G. Boissier of Derby and grandson of Canon F.S. Boissier, vicar of Denby (1855–1951). Mr Boissier's brother, Martin, lives at Idridgehay.

Bonell. Duffield. *Or crusilly a lion rampant sable*; crest: *a demi-lion sable* (Thompson III.13; Lysons, cxix). Used by Thomas Porter Bonell of Duffield Hall, heir of Henry Porter *alias* Sherbrook, who inherited from the Coapes.

Bonnington. Bearwardcote; Burnaston. *Sable a chevron or between three roses argent* (Vv. 1569, 1662). Some MSS give the roses as *or*. Borne by William Bonnington of Bearwardcote 1569 and by Ralph (Bearwardcote Hall) and Peter (Burnaston) in 1662. In V. 1611 William Bonnington the yr was branded as 'an usurper' and it is noted that he 'promised to come to London' with his proofs, which presumably he did.

Bonsall. Alfreton. *Argent on a fesse gules three crystals and a bordure ermine* (*Rel.* V (1865) 229). These are the arms of a Welsh family, originally from Staffs., used by George Bonsall of Alfreton gent. (1719–97) and his son, John (1751–1810), and are commemorated in the church there.

Booth: see Bothe.

Boothby. Ashbourne; Broadlowash (Thorpe). *Argent on a canton sable a lion's gamb erased and erect or*; crest: *a lion's gamb erased and erect or*; motto: *'Mors Christi mors mortis mihi'* (V. 1662). Arms borne by Henry Boothby of Broadlowash, cr. a bt at Oxford

1644 (when it failed to pass the great seal). The title was re-cr. for his eldest son, William, 13 July 1660.

Borough

Borowe (later Borough). Castlefields (Derby); Hulland Hall. *Argent on a mount vert in base the trunk of an oak tree sprouting out two branches proper hanging thereon the shield of Pallas or fastened by a belt gules*; crest: *an eagle proper holding in its talons the shield of Pallas or*; motto: *'Virtute et Robore'* (MI at St Werburgh, Derby). Gr. 2 Oct. 1702 to John Borowe (of Castlefields) son of Humphrey 'late of Gotham Notts. dec'd' with remainder to Samuel, his yr brother, of Mansfield, Notts. John Borowe of Hanson Grange (Newton Grange) and Alvaston Fields assumed the surname and arms of Tempest additionally to his own early C18, and the field of the Borowe arms as borne by him was *azure*. Another member of the family, Charles, assumed by RL 1875 the surname and quartered arms of Roberts-Gawen (grant in Derby Local Studies Library, uncatalogued). The senior line moved to Chetwynd Park, Newport (Salop), and its last male heir, Burton Borough, dsp. The last heir male of the family as a whole, Canon R.F.

Borough, bore (with numerous quarterings) the arms *with a bordure wavy gules.*

Bossley. Bakewell; Chesterfield. *Argent on a fesse engrailed between three cinquefoils sable as many fleurs-de-lys of the field.* (V. Staffs. 1583). Borne by 'J.S. Bossley, vicar of Chesterfield' (*Rel.* V (1865) 229) (in error for George Bossley (1754–1822)), youngest son of William, of Bakewell, whose mother was heiress of the Breretons through the Barkers.

Bosville. Beighton; Loscoe; Ripley. *Argent five fusils in fesse gules in chief three bears' heads erased sable*; crest: *an ox issuant from a knot of trees proper*; motto: *'Intento in Deum animo'* (V. 1569). Borne by Thomas Bosvile (or Boswell) in 1569; his heir, George, disclaimed in 1611. The heiress of Col. William Bosville marr. Sir Alexander MacDonald of Sleat, 9th bt (cr. 1st Lord MacDonald of Slate in Ireland) and their third son (later 3rd Lord) assumed the additional surname and arms of Bosville in 1814. The arms, *sans boars' heads*, appeared in glass at Staveley church (Cox I.353) – those of the Bosvilles of Chevet. Lysons (cxix) blazon the bears' heads muzzled of the field; Lord MacDonald quarters arms wherein they are *muzzled or* (J. Foster, *Peerage* (1881), 439).

Boswell. The Grey House (Ashbourne). *Quarterly i, argent on a fesse sable three cinquefoils of the field and a canton of Caithness: azure a ship at anchor sails furled within a double tressure flory counter-flory or,* for Boswell; *ii, argent three bars sable* for Auchinlech of that Ilk; *iii, argent a lion rampant azure armed and langued gules quartering argent a saltire and a chief gules,* for Bruce, Earl of Kincardine, and *iv, azure a bend between three pelicans in their nests feeding their young argent,* for Cramond; crest: *a falcon proper hooded gules jessed and belled or*; motto: *'Vraye foy'* (FD (1929) I.190). Matriculated (LO) 1773 to James Boswell 9th of Auchinleck, the biographer of Dr Johnson (with supporters: *on either side a greyhound proper collared collar charged with three cinquefoils argent leash passing between the forelegs and reflexed over the back of the last on a compartment charged with a lion's head affrontée also of the last suppressing a saltire argent)* whose brother's descendant was Dr Alexander Boswell, who lived and practised in Ashbourne for many years from the late C19.

Botetourt. Bakewell. *Or a saltire engrailed*

sable; crest: *out of a mural crown six spears in saltire proper* (Caerlaverock Roll, 1300). These arms were borne by the future 1st Lord Botetourt (cr. 1308) whose brother John was *jure uxoris* of Bakewell, and some sources difference the arms for him with *a crescent.* His heiress marr. Swinbourne, which family (qv) occasionally bore these arms in lieu of their own.

Botham. Derby; Mickleover. *Argent six pellets two two and two.* (Thompson IV.50; Burke). Used by William Botham gent. of Derby 1596 (bur. at Mickleover 1636) and by his kinsman, Robert, of Mickleover and Littleover, who nevertheless disclaimed 1662. John Botham was bailiff of Derby 1556 and 1566; William, his son, in 1581, 1590 and 1598.

Bothe. Arleston; Barrow upon Trent; Charlesworth; Sinfin. *Argent three boars' heads erect sable* (seal of Henry Bothe C14, Local MS 6341; cf. V. Cheshire 1580). Borne by Sir Henry Bothe of Arleston, Barrow and Sinfin (d. 1446). Thomas Bothe (Bouth) of Fawley, Berks., grandson of Thomas, of Charlesworth, gent., bore the arms differenced by a *mullet* (V. Berks. 1623).

Bothe. Sawley. *Argent a tun fesseways charged with a mullet between three boars' heads erect sable* (MI at Sawley church). Borne by Roger Bothe of Mollington, Cheshire, and Sawley and his heirs; he was 6th son of Sir John of Cheshire, who assumed the arms (without the tun) of Barton of Barton (Lancs.) in 1403 in lieu of the original Bothe arms: *argent a chevron engrailed gules on a canton a mullet*; crest: *a Catherine wheel* (sometimes: *an Agnus Dei)* (Cox IV.332n.; V. Cheshire 1580, Harl.MSS 1424, 1505, suggest that they were the other way round)

Bott. Derby. *Or a chevron pean between three mullets sable*; crest: *on a glove a falcon proper* (MI at Holy Trinity Church, Coventry, impaled by Holland). Borne or used by Thomas Bott of Derby, mayor in 1705: descendants were of Burton on Trent, Coton in the Elms and Tutbury, Staffs. They came from Handsworth, Staffs.

Boultbee. Derby. *Or a pile azure overall a chevron invected between two garbs in chief and in base a mullet of six points all counterchanged* (FD (1905) 217). Gr. as a quartering to the Cantrell-Hubberstys (qv). Borne by Joseph Boultbee of Leicester, who was close kin to Revd Thomas Boultbee of Derby, a c18 divine, who actually used: *azure a chevron between three garbs or*; crest: *out of a ducal coronet a demi-boar proper* (*Rel.* V (1865) 229).

Boun (Bown). Blackwell. *Azure on a bend argent cotised between six lioncels rampant or three escallops gules* (Thompson IV.50). Apparently borne by Ralph Boun of Coventry and London, directly descended from another Ralph, of Blackwell, living in the reign of Henry VI. The arms are a differenced coat of Bohun, of which surname Boun is plainly a phonetic mutation. Sleigh (*Rel.* V (1865) 229) gives another coat for Boun (which he spells Boam): *argent on a bend azure three fleurs-de-lys or*. This coat was used by the Bowns of Matlock c17.

Bourne. Ashover; Chesterfield. *Argent on a chevron gules three lions rampant or* (Burke). Used by Revd Obadiah Bourne (d. 1711) impaling Beckingham. This represents the marriage of his father, Revd Immanuel Bourne, rector of Ashover 1621–42 and owner of Eastwood Hall there, to Jemima, dau. of Sir Thomas Beckingham of Tolleshunt, Essex.

Bowdon. Beighton; Bowden (Chapel en le Frith); Clowne; Southgate House (Clowne). *Quarterly sable and or in the first quarter a lion passant argent langued gules*; crest: *out of a ducal coronet a demi-eagle displayed above its head a cross formée sable* (Vv. 1569, 1611). Gr. *c.* 1597 to George Bowdon of Bowden, his father's arms having been entered at V. 1569 with a dubit. This family eventually became heirs of Butler of Pleasington Hall, Lancs., and John Bowdon assumed the additional surname and quarterly arms of Butler (qv), by RSM 21 Jan. 1841. By this grant the crest of Bowdon was changed to: *a heron's head erased proper beaked and charged on the neck with three ermine spots sable* borne with the crest of Butler (qv) and motto: *'Vanus est Honor'* (BLG (1937) 214). John Butler-Bowdon became, by the termination of abeyancy in 1940, 25th Lord Grey de Ruthyn and bore arms (bearing no coat of Bowdon at all!): *Quarterly of eight: 1 & 8 Clifton (qv), 2 Hastings (qv) quarterly with Rawdon, 3 & 5 Yelverton, 4 Gould, 6 Barnardiston, 7 Grey (qv)* crest: *a dexter arm embowed in armour holding a sword proper*; supporters: *dexter a wyvern collared and lined gules, sinister a lion rampant reguardant gules*;

motto: *'Mortem aut triumphum'* (Pine, 136). On Lord Grey de Ruthyn's death in 1963 the barony again fell into abeyance, out of which it has yet to be called.

Bower. Tideswell. *Sable a cross patée argent* (MI at Tideswell church, now lost). Arms restored as allegedly borne by 'Sir' Thurstan de la Bower of Little Longstone and Tideswell, living 1403 and quartering Edensor, his mother being supposedly a coheiress of the Longstone branch of that family.

Bower. Chesterfield; Darley Hall (Darley); Ollersett Hall (New Mills); Taxal. *Sable a cross patée and in dexter chief an escallop argent* (*Rel.* XII (1872) 93). Arms, plainly inspired by those given above, used by Francis Bower of Darley, his kinsman Samuel of Chesterfield, and Buckley Bower of Ollersett. The Bowers of Goss Hall, Ashover, were also kin of those of Chesterfield, but the arms they used, if any, are uncertain. Foster Bower of Taxal, Cheshire, assumed the surname and arms of Jodrell 5 April 1775 (qv), thus regularising his position heraldically.

Bowles. Abney; Bradshaw Hall (Chapel en le Frith); Wirksworth. *Azure three cups in each a boar's head or*; crest: *a demi-boar salient azure vulned in the left breast with an arrow proper*; motto: *'Ut tibi sic alteri'* (BLG (1898) I.156). Arms conf. 1817 to Humphrey Bowles of Sheen, Surrey, and *jure matris* of Abney and Bradshaw. His grandson, C.E. Bradshaw Bowles, was of Wirksworth and a noted local antiquary early c20.

Bowman. Hartington; One Ash Grange (Monyash). *Or a chevron between three bows bent in pale gules* (*Rel.* V (1865) 229). Arms of a Dorset family used by Ebenezer Bowman of One Ash, of a Hartington family.

Bowyer. Roston; Snelston Hall; Waldley (Marston Montgomery). *Argent a lion rampant between three crosses crosslet fitchée gules*; crest: *out of a tower gules a demi-dragon rampant or* (seal in a local collection). Arms used by William Bowyer of Marston Montgomery (d. 1769), who purchased Snelston Hall. Despite the use of the arms of the Bowyers of Knypersley, Staffs., the families were apparently unrelated. William Bowyer esq. of Roston Hall, a kinsman of the c17, used the same coat.

Boyle. Bradley Hall. *Per bend embattled argent and gules*; crest: *out of a ducal coronet or a lion's head per pale embattled argent and* *gules*; motto: *'God's providence is my inheritance'* (V. Herefs 1586). Conf. (UO) 1603 to the future 1st Earl of Cork (cr. 26 Oct. 1620). His descendant, the Hon. John Boyle, was of Bradley Hall prior to 1973.

Boyleston. Boyleston. *Gules six crosses crosslet fitchée argent on a chief or three pellets.* Borne by Thomas de Boyleston of Boyleston, grandson of Roger de Instanval, huntsman to Earl Ferrers. Quartered by Ridware and Cotton (Harl.MS 6592).

Bozon. Edensor. *Argent three bird bolts one in pale erect between two pilewise gules heads sable* (Charles Roll). Borne in Henry III's reign by Ralph de Bozon; Robert de Bozon marr., a generation or so later, the heiress of Sir Adam de Edensor and his grandson was there in 1353.

Brabazon. Croxall. *Gules on a bend argent three martlets sable*: crest: *on a mount vert a falcon volant or* (Arms: seal *c.* 1446, Local MS 6341, and as quartered by Curzon of Croxall; Crest: Berry). The seal (quoted above) of Sir William Brabazon included *a label of 3 points* (ibid.). The Parliament Roll gives the bend as *or* for Sir Roger Brabazon of Leicestershire, 1347. In 1296 Robert de Brabazon held Croxall under Ralph de Bakepuize; his heiress marr. Curzon.

Brace. Doveridge Hall. *Sable a bend argent between two dexter cubit arms in bend vested of the second hands proper*; crest: *an arm embowed vested in mail argent the hand grasping a scimitar proper hilt and pommel or* (FD (1910) 176). Arms borne by Frank Addison Brace (1859–1912) of Doveridge Hall; there seems to be no authority for the use of the crest. He was son of Henry, of Walsall, Staffs.

Bracebridge. Twyford. *Vairé argent and sable a fesse gules*; crest: *a ragged staff erect or*; motto: *'Be as God will'* (arms, Parliament Roll, 1308; rest: BLG (1937) 223). The crest and motto are anachronistic. The arms were borne c16 by Simon Bracebridge of Twyford, whose dau. and heiress marr. Beaumont. Simon's wife was the heiress of Crewker (qv). These arms are found quartering Burton (Papworth 764). Whole achievement conf. 1808 to the Bracebridges of Warwickshire. In 1308, Sir John, the bearer, was of Lincs.

Bradbourne. Bradbourne; Hulland; Lea Hall. *Argent on a bend gules three mullets pierced or*; crest: *a beech tree proper* (V. 1569, The Hough (Hulland); V. 1611, Bradbourne).

Jenyns' Ordinary (*c.* 1380) gives mullets *pierced vert* for Sir John Bradbourne of The Hough. Lysons (clv) give for crest: *a pine tree fructed vert.* Papworth (268) gives the above coat *cotised sable* which is unknown otherwise, and may represent a misinterpretation of arms in church glass, the bend picked out in leaden strips. Burke gives another coat entirely for 'co. Derby': *argent three pallets azure and a chief gules.* A device similar to this (but, inevitably, without tinctures) was used on the seal of John Bradbourne esq. of Burton on Trent, *c.* 1713 (Every Deeds in private hands).

Bradbury. Ollersett (New Mills); Youlgreave; Dinting (Glossop); Tideswell. *Sable a chevron ermine between three round buckles points downwards argent and a fleur-de-lys or for difference*; crest: *a demi-dove volant argent fretty gules holding in the beak a slip of barberry vert fructed of the second* (V. 1569). Conf. 1569 to Nicholas Bradbury of Ollersett Hall, the fleur-de-lys indicating either that he was not the eldest son, or that a senior line existed. At V. 1611 Nicholas Bradbury (the grandson of the last) 'promised to come to London' and in 1662 Edmund's arms were respited for proof; he disappears from record after 1682, however. There is a record of the grant of a crest to a Bradbury by Christopher Barker, when Norroy (i.e. before 1536) but whether it was to this family or the Bradburys of Essex and Suffolk who bore similar arms, but without the difference, is not clear. Francis Bradbury of Youlgreave (yr brother of Nicholas, of V. 1611) disclaimed at the Visitation.

Bradley. Butterley Park (Ripley); Chesterfield; Rowtor Hall (Birchover). *Gules a chevron between three boars' heads couped or* (*Rel.* XII (1872) 93). Borne or used by John Bradley of Rowtor 1745 and by Henry and James Bradley three generations later.

Bradshaw. Abney; Barton Blount; Bradshaw Hall (Chapel en le Frith); Eyam; Duffield; Holbrook; Makeney etc. *Argent two bendlets between as many martlets sable*; crest: *on a mount vert a stag at gaze russet under a vine of the first fructed purpure*; motto: *'Qui vit content tient assez'* (V. 1611). Borne 1611 by Francis Bradshaw of Bradshaw as senior representative of this extensive and complex family (see *DAJ* XXV (1903) 13). Edward Bradshaw of Litton, although entitled to these arms, did not appear at V. 1662.

Bradshaw. Windley. *Argent two bendlets between as many martlets sable an annulet in chief* (V. 1569, Local MS 6341). Borne by John Bradshaw of Windley, of a little understood family, consanguineous (if the difference mark is to be believed) with the preceding. An ancestor had marr. the heiress of Folcher and quartered their arms and those of the Champeynes. Both *bendlets gules* in some MSS and Tilley II.307.

Bradshaw. Duffield; Idridgehay Wirksworth. *Argent two bendlets the uppermost sable the other gules* (*Rel.* XII. (1872) 93). Apparently borne by Robert Bradshaw of Idridgehay, d. 1556, and his son, Anthony, of Wirksworth (d. 1608). Also quartered by Lord Waterpark (see Cavendish) by the marriage of Sir Henry Cavendish, 2nd bt of Doveridge, with Sarah, dau. and heiress of Richard Bradshaw, cr. 1792 Baroness Waterpark in the Irish peerage. The arms were conf. 1791. For the supporters, see Cavendish.

Brailsford. Brailsford; Bradley; Wingerworth; Birchitt (Coal Aston); Bupton (Longford); Burnaston; Culland (Brailsford); Osmaston (by Ashbourne) etc. *Or a cinquefoil sable*; crest: *out of a ducal coronet or a stag's head affrontée proper.* (Jenyns' Ordinary; crest: Local MS 6341). Borne 1356 by Sir Henry de Brailsford of Brailsford (seal, Local MS 6341). The cinquefoil is sometimes shown as *pierced*. A seal of Ralph Brailsford kt (d. 1344), father of Sir Henry, gives an alternative coat, *on a bend three cinquefoils* (Local MS 6341; see next entry). Branches which settled early at Birchitt, Culland and Osmaston assumed those names; the Osmastons ended in heiresses in 1431, leaving their estates divided between the Franceis, Bradshaw and Bothe families, the former known to have quartered Brailsford: thus it must be assumed that these branches of this family – one of only two in the county provably descended from a Saxon-named tenant mentioned in Domesday Book – also used or bore the above arms.

Brailsford. Duffield; Seanor (Ault Hucknall); N. Wingfield etc. *Argent on a bend gules three cinquefoils or* (V. 1611, Egerton MS 996; V. 1634). These arms, occasionally given for the Brailsfords of Seanor, plainly derive from the seal of Sir Ralph Brailsford given above. More often the arms were as for Brailsford of Brailsford, with *a martlet for difference* (Local

MS 6341, Vv. 1611, 1662), as borne by Thomas Brailsford of Seanor (1554–1625). This man marr. one of the heiresses of Clay of Crich, and glass once in Crich church showed the *bend* version of the arms impaling Clay (Cox, IV.58 and n.) Sometimes the bend is given (as Burke) as *sable*.

Brailsford. South Normanton. *Or a cinquefoil sable on a chief indented ermine two pommes on each a cross argent*; crest: *a unicorn's head argent erased gules armed and crined or entwined with a snake vert and charged on the neck with a pomme as in the arms*; motto: *'In Jehova spes mea'* (Burke). Gr. to Thomas Brailsford of East Barkwith, Lincs., and South Normanton 1825, marr. to the heiress of Heathcote of Stancliffe (Darley), hence the *chief* of Heathcote. He was descended from Brailsford of Hill, Tupton, 1630. The Brailsfords of Wellow, Notts., cadets of those of Seanor, bore *or a cinquefoil pierced and a canton sable* (V. Notts. 1662).

Braithwaite: see Oxley.

Bramhall. Norton. *Argent three pelicans' heads erased azure vulning themselves gules* (*Rel.* V (1865) 229; Local MS 4556). Arms used by John Bramhall of Norton House, which he sold 1712.

Brailsford

24

Brampton. Tideswell. *Azure a lion rampant or* (brass at Tideswell church, Cox, II.301). Paulinus de Brampton marr. the dau. and heiress of Thomas de Lamely (Ibid., 300) and their heiress marr. Daniel (qv).

Brandram. Alvaston; Weston upon Trent. *Azure a pile wavy ermine between two bees volant in fesse or*; crest: *a lamb passant proper on the body a pile wavy between two millrinds sable the pile charged with a bee volant or*; motto: *'Persevere'* (BLG Supplement (1954) 55–7). Gr. 1 June 1795 to Samuel Brandram of Size Lane, London, and Lee Grove (Lewisham), Kent, to the descendants of his father, James, of Alvaston and Weston, of a family long settled at the latter place. Maj. R. Brandram marr. in 1947 Princess Katharine of Greece and Denmark.

Branston. Co. Derby. *Argent on a fesse sable three bezants* (Local MS 4556; Burke; Berry). Efforts to provide this coat with a name and place in this county have proved fruitless.

Brazier-Creagh. Netherseal Old Hall. *Quarterly per fesse indented or and sable four cinquefoils counterchanged (quartering Creagh: argent a chevron between three laurel branches vert on a chief azure as many bezants)*; crest: *a demi-lion rampant per pale or and sable*; motto: *'Amor Patriae'* (Burke, IFR 285). Gr. 24 May 1665 by Ulster to Brasier (sic) of Coleraine, whose descendant, Kilner Charles Brazier-Creagh (1869–1956) lived at Netherseal Old Hall.

Brereton. Hurdlow (Hartington). *Argent two bars sable a crescent for difference*; crest: *a cameleopard's head erased* (V. 1662; V. Staffs. 1663). The arms of the Breretons as recorded to Andrew de Brereton of Brereton, Staffs., *c.* 1465 (Ballard's Book), and borne as above by Edward, of Hurdlow and his son, William. In 1687 *(DAJ* XXXII (1910) 67 n. 4) William was recorded as having his arms respited for proof, and, indeed the connection with the Breretons of Brereton has never satisfactorily been established, although two possibilities exist.

Breton. Walton; Rowditch (Derby). *Argent a chevron between three escallops gules* (Jenyns' Ordinary). Borne by Roger le Breton kt of Walton 1339, whose grand-dau. and ultimate heiress marr. Loudham, both arms being quartered by Foljambe and visible in Chesterfield church.

Brewer: see Briwere.

Brighouse. Derby; Spondon. *Sable on a fesse between three lions rampant or as many crescents of the field*; crest: *out of a mural coronet or a tiger's head argent*; motto: *'Dei Regi Patriae'* (C19 letterhead in writer's possession). Gr. to Martin Brighouse of Coleby (Kesteven), Lincs., 1 Dec. 1590; used by Joseph Brighouse of Spondon, Midland Railway accounts controller and organist of St Andrew's church, Derby, 1892. His ancestor was John Brighouse (d. Derby 1736), who came from Yorks.

Bright. Chesterfield; Overton Hall (Ashover); Staveley. *Per pale azure and gules a bend or between two mullets argent*; crest: *a mass of clouds therefrom a sun issuant all proper*; motto: *'Clarior e tenebris'.* (MI in Sheffield Cathedral, 1765). Gr. 1660 to Col. John Bright of Carbrook, Yorks., on his being made a bt 16 July that year (ext. 13 Sept. 1688). The nephew was Ald. John Bright of Chesterfield (1657–1734), who actually used these arms with the *bend argent*. Thomas Bright of Inkersall (Staveley) was a cadet of Ald. Bright's and bore (or used) these arms with the colours of the field reversed; he was ancestor of Sir Charles Tilston Bright MP, whose arms were the same. His C19 kinsman, Dr John Bright of Overton Hall, bore likewise.

Bristowe. Twyford; West Hallam. *Ermine on a fesse cotised and all engrailed sable three crescents or*; crest: *issuant from a crescent argent a demi-eagle displayed azure wings expanded barry of four argent and of the first*; motto: *'Splendeus et crescens'.* (BLG (1937) 241). Allowed to Thomas Bristowe of Besthorpe Hall, Notts. (V. Notts. 1662–4), and borne by Simon Bristowe of Twyford Hall (1615–81) and his heirs (MIs at Twyford church). The two branches of the family are difficult to reconcile genealogically and one suspects that Bristowe of Twyford were only users of these arms. Lysons (lxxix) blazon them without engrailments (as at Twyford church) and with the motto *'Vigilantibus non dormientibus'.*

Briwere. Castleton; Chesterfield. *Gules two bendlets wavy or* (glass in window at Hassop Hall, cf. Burke). William Briwere was constable of the Peak, *c.* 1210, and he and his son William were lords of Chesterfield. Both sealed with *a mermaid holding her tail,* *although another seal shows the mermaid holding an additional tail, and so the device was presumably a mermaid with two tails* (RBC 49, 101, 260). The hereditary nature of this device is heraldic, although it may be a badge. Heiress marr. Wake.

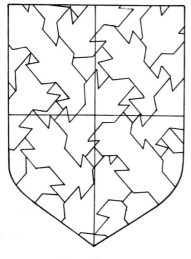

Broadhurst

Broadhurst. Duffield; Foston Hall. *Quarterly azure and or fretty raguly counterchanged*; crest: *a swan ermine naiant in water proper and charged on the breast with an estoile sable wings expanded or fretty raguly azure*; motto *'Sapere et tacere'* (BLG (1875) I.147). Gr. 1809 to John son of John Broadhurst of Foston (d. 1861), whose father was alleged to have once been a footman to Lord Portmore.

Brocklehurst. Glossop; Taxal. *Per pale argent and sable three chevronels engrailed between as many brocks all counterchanged*; crest: *a brock sable holding in the mouth a slip of oak fructed proper in front of a mount vert thereon two oak trees also proper*; motto: *'Veritas me dirigit'*. Conf. to Sir Philip Brocklehurst of Swythamley Park, Staffs., on his being made a bt 27 Aug. 1903. He was descended in the 7th generation from George Brocklehurst of Glossop and Gap House, Taxal, which he sold in 1623. Sir Philip's bro-

ther John was in 1914 cr. Lord Ranksborough, being gr. supporters: *on either side a Roman soldier reguardant resting the exterior hand on a shield all proper* (Pine, 226). Arms originally gr. 1879 to Thomas Unett Brocklehurst and the descendants of his father, Thomas.

Brocksopp. Ashover; Hasland; N. Wingfield; Shirland Park. *Azure on a saltire ermine between a garb in chief two cinquefoils in flaunch or and a greyhound courant in base argent five cross crosslets gules*; crest: *a cross potent gules thereon a dove wings elevated in the beak three ears of wheat proper*. (College of Arms, Grants XXIV.201–2.) Gr. 11 May 1807 to Edward Brocksopp of London, N. Wingfield, Hasland and Ashover; his kinsman John, an ironmaster, was of Shirland Park.

Bronham. 'Co. Derby'. *Sable six plates two two and two* (Local MS 4556). These arms are either a variant of those used by the Bothams (qv) or intended for those of Alwin Bronson, recorded (Burke, DFUSA 2580) as an 'adherent of Mary, Queen of Scots, living in co. Derby 1568'. No Bronham family is traceable in local records: a misreading of an MS seems likely.

Brookhouse. Derby. *Sable a lion rampant guardant or* (Jeavons, 291). Used by Robert Brookhouse of Derby, gent., whose dau. marr. the Revd Dr Samuel Crossman of Bristol. The arms appear impaled by Crossman's on plate given to St Werburgh's church, Derby, dated 1717. The family provided several bailiffs of Derby from the early C16.

Brooks. Derby; Coxbench (Holbrook); Ingleby. *Argent on a bend sable a hawk's lure or and a chief of the second*; crest: *a lure with the line formed into a bow knot between two wings all proper* (Cox & Hope, 147; crest: Burke). Borne or used by Revd Ley Brooks of Derby (MI at All Saints), d. 1844. He was descended from John Brooks of Ingleby, living *c*. 1625; it is therefore unlikely that he was entitled to these arms, conf. 1605 to the family of Brooke of Bucks.

Broomfield. Morley. *Azure a lion passant guardant or*; crest: *a lion passant guardant or gorged with a wreath of the first and azure* (Tilley IV.155). Thomas Broomfield, of a Staffs. family 'descended out of Wales' (Berry) was of Morley (presumably in the Broomfield Hall area) in 1495.

Broster. Wirksworth Manor. *Sable three antelopes' heads couped or*; crest: *a buck trippant* (arms: quartered by Shalcross on a seal, 1478; crest: livery button in a private collection). Used by Dr A.E. Broster of Wirksworth about 80 years ago. The above is not the usual achievement of Broster, a Chester family. The family originated at Broster Field (Foolow).

Brown. Compton. *Per pale argent and sable within two bendlets as many lions passant all between two fleurs-de-lys and all counterchanged*; crest: *in front of a griffin's head erased per pale sable and argent gorged with a collar flory counterflory counterchanged five bezants fessewise*: motto: *'Si sit prudentia'* (FD (1910) 203). Gr. to David Brown of Compton and Southport, Lancs. (b. 1833), son of William, of Compton. Borne by his sons, Frederick and Alleyne.

Browne. Hungry Bentley; Chesterfield. *Ermine on a fesse embattled counter-embattled sable three escallops argent*; crest: *out of a mural coronet gules a crane's head and neck issuant ermine beaked azure*; motto: *'Esse quam haberi'* (V. 1662). Conf. by Camden before 1623 to Thomas Browne of Shredicote (Bradley), Staffs., and borne at V. 1662 by his fourth son, Edmund, of Hungry Bentley (1611–84). V. 1662 adds 'not proved'.

Browne. Boyleston; Burnaston; Egginton; Etwall; Hilton. *Ermine on a fesse embattled counter-embattled sable three escallops or*; crest: *out of a mural crown gules a stork's head and neck issuant ermine beaked and charged on the neck with an escallop azure*; motto: *'Verum atque decens'* (MI at Uttoxeter church, Staffs.; bookplate, I.H. Browne, Local MS 7769). Gr. 14 May 1779 (and previously used by) Isaac Hawkins Browne MP of Bridgnorth, Salop (1745–1818), who helped to found the Derbys. General Infirmary, and owned much property in Derbys. He was 5th in descent from William Browne of Etwall (1562–1633), who claimed descent from Browne of Shredicote.

Browne. Lings (N. Wingfield); Newbold. *Sable three lions passant in bend between two double cotises argent*; crest: *an eagle displayed vert*; supporters: *two wolves argent collared and chained or*; motto: *'Suivez raison'* (formerly on (lost) MI at Newbold chapel, near Chesterfield (Cox, I.179); cf. V. Surrey 1623). Borne, probably legitimately, by Maj. the

Hon. Anthony Browne, estranged elder son of 3rd Viscount Montagu (cr. 1544) and *soi disant* or *de jure* 4th viscount. The peerage claim post-1660 failed for want of proof of a marriage contracted in York during the siege, 10 Jan. 1644; subsequently, poverty prevented further claims. The heir male of this family lived at Chorleywood, Herts., 1977.

Browne. Marsh Hall (Chapel en le Frith). *Argent on a chevron gules three roses of the field*; crest: *a lion rampant argent ducally crowned or supporting an upright spear proper headed of the first* (V. 1611). Displayed at V. 1569 (with a dubit) by Nicholas Browne of Whitfield (Glossop) and Marsh, and conf. to him 4 Nov. 1582.

Browne. Snelston. *Sable three lions passant in bend between two cotises argent in chief a trefoil slipped ermine*; crest: *a griffin's head erased sable ears, beak and collar or charged on the neck with a trefoil ermine* (V. 1569). Exemplified 15 Aug. 1551 to Nicholas Browne of Snelston, of a family settled there from C14. William son of Henry Browne of Marston Montgomery showed the same arms at V. 1611, but was labelled 'an usurper' and 'promised to come to London'. A descendant, Thomas Browne of Little Wimley (Stevenage), Herts., and Snelston, Norroy King of Arms (1761–73), was gr. 1761 a different crest, with remainder to his brothers Henry and John, sons of John son of William Browne.

Browne. Derby. *Sable a lion passant in bend between two cotises argent in the sinister chief a trefoil slipped ermine* (Local MS 4556). Used by Ald. Henry Browne, mayor of Derby 1799 and 1808, of a Loughborough family; he was an ancestor of Sir George Buckston Browne (b. 1850), the surgeon.

Browne. Compton. *Sable three lions passant in bend between two cotises argent all between as many trefoils slipped ermine* (Thompson IV.2). Gr. (at a date unknown) to Edward Browne of Compton, 'supposed descendant of Sir Anthony Browne KG ancestor of Thomas Browne, Norroy' (later Garter, 1774–80, on whom see Browne of Snelston (sic)). This may be due to confusion in Thompson's handling of his sources.

Browne. Stretton en le Field. *Azure a chevron between three escallops or*; crest: *a stork azure collared beaked ringed and membered argent* (V. 1662). Borne 1662 by John Browne of Stretton, whose grandfather, John, first settled there; he was son of Sir William and grandson of John, both Lord Mayor of London. The arms were exhibited 'sans proof' in 1662 (although, apparently, borne by both mayors) but were conf. 1664 and again in 1838 when their heirs, the Caves assumed the additional surname and quartered arms of Browne. *A bordure engrailed gules* was added by the Caves at first, and the crest was altered: *stock, proper, winged and ducally gorged or beaked and membered gules*. See also Cave.

Brownell. Derby. *Ermine on a chevron cotised sable three escallops argent*; crest: *out of a ducal coronet a triple plume of feathers five, four and three* (Berry). Gr. 8 Feb. 1682 to Mary, dau. and heiress of John Brownell of Derby, and wife of Sir Robert Dacres of Clerkenwell kt.

Brownell. Cliffe Field (Hope). *Ermine on a chevron cotised sable three escallops argent*; crest: *an escallop argent* (*DAJ* XLV (1923) 91). Gr. 1775 to Robert Brownell of Cliffe Field, and London, son of Peter, of Newfield (Chapel en le Frith).

Brownlow. Heanor; West Hallam. *Or eight martlets sable*; crest: *on a cap of maintenance a greyhound or collared gules* (*Rel.* VII (1867) 19). Arms allowed to John Brownlow of Enfield, Middlesex, 1634, son of Christopher of 'co. Derby'. He had a brother, John Brownlow gent. of Heanor, with a son, Martin, of West Hallam. Two grandsons of John were cr. bts: Sir John, of Belton, Lincs. (26 July 1641), and Sir William, of Humby, Lincs. (27 July 1641). The 5th bt of Humby was 1718 cr. Lord Charleville and Viscount Tyrconnel in Ireland. By this time the arms were *or an orle of eight martlets and an inescutcheon sable*; supporters: *on either side a lion rampant reguardant argent* (UO). Honours ext. 1754; btcy of Belton ext. 1679.

Brucknall. Spondon. Arms usurped in 1611 unknown (V. 1611).

Bruckshaw. Dalley (Belper). *Argent a chevron between three crosses moline gules*; crest: *sea chart proper* (Burke). Entered by John Bruckshaw (Brookshaw) of Belper V. 1611 and by Francis Bruckshaw of Belper, Dethick and Matlock in 1662. Both 'usurpers', although the former 'promised to come to London'; the fact that he appears not to have done so suggests that he was unconnected

with Bruckshaw of Harrytown, Cheshire.

Bruninge: see Briwere.

Buck. Derbys. *Per fesse nebulée argent and sable three bucks' attires fixed to the scalp counterchanged* (Local MS 4556). These arms are attributed neither to a period nor a locale in the MS. The arms belong to a Worcs. family of this name.

Buckston: see Buxton.

Bulkeley. Stapenhill. *Sable a chevron between three bulls' heads caboshed argent and a canton or*. This is the form taken by the arms of Thomas Bulkeley of Leek, Staffs., 1557, supposedly the ancestor of this family, and quoted in most references (e.g. Lysons, clvii). However, the D369 MS of V. 1662 shows the arms with no canton, and in fact these arms, but with *two chevronels and a canton or*, were allowed 1662 to Thomas Bulkeley of Stapenhill, son of Alexander, 2nd son of Thomas of Stoke, Salop. Thomas had exhibited arms 'sans proof', V. 1662, but later established them.

Bullock. Brampton; Darley; Derby; Norton; Unstone. *Ermine on a chief gules a label of five points or*; crest: *seven arrows six in saltire and one in base gules feathered and headed argent enfiled with a mural coronet of the last* (MI at St Alkmund, Derby; V. 1611). Arms conf. and crest gr. 20 June 1609 to John Bullock of Derby (and Darley). Inexplicably, therefore, the remark 'promised to come to London' was attached to his pedigree in V. 1611. The Unstone branch showed arms V. 1569 'with a dubit', V. 1611 without comment, and as above, and V. 1662 'sans proof'. Likewise, Bullock of Norton. Note the armorial similarity with the arms of Morteyne (qv).

Bullock. Ashford; Hurdlow (Hartington). *Sable two swords in saltire between four fleurs-de-lys or*; crest: *a squirrel cracking a nut proper* (MI at Ashford church). Used by Revd John (1730–89) of Ashford and Dr William Bullock (1735–84) of Hurdlow, but actually the arms of Barrow, here impaling Swan of Kent.

Burdett. Foremark; Knowlehill (Ticknall). *Azure on two bars or six martlets gules*; crest: *a lion's head erased sable* (V. Warwicks. 1619). Conf. to Sir Thomas Burdett when he was made a bt 25 Feb. 1619, of Bramcote (Polesworth), Warwicks. The family had earlier borne *azure two bars or* (as quoted in V.

1662, D369 version) and in glass once at Kirk Hallam church (Cox, IV.215), and had previous Derbys. connections, despite being for a long time seated in Leics. They also bore (irregularly) in C17 *azure two bars and in chief three mullets or* (V. 1662). Thomas Burdett of Dunmore, Co. Carlow, was cr. a bt 11 July 1723; he was descended from the 2nd bt of Foremark. The title was remaindered to the heirs male of his sister, the Weldons, who used the Burdett arms for some time before reverting to their own. Angela Georgina, sister and heiress of the 6th bt of Foremark, was gr. the arms and assumed the surname of Coutts in addition to her own 14 Sept. 1837: Coutts – *argent a stag's head erased gules between the attires a pheon all within a bordure embattled azure thereon four buckles or* – quartering Burdett. In 1871 she was cr. Baroness Burdett-Coutts of Highgate and Brookfield, Middlesex, and was gr. supporters: *dexter a stag proper gorged with a riband argent pendent therefrom an escutcheon of the arms of Coutts; sinister a lion proper pendent from a like riband an escutcheon of the arms of Burdett* (Pine, 45). Ext. 1906. One of Lady Burdett-Coutts's heirs, Herbert Ashmead-Bartlett, assumed in 1922 by RL the surname of Burdett-Coutts and the arms quarterly with his own: the shield of Burdett was herein *charged in the centre chief point with a cross patée or (for distinction)* and likewise the crest of Burdett (FD (1929) I.260). Btcy of Bramcott ext. 1951.

Burgilon. Weston Underwood. *Quarterly or and gules a bend sable between six annulets argent three each in the second and third quarters two and one* (Burke). Perhaps borne by Ralph Burgilon of Weston Underwood *c.* 1380, of the 5th generation of his family there. But note *argent on a bend sable three martlets of the first* impaled by Thomas Twyford of Langley seen by Bassano in Kirk Langley church, 1710, for Bourgheron: possibly the same family, and Burke's solitary entry for this name (and its mutations) may refer to Burgilon of Worcs.

Burnaston. Burnaston. *Gules a cross flory or* (Cox IV.307). Cox made this attribution of these arms carved on a boss at All Saints' church, Mickleover. Nicholas son of Henry de Burnaston marr. Isabella Riboef of Etwall in the later C13.

Burrow. Morton; N. Wingfield. *Azure three fleurs-de-lys ermine*; crest: *a falcon ermine with wings expanded* (Burke). Borne by Revd Benjamin Burrow, rector of Morton (1765–9) and chaplain to 5th Duke of Devonshire. Marr. Mary dau. of Henry Bourne (qv) and d. 1779. Coheiresses marr. Turbutt and Holland (qqv). Hatchment at Morton church; seal of Turbutt impaling Burrow.

Burton. Bakewell. *Azure on a fesse ermine between in chief two talbots' heads erased or and in base a cypress tree proper issuant from a ducal coronet of the third three fleurs-de-lys gules*; crest: *issuant from the battlements of a tower argent charged with an estoile within a crescent gules a beacon fired proper*; motto: *'Lux vitae'* (BLG I (1965) 111). A grant made *c.* 1950 to the descendants of George Burton of Bakewell (d. 1667) whose great-grandson removed to Aynhoe, Northants.

Burton. Chesterfield etc. *Azure semée d'estoiles and a crescent argent; crest: a serpent winged legs azure scaled argent statant upon a crown or in front of a beacon and a cypress tree proper* (Glover, II.288). Arms borne from C14 by the ancestors of Richard Burton of Chesterfield, and numerous of his kin in that area; crest looks like a formal grant, but the date has not been found. William son of Richard Burton of Fauld, Staffs., of this family, standard bearer to Henry VI, discarded the above coat in favour of *azure a fesse between three talbots' heads erased or*; crests: *a beacon argent burning proper standing on a mount vert and a cypress tree proper in a coronet or*; motto: *'Lux Vitae'* (Burton of Tutbury, Vv. Staffs. 1583, 1614). Sir Thomas Burton of Kinsley, Yorks. brother to Richard, of Chesterfield, who d. 1465, left descendants who bore: *quarterly one and four argent a bend wavy sable and two and three azure a fleur-de-lys* (RL of 1866, change of name and quarterly arms of North).

Burton. Dronfield; Derby; Heanor; Holmesfield. *Azure a crescent argent within an orle of estoiles or; crest: out of a ducal coronet or a wyvern azure collared of the first* (V. 1634). Borne by Francis Burton of Dronfield in 1662 and shown on the MI of Samuel Burton of Thorntree House, Derby, and Aldercar Park (Codnor Park), St Alkmund, Derby, 1751, see Simpson I.322). The Harl.MS 6104 version of V. 1662 gives (quite erroneously): *gules a crescent within an orle of estoiles and a bordure or; crest: a cockatrice gules scaled ar-*

gent collared or. Lysons (cxxii) and V. 1662 give the arms with a bordure or (see next entry). The heiress of the senior line marr. Borowe (Borough) (qv).

Burton. Holmesfield. *Azure a crescent within an orle of estoiles argent and a bordure or.* Gr. to Michael Burton of Holmesfield Hall 1646. He was 2nd son of Thomas Burton of Cartledge Hall (Holmesfield), and dsp 1656. His immediate ancestors bore (or used) *azure semée d'estoiles a crescent and a bordure argent* (Papworth 596).

Burton. Ingmanthorpe (Brampton). *Sable a fesse nebulée between three cinquefoils argent*; crest: *on a mount vert a tower triple towered or* (Thompson IV.24). Gr. 6 March 1582 to Nicholas Burton of 'Inglethorpe or Ingelsthorpe'. Ingmanthorpe is undoubtedly the place intended.

Burton. 'Co. Derby'. *Argent a chevron between three bears' heads couped sable armed or*; crest: *a tower triple towered argent* (Burke). No name or locale has yet been identified for these arms. It may, however, refer to the arms which Francis Burton of Weston Underwood bore when he failed to appear at V. 1662. He was high sheriff 1669, and a 'person for a grant' in 1686.

Burun. Alton (Idridgehay & Alton); Horsley etc. *Argent three bendlets sinister gules* (in glass at Burton church, V. 1611). Borne by Hugh and Roger sons of Hugh de Burun of Horsley, c. 1200 (if quartering evidence is to be believed) and by Sir Nicholas Byron of Alton (d. 1503), 5th in descent from Richard de Burun of Alton, c13. See also Birom and Byron.

Bushey. North Wingfield. *Barry of six argent and sable* (glass at Chesterfield church, seen 1596; Cox, I.419). Sir John Bushey was patron and joint lord of N. Wingfield c15.

Busli. Norton etc. *Gules a bezant* (Chester Waters (1886) 35). Tenants-in-chief in Derbys. at an early date, and lords of those parts of Hallamshire in the county c. 1147–1214.

Butler. Beighton Fields (Barlborough). *Azure a chevron between three covered cups or in the centre chief point a cross crosslet of the last*; crest: *a covered cup or charged with an ermine spot sable* (BLG (1937) 214). Conf. 21 Jan. 1841 to John Bowdon of Beighton (qv), quarterly with his own.

Butler. Chilcote; Somersall (Brampton); Sutton Scarsdale etc. *Quarterly of 4: 1: or a chief indented azure* (Walter *alias* Butler) *2: gules three covered cups or* (High Butler of Ireland) *3: argent a lion rampant and on a chief gules a swan close of the field between two annulets or* (Earldom of Carrick) *4: ermine a saltire engrailed gules* (Fitzgerald of Desmond); crest: *out of a ducal coronet from a plume of five ostrich feathers a falcon rising argent beaked and membered or*; supporters: *dexter, a falcon wings expanded argent beaked and membered or and sinister, a male griffin argent armed beaked rayed ducally gorged and chained or*; motto: *'Comme je trouve'*. (UO, various dates). Borne by Walter Butler KP, 18th Earl (cr. 1328), 1st Marquess of Ormonde (cr. 1816, ext. 1820) and 19th Earl of Carrick (cr. 1315) all in the peerage of Ireland as heir of the Clarkes of Somersall.

Butler. Handley (Staveley). *Argent three covered cups sable between seven crosses crosslet gules*; crest: *an arm embowed habited azure cuffed argent holding in the hand a bunch of grapes proper* (Thompson IV.70; Burke). Gr. 1606 but no member of the family appears at any V.

Butler-Clarke-Southwell-Wandesford. Chilcote; Eaton Dovedale (Doveridge). *Or a lion rampant double queued azure armed and langued gules* (Wandesford); quartering: *argent three cinquefoils gules on each six annulets or* (Southwell, UO 1603), Clarke of Somersall and Butler, Marquess of Ormonde (qqv); crest: *a church proper, spire azure*; motto: *'Tout pour L'église'* (BP (1956) 1675). The Hon. Charles Butler, brother and heir of the 1st Marquess of Ormonde, inherited the latter's Derbys. properties and assumed the additional arms and surname of Clarke by RSM 1820. In June 1830 a further RL enabled him to add the surnames of Southwell and Wandesford, with arms as above. He d. 1860, when Henry, his nephew, inherited more than 1,300 acres in Derbys.

Buxton, Borough of. *Vert the rod of Aesculapius or within an orle of eight fountains*; crest: *on a rock a buck at gaze proper*; motto: 'Benedicite fontes Domino' (Scott-Giles 88). Gr. 31 Jan. 1917 to replace the unauthorised use of: *or a fesse barry wavy azure and argent overall on a pale embattled gules a fasces of the field on a chief a scenic representation of Buxton from the North proper*; crest: *out of a mural crown argent a stag's head affrontée proper regally crowned or*; supporters: *on* *either side a stag proper ducally gorged or*; mottoes: (above) *'Bawkestanes 1080'* (below) *'Buxtona quae calidae celebrabere nomine lymphae forte mihi posthac non adeunda value'* (postcard in author's collection, 1907).

Buxton. Ashbourne; Brassington; Youlgreave. *Sable two bars and on a canton argent a buck trippant of the field*; crest: *a pelican or vulning herself gules* (Vv. 1611, 1634, 1662). Borne by John Buxton of Brassington 1611 and his grandson Henry in 1662. John, the latter's first cousin, seated at Youlgreave, was marked as displaying arms 'sans proof' in 1662. One version of V. 1611 (D369) gives the buck *at gaze* (which is how it is usually shown anyway) and the crest *or*.

Buxton (Buckston). Bradbourne; Carsington; Kirk Ireton; Sutton on the Hill. *Sable three mullets between two bars and on a canton argent a buck trippant of the field*; crest: *a pelican volant wings or gouttée-de-sang nest argent*. Conf. to Henry Buxton of Bradbourne (as previous entry) 1662, but later conf. as above. Buxton claimed descent from Thomas de Buxton of Buxton, sheriff of Notts. and Derbys. 1415 (allegedly) who is supposed to have borne arms: *sable three mullets in fesse between two cotises argent*. Revd German Buxton of Bradbourne and *jure uxoris* of Sutton (1797–1861) changed the spelling of his name to Buckston in the 1820s.

Byron. Bolsover etc. *Argent three bendlets enhanced gules*; crest: *a mermaid proper*; motto *'Crede Byron'* (V. Lancs. 1613). Sir John Byron, of Clayton, Lancs., was gr. a 50-year lease in 1552 of Bolsover Castle by the Crown. He and his family had many other territorial interests in Derbys.

Cachehors. Staveley Woodthorpe. *Argent a chevron between three cross crosslets sable an annulet for difference* (as quartering of Rodes, V. 1611). Borne by John Cachehors of Staveley Woodthorpe, whose heiress Anne marr. William de Rodes *c.* 1440.

Cade. Spondon; Eckington. *Argent a fesse azure between two lions passant guardant gules*; crest: *a demi-lion rampant gules* (C19 bookplate in a local collection; Burke). Used by James Cade of the Homestead, Spondon (1772–1840), whose wife was the heiress of the painter Joseph Wright.

Cadman. Cowley (Wensley and Snitterton);

Darley. *Or three buds of columbine vert*; crest: *a stork's head regally crowned proper* (Burke; also on seal of 1530, now lost, in Local MS 7769; quartered by Needham, D369). Quartered by Needham of Cowley, Otwell Needham having marr. the heiress of Nicholas Cadman who died *c.* 1545. Some Needhams (qv) bore this coat in lieu of their own C17, sometimes with the field *argent*. Benjamin Cadman of Spinkhill Manor (Eckington), living 1745, and claiming descent from the Cadmans of Cowley, was great-great grandfather of Col. W.E. Cadman of Westbourne House, Hope (b. 1838), a claimant to the Earldom of Newburgh. The latter is credited with the arms of Cowley, with the motto: *'Deus et Patria'*, in BLG (1898) I.217, although on what authority is unclear.

Calcroft. Chesterfield. *Ermine three lions passant guardant in pale gules* (D369). Arms recorded in two MSS of V. 1611.

Calton. Calton (Edensor); Chesterfield; Stanton in Peak. *Or a saltire engrailed between four cross crosslets sable*; crest: *a boar passant argent* (MIS at Chesterfield church, 1756, 1758, 1784). Borne by Richard, son of John Calton of Chesterfield, and his heirs, descended from Ralph Calton of Stanton, and allegedly borne by William Calton of Calton, 'Cock Matcher and Servant of the Hawks to Henry VIII', who sold Calton to Bess of Hardwick *c.* 1552 (Lysons, lxxx).

Cammell. Brookfield Manor (Outseats); Norton Hall. *Sable on a chevron argent cotised or between three camels statant of the second as many trefoils slipped of the field*; crest: *a camel's head erased argent gorged with a collar gemel sable holding in the mouth a trefoil as in the arms*; motto: *'Perseverando'* (BLG (1952) 353; carved on lodges at Hathersage). Gr. 1877 to Charles Cammell of Norton (1810–79); previously the family had used: *argent a chevron between three camels sable* (Burke).

Campion. Derby. *Per fesse azure and argent in chief an eagle displayed and in base two fleurs-de-lys counterchanged all witin a bordure wavy ermine*; crest: *upon the trunk of a tree fessewise eradicated and sprouting a turkey cock proper charged on the breast with a saltire wavy azure*; motto: *'Ne tentes aut Perfice'*. Gr. 22 June 1867 to Frank Campion of The Mount, Duffield Rd, Derby, and issued to him by RL 23 July 1867 authorising him to take the surname of Campion in lieu of Eason. Sir Colin Cole (pers.comm.) comments: 'The *wavy bordure* would indicate that Frank Eason's true father's name was Campion'.

Cantilupe

Cantilupe. Ilkeston. *Gules a fesse vair between three leopards' faces jessant-de-lys or* (ASP II.120). Adopted by William de Cantilupe of Ilkeston (cr. by writ of summons 29 Dec. 1299 1st Lord Cantilupe of Ilkeston), combining the arms of his mother's grandfather, Hugh fitz Ralph (qv) with those adopted by his father, Nicholas, 4th son of Sir William de Cantilupe: *three leopards' faces jessant-de-lys between as many cross crosslets* (seal, C13, Birch 8308). Nicholas's elder brother William bore: *three leopards' faces jessant-de-lys* (Glover's Roll, 1st version, 27), which appears anomalous, for the senior line of the family – this William, his father, and descendants – customarily bore *gules three fleurs-de-lys or* (Matthew Paris Shields, I.54, II.26). John, youngest bother of William and Nicholas, bore *azure three leopards' faces inverted jessant-de-lys or* (Heralds' Roll, 142). Each version plainly represents a brisure of

cadency. The issue of the 1st Lord Cantilupe became entirely ext., with the peerage, *c.* 1376, when the estates passed to the senior line, and 2nd Lord Zouche of Harringworth (d. 1382), its representative. A member of this branch was St Thomas of Hereford, who bore yet another variant: *gules three leopards' faces reversed jessant-de-lys or* (Wagner 1939, 43–4). Wagner suggests that the leopards' heads should really be wolves' heads, in allusion to the name Canti*lupe*.

Cantrell. Alvaston Fields; King's Newton (Melbourne). *Argent a pelican in her piety in chief two roses all between as many flaunches sable*; crest: *in front of a tower argent on a rock proper a boar passant sable armed or charged on the body with two roses of the first*; motto: *'Pectus fidele et apertum'*. (FD (1905) 217). Gr. and conf. by RL 1893 and 1894 to Col. Albert Cantrell Cantrell-Hubbersty, and quartered by Hubbersty (qv). Col. Hubbersty's mother, Anne Augusta, was heiress of the Cantrells who previously used *argent a pelican in her piety sable* (*Rel.* V (1865) 230).

Capell. Markeaton. No arms known; 'an usurper' V. 1611 (Local MS 6341).

Capps. Eyam. *Argent on a chevron between three trefoils slipped sable an escallop of the field* (*Rel.* V (1865) 230). Borne by Cappus, a Kentish knight in Henry VI's time, according to the Military Roll, without *escallop*. Doubtless the user of these arms was William Capps of Stony Middleton, who paid tax on three hearths there 1670, or a relative.

Carleill. Longstone Hall (Great Longstone); Little Hucklow. *Argent on a chevron sable between three Cornish choughs proper beaked and legged gules as many mullets of six points or*; crest: *a moor's head in profile couped at the shoulders proper* (*Rel.* V (1865) 230). Allowed at V. Yorks. 1612 to Tristram Carleill of Sowerby, from whom descended Capt. Randolph Carleill of Broster Field (Foolow), ancestor of the Derbys. family of this name.

Carnac: see Rivett.

Carpenter. Bradway (Norton); Millthorpe (Holmesfield). *Per pale indented or and azure an eagle displayed and in chief two roundles all counterchanged*; crest: *an arm embowed proper hand grasping a staff or between two wings of the last semée d'estoiles azure*; motto: *'Spernit pericula vertus'*. (BLG (1875) I.210). Borne by the radical philosopher Revd Edward Carpenter (1844–1929); conf. by RL 1864.

Carr. Holbrook; Parwich. *Per pale gules and sable on a chevron invected plain cotised argent between two mullets of six points of the second in base and a like mullet of the third a stag's attires proper*; crest: *a stag's head erased proper charged on the neck with a mullet of six points or between two thistles slipped and leaved proper*; motto: *'Tout droit'*. (BLG (1937) 359). Gr. to Revd Edmund Carr of Holbrook 1896.

Carrier. Wirksworth. *Sable a bend between three spear heads or* (Berry). Conf. by RL 1773 as a quartering of Anson to George Anson of Orgreave, Staffs. (qv). Previously these arms were borne or used by Charles son of Richard Carrier of Wirksworth, one of whose coheiresses marr. William Anson *c.* 1695.

Carill-Worsley: see Tindall-Carill-Worsley.

Carrington. Brookfield (Brampton); Holywell House (Chesterfield). *Argent on a bend azure cotised sable between two horseshoes of the second a unicorn's head erased or between two bezants a crescent for difference*; crest: *three horseshoes or thereon a unicorn's head erased sable*; motto: *'Semper paratus'* (FD (1929) I.319). Gr. to Maj. Arthur Carrington of Holywell House 14 April 1874; the family were of Brookfield in the 1920s.

Carsington. Carsington. *A boar's head* (*DAJ* XXVI (1904) 168). Found on a seal believed to be late C13 in the ruins of a house in Haverfordwest, Pembs.; borne, whether as a crest or on arms is unclear, by Roger de Carsington, cf. Nicholas son of Roger de Carsington, 1276.

Cartwright. Derby. *Per chevron or and azure three pelicans counterchanged*. Conf. 1574 to Rose, dau. of John Cartwright of Derby, Mrs John Trott.

Carver. Chesterfield. *Or on a chevron between three crosses clechée sable a fleur-de-lys between two stags' heads caboshed of the field*; crest: *on a mount vert a cross clechée or charged with a fleur-de-lys sable* (Burke). Gr. 1742 to John Carver of Morthen Hall (Whiston), Yorks. His ancestor, Marmaduke (1662–1756), was of Pump House, Chesterfield, son of a Yorks. priest. They assumed the surname Middleton 1795. John Carver was gr. quarterings 1822. See also Gregory; Middleton.

Case: see Morewood.

Castlyn. Hemsworth (Norton). *Sable on a chevron or between three castles argent each with demi-lion issuant from the battlements three anchors azure* (V. London 1568). Allowed to James Castlyn of London, son of James, of London and Norton, son of John son of Robert Castlyn of 'Lymesworth' by which Hemsworth is intended. This is odd, for the same document gives: *Azure on a bend or three castles sable*; crest: *on a tower proper a flag gules* (crest: on a C18 Crown Derby plate in Derby Museum, DBYMU 1951-78) for Edward son of William Castlyn of Hemsworth (Norton) and London, 1st cousin of James (qv). Crest presumably assumed without authority C18.

Catt. Outwoods (Little Eaton). *Gules three cats-à-mountain passant guardant in pale argent between two flaunches of the last on each a rose of the first barbed and seeded proper*; crest: *in front of an esquire's helm a gauntlet fessewise all proper*; motto: *'Fortis qui pudens'* (FD (1929) I.329; livery button in private collection). Gr. to John Catt of Lewes, Sussex, and Edmund Catt of Brighton, 1864, and borne by Charles William, of Outwoods, 1908.

Cauz. Bradbourne; Caus Hall (Brampton). *Per chevron or and gules three human hearts counterchanged* (Lysons, ci). Borne by Sir Geoffrey de Caus of Caus Hall 1232.

Cave. Stretton en le Field; Ravenstone. *Azure fretty argent*; crest: *a greyhound courant sable collared argent*; motto: *'Guardez'* (arms: Jenyns' Ordinary; BP (1970) 503). Borne by William Cave *c.* 1380; coat conf. and crest gr. *c.* 1536–50 to Cave of Stanford Hall, Leics., cr. bt 30 June 1641. Roger Cave marr. the heiress of Browne of Stretton (qv), whose descendant added the surname of Browne by RL 1752, quartering the arms, but adding (to Browne) *a bordure engrailed gules*. The surname became Cave-Browne-Cave (through another RL) 1838. Roger Cave of Eydon (Northants.) built the present Ravenstone Hall *c.* 1730.

Cavendish. Chatsworth; Edensor; Owlcotes (Heath) etc. *Sable three stags' heads caboshed argent attired or*; crest: *a serpent nowed proper*; motto: *'Cavendo Tutus'*. (Vv. 1569, 1611). Borne by Sir William Cavendish, 2nd husband of Bess of Hardwick, claiming descent from Gernon (qv). Sir William, the 2nd son, was cr. Lord Cavendish of Hardwick (1605) and Earl of Devonshire (1618); the 4th earl was raised to a dukedom in 1694. Supporters were gr.: *on either side a buck proper wreathed about the neck with a chaplet of roses alternately argent and azure.* An alternative crest was sometimes employed: *a stag statant proper attired or gorged with a garland of roses argent and azure barbed proper.* Lord George Cavendish was cr. (1831) Lord Cavendish of Keighley and Earl of Burlington and his 4th son, Hon. C.C. Cavendish, was in 1858 cr. Lord Chesham, varying the arms with the substitution for the *sinister* supporter for: *a greyhound argent gorged with a plain collar gules thereon three buckles or* (BP (1970) 530).

Cavendish. Bolsover etc. Same arms, crest and motto as previous, but supporters: *dexter, a bull or ducally crowned gules* and *sinister a lion rampant guardant gules crined and ducally crowned or* (Burke). Gr. to Sir William Cavendish (son of Sir Charles) 1620 when he was cr. Lord Ogle and Viscount Mansfield. Lord Mansfield was further elevated as earl (1628), marquess (1644) and Duke of Newcastle under Lyme and Earl of Ogle (1664). Honours ext. on death of 2nd duke, 1691.

Cavendish. Doveridge. *Sable three stags' heads caboshed argent attired or within a bordure of the second;* crest: *out of a marquess's coronet a snake nowed and encircled or head reguardant vert;* motto: *'Cavendo tutus'* (BP (1970) 2765). Gr. 20 May 1664 to Henry and Charles Cavendish of Doveridge sons of Francis son of Henry, natural son of Henry Cavendish of Tutbury. Prior to 1664 (e.g. V. 1662, 'sans proof') they used Cavendish *differenced overall with a baton sinister or* (sometimes *gules*); crest: *a serpent nowed proper gorged with a ducal coronet debruised by a baton sinister gules.* Henry Cavendish was made a bt of Waterpark, Co. Cork (GB 7 May 1755), and his son, Sir Henry, marr. Sarah, dau. and heiress of Richard Bradshaw, she being in 1792 cr. *sua jure* Baroness Waterpark (Irish Peerage) and gr. the quarterly arms of Cavendish and Bradshaw in 1791, both remaindered to her heirs male by Sir Henry.

Cavendish-Bentinck: see Bentinck.

Cecil. Broadlowash (Thorpe); Exeter House (Derby). *Barry of ten argent and azure overall six escutcheons sable on each a lion rampant of the first;* crest: *on a chapeau gules turned up ermine a garb or supported on either side by a lion that on the dexter argent and that on the sinister azure;* supporters: *on either side a lion ermine;* motto:'Cor unum via una' (plate at All Saints', Derby). Brownlow Cecil, 8th Earl of Exeter, inherited Chambers's house in Full St, Derby, and gave his name to it. He also owned Broadlowash. Supporters were gr. on his ancestor Sir William Cecil's elevation to the peerage in 1571 as Lord Burghley. The earldom was gr. to Lord Burghley's son in 1605. The arms were apparently conf. from a controversy as to arms decided by Edward de Beaulile and John de Moubray, 4 June 1332, in favour of Sitslilt (sic) of Duncombe (Orcop), Herefs. (A. Collins, *Peerage*, II.584–5, cf. Harl.MS 1140 f. 57b). The 10th earl was raised to marquess, 4 Feb. 1801.

Chaddesden. Chaddesden; Hognaston; Spondon. *On a chevron rompu two mullets* (Cox, III.308n.). Arms seen by Bassano in 1710 carved in Chaddesden church.

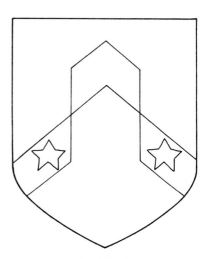

Chaddesden

Chadwick. Callow; Edingale, Staffs. *Gules an inescutcheon and an orle of martlets argent;* crest: *a talbot's head gules vulned and bleeding at the mouth proper pierced through the neck with an arrow or barbed and flighted argent point embrued also proper gorged ermine runmed and mowed of the third and charged with three chessrooks of the first;* motto: *'Juxta Salopiam'* (Glover, II.189) Borne by Col. John Chadwick of Edingale (1719–1800) who was gr. the crest of the Malveysins (whose heir he was), 1 Aug. 1791. His half-brother, Charles of Callow Hall (1705–79), bore similar arms with a plainer version of the Malveysin crest. Their great-grandfather, John Chadwick of Healey Hall, Lancs., *jure uxoris* of Edingale, bore the original crest of Chadwick: *a lily argent, stalked and leaved vert,* motto: *'Stans cum Rege'* (V. Lancs. 1664).

Chaloner. Boyleston. *Sable a chevron engrailed between three cherubs' heads argent;* crest: *a cherub argent* (Cox, III.23). Arms used by William Chaloner of Boyleston (d. 1665). His son, William (1630–75), and grandson, John (1670–1701), claimed descent from a 2nd marriage of Sir Thomas Chaloner of Guisborough with a lady of the Mountjoy Blounts. Sir Thomas's arms, given erroneously by Tilley (II.307), were in fact: *sable a chevron between three cherubs' heads or;* crest: *a demi-sea wolf rampant or.*

Chaloner. Duffield Park. *Azure a chevron engrailed between three cherubs' heads argent;* crest: *a cherub argent* (V. 1634). Borne by Thomas Chaloner of Duffield Park (b. 1619), whose dau. and heiress marr. Nicholas Wilmot. It is likely that the Boyleston and Duffield families were related.

Chambers. Derby. *Argent a chevron ermine fimbriated sable between three chamber pieces fessewise of the third fired proper;* crest: *an ass's head argent* (hatchment in All Saints', Derby; crest: Burke). Used by John Chambers of Derby (1691–1751) and his son, Lancelot. John's father was considered 'a person for a grant' in 1686, when it was recorded that for arms 'he hath used something of a cannon'. Thomas Chambers of Exeter House was close kin (qv). The arms are borrowed from the Sussex family of de la Chambre of Rodmell (Huxford, 83, and as borne in pretence, by Sir William Wolseley of Wolseley, Staffs, 7th bt, in glass at Wolseley Park).

Chamber(s). Derby. *Argent a fesse chequy or and azure between three lions' heads erased sable* (V. 1634). Borne by Gabriel Chamber esq. of Coventry, who came to Derby, and by his descendant, Mr John Chamber(s), living 1722.

Chambers. 'Co. Derby'. *Gules a chevron between three cinquefoils or* (Berry). The bearer or user of these arms in the county is so far unidentified. They were allowed V. Essex 1634 to a family of this name, and possibly refer to the Mr Chambers of Derby whose daus. and coheiresses marr. Sir John Shore and Joseph Parker (qqv).

Chambers. Exeter House (Derby). *Ermine three copper cakes proper on a chief gules a chamber piece or;* crest: *in a cave a miner wielding his pick proper the sign of Mars above or* (MI in All Saints', Derby, 1726). The copper cakes are sometimes blazoned as *quadrants.* Gr. 26 July 1723 to Thomas Chambers of London and Exeter House (1660–1726); his daus. and coheiresses marr. William Bate of Foston and 8th Earl of Exeter (qqv).

Chambers. The Hurst (Tibshelf). *Argent on a fesse engrailed sable three cinquefoils or in chief two squirrels sejant proper;* crest: *in front of a fret or a stork wings expanded proper on each a cinquefoil also or;* motto: *'In fide fortis'.* (FD (1929) I.345). Gr. 1869 to John Chambers of The Hurst, Tibshelf (1836–1901), owner of Hardwick Colliery, Ault Hucknall. See also Bagshawe.

Champeyne. Champeyne Park (Champion, Windley). *Or fretty sable* (Lysons, cii). Above are the arms as quartered by Bradbourne (via Turville) V. 1611 and on an MI at Ashbourne church. The Powell Roll, however, gives for Sir William de Champeyne of Champeyne c. 1375, *or fretty sable crusilly fitchée at the joints argent,* which is probably the more correct version (see also PRO, P.179 of 1336).

Champer(k)nowne: see Willington.

Champion. Champion House (Edale); Hopton. *Per saltire argent and or three mullets in fesse between as many trefoils sable;* crest: *a cubit arm erect in armour proper encircled by an annulet or the hand gauntletted of the first surmounted by a mullet of six points of the second and holding two branches of laurel in saltire slipped also of the first;* motto: *'Le camp vaux mieux que l'or'* (FD (1929) I.347). A C20 grant obtained by W.N.L. Champion of Edale and Hopton (1850–1939), grandson of John Champion of Edale. Previously the family had used *Argent three trefoils slipped sable* (*Rel.* V (1865) 230).

Chandos. Radbourne. *Argent a pile gules* (glass at Mugginton church, V. 1611; seals 1329, 1420, PRO, P.1181–2). Borne by Edward Chandos of Radbourne (d. 1346) (Jenyns' Ordinary), father of Sir John Chandos, whose arms on his Garter stallplate (and Willement Roll) are *Or a pile gules* – the arms of the senior line of Chandos of Chandos in Snodhill (Peterchurch), Herefs. Froissart's *Chronicles* (Lettenhove Ed., VII.196) and the Navarre Roll confirm the field of the Derbys. branch as *argent* (cf. Wagner (1939) 52).

Chandos-Pole: see Pole.

Chandos-Pole-Gell: see Gell; Pole.

Chapel en le Frith Rural District Council. *Vert a stag's head caboshed between the attires a cross formée on a chief dancettée or a lion passant gules*; crest: *out of a circlet vert charged with four gouttes-de-l'eau the battlements of a tower issuant therefrom a demi-lion argent collared vairé or and gules and holding an inescutcheon per pale argent and azure thereon a rose gules barbed and seeded proper* motto: *'Cave et spera'* (Briggs, 100). Gr. 8 April 1954 to an authority cr. in 1894 and abolished in 1974.

Chappell. Riber (Matlock). *Or an anchor in pale sable a fleur-de-lys for difference*; crest: *an arm vested holding a viper proper passing through the cup of an obsidian figure* (Tilley, II.311). Borne or used by John Chappell, who bought Riber 1681, and his son, John. Their kinsman, Rt Revd William Chappell, Bishop of Cork, d. Derby 1649. The arms are given in Vincent's MS 154 at the College of Arms, where the crest includes an *obicular figure*.

Charge. Chesterfield. *Erminois on a fesse engrailed between three bucks' heads erased gules as many cinquefoils pierced argent* (*Rel.* XII (1872) 94). Borne by John Charge of Spital House, Chesterfield, a former mayor of the town who d. 1849. Gr. to his father Robert (then of Yorks.), 1811.

Charlton. Breaston; Sandiacre; Risley. *Azure on a chevron or between three swans argent as many cinquefoils gules*; crest: *a swan's head and neck erased argent beaked gules gorged with a chaplet vert*; motto: *'Stabit conscius aequi'* (V. 1662; V. Notts. 1662–4). Arms conf. and crest gr. 23 May 1612 to Thomas Charlton of Breaston, Risley and Sandiacre,

also of Bardon Park, Leics. (1562–1631). His father, Thomas, was younger son of Sir Thomas Charlton of Hillingdon, Middlesex, Speaker in 1453, who bore the arms as above, but without *cinquefoils*. At V. 1611 Thomas exhibited the arms in the same way and *all within a bordure of the second*, and 'Promised to come to London' – hence the grant. The D369 MS of V. 1662 varies slightly.

Charlton. Wheston Hall. *Or a lion rampant gules*; crest: *a lion's face caboshed gules* (MI at Tideswell church). Used by Robert Charlton of Wheston Hall (d. 1787). The arms are those of Charlton of Lea Hall, Northumberland, to which family he could perhaps have been related.

Chatterton. Derby. *Argent a griffin segreant gules holding in its claws an escutcheon azure charged with a demi-griffin argent* (impaled by Barnes, Simpson, I.423). Arms of Ald. John Chatterton (1771–1857), mayor of Derby, as used by his father, John (1742–1800). Their kinsman, Edward, also added for crest: *a dove wings elevated holding in the beak a slip of olive all proper*; motto: *'Fides et Fiducia'* (Local MS 9555.194).

Chawner. Lees Hall and Muse Lane (Church Broughton); Vernon's Oak (Sudbury); Hill House (Tupton). *Sable a chevron between three cherubs' heads or*; crest: *a seawolf's head erased proper*; motto: *'Nil desperandum'* (BLG (1952) 422). Used by John Chawner of Hare Hill and Muse Lane and his son Thomas of Sudbury Wood and Lees Hall (1700–73) whose MI at Boyleston bears these arms. This numerous family also claims descent from a son of Sir Thomas Chaloner of Guisborough, Yorks. (the 4th by his 1st marriage, usually thought to have been childless and unmarr.). Thus they not only claim kinship with the Chaloners of Boyleston (qv) but use the Guisborough family's arms (Derbyshire Family History Society, *Branch News*, No 26 (Sept. 1983), 10–13).

Chaworth. Alfreton. *Azure two chevronels or*; crest: *from a tower five ostrich feathers argent* (Local MS 6341 includes crest; arms: FitzWilliam Roll 632). William de Chaworth marr. Alice, sister and coheiress of Thomas de Alfreton, and assumed the Alfreton (qv) arms in lieu of his own early C13. His grandson, Thomas, was summoned to Parliament as 1st Lord Chaworth 1299, and he bore the above crest, usually associated with the

Chaworths. See also Musters.

Chederton. Unstone. *Gules a cross potent or* (Tilley, II.268; Harl.MSS 1093, 1486, 1537; Egerton MS 996). Borne *c.* 1443 by a member of this family who held Unstone in the right of his wife, heiress of Belfield, qv.

Chellaston. Chellaston. *Azure two chevronels or* (Jewitt's Notes, Box 57). The attribution of these arms to this family is highly unlikely, and is based on there having been two Robert fitz Ralphs living early C13: one of Alfreton, whose arms these were; the other the ancestor of the de Chellastons who seem to have become ext. in the senior line by 1272, and probably never bore arms, although cousins of de Heriz (qv).

Cheney. Ashford; Kirk Langley; Monyash. *Azure six lioncels rampant argent and a canton ermine*; crest: *a bull's scalp proper*; motto: *'Fato prudentia maior'* (Bassano's MS, Local 3525). Borne by Thomas Cheney of Ashford, whose hatchment Bassano painted 5 Oct. 1723. He was 4th in descent from Sir Oliver Cheney (C16) and his posterity were ext. later C19. Burke gives two other Cheney coats for Derbys.: *ermine on a bend azure three martlets or* and *chequy or and azure a fesse gules fretty argent*. These represent out-county alliances, quartered by Shirley (V. 1569 – Cheney of Toddington) and Rollesley (V. 1569 and MI at Darley – Cheney of Bucks.).

Cheney. Beeley. *Azure six lioncels and a quarter ermine*; crest: *a bull's scalp argent*; supporters: on either side a greyhound (Burke). Speaker Sir John Cheney of Shurland, Kent, purchased the manor of Beeley and settled his son Thomas there. The former was cr. (by patent) Lord (Cheney of) Shurland 1487 and d. 1489. The son pre-deceased his father. The heiress of Lord Shirland's nephew, Sir Thomas Cheney, who also bore these arms (without supporters) passed the estate to Vaux (qv).

Chester. Derby. *Ermine on a chief sable a griffin passant argent* (*Rel.* XII (1872) 94). Supposedly borne by Simon, Roger and William de Chester of Derby, successively MPs for Derby 1318–44, 1340 and 1353–72, who derived their surname from Little Chester. They were allegedly ancestors of Chester of Bush Hall (Barkway), Herts., who added to the arms a crest: *a demi-griffin segreant ermine*; and motto: *'Vincit qui Partitur'* (BLG (1846) I.212). Numerous other branches

existed, apparently. A John de Chester bore *a griffin passant* (seal 1301, PRO, P.186)

Chester, Earls of. Markeaton; Repton; Walton upon Trent etc. *Azure three garbs or* (FitzWilliam Roll 48). The above are the traditional and later arms of the medieval Earls of Chester, first borne by Ranulph de Blundevill, 4th Earl of Chester of the 3rd (1121) creation, and adopted by his heir, John le Scot, 1st Earl of the 4th (1232) creation. When the county palatine of Chester was cr. in 1070 much of the remaining lands, including some in Derbys., of the Saxon Earls of Mercia were merged into it (CP II.221). The arms of the earls varied: Hugh d'Avranches, called Lupus (1st Earl, second (1071) creation): *Azure a wolf's head erased argent*. This man's career predates heraldry, and this is an invented coat alluding to his name. Ranulph le Meschin de Briquessart (1st Earl, 3rd creation): *or a lion rampant gules*. Whilst this coat is also pre-heraldic, the bearing of a lion and the use of the tinctures *or and gules* suggests the relic of a genuine tradition of association with these emblems, even if not in a strictly heraldic way. To this man's grandson, Hugh Kevelioc (3rd Earl of this creation), is plausibly attributed: *azure six garbs or, three two and one* (Jenyns' Ordinary; Burke), and his son bore as at the head of this entry. Burke attributes John le Scot, 1st Earl of the 4th creation with *or three piles gules* (Matthew Paris Shields, II.19, as Earl of Huntingdon), but he adopted the arms of his predecessor (ibid., IV.34). Even though some of these coats are retrospective, they do occur in local sources.

Chesterfield, Borough of. *Gules a representation of a pomegranate tree as depicted on the common seal of the borough leaved and eradicated proper flowered and fructed or*; crest: *issuant from a mural crown gules masoned or a mount vert theron a Derby ram passant guardant proper*; supporters; *dexter a cock and sinister a pynot proper each ducally crowned or*; motto: *'Aspire'* (Briggs, 106). Gr. 10 Nov. 1955. The previous arms were: *azure on a fesse gules* (sic) *a lozenge fesseways argent* (Ford, 18). Status of arms unclear since 1974.

Chesterfield Rural District Council. *Or a miner's pick sable surmounted of a Tudor rose barbed and seeded proper on a bordure engrailed of the second eight annulets of the field.*

37

Gr. 20 Sept. 1954; authority abolished 1974.

Chesterfield Grammar School. *Azure a bend between six escallops argent impaling gules a bear rampant between three mullets argent*; motto: *'Schola Cestrefeldensis'* (medalet of 1905 for school attendence, DBYMU 1985-290/2). Unauthorised combination of Foljambe impaling Clarke of Somersall (qqv); not very original.

Chetham. Ash; Etwall. *Sable a griffin segreant wings displayed or a bordure gules bezantée* (on church plate at Sutton on the Hill 1748 and Dalbury Lees 1749; V. Lancs. 1613). Borne by Humphrey Chetham of Castleton, Lancs., patron of Sutton and Dalbury c18. His brother, Canon James Chetham, vicar of Etwall, bore *or a griffin segreant gules and a bordure engrailed sable* (MI at Etwall 1740), which is surely incorrect. Lysons (cxxii) give *argent a chevron gules between three fleams sable*, which coat quartered the *sable/griffin* arms, V. Lancs. 1613.

Chetham. Duffield; Mellor Hall. *Argent a griffin segreant gules a bordure sable bezantée*; crest: *a demi-griffin gules charged with a cross potent argent*. Conf. to Randle Chetham-Strode of Mellor 1808, 'now prisoner at Verdun, France', quarterly with Strode of Southill, Somerset, with further exemplifications in 1828 and 1845. The first of the family was James Chetham of Duffield, who marr. the heiress of Radclyffe of Mellor; he was allegedly from Lancs.

Christian. Riddings (Alfreton); S. Wingfield; Derby. *Azure a chevron humettée between three covered cups or on a canton argent an anchor erect with part of a cable round the stock proper*; crest: *out of a naval coronet or a unicorn's head argent collared gules*; motto: *'Perseverando'* (FD (1929) I.367). Gr. 17 Dec. 1796 to Admiral Sir Hugh Cloberry Christian with supporters *on either side a unicorn argent crined and gorged with a collar invected gules*; motto: *'Volovisse sit est'*. The admiral was in 1798 cr. Lord Ronaldsway, which title has ever since lain dormant due, we are told, to the patent not reaching Sir Hugh before his death on station in the West Indies. The arms were borne by his descendant, Reginald (son of Revd Fredrick Christian, vicar of S. Wingfield), who marr. a coheiress of Strelley of Oakerthorpe, and currently by Roy Christian of Littleover, Derby. The arms, without canton and with the motto: *'Salus per Christum'*,

Christian

had been gr. initially in 1788 (with remainders) to John Christian Curwen of Ewanrigg (1756–1828) and conf. in 1945 to John Monsell Christian of Stonerwood Park (Petersfield), Hants. (b. 1911).

Christie. Darley; Edale. *Or a saltire wavy between four spur-rowels pierced sable*; crest: *a withered branch of holly sprouting out leaves proper*; motto: *'Sic viresco'* (on lodge at Darley House; FD (1905) 267). Gr. (LO) 1866 to Lorenzo Christie of Darley House and Edale (1802–92).

Clark: see Darcy-Clark.

Clarke. Ashgate (Brampton); Chesterfield. *Gules a bear rampant argent collared of the field between three mullets of the second*; crest: *a bear rampant argent collared and chained sable holding a poleaxe erect azure* (V. 1662). Gr. at the time of the Visitation 12 May 1663 to Samuel Clarke of Ashgate and his brother Cornelius of Cutthorpe (Brampton), sons of Ralph of Ashgate.

Clarke. Chesterfield; Durrant Hall (Chesterfield). *Argent on a bend gules three swans of the field between as many pellets* (Bassano's MS, Local 3525). Borne by Sir Talbot Clarke

Bt, who marr. a Gladwin and d. at Durrant Hall 16 Feb. 1723 leaving a son, Sir Talbot, of Durrant Hall. The arms were borne by the family in Devon and are recorded to Sir Clement Clarke (cr. bt, of Launde Abbey, Leics., 18 June 1661), V. Northants 1681. Ext. 1750.

Clarke. Chilcote; Somersall (Brampton); Sutton Scarsdale. *Azure three escallops in pale or between two flaunches ermine*; crest: *within an annulet or enriched with an escallop sable a pheon argent.* (Vv. 1611, 1662). Arms conf. and crest gr. to Godfrey Clarke of Somersall Hall 19 April 1608, and conf. to Job Hart Price of Sutton Scarsdale and Chilcote (marr. to the heiress) who assumed the surname and arms of Clarke 18 Nov. 1786, the crest then being enriched with *a ruby proper.*

Clarke. The Elms (Derby); Masson House (Matlock). *Gules a saltire engrailed erminois between two fleur-de-lys in pale and as many horses' heads couped in fesse argent;* crest: *in front of an heraldic tiger's head erased sable maned or gorged gemel two fleurs-de-lys argent*; motto: *'Vincit qui partitur'* (FD (1905) 274). Gr. 1890 to Thomas Clarke of Masson House, son of Ald. Thomas (1815–77), mayor of Derby 1862.

Clarke. Shirland. *Gules three swords erect in pale argent hilts and pommels or*; crest: *a hand couped at the wrist proper holding a sword as in the arms* (J. Foster, *Baronetage* (1882), 120): see Clark of Abbot's Salford, Warwicks., V. Warwick 1619, and borne by Clarke bt of Salford and 'Shirland, Co. Nottm', cr. 1 May 1617, ext. 1899. Shirland is in Derbys. but the connection is elusive.

Clarke-Maxwell. Mackworth; Markeaton. *Argent an eagle double-headed displayed sable charged on the breast with a saltire of the field, for Maxwell, quartering: sable a spur-rowel or within a bordure argent charged with three cross crosslets fitchée of the field;* crest: *a stag lodged before a hollybush all proper;* motto: *'Reviresco'* (BLG (1972) III.636). Gr. (LO) as a result of Revd W.G. Clark (1865–1935), heir of Mundy of Markeaton (qv), assuming the additional surname and quarterly arms of Maxwell in 1897. The crest was granted (LO) in 1848.

Clay. 'Chapel' (en le Frith?); Crich. *Argent a chevron engrailed between three trefoils slipped sable*; crest: *two wings expanded argent semée of trefoils slipped sable* (MI at Crich). Gr. to John Clay of Crich son of Robert son

Clay

of John, of 'Chappell' 1588, and exhibited by him V. 1611. These arms also appear on church plate dated 1698 at Heath given by Mrs Barbara Claye (of a N. Wingfield family), impaling *an escallop*. Sir William Clay of Fulwell Lodge, Middlesex, claiming to be a cadet of 'Chapel and Crich', was cr. a bt 20 Sept. 1841 and had a grant the same year: *Argent a chevron engrailed paly sable and or between three trefoils of the second*; crest: *two wings expanded argent each charged with the arms of Clay of Crich proper*; motto: *'Per orbem'* (BP (1970) 568).

Clay. Dalbury Lees; Duffield; Sudbury Hall. *Argent a chevron indented between three trefoils slipped and in centre chief point a wing sable*; crest: *in front of two wings argent semée of trefoils slipped sable a mount vert thereon as many estoiles gules*; motto: *'Clarior virtus honoribus'* (BLG (1937) 423). Gr. 1884 to Henry Clay of Piercefield Park, Mon. (1825–1921), grandson of Joseph, of Dalbury Lees (where he was born), later of The Bank, Burton upon Trent, which his father purchased, and claiming descent from Joseph, of Duffield, 1741.

Clay. Darley Hall (Darley). *Argent gouttée-de-poix on a chevron engrailed between three trefoils slipped sable a rose between two martlets of the first*; crest: *an annulet sable surmounted of a martlet argent between two wings also argent goutée-de-poix each charged with five trefoils, three, one and two, sable* (FD (1905) 275). Gr. also in 1884 to Joseph Travis Clay of Rastrick, Yorks.; his 2nd son Alfred was of Darley Hall.

Clayton: see Every.

Clayton. Bowden Edge (Chapel en le Frith); Strines Hall (New Mills). Arms not known, but 'an usurper' V. 1611 who 'promised to come to London'.

Clifford. Chaddesden; Edensor; Staveley etc. *Chequy or and azure a fesse gules a crescent for difference*; crest: *out of a ducal coronet or a wyvern rising gules* (arms: Glover's Roll, 1st Version, 31; crest: Burke). This coat was first adopted by Roger, nephew and heir of Walter de Clifford of Clifford; the arms had previously been: *chequy or and azure a bend gules* (ibid., 30). Borne by Robert, 1st Lord Clifford of Clifford Castle, Herefs., summoned to Parliament as a peer 1299, at Caerlaverock a year later. His descendant, Hon. Sir Ingram Clifford (d. 1578), held (by inheritance from his mother, a dau. of 4th Earl of Shrewsbury) considerable estates in Derbys. On his death, these passed to his nephew, George, 3rd Earl of Cumberland (cr. 1525; *supporters: on either side a wyvern gules).* Earldom ext. 1644.

Clifton: see Abney; Bowdon; Hastings.

Clifton-Hastings-Campbell. S. Derbys. *Gyronny of eight ermine and gules* (Campbell) quartering (2) Hastings (qv) and (3) *sable on a bend argent three mullets gules* (Clifton); crests: (1) *issuant from flames or an eagle with two heads displayed gules on an escroll above,'I byde my time'* (Campbell), (2) as Hastings (qv) and (3) *a dexter arm embowed in armour proper the hand also proper in a gauntlet or grasping a sword argent hilt and pommel of the second* (Clifton); motto: *'Trust Winneth Troth'* (FD (1910) 330). Gr. under RL 2 Jan. 1896 to Hon. Gilbert Abney-Hastings, 3rd son of Lady Loudoun (see Rawdon-Hastings) who later succeeded as 3rd Lord Donington (with some 3,000 acres in Derbys.), whereupon he assumed the supporters. gr. to the 1st baron 4 May 1880: *dexter a mantygre affrontée or the visage resembling a human face proper gorged with a chain of the first pendant therefrom a like escutcheon bearing the arms of Clifton (viz. sable on a bend argent three mullets gules), sinister, a bear argent muzzled gules gorged with a chain or pendant therefrom a like escutcheon bearing the arms of Clifton as on the dexter holding between the forepaws the trunk of a tree erect proper.* Motto (latterly): *'Tenebras Meas'* (Pine, 104). Title ext. on his death 31 May 1927. Debrett ascribed to the present Countess of Loudoun, who has assumed the surname of Abney-Hastings by deed poll: *argent a maunch sable* (for Hastings) quartering *or on a chief gules a demi-lion issuant argent*; supporters: *dexter a man in armour plumed on the head with three feathers gules and holding in the right hand a spear in bend proper*; sinister: *a lady rich apparelled plumed on the head with three feathers argent and holding in the sinister hand a letter of challenge* (Debrett, *Peerage* (1980), 744). These supporters are those originally gr. (LO) to 1st Lord Campbell of Loudon in 1601.

Clinton. Tissington, Repton. *Argent on a chief azure two mullets or a label of three points ermine* (as quartered by Franceys of Foremarke, V. 1569; Willement's Roll). Borne by Sir William Clinton, *c.* 1330, ancestor of Sir Thomas de Clinton, *jure uxoris* of Tissington *c.* 1400. A coheiress of his son, Thomas, carried it to Robert Franceys of Foremark. The William of the Willement Roll held a moiety of the manor of Repton *jure uxoris* as representative of the Earls of Chester.

Clowes. Clifton; Cubley; Norbury Hall; etc. *Azure on a chevron cotised between three unicorns' heads erased or three crescents gules*; crest: *a demi-lion rampant ducally crowned or holding a battleaxe in bend sinister and charged on the shoulder with an increscent and a decrescent in pale sable* (BLG (1937) 436). Gr. to Ernest William Clowes of Bradley Hall 11 Nov. 1921 and to the descendants of Col. William Legh Clowes of Broughton, Lancs. Prior to the grant the arms used were *azure on a chevron between three unicorns' heads erased or as many crescents gules* (actually gr. to William Clowes of London, descended out of Tutbury, Staffs., 28 Oct. 1576). As the Derbys. Clowes were descended from Lawrence, of Rudyard, Staffs., they may have considered themselves to have had a claim to these arms.

Coape. Duffield; Brassington. *Argent on a chevron azure between three roses gules stalked and leaved vert as many fleur-de-lys of the field*; crest: *a fleur-de-lys argent* (Woolley, 56; Lysons, cxxiii). Henry Coape, descended out of Shatton, purchased Duffield property and bore these arms, allowed to his relatives of Ranton, Staffs. (V. 1663).

Coape. Farnah Hall (Windley). *Argent on a fesse embattled between three roses gules slipped proper as many fleur-de-lys of the field* (Lysons, cxxiii). Conf. to Wiliam Coape (son of William, of Farnah) in 1810 when he assumed the surname and arms of Sherbrooke. Allowed also to Maj.Gen. Sir John Coape-Sherbrooke quarterly with supporters 1868. Another line of descent from the Coapes of Farnah assumed this surname and arms additionally in 1867 and of Arnold in 1898.

Coates. Wirksworth. *Argent fretty azure on a canton sable a lion rampant or* (*Rel.* XII (1872) 283). Used by Eleazer Coates of Wirksworth 1667 on his trade tokens (Derby Museum, DBYMU, 1936-601, W.118); his father was vicar of S. Wingfield.

Cochrane. Etwall. *Per pale or and gules two crosses botonnée dimidiated and issuant from the dexter and sinister counterchanged*; crest: *a horse passant argent ducally gorged or*; motto: *'Virtute et Labore'* (MI at Etwall). An early C20 grant to Revd David Cochrane of Etwall Lodge, whose son A.W.S. Cochrane was a distinguished officer of arms.

Cochrane. Hopton. *Argent a chevron gules between three boars' heads erased azure armed and langued of the second and a bordure contre-ermine* (quartering Crawford of Kilbirnie, Lindsay of the Byres and Blair); crest: *a horse passant argent between two stags' attires gules*; motto: *'Virtute et Labore'* (BP (1970)). Exemplified (LO) 1919 to Lord Cochrane of Cults, and borne by Hon. Julian Cochrane of Hopton, 3rd son of 2nd Lord Cochrane, with appropriate difference.

Cochrane. Derby; Long Lee (Hayfield); Rowarth (New Mills). *Argent a chevron gules between three boars' heads erased azure armed and langued of the second quartering Blair*; crest: *a horse passant argent*; supporters: *on either side a greyhound argent collared and lined or*; motto: *'Virtute et Labore'* (BP (1956) 713). Gr. (LO) and exemplified 1672, 1677 and 1774. In the mid-C18 a large estate

centred on that of the Hydes at Long Lee was purchased by 8th Earl of Dundonald (cr. with Barony of Cochrane of Paisley and Ochiltree (S) 1669 and Lord Cochrane of Dundonald (S) 1647). He also had a house in Derby.

Cock(s). Stapenhill. *Argent on a chief gules two pansies of the field*; crest: *on a log of wood a cock gules beaked and combed or holding in its beak a pansy azure stalked and leaved vert* (V. 1662). John Cocks exhibited these arms 'sans proof' in V. 1662 but this comment does not figure in D369. In some MSS the *pansies* are *roses argent*.

Cockburn. Sutton Rock (Sutton Scarsdale). *Argent three cocks gules, quartering gules six mascles or, for Weapont, all within a bordure vert*; crest: *a cock crowing proper*; mottoes: (above) *'Accendit Cantu'*; (below) *'Vigilans et audax'* (FD (1929) I.395). Arms of Cockburn of that Ilk bt. (cr. 24 May 1671); Charles Edward Stuart Cockburn (1867–1917) was of Sutton Rock and was grandson of the 2nd bt.

Cockfield: see Cofield.

Cockshutt. The Pastures (Mickleover). *Argent a chevron between three moles sable*; crest: *a dexter arm embowed vested sable turned up argent holding in the hand proper a molespade or headed and armed of the second* (FMG II.924). Conf., on taking the name Twistleton by Josias Cockshutt of the Pastures, 1801; these are the arms of Twistleton, indeed; he had also claimed the baronies of Saye and Sele (unsuccessfully) 1781. Heiress marr. Heathcote. On his funeral hatchment he quartered Cockshutt (Lancs.): *gules six gouttes three, two and one argent on a chief or a griffin passant sable* (Pierrepont, 42).

Coddington. Bennetston Hall (Chapel en le Frith). *Ermine a cross sable fretty or between a trefoil slipped in the first and fourth quarters a wolf's head erased in the second and third*; crest: *in front of a wolf's head erased or fretty sable a trefoil slipped vert*; motto: *'Nil Desperandum'* (FD (1910) 337). Gr. 1896 to Sir William Coddington 1st bt (cr. 17 Feb. 1896) and borne (presumably under remainder) by his nephew, Reginald, whose seat was Bennetston Hall.

Codinton. Codinton (Normanton by Derby). *Gules a cross countercompony or and azure* (Burke). Arms presumed to have been borne by Ralph de Codinton of Codinton, living late C13, the descendant of Sir Robert, 1156; the heiress marr. Folcher.

Coffyn. Haddon; Youlgreave. *Azure three bezants and nine cross crosslets or*; crest: *a martlet azure charged on the breast with two bezants* (MI at Hathersage; Local MS 6341). Arms conf. and gr. to William Coffyn of Haddon 24 Aug. 1522 of the family from Portledge (Fairy Cross, Bideford), Devon; he and his family had been dealing in lead for a couple of decades; one member was Sir Arthur Eyre's 3rd wife; another was allied to the Gilbert *alias* Knivetons and included with them in some MSS of V. 1569.

Co(k)field. Alfreton; Chaddesden. *Azure a cross compony argent and gules* (once in glass at Basford church, Notts.; cf. a seal of 1319: Thoroton, *Notts.* (1793), II.229, 253). Borne by John de Cokfield or Cofield of Nuthall, Notts., whose father and grandfather held also at Alfreton. A cadet branch held at Chaddesden 1431.

Cokayne. Ashbourne; Harthill; Sturston etc. *Argent three cocks gules combed and wattled sable*; crest: *a cock's head erased gules combed and wattled sable*; motto: *'A tribulacione'* (Willement Roll; seals of John 1334 and Sir John 1405, 1420, latter with crest, all from Local MS 6341; motto from same source); crest: *a cock gules* (Vv. 1569, 1611, 1662; Beds. 1566, 1582, 1634; Northants., 1681). Borne from an early date by this family. The last of the senior line, Sir Aston Cokayne, was cr. a bt 10 Jan. 1642 (ext. 1684). Charles, of the Sturston branch, was in 1642 cr. Baron and Viscount Cullen in the Irish peerage, being gr. supporters: *dexter a lion guardant per fesse or and argent, sinister an ostrich argent holding in the beak a horseshoe proper*; motto: *'Virtus in arduis'* (Burke). After the title became ext. (or dormant) in 1810, George Edward Adams, 4th son of one of the heiresses, assumed in 1845 (arms conf. 1873) the surname and arms of Cokayne; his second son was in 1920 cr. Lord Cullen, of Ashbourne, with arms as Viscount Cullen, but the similar supporters varied with *a collar or pendant therefrom an escutcheon argent thereon two bars vert* on each (for Harthill; BP (1970) 701). Andreas E. Cokayne C19 had as motto: *'En bon Espoir'* (bookplate, Local MS 7769). Sir John, 1421, was not unusual in bearing Harthill (qv) alone with the same motto (seal, PRO, P.199).

Cokayne. Ballidon; Chaddesden; Derby. *Ermine three cocks gules* (*DAJ* III (1881)

Cokayne

109). Arms used by George Cokayne of Ballidon, 2nd son of Sir Edward of Ashbourne, *c.* 1606. A younger son of George marr. the heiress of Angell of Chaddesden and some descendants used these arms quartered by Angell (qv), according to Tilley (II.197). Francis Cokayne of the Chaddesden family, lord mayor of London 1751 (Robert Bakewell the gatesmith's brother-in-law), also used these arms (Burke). One MS of V. 1569 was annotated by Bassano 'This family bear the arms with Cokayne of Ashburne with a sinister bend' (*DAJ* III (1881) 130).

Coke. Longford. *Per pale gules and azure three eagles displayed argent*; crest: *an ostrich argent holding in its beak a horseshoe or*; motto: *'Prudlens qui patiens'* (V. 1662). Harl.MS 6104 avers that these arms were borne by the Cokes 'sans proof' and that the *horseshoe* in the crest is *argent*: this is unreliable. Sir Thomas Coke was cr. Lord Lovell of Minster Lovell, Oxon., 1728 and in 1744 was advanced to Viscount Coke and Earl of Leicester. He was gr. supporters (on his appointment as KB) 1725: *on either side an ost-*

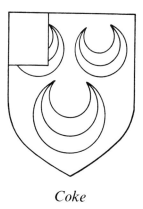

Coke

rich *argent ducally gorged per pale gules and azure lined the dexter of the first the sinister of the third* (J. Foster, *Peerage* (1881), 402); title ext. 1759 when Lord Leicester's nephew, Wenman Roberts, assumed the surname and arms of Coke. His son was made Earl of Leicester and Viscount Coke 12 Aug. 1837 with arms as above.

Coke. Trusley; Derby; Brookhill (Pinxton); Melbourne etc. *Gules three crescents and a canton or*; crest: *a sun in splendour or*; motto: *'Non aliunde pendere'* (V. 1662). Arms conf. to Richard Coke of Trusley 1573. Harl.MS 6104 of V. 1662 omits the *canton* and gives as crest: *a crescent or* (which may represent the pre-1573 usage inadvertently exhibited in 1662). The V. 1634 gives, for the Melbourne branch, *a fleur-de-lys of the field* on the *canton* (doubtless for difference; not in V. 1662). Local MS 6341 gives *argent two bars and a canton gules* as the arms of Coke of Trusley in 1611: the arms of Kirkby of Kirkby in Ashfield, Notts., whose heiress had marr. into the family. On the extinction of the Trusley branch in the 2nd World War, the heiress's husband assumed the surname and arms of Coke by RL in 1945. The arms as then gr. were: *gules three crescents and on a canton or a caltrap of the field* (Coke of Trusley in pretence); crest: *in front of a sun in splendour or a caltrap as in the arms*, as seen in Trusley church. V. 1569 quarters *per chevron or and azure in chief two roses gules* for Owen, a putative ancestor.

Cokerham. Buxton. *Azure on a bend sable three leopards' faces of the first (Rel.* V (1865) 230). Borne or used by John, son of James Cokerham, living the Buxton area *c.* 1580. The arms were gr. to Philip Cokerham of Wigmore, Herefs., 10 July 1549.

Cokesay. Catton; Eaton Dovedale; Walton upon Trent. *Argent on a bend azure three cinquefoils or* (Willement Roll). Borne by Sir Walter Cokesay of Upton Warren, Worcs., *jure uxoris* of Eaton. Sir Thomas Greville kt bt of Chipping Campden, Gloucs., who marr. Walter's grandson's heiress, seems also to have assumed these arms in lieu of his own (qv), 1445.

Colledge: see Colwich.

Collier. Allestree; Derby. *Argent on a chevron azure between three demi-unicorns courant gules as many acorns slipped or* (D369). Arms used by Mr Collier of Allestree, who failed to appear at V. 1662; the arms are those of Collier of Darlaston (V. Staffs. 1664). Collier's ancestor, Ralph, was bailiff of Derby 1568, which does not square with the Staffs. pedigrees, thus branding him as a usurper.

Collingwood. Caldwell. *Argent a chevron between three stags' heads erased sable* (quartered by Sanders on MI at Caldwell church, Glover II.182). Richard Collingwood of Caldwell, who used these arms, was labelled 'an usurper' V. 1611. They are those of Collingwood of Lilburn Tower, Northumberland.

Collingwood. Trusley. 'An usurper' at V. 1611. Presumably used arms as above.

Columbell. Nether Hall and Stancliffe (Darley); Sandiacre. *Sable three doves argent in their beaks an ear of wheat proper*; crest: *on a chapeau argent turned up sable a dove of the first in its beak an ear of wheat proper.* (Vv. 1569, 1611). Two of the MSS of V. 1569 (Harl.MSS 1484 and 6592) omit the chapeau in favour of a wreath; Harl.MS 886 alone shows both: Roger Columbell of Darley was the representative then. His ancestor, Henry of Nether Hall, was described as 'gentleman' in 1480: perhaps the original grantee. William Columbell of Derby (1733–1814) also bore (or used) these arms (MI formerly in St Michael's church, Derby). Mr Columbell of Matlock was a usurper in 1611.

Colville. Duffield; Lullington. *Azure a lion rampant argent a label of five points gules*; crest: *on a chapeau a lion statant tail extended argent gorged with a label of five points gules*; motto: *'Persevere'* (Parliament Roll; V. Cambs. 1619). Arms borne by Sir Geoffrey Colville of Carlton Colville, Suffolk, 1317, replacing a coat *argent a cross fleury gules* borne by Sir Roger, Geoffrey's father or grandfather. Arms conf. and supporters gr. 7 April 1815 to Sir Charles Henry Colvile (sic) of Duffield (1759–1833).

Colwich. Darley Moor (Snelston); Stydd Hall (Yeaveley). *Argent a fesse between three bats displayed sable*; crest: *a bat displayed proper* (V. 1611; V. Staffs. 1614). The gloriously mis-spelt 'Mr College of Steed' of V. 1611 was Anthony son of William. His son Francis was respited for proof in V. 1662, however; in 1687 they were 'all sold and dead'.

Comyn. Smisby. *Argent three garbs gules* (glass at Smisby noted V. 1611). Sir John Comyn of Lincs. bore *argent crusilly and three garbs gules* (*temp.* Edward II: Parliament Roll), and in both forms the arms are found as quarterings of Foljambe of Walton (V. 1569): the crusilly version is probably right.

Constable. Barlborough; Upper Hall (Darley). *Sable a cinquefoil between eight cross crosslets or quartering (argent) two bars of five lozenges gules* (glass once at Barlborough church, V. 1611). In fact, Constable of Freshmarsh (Yorks.), quartering those of Catfoss (Yorks.). Stephen of the latter marr. the heiress of the former, inheriting a moiety of Barlborough, but marshalling his wife's arms before his own, because, it is suggested, of the seniority of the Freshmarsh Constables over those of Catfoss.

Conway. Marston Montgomery. *Per fesse sable and gules an eagle displayed argent on a chief or a rose between two annulets of the second*; crest: *a reindeer's head couped proper collared and chained or*; motto: *'Semper Fidelis'* (BLG (1937) 680). Invariably shown quartering, and adding the crest of, Hurt of Alderwasley (qv); gr. 1848 to Capt. James Hurt of Strelley, as successor of Richard Conway of

Marston Montgomery and Strelley Hall, Notts., who assumed these arms and the surname of Edge (to which they apply) by RL in 1708 (Local Deed 5460). Conway's grandfather, John, of Marston, marr. the ultimate heiress of Edge, 1660s.

Cook. Ashbourne. Crest: *out of a ducal coronet a dexter arm in armour embowed to the sinister holding a scimitar* (Fairbairn, I.131). Used or borne by J. Reginald Cook of Asbbourne, solicitor, living 1892.

Cook. Melbourne. *Per chevron argent and sable in chief two boars' heads gules langued and armed argent and in a base a demi-eagle displayed or*; crest: *on a plate a boar's head erect gules armed and langued argent*; motto: *'Trwy Rhinwedd Onestrwydd'* ('Through virtue honesty') (BLG (1937) 473). Gr. C20 to a descendant of Thomas Cook of Melbourne (1808–84) the travel pioneer, then of Sennowe Park, Norfolk.

Cooksey: see Cokesay.

Cooper. Culland Hall (Brailsford). *Purpure on a chevron engrailed or between two lions statant in chief and a griffin's head erased in base of the second three gads proper*; crest: *on a mount vert in front of two battleaxes saltirewise a lion sejant sable collared or resting the dexter forepaw on a gad proper*; motto: *'Tout vient de Dieu'* (FD (1929) I.426). Gr. C20 to Arthur Francis Thomas Cooper of Culland (1857–1918).

Cooper. Derby; Sandybrook Hall (Offcote and Underwood). *Azure a saltire or between four trefoils and on a chief argent three dolphins embowed of the field*; crest: *a lion's head erased gorged with a chaplet of holly proper*; motto: *'Spero'* (BLG (1952) 522). Gr. C20 to Maj. V.B.D. Douglas-Cooper of Blakeney, Gloucs., descended from Capt. John Cooper of Derby (1745–1818), who marr. the coheiress of Douglas (qv); the eldest son, Joseph, was the Derby Regency architect. See also Gilbert.

Coote. Butterley Hall (Ripley). *Argent a chevron sable between three coots close proper*; crest: *a coot close proper*; mottoes: *'Vincit veritas'* and *'Coute que coute'* (FD (1929) I.426). Borne by Arthur Philip Coote (1887–1954), a director of the Butterley Co.; he was 5th son of Sir Algernon Coote of Castlecuffe (Co. Laois), 12th bt, the title having been cr. 2 April 1621 (Irish baronetage). Arms conf. (UO) 16 Jan. 1764 and 28 June

1770.

Copeldicke (Copuldick). *Argent a mullet sable and a chief per fesse indented of the field and of the second* (Local MS 6341). Not at present assignable but apparently belonging to Derbys.

Copestake. Copestake House (Kirk Langley); Marston Montgomery. *Sable semée of mullets and on a pile or an eagle displayed gules*; crest; *a demi-eagle displayed gules within a wreath argent and azure*; motto: *'Memor beneficii'.* Thomas Goodall was heir to his uncle Sampson Copestake of Kirk Langley (1736–1816), assumed his surname additionally to his own, and was gr. the above arms in 1827 by RSM

Copwood. Bakewell; Bubnell Hall. *Argent a pile in bend sable fimbriated and engrailed between two eagles displayed gules*; crest: *an eagle displayed vert* (*Rel.* XII (1872) 94). Used or borne by Richard Copwood of Blore, Staffs., heir of the Bassets, whose son, Basset Copwood, was of Bubnell and Bakewell. The eagles may be actually *vert*, not *gules*, as given in Burke. They have suggestive Basset (qv) imagery.

Corfield. Ormonde Fields (Codnor and Loscoe). *Per chevron gules and argent in chief two escutcheons of the second and in base a like escutcheon ermine on each a human heart of the first*; crest: *in front of a cubit arm erect the hand grasping two palm branches all proper a heart as in the arms*; motto: *'Serva fidem'* (BLG (1952) 531). Gr. 1897 to Frederick Channer Corfield of Ormonde Fields and Chatwall Hall, Salop. Previously the family had used: *argent three hearts gules*; crest: *a leopard passant collared and chained or holding in the dexter paw two palm branches all proper*; same motto (Tilley, IV.156).

Cotchett. Derby; Mickleover. *Azure a bend argent*; crest: *a talbot passant sable spotted argent* (Burke). Used by Thomas Cotchett of Mickleover, attorney and would-be silk throwster but who disclaimed V. 1662, and sealed with *a bend*.

Cotterell. Darley; Priestcliffe (Taddington). *Argent a bend between two escallops sable*; crest: *a talbot's head sable collared and lined or collar charged with three escallops of the first* (Tilley, IV.156). Attributed to Lawrence Cotterell of Priestcliffe and Darley C14 by Tilley on the strength of a presumed descent of Cotterell of Southrepps, Norfolk, from this family.

Cotton. Ash; Etwall. *Azure a chevron argent between three hanks of cotton proper*; crest: *a falcon proper beaked, legged and belled or the dexter claw supporting a belt also proper, buckle gold*; motto: *'In utraque fortuna paratus'* (MIS in Etwall church; V. Cheshire 1663). Borne by Roland Cotton of Bellaport, Salop, and (*jure uxoris*) Etwall (1674–1753) and conf. 1820 to Joseph Green of Hall Green, Worcs., who assumed the surname and arms of Cotton in lieu of his own, having marr. the heiress.

Cotton. Boyleston. *Azure an eagle displayed argent armed gules*; crest: *an eagle displayed argent* (as glass in church at Chesterfield, V. 1569). Assumed by William Cotton *jure uxoris* of Hamstall Ridware, Staffs., being his wife's family's (Ridware) arms, and replacing those previously borne by his family *argent a bend sable between three ogresses* which his descendants usually quartered with the above (both quartered by Bradbourne: MIS at Ashbourne church and V. 1569). William's wife also brought him Boyleston.

Cotton

Cotton. Derby. *Sable a chevron between three griffins' heads erased argent*; crest: *a griffin's head erased argent*; motto: *'Fidelitas Vincit'* (R. Broun, *Baronetage* (1844), 37). Rowland Cotton of Derby, descended from Cottons of Landwade, Cambs., d. 1604. He and his son, John (who went to America 1620) bore these arms. See also Jodrell.

Couling. Willington. *Argent a griffin segreant sable* (on plate at Willington church, dated 1699). Borne by Mrs Katherine Couling of Willington C17. Shown impaling *ermine(s) on a chief argent three lions rampant and a bordure vert* (Jeavons, 236, 251). As her marriage entry is untraced, it impossible to identify her family, as these arms do not appear in Papworth.

Cowley: see Culey.

Cowper. Melbourne; Over Haddon. *Argent three martlets and on a chief gules as many annulets or*; crest: *a lion's gamb erect and erased or holding a branch of cherry vert fructed gules*; supporters: *on either side a light dun horse a large blaze down the face mane close shorn except for a tuft on the withers a black list down the back a bob tail and three white feet, viz.: the hinder ones and the near forefoot*; motto: *'Tuum est'* (Pine, 88). Gr. 9 Feb. 1615 to John son of John grandson of John Cowper of Ditcham (Hants.) and Kent and supporters gr. to Sir William Cowper, 3rd bt (cr. 4 March 1641), 9 Nov. 1706 on his elevation to the peerage as Lord Cowper of Wingham, Kent. He was raised to an earldom and viscountcy of Fordwich, Kent, 1716, and the 5th earl (also a Prince of the Holy Roman Empire, cr. 31 Jan. 1778) inherited the Lambs' Melbourne estates. The 7th (and last) earl also became, by inheritance, Lord Dingwall (Scotland, cr. 1609), Lord Butler of Moore Park (England, cr. 1666) and Lord Lucas of Crudwell, Wilts. (England, cr. 1663). Original titles ext. 1905.

Cox. Brailsford; Culland (Brailsford); Derby; Field House (Spondon). *Argent three moorcocks proper*; crest: *a gamecock proper*; motto: *'Vigilantia praestat'* (Glover, II.140); moorcocks sometimes *gules*. Used by the extensive family of Cox, vintners and lead merchants, C19. T.W. Cox of Spondon (1841–89) used on his carriage: *per chevron gules and azure a bezant between in chief two roses and in base as many cocks respectant argent*; crest: *a cock gules*; motto: *'Vigilantia praestat'* (Local MS 9555.120).

Craven-Smith-Milnes. Dunston Hall (Newbold). *Argent a fesse couped indented between five cross crosslets fitchée gules*; crest: *on a coronet composed of five roses set on a rim or a griffin statant wings elevated ermine beaked formembered and charged on the wings with a cross crosslet of the first*; motto: *'Fortiter et Recte'* (BLG (1937) 1600). Gr. with crests and quarterings of Milnes and Smith of Dunston (qv) 1932 to Lawrence Barrington Craven (1874–1933) on his assuming the surname and arms of Smith-Milnes additionally to his own.

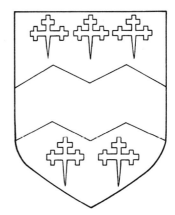

Craven-Smith-Milnes

Creagh: see Brazier-Creagh.

Cresswell. Edale; Ford Hall and Malcoff (Chapel en le Frith). *Per fesse gules and or a pale with three squirrels sejant two and one and as many trefoils slipped one and two all counterchanged*; crest: *between two wings gules goutée d'or a bird bolt fessewise of the second thereon a squirrel sejant proper holding in its paws a trefoil slipped vert*; motto: *'Vincit amor Patriae'* (FD (1929) I.458). Gr. 2 Feb. 1895 to George Cresswell of Ocle Pychard Court, Herefs., who was descended from the Cresswells of Ford and Malcoff (*DAJ* XXX (1909) 170).

Cressy. Alfreton; Beighton. *Argent a lion rampant queue fourchée sable* (St George Roll, 594; V. Notts. 1614; seal of 1292, PRO, P.1251). Borne by Sir William Cressy, who held moieties of Beighton and Alfreton; the arms are supposed to be 'recorded from before 1189'. They were adopted by William de Cressy of Hodsock, Notts., whose father had borne the canting *or three cressets gules* (Matthew Paris Shields, II.30). They were conf. 21 June 1580 to Henry Cressy of Owlcotes, Notts.; his kinsman Abraham held property in Brampton and Alfreton later C17. In V. Notts. 1663 the arms are shown with *a cinquefoil gules* in the dexter canton: for difference?

Crewe: see Harpur.

Crewcher (Crewker). Twyford; Stenson. *Argent a fesse between six martlets sable* (*Rel.* VII (1867) 23). Sometimes found as above and *a bordure of the second*, e.g. as a quartering of Beaumont of Barrow. Borne by John Crewker esq., whose ancestor, William son of Nicholas Crewker, acquired Twyford and Stenson early C14. Anne, dau. and heiress of John Crewker of Twyford, marr. John Tevery of Stapleford, Notts. (d. 1603). On their son's MI in the church there the arms quartered as Crewker are: *or fretty sable on a chief gules a lion passant guardant of the first* (Thoroton, *Notts.* (1793), III.195). This coat is strongly remiscent of that of St Amand and might suggest a connection with an heiress of that family, perhaps explaining its adoption in lieu of the coat above.

Criche. Stubben Edge (Ashover). *Ermine on a pale sable three crosses patée fitchée or* (Vv. 1611, 1634). Borne by William Criche of Stubben Edge (1611) and his son Ralph (1634). The above arms and *a mullet for difference* were gr. 1619 to Edmond Criche of London, draper, and of Oxon. He was master of the Merchant Taylors in 1624.

Criche. Crich. *Azure a chevron between two crescents in chief and a pelican in its piety in base or* (V. 1611). Allowed to Henry Crich 1611, allegedly borne C14 by his ancestors of Crich. Lysons (cxxiv) gives a *sable* field, due to use of 'B' for both *azure* and *sable* in C17 tricks.

Cromford & High Peak Railway Co. *A fesse and in chief a railway wagon*; motto: 'Divina

palladis arte' (as carved on Jessop's Bridge, Cromford). Dow (p. 31) assigns the arms to the company's foundation in 1825; it was later absorbed by the London & North Western. No authority.

Crompton. Durrant Hall (Chesterfield); Flower Lilies (Windley); The Friary (Derby); Stanton Hall (Stanton by Dale). *Vert on a bend argent double cotised ermine between two covered cups or a lion passant gules on a chief azure three pheons of the fourth*; crest: *a demi-horse rampant vulned in the breast with an arrow sable headed and feathered argent*; motto: 'Love and Loyalty' (Glover, II.578; motto: Burke). Gr. to Samuel Crompton of Derby, banker, 1751. A grandson inherited the Yorks. estates of the Stansfields, the son taking the surname and arms of Stansfield 1832, conf. 1872. Another confirmation was gr. to the widow of Samuel Crompton's brother, 1771.

Cromwell. S. Wingfield; West Hallam etc. *Argent a chief gules overall a bendlet azure* (Jenyns' Ordinary). Borne by John, 1st Lord Cromwell, summoned to Parliament as a baron 1308. The Caerlaverock Roll gives the field as *or*. The 4th baron quartered the field *argent* version with Tattesall: *chequy or and azure a chief ermine*. In glass at S. Wingfield church was *argent a bend azure* for Cromwell (Cox, I.443), plainly an earlier version. Bassano recorded in glass at Dronfield (1710) *azure a lion rampant double queued argent*, also found on a harness pendant of C14 date found at Swarkestone in the 1970s.

Cromwell. Tideswell. *Quarterly per fesse indented or and azure four lions passant counterchanged*; crest: *on a chapeau a pelican or goutée azure vulning herself proper*; supporters: *on either side a bull gules winged argent crined and unguled or*; motto: 'Semi mortus qui timet' (V. Staffs. 1663). Gr. 1543 to 1st Lord Cromwell of Oakham, son of the attainted Thomas Cromwell, Earl of Essex, on his rehabilitation; title originally cr. 1536. The 4th baron, cr. (1624) Viscount Lecale and (1645) Earl of Ardglass (Irish Peerage) marr. the heiress of Meverell of Tideswell. Ext. 1687. The Earl of Essex's shield was different: *azure on a fesse between three lions rampant or a rose gules between two Cornish choughs proper* (crest as above; Parliament Roll 1539–40).

Cross. Spondon. Arms if used not known. Richard Crosse did not appear at V. 1662.

Crossley. Priory Flatte (Breadsall). Crest (?): *on a rock a swan statant close proper* (livery button in a local collection). Used (or borne if the person was descended from the recipient of a similar grant of 1821) by H. Crossley JP *c.* 1908.

Crowshawe. Derby; Markeaton. *Argent on a chevron engrailed gules between three crows proper as many mullets or, a crescent for difference* (MI at All Saints', Derby). Presumably any grant (so far not traced) must have been to Richard Crowshawe's elder brother, father of Richard's heir, John in 1631; hence the difference mark, unless the arms were unauthorised and this was assumed for effect.

Croxden Abbey. Staffs. *Or a bend between six martlets sable* (Burke). Founded *c.* 1188 by Bertram de Verdon (qv); held land extensively W. of Derby and S. of Ashbourne, e.g. around Longford.

Cubley. Cubley. *Argent on a chevron sable three acorns or* (*Rel.* V. (1865) 231). Entered by John Sleigh under Cuderley, but this name in Derbys. is not known. It is suggested that the name was Cubley, a cadet branch of Montgomery whose heiress marr. Clifton of Clifton by Ashbourne *c.* 1381. Another spelling of the name is 'Cobile', given by Burke: *per pale indented or and argent a chevron gules:* arms which perhaps derive from those of Stafford.

Culey (Cuilley, Colleigh, Cowley). Cowley (Dronfield Woodhouse). *Argent a chevron between three mullets pierced sable* (Berry; Burke). Given as borne by Sir Hugh de Culey (sic) on a list of knights of Notts. and Derbys. *temp.* Edward III (Glover, Appendix, p. 55). Almost certainly the arms of Cowley of Cowley, where they held a knight's fee C12. In glass at Walton on Trent church (Wyrley's notes to V. 1569) they were given as above, and they are also found with *pellets* instead of *mullets*. Berry also gives for 'Co. Derby' *argent a chevron sable cotised azure between three mullets pierced of the second.* Heiress marr. Cadman.

Cumming. Foston Hall. *Azure an oval buckle between three garbs and a bordure or;* crest: *a lion rampant proper holding a dagger in bend sinister point upwards argent hilt and pommel or;* motto: *'Courage'* (arms: Burke; with crest and motto: Local MS 9555). Borne by Sir Henry Cumming, whose son, Adm. Sir A.C. Cumming inherited Foston Hall from

John Broadhurst, his sister's husband: presumably a grant of before 1874 by Lord Lyon.

Curteis. Summerley Hall (Unstone). *Per saltire argent and sable four bears passant counterchanged in the centre a bezant* (V. 1662 (D369)). Borne by Robert son of Francis Curteis of Summerley, although 'sans proof' in some MSS. The descendants of William Burton of Fauld, Staffs., quartered *or three mullets gules* (Burke) for William Curteis of this family, whose heiress he marr.

Curtis. Ford (Stretton). John Curtis disclaimed V. 1611.

Curzon. Breadsall. *Gules on a bend azure three horseshoes argent* (as quartered by Dethick of Breadsall, V. 1569). The arms breach the 'rules' of tincture, and bear the Ferrers horseshoes. Borne by Thomas Curzon, whose heiress marr. Dethick.

Curzon. Croxall. *Vairé or and gules on a chief sable three horseshoes argent;* crest: *a cockatrice gules legged beaked combed and wattled sable* (Cox, II.358; crest: V. 1569). Ancient arms, replete with Ferrers motifs, presumably discarded after the disgrace of that family for they later bore: *azure on a bend between two lions rampant argent three popinjays vert* (V. 1569; crest as above). This family also bore the arms of Camville (*gules on a bend argent three martlets sable* (MI at Croxall church)) and Foliot (*gules on a bend argent in dexter chief a martlet sable* (Cox, loc.cit.)) from heiresses. Senior line of Curzon.

Curzon. Kedleston; Derby. *Argent on a bend sable three popinjays or collared gules;* crest: *a popinjay rising or collared gules;* motto: *'Let Curzon holde what Curzon helde'* (Vv. 1569, 1611). Before the fall of the Ferrers, the Kedleston branch bore *vairé or and gules on a bend sable three popinjays or collared gules.* Robert Curzon of this branch was in 1500 cr. a baron of the Holy Roman Empire and was gr. a new and highly complex coat of arms (Harleian Soc. LXXVI (1925) 56), 30 Aug. 1500. According to Beckwith's MS (Local 3562) his great-grandfather, Henry, 3rd son of John of Kedleston (and brother of Walter, of Waterperry, Oxon), bore: *argent on a bend sable between three tigers' heads erased gules as many popinjays of the field collared of the third.* In 1761 Sir Nathaniel Curzon, 4th bt (Nova Scotia, 18

Curzon

June 1636; England, 11 Aug. 1641), was cr. Lord Scarsdale, being gr. supporters 9 April 1761 *dexter a figure of Prudence habited argent mantled azure holding in the sinister hand a javelin entwined with a ramora proper sinister a figure of Liberality mantled purpure holding a cornucopia also proper* with additional motto: *'Recte et Suaviter'* (BP (1970) 2386). His brother Assheton was cr. (1802 and 1791) Viscount and Baron Curzon of Penn; his grandson succeeded to his mother's barony of Howe of Langar, being cr. 7 July 1821 Earl Howe. He bore Howe quartering Curzon with supporters: *on either side a Cornish chough proper round their necks a chain or* (ibid.), gr. 1794. 5th Lord Scarsdale was further cr. 1898 Lord Curzon of Kedleston in the Irish Peerage (the last such); Earl Curzon, Viscount Scarsdale (the latter in remainder to his father's heirs male) and Lord Ravensdale (with remainder to his daughters and their heirs male successively) and in 1922 Marquess Curzon. (2nd) Baroness Ravensdale was cr. for life in 1958 Lady Ravensdale of Kedleston Hall and her son and successor in the original peerage established his arms

(1966) as Mosley (qv) and Curzon quarterly with Mosley crest; supporters: *dexter a raven proper and sinister a popinjay also proper collared gules* motto: as Mosley. Numerous Curzon coats borne by descendants of the Derbys. family exist: *Vairé or and gules on a bordure sable eight popinjays argent* (Stephen, of Fauld, Staffs., and W. Lockinge, Berks.; Papworth); as Curzon of Kedleston (ancient) for the Waterperry, Oxon, branch (cr. bt 30 May 1661, extinct 1750) conf. to Lord Teynham's ancestors 1788, and *argent on a bend gules three bezants* (Weston on Trent church V. 1611, Local MS 6341) for Curzon of Besthorpe, Norfolk.

Curzon. Derby. *(Argent?) on a bend sable three popinjays vert*; crest: *a popinjay rising.* (Glover, 2nd Ed. II.587). Borne (incorrectly) by John Curzon of Derby, a scion of Curzon of Breedon, Leics., cadets of Kedleston, *c.* 1800. A Chinese armorial plate of *c.* 1730 bears the unrecorded *Azure on a bend or three popinjays vert*; crest: *a pelican vulning herself vert*; motto: *'Prodesse conor'* (Howard, A5, E7). The Cursons of Letheringsett, Norfolk, bore: *Ermine a bend counter compony argent and sable*; crest: *two arms in armour proper couped at the shoulders garnished or holding a sword fesseways hilt in the dexter gauntlet point to the sinister* (Burke); they descended from a common ancestor with the Derbys. branches. Burke also gives for Curson, Derbys.: *Chequy or and sable a fesse argent* and for Derby: *quarterly argent and or on 1st and 4th a martlet sable and 2nd and 3rd a bend chequy of the second and third cotised of the last.* Neither of these has been traced.

Cutler. Breadsall. *Azure three dragons' heads erased and a bordure engrailed or*; crest: *a dragon's head erased or gorged with a ducal coronet azure* (Le Neve, 151, cf. V. Yorks. 1664–5). Borne by Sir Gervase Cutler, who marr. the heiress of Bentley.

Cutlove. Staveley. Arms not known; Francis Cutlove of 'Stabley' disclaimed V. 1611. Thomas Cutlowe of London, pewterer (d. 1680), used on his wares a crazy combination of bezants, mullets and fleurs-de-lys.

D'Abitot: see Barlow.
Daintree. Hatton. *Sable a bend ermine between two cotises engrailed on their exteriors or*; crest: *a bull's head ducally gorged proper*

(Burke). Used by Tristram Daintree who disclaimed at V. 1611 where the place is given as Halton, a mistake repeated by Sleigh (*Leek*, 9) where he gives the arms as finally gr. to the Daintrees of Macclesfield, Tristram's descendants: *quarterly sable and or a bend ermine between two cotises engrailed of the second* (1809). D369 gives the *bend* of the disclaimed coat as *argent*.

Dakeyne. Biggin (Hartington Nether Quarter); Chelmorton; Holt House (Darley); Stubben Edge (Ashover). *Gules a lion passant guardant between two mullets in pale or between as many flaunches argent each charged with a griffin segreant sable*; crest: *issuant from a palisado coronet or a dexter arm embowed proper holding a battleaxe of the first around the wrist a riband azure*; motto: *'Strike, Dakins, strike, the Devil's in the hemp'* (Vv. 1611, 1662). Gr. 12 Oct. 1563 to Arthur Dakeyne of Stubben Edge, Ashover, whose kinsman, Arthur, son of Richard, received a confirmation 27 Aug. 1611. George Dakeyne(s), a Yorks. kinsman, was gr. 15 Dec. 1548 arms as above but with *lions rampant sable* on the flaunches. Another kinsman, Arthur, of York, was gr. 12 Oct. 1563 *argent an anchor sable* (MI at Hackness church, Yorks.). The family had an alleged 'ancient arms' which Sleigh (*Rel.* V (1865) 231) gives as: *argent a cross between four lioncels gules* which contrast with Dakeney, Norfolk, *azure a cross between four lioncels or* (*DAJ* XL (1918) 87). William Dakeyne of Ashover was a *soi disant* Norroy, making 'grants' in the 1570s and 1580s: MI at Ashover.

Dalby. Ockbrook. *Ermine a cinquefoil gules* (seal in private collection). Used by Edward Dalby of Ockbrook (1635–96): for grant of 1853 to his descendant Robert and 1886 to Sir W.B. Dalby, representing the Dalbys of Castle Donington, Leics., see BLG (1952) 593 and FD (1910) 410 respectively.

Dale. Ashbourne; Flagg Hall; Parwich. *Paly of six gules and argent a bend ermine on a chief azure three garbs or*; crest: *on a mount vert three Danish battleaxes two in saltire one in pale proper staves azure enfiled with a chaplet of roses alternatively gules and argent banded or* (V. 1662). Allowed to Robert Dale of Flagg Hall, 1662 (but 'sans proof' in the Visitation papers at the College of Arms: Harl.Soc. new series 8 (1989) 76–7) and conf. to Robert, of Ashbourne 22 Aug. 1816.

Dale. The Pastures (Mickleover). *Azure a swan argent between four bezants saltireways*; crest: *in front of two eagles' heads erased and addorsed proper an escutcheon azure charged with a bezant*; motto: *'I byde my tyme'* (FD (1910) 411). Gr. to David Dale of Darlington 1874 and borne by Sir James Backhouse Dale, 2nd bt, of The Pastures. Title cr. 13 July 1895, ext. 1922.

Dalrymple. Barrow Hall (Barrow on Trent); Caldwell Hall; Ravenstone Hall. *Or on a saltire azure nine lozenges of the field*; crest: *a rock proper* (Tilley IV.156, and carved on gable at Barrow School). Borne by Daniel Dalrymple of Barrow *c.* 1800, who, if Tilley's attribution is correct, was of the house of Stair.

Dalton. The Friary (Derby). *Azure crusilly and a lion rampant guardant or* (MI once at All Saints' Derby as impaled by Bateman; Cox & Hope, 143). Arms used by John Dalton of Derby 1662 given in V. 1662 without tinctures 'said to be ex antiquo sigillo'. In the notes in preparation for a V. 1688 a note says of his son: 'a young barr[ister]; not rich no title to arms ... not connected to the Yorkshire family who bore *azure crusilly a lion rampant guardant argent'*.

Damport: see Davenport.

Daniell. Tideswell. *Azure a bend between six escallops or* (St George Roll). Borne *c.* 1295 by John Daniell. Note the striking similarity between these arms and those of Foljambe, Frecheville and Tideswell. Quartered by Meverell, V. 1569.

D'Arcy. Eckington. *Azure crusilly fitchée and three cinquefoils argent* (Calais Roll). Borne by Sir William d'Arcy 1345–48, and by Philip, 1st Lord d'Arcy of Knayth, Lincolnshire, who was gr. Eckington by Edward III, and summoned to Parliament as a baron 1331. The latter bore the *cinquefoils pierced* (seal 1349, PRO, P.1276).

D'Arcy. Newhall. *Azure crusilly and three cinquefoils argent*; crest: *a bull passant sable armed unguled maned and tufted or*; motto: *'Je loue Dieu grace attendant'* (Harl.MS 1093; Egerton MS 996). Borne by Sir Robert d'Arcy of Dartford Place, Kent, and *jure uxoris* of Newhall, great-grandson of 1st Lord d'Arcy of Temple Newsam (summoned to Parliament as a baron 1509, attainted 1538), a root of the Knayth branch. See also Jessop.

Darcy Clarke. Bearwardcote; Burnaston; Etwall; Derby. *Gules a saltire invected plain cotised or between three horses' heads couped one in chief and two in fesse erminois*; crest: *in front of a horse's head couped erminois a spur erect leathered gules*; motto: *'Fortis in arduis'* Used by George Darcy Clarke (1839–1901) co-founder of Alton's Brewery, Derby; his kinsman, Capt. J.N. Darcy Clarke, had livery buttons bearing a crest: *a horse's head erased.*

Darley Abbey. *Argent six horseshoes sable* (Tilley, III.269). Doubtless the tinctures represent a Tudor herald's idea of those borne by the Ferrers Earls of Derby, co-founders of this house. Only known in monochrome from encaustic tiles and seals.

Darley. Nether Hall (Darley). *Gules six fleurs-de-lys argent and a bordure ermine* (Burke). Borne, apparently, by the yr branch of the Darleys, whose heiress marr. Kendall (qv).

Darling: see Bagshawe.

Darwin. Breadsall Priory; Derby; Fern (Hartington); Sydnope Hall (Darley). *Argent on a bend gules cotised vert between two mullets each within an annulet of the second three escallops or*; crest: *in front of a demi-griffin segreant vert holding in its claws an escallop or three escallops fessewise argent*; motto: *'Cave et Aude'* (BLG (1937) 564). Gr. 1890 to Reginald Darwin of Fern, grandson of Dr Erasmus Darwin of Derby and Breadsall who used arms: *argent on a bend gules cotised vert three escallops or*; crest: *a demi-griffin segreant vert holding an escallop or*; same motto (Glover, II.154). Dr Darwin is said by Anna Seward to have had painted the motto *'E Conchis Omnia'* beneath his arms on his carriage, 1770: a reflection of his evolutionary inklings. It upset churchmen at Lichfield and had to be painted out (D. King-Hele, *Doctor of Revolution* (1977), 75). Francis Darwin, formerly Rhodes, of Elston, Notts., representing the senior branch of Dr Darwin's family, had a confirmation in 1850: *Ermine a leopard's face jessant-de-lys between two escallops all within two bendlets gules in chief a cross patée of the last*; crest: *a demi-griffin sable semée of mascles or resting the sinister claw on an escutcheon argent thereon a leopard's face jessant-de-lys gules and a cross patée or*; same motto (BLG (1937) 566).

Davenport. Codnor. *Argent a chevron between three cross crosslets fitchée sable and a bordure gules bezantée* (Local MS 6341.3v). Cadets of the Cheshire family (arms as above, *'sans bordure'* (William Davenport) Military Roll *c.* 1460) holding at Codnor *c.* 1490; cf. V. Cheshire 1580.

Daventry: see Daintree.

Davie: see Thornhill.

Dawes. Ingleby. *On a bend cotised between six cross crosslets fitchée three swans* (King, p. 67). 'Mr John Dawe bur[ie]d with these arms 1684'. He represented a family which had held at Ingleby mid-c15; authority for arms uncertain.

Dawson. Melbourne. *Ermine on a fesse engrailed sable three mullets or* (MI at Melbourne church). Used by William Dawson of Melbourne, d. 1603, of a south Derbys. yeoman family, a branch of Dawson of Long Whatton, Leics.

Dawson. Appleby; Melbourne; Smisby. *Azure on a bend engrailed argent two martlets sable* (Glover, 2nd Edn.II.26). Borne or used by Edward Dawson of Long Whatton, Leics., and Appleby, as on his C18 hatchment in the church at Appleby.

Day. Chellaston. *Per chevron or and azure three mullets counterchanged*; crest: *two winged hands clasping each other dexter or sinister azure on each a mullet counterchanged* (on church plate at Chellaston). Gr. to William Day, provost of Eton, 28 Oct. 1582, son of Richard, and used by Benjamin Day of Chellaston and London, whose father, John, of Norwich was born in Chellaston in poor circumstances. Plate dated 1771.

Day. 'Derbys.' *Gules two flaunches ermine on a chief azure three suns or*; crest: *a greyhound's head erased argent collared ringed and lined gules, the end nowed* (Burke). Gr. 28 Feb. (or 20 March) 1583 to 'Edward Day of London, Gent. f. Edmund f. William of Derbys.'. The latter's provenance is untraced.

De, D': see under second word.

Deane. Beeley; Matlock. *Or a fesse dancettée and in chief three crescents gules* (Lysons, clix). Disclaimed by Robert Deane of Beeley, V. 1611; in fact the arms of Deane of Deane Hall, Cheshire.

Deane. Hartshorne. Arms used not known. Thomas, son of Walter Deane of Hartshorne, 'promised to come to London' V. 1611, but see Debanke.

Deane. Ashbourne. Arms used not known. Mr Deane 'promised to come to London' V.

Day

Degge

1611.

Debanke. Hartshorne. *Azure a saltire between four escallops or*; crest: *an escallop or* (Sleigh, *Leek*, p. 34; Harl.MS 1537). Thomas, son of Walter Debanke of Hartshorne, entered these arms V. 1611 (Harl.MS 1093). The entry (above) for Deane of Hartshorne is probably a double for this one, which is undoubtedly correct.

Deeley. Melbourne House (Derby). *Gules a lion rampant argent ducally crowned between two fleurs-de-lys in pale or all between two flaunches bendy of six of the last and azure*; crest: *in front of a demi-eagle displayed sable an escallop between two fleurs-de-lys or*; motto: *'Ut vitrum sic vita'* (BLG (1937) 596). Gr. 6 April 1924 to Richard Mountford Deeley, formerly locomotive superintendent, Midland Railway, of Melbourne House, with remainder to the heirs male of his homonymous father (1825–1909).

Deincourt: see D'Eyncourt under E.

Degge. Abbott's Hill House (Derby); Fenny Bentley. *Or on a bend azure three falcons arousant argent belled and jessed of the field*; crest: *out of a ducal coronet or a falcon reclaimed argent beak and legs or* (V. 1662). Gr. 9 May 1662 to Sir Simon Degge of Stramshall, Staffs., and Derby, recorder of the latter; proposed as a kt of the Royal Oak, 1661. Simon Degge FRS, also of Derby, bore his falcons or and a crescent for difference.

Delves. Walton on Trent. *Argent a chevron gules fretty or between three delves sable* (Cox, III.100). Borne by Sir John Delves of Doddington, Cheshire (d. 1369) who was gr. Walton on Trent. A coat of Delves appeared on a Babington MI at Barlborough church: the *delves* there were replaced by *fleurs-de-lys* (Cox, I.55); at Cubley they also appear as *billets*. The arms incorporate elements of Audley (qv) from whom the Delves may have received a grant, cf. Mackworth.

Denman. Bakewell; Buxton; Derwent Hall; Stony Middleton Hall. *Argent on a chevron between three lions' heads erased gules as many ermine spots or*; crest: *a raven rising proper in the beak an annulet or*; motto: *'Prudentia et constantia'* (BP (1970) 766). Gr. to Lord Chief Justice Denman in 1834 when he was cr. Lord Denman of Dovedale: he was gr. supporters at the same time: *on either side a* *lion gules charged with five ermine spots in cross or.*

Derby. Derby etc. *A chevron between ten billets six in chief and four in base* (seal of 1379, Local MS 6341.23v). Borne by Alice dau. of John de Derby, wife of 5th Lord Basset of Sapcote, Leics., and widow of her kinsman, Robert Touchet of Markeaton. Of the family of Hugh, Dean of Derby C12. Note also *argent three cinquefoils and a canton gules* borne C14 by Derby or Dryby of Tattershall, Lincs., and attributed to the above family by Williamson (Box 57).

Derby Aluminium Company. *On a charger a boar's head couped.* In use Jan. 1989 (*Derby Evening Telegraph,* 12 Jan. 1989); no authority.

Derby, Bishopric of. *Purpure a cross potent quadrate argent in chief three fountains* (Briggs, 134). Gr. 1927 on the foundation of the diocese and impaled by Pearce over the door of Breadsall Mount (demolished 1967).

Derby, City of. *Argent on a mount vert within park pales a buck lodged between two oak trees fructed proper*; crest: *a ram passant proper collared or between two sprigs of broom also proper*; supporters: *on either side a buck charged on the shoulder with a sprig of broom proper*; motto: *'Industria virtus et fortitudo'* (e.g. on Derby Council House; Briggs, 134). Gr. 12 May 1939 to the then County Borough of Derby. Previously the town had used: *azure on a mount vert a buck lodged within park pales proper* as on the mid-C15 common seal (V. 1569, Local MS 6341). In 1974 Derby became a district council with the style of a borough and these arms were exemplified by Order in Council 2 June 1975. Derby became a city in 1977.

Derbyshire County Council. *Or a rose gules surmounted of another argent both barbed and seeded proper on a chief sable three stags' heads caboshed of the third*; crest: *out of a ducal coronet or a demi-griffin sable collared and chained argent holding a miner's pick in bend sinister of the first*; supporters: *dexter a stag and sinister a ram both proper gorged with a chain or pendent therefrom a Tudor rose proper*; motto: *'Bene consulendo'* (e.g. on County Council Handbook). Arms gr. and motto recorded 17 Sept. 1937; crest and supporters gr. 1978. Prior to the grant the arms used were: *or a Tudor rose slipped and ensigned with a regal crown all proper*; occasionally the rose is

shown with three blooms. Not officially in use since 1981.

Derbyshire Constabulary. *Sable on a fesse between in chief two stags' heads caboshed and in base a ram passant argent a Tudor rose proper*; motto: *'Vis unita fortior'* (Briggs, 134). Gr. 20 Sept. 1968.

Derby Lonsdale College: see Diocesan Training College.

Derby School. *Per pale argent and sable an open book proper edged and clasped or bound gules pages inscribed 1554 in Arabic numerals ensigned by an ancient crown of the fourth on a chief of the 5th between two crosses potent quadrate a stag lodged in a park also of the fourth*; motto: *'Vita sine litteris mors'* (Briggs, 134, and on the building.) Gr. to this former C16 grammar school 20 Nov. 1962, to the design of which Messrs T. Wrigley and R. Christian (qv) made the main contribution. Arms lapsed with institution, July 1989.

Derbyshire Building Society. Derby; Duffield Hall. *Or a Tudor rose proper on a chief vert between two sprigs of thrift each of three flowers a castle of as many towers portcullis raised all of the field*; crest: *on a mount vert a ram passant proper resting the dexter forehoof upon an escutcheon purpure thereon a mitre or*; supporters: *on either side a stag proper gorged with a collar of park pales or holding in the mouth a sprig of broom also proper*; motto: *'Bene Serviendo'.* This amusing burlesque of the arms of Derby – diocese, city and county – was gr. 20 March 1959.

Derwent. Derwent. *Argent two bars and on a canton gules a rose or* (Glover's Ordinary). Included by Sleigh in his list (*Rel.* XII (1872) 94), perhaps on the strength of the suggestive surname in Glover; no person of the name can be identified as holding at Derwent.

Desborough: see Disbrowe; Grenfell

Des Voeux. Caldwell Hall; Ravenstone Hall; Barrow Manor. *Gules on a pale or a squirrel sejant in chief a moor's head couped in base proper*; crest: *a squirrel sejant proper*; motto: *'Altiora in Votis'* (on porch at Caldwell Hall; FD (1929) I.536). Conf. (UO) 3 Aug. 1811 to Sir Charles Des Voeux who was made a bt (of Ireland) 1 Sept. 1787, the arms having been borne by his ancestors, the Vinchon de Bacquencourts of Rouen. Title ext. 1944.

Dethick. Breadsall; Derby; Newhall etc. *Argent a fesse vairé or and gules between three*

Dethick

water bougets sable; crest: *a horse's head couped argent* (Jenyns' Ordinary; Vv. 1569, 1611). Borne by Sir William de Dethick of Dethick (seal 1402, Local MS 6341). Sir William, yr son of another Sir William (qv) marr. the heiress of Curzon of Breadsall and assumed arms combining those of both houses: *on a bend between three water bougets as many horseshoes* (as carved in Breadsall church (now lost, Cox, III.61), with Dune irregularly in pretence); both coats contain elements of Ferrers armory. Lysons (cxxv) give the crest: *a nag's head erased argent*. William Dethick, Garter, and his family used these arms (or bore: as Garter it was presumably his right to legitimise the situation) with crest: *an eagle reguardant wings expanded and inverted proper*. He was, however, grandson of a Dutchman.

Devas. Field House (Spondon). *Argent on a chevron between three boars passant sable maned and unguled or langued gules a bee volant proper between two bulls' heads caboshed of the field*; crest: *a lion rampant sable collared or langued gules holding in the paws an escutcheon argent thereon a spearhead in pale sable*;

motto: *'Virtute et opera'* (FD (1905) 382; motto: Burke, FR 217–18). Gr. to Devas of Newgate St, London, 1812, and to kinsman Thomas son of Thomas Devas of London 1820. Horace (1826–1903), a son of the latter, settled at Spondon.

Dickens. Bakewell; Hazlewood. *Ermine on a cross flory sable a leopard's face or*; crest: *a lion couchant or holding a cross patonce sable* (*Rel.* V. (1865) 231; crest: Burke). Gr. 26 June 1629 (16 June 1625 in some MSS) to William Dickins (sic) of Fleet St, 'descended out of Derbyshire from Hazlewood'. Sleigh gives Bakewell as his origin (did he notice a kinsman there using these arms?) and Burke gives the *cross* in the arms as *patonce*.

Digby. Ravenstone. *Azure a fleur-de-lys argent*; crest: *an ostrich holding in its beak a horseshoe all proper* (Parliament Roll; crest: Burke). Borne by Sir John Digby of Leics. C14 and by his descendant, Henry, who purchased Ravenstone 1542, being allowed to Thomas of the same, V. Leics. 1619.

Digby. Stancliffe Hall (Darley). *Azure a fleur-de-lys argent a canton or*; crest as above (V. Notts. 1663). Sir John Digby of Mansfield Woodhouse sold Stancliffe 1655.

Dillon. Derby? *Argent a lion rampant between three crescents each surmounted of an estoile gules overall a fesse vert an annulet for difference* (V. 1611). These are the arms of Dillon of Northants., and are given in most Derbys. collections, including some Vv. The *estoiles* are omitted in Local MS 6341.3v. The representative in 1611 (who presumably had interests in Derbys.) was John son of Robert Dillon. A 'Mr Dillon' appears on a Derby rent roll of that year (*DAJ* XXXVI (1914) 94).

Diocesan Training College. Derby. *Argent on a pale purpure a cross potent quadrate of the field between a mitre or and a fountain on a chief sable an open book proper edged and clasped of the third*; crest: *a cross potent quadrate argent thereon a fountain*; motto: *'Nisi Dominus frustra'* (Briggs, loc.cit.) Gr. 20 Dec. 1950; college founded 1852. Became Bishop Lonsdale College 1964, Derby Lonsdale College 1977, now part of Derbyshire College of Higher Education. The late T. Wrigley advised in the adoption of the design. The validity of this achievement would appear to have lapsed.

Disbrowe. Walton Hall (Walton on Trent).

Argent a fesse between three bears' heads and necks couped sable muzzled or; crest: *a bear's head as in the arms* (Tilley, IV.161). Borne by Maj.Gen. John Desborough, cr. a peer by Cromwell 1658 (CP II.85n). His descendant, Gen. Sir Edward Cromwell Disbrowe, was of Walton C18. See also Wise.

Dixie. Appleby Parva; Normanton by Derby. *Azure a lion rampant and a chief or*; crest: *an ounce sejant proper ducally gorged or*; mottoes: *'Quod dixi dixi'* and *'Dei gratia grata'* (FD (1929) I.549; V. Leics. 1619). Sir Wolstan Dixie of Market Bosworth had acquired the Appleby Parva estate and was cr. a bt 14 July 1660; his son sold it, but a branch settled at Normanton Hall, which they replaced with Normanton House C18.

Dixon. Whittington Hall; Brampton Hall. *Per bend gules and azure a bend engrailed argent between two plates on a chief of the third a rose of the first between two torteaux*; crest: *an arm embowed habited azure platée cuffed argent hand proper holding a chaplet also proper*; motto: *'Fide et constantia'* (Local MS 9555.112). Used on his carriage by John Dixon of Whittington and Brampton C19.

Docksey (Doxey). Snelston Hall. *Or a lion rampant azure debruised by a bendlet gules* (seal in Derby Museum, 1928-407/2). Used by Robert Doxey, goldsmith and sugar-baker of London, who purchased Snelston Hall 1682 and d. 1704. The tinctures are supplied from Burke.

Dod: see Wolley.

Douglas. Douglas House (Derby); Sandybrook Hall (Offcote & Underwood). *Argent a human heart gules crowned or on a chief azure three mullets of six points of the field* (BLG (1952) 522). A much later confirmation as a quartering of Cooper (qv) representing the arms of Ald. Archibald Douglas of Derby, and tenant of Sandybrook. Coheiresses marr. Strutt, Fox and Cooper (qqv).

Douglas-Cooper: see Cooper.

Dovedale (Downdale): see D'Uvedale.

Downes. Downes Hall, Overton Hall (Taxal). *Sable a hart lodged argent* (seal on death warrant of Charles I (Harl.MS. 139, f. 38); V. Cheshire 1580 says a *buck*). Allowed to Reginald Downes of Taxal, 1580.

Drake. Beighton. *Paly of six argent and ermine a wyvern gules a chief of the first fretty of the third* (as quartered by Wright of Bilham House, Yorks.; College of Arms, Grants XXXVIII.170) Gr. 12 Jan. 1831 to be quartered by Wright of Bilham House (Beighton), with the latter crest, to Revd Godfrey Wright of Bilham House, son of Thomas, of Kimberworth, Yorks., by Dorothy, dau. of Revd John Drake, vicar of Beighton, and coheiress of her brother, Marmaduke, also of Beighton. They were the family of Drake of Yorks., allegedly male line descendants of Shepden of Shibden, Yorks.; cf. BLG (1952) 2799.

Draper. Culland Hall. *Argent on a fesse between three annulets gules as many covered cups or a crescent for difference* (V. 1662). Allowed to Robert Draper of Culland, although in some MSS 'respit given for proving the armes' and 'usurpers' in V. 1611, despite descent from Draper of Hants.

Draycott. Croft Hill (N. Wingfield); Loscoe Hall; Stanley Grange (Dale Abbey). *Paly of six or and gules a bend ermine*; crest: *a dragon's head erased gules*; motto: *'Justus esto et non metui'* (Vv. 1569, 1611, 1662; motto: pers.comm., W.M. Draycott of N. Vancouver, BC). Usually quartering *or a fret (or fretty) gules on a canton azure a cross patonce (or crosslet) argent* being the arms of the senior line of the family, of Paynsley (Draycott in the Moors), Staffs. (V. Staffs., 1614, 1663). This coat may derive from a Draycott–Touchet match late C12, although the two Draycott branches split c. 1250–75 when Philip son of Sir Richard settled at Wilne. Alternatively, the Loscoe branch coat may derive from the unknown heiress who brought Philip the Wilne estate. A third possibilty is that the Draycotts derive from Draycott, Derbys., and the *fretty* coat derives through an Audley connection in Staffs.

Draycott. Sedsall (Doveridge). *Or a fret gules on a canton azure a cross patonce argent a crescent for difference* (V. 1611). The 2nd son of Sir John Draycott of Paynsley bore these arms and inherited Sedsall from FitzHerbert.

Drury. Darley. *Argent on a chief vert two mullets or* (Military Roll). Sir William Drury bore these arms and inherited one moiety of Darley from Sotehill, buying the other. Sold 1547. See also Lowe.

Duckmanton. Duckmanton; Goss Hall (Ashover). *Sable a fesse dancettée ermine between six cross crosslets or* (V. Cheshire 1612). Borne by the Barnestons from as early as

1377, a family which represents the senior line of Gervase de Barneston, whose yr brother Robert de Duckmanton apparently was of Duckmanton later C12. The senior descendants of Richard son of Nigel of Malpas, Cheshire, Gervase's father, bore *gules a pale fusilly or*.

Duncombe. Norbury; Roston; Snelston. *Per chevron fleur-de-lysée argent and gules three talbots' heads erased all counterchanged*; crest: *a talbot's head erased gules collared or* (D369). Borne by William Duncombe of Bucks. and Ellastone, Staffs., whose Derbys. holdings included property around Ashbourne and Haselbarrow.

Dune (Duyn). Breadsall. *Or four pallets gules* (as a quartering of Dethick, V. 1569). Borne by Robert de Duyn who divided Breadsall into moieties before 1244, for the arms were quartered by the heirs of both branches.

Dunston: see D'Oyly under O.

Durant. Durrant Hall (Chesterfield); Tapton. *Sable a cross crosslet ermine and a crescent for difference*; crest: *a boar passant argent bristled armed and unguled or pierced in the side with a broken spear proper vulned gules* (Harl.MS 6095.76, quartering St Liz). Granted July 1606 to Rowland Durant of Durrant Hall (the modern spelling, preserved in nearby Durrant Road), whose heiress marr. Alsopp. The grantee's probable ancestor, Thomas Durant of Chesterfield, sealed with: *a fesse dancettée in chief three cross crosslets fitchée* (RBC 127, 1392). It is noteworthy that one John Durant of Yarnton, Oxon., bore the 1606 arms without difference, implying that the Chesterfield family were their cadets. The Oxon. branch were ultimately descended from Walter Durant, bailiff of Ashdown Forest, Sussex, c. 1300 (V. Rutland 1618; V. Oxon. 1574). Local MS 6341, however, ascribes the undifferenced coat to the Derbys. Durants, and that charged with a crescent to a cadet, Francis, of Tapton. In spite of the evidence of the 1606 crescent, the Chesterfield branch has no known connection with those of Oxon. The crescent may, therefore, be a charge, not a difference.

Durrant. 'Co. Derby'. *Sable a fesse dancettée and in chief three fleurs-de-lys argent*; crest: *a lion rampant argent holding in the dexter paw a fleur-de-lys or and in the mouth a sword proper hilt and pommel of the second point*

downwards (shield: Thompson IV.70; crest: Burke). It is quite unclear to whom in Derbys. these arms pertained, nor can authority be found for them. The shield is that of Durrant of Tong, Salop, but not the crest. The former arms are clearly based on the seal of Thomas Durant of Chesterfield (qv) and the achievement may represent the device used by one of his posterity.

Dury. Bonsall. *Azure a chevron argent between three crescents or*; crest: *a demi-lion rampant argent*; motto: '*Confido*' (BLG (1952) 721). Gr., apparently, to Charles du Ry (1550–1637) of Verneuil-sur-Oise, Valois, France, architect to Louis XIII. Borne (whether with the approval of the College of Arms is unclear) by his descendant, Maj.Gen. Alexander Dury, who marr. the heiresses of Turnour and Ferne, 1753.

Du Sautoy: see under S.

Eadie. Barrow Hall (Barrow on Trent). Crest: *a cross crosslet fitchée gules and a skean in saltire proper* (livery button in a local collection). This device was used (or borne) by James Eadie of Barrow, a brewer, c. 1900 and is the crest of Edie of Moneaght, whose arms are: *argent three cross crosslets fitchée gules* (Burke).

Eam: see Eyam.

East Midlands Electricity Board. *Azure a cross raguly couped between in the first quarter an antique crown in the fourth quarter a fetterlock or in the second and third a rose argent barbed and seeded proper on a chief of the second a bear supporting a staff raguly sable between two cinquefoils ermine*; crest: *a Viking ship oars in action or sail argent charged with a horseshoe sable pennant flying gules*; supporters: *on either side a stag proper that to the dexter charged on the shoulder with a plate thereon a Stafford knot sable that to sinister charged with a roundel per chevron a cross at the point vert and argent*; motto: '*Feliciter servimus*' (*EMEB Journal*, I(7), 242). Gr. 10 March 1950.

East Midlands Gas Board. *Or on a cross raguly vert a fleur-de-lys of the field on a chief gules a tiered castle between two rams' heads caboshed argent*; crest: *in front of flames a demi-figure of Vulcan holding in the dexter hand four arrows and over the sinister shoulder a hammer all proper*; supporters: *on either side* *a panther gardant gules incensed and charged on the shoulder with a cinquefoil pierced ermine;* motto: *'E mulcibere garae'* (pers. comm.). Gr. 19 March 1953. It is unclear how the privatisation of this board (and the EMEB, qv) has altered the status of their arms.

Eaton. Derby. *Argent a griffin segreant sable* (Heard's MS Pedigree, Blackwall Hall). Used by Ald. Thomas Eaton of Derby, who marr. Elizabeth dau. of Richard Blackwall of Blackwall (Kirk Ireton) *c.* 1730. Having been included in the pedigree drawn up by Heard 1764 for the Blackwalls, these arms have presumably been endowed with a sort of legitimacy.

Eaton. Sawley; Wilne Mills (Draycott & Church Wilne); Wilsthorpe (Sawley). *Or a fret azure;* crest: *an eagle's head erased sable in the beak a sprig vert;* motto: *'Vincit omnia veritas'* (Burke). Arms of Eaton of Nottingham, used by the sons of William Eaton of Wilne.

Ecclesbourne School. Duffield. *On a lozenge a fesse wavy between in chief on a mount a tower and in base a tree eradicated.* On contemporary notepaper; no authority.

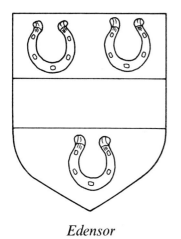

Edensor

Edensor. Edensor; Tissington. *Argent a chevron gules between three horseshoes sable* (as quartered by Cokayne, V. 1569, cf. MI at Youlgreave, Cox, III.327 & n.). A cadet branch (holding at Tissington) were of Comberford, Staffs., and bore *argent a fesse gules between three horseshoes sable;* crest: *a dexter arm erect holding a sword argent hilt and pommel or* (V. Staffs., 1583; quartered by Heathcote of Longton Hall, Staffs., qv.). Arms of this family – consanguineous with the Shirleys – are full of Ferrers motifs.

Edge: see Conway; Hurt; Strelley.

Edwards. Derby. *Argent a fesse between three martlets sable;* crest: *out of a ducal coronet argent a tiger passant or langued maned and tufted sable* (Glover, 2nd Edn., II.570-1). Borne (or used) by Nathaniel son of Thomas Edwards of Wilts. (1683–1745), who was mayor of Derby 1731; his son was mayor 1773, 1785, 1798. Ultimate ancestors from Pembs., although the arms seem to pertain to a London family.

Eley. Alport (Youlgreave); Winster. *Argent a fesse engrailed between six fleurs-de-lys gules;* crest: *an arm in armour holding in the hand a hawk's lure all proper* (Burke). Borne (if members of a Yorks. family) or used by William Eley of Winster (d. 1758) and his nephew John, of Alport in Youlgreave (d. 1793). On a tombstone in Winster churchyard T.N. Ince recorded the above arms combining the crest of Eley of Scropton (qv) 26 July 1824 (Local MS 8022).

Eley. Scropton. *Argent a fleur-de-lys within a mascle between four other fleurs-de-lys sable;* crest: *in front of a cubit arm vested ermine cuffed argent holding in the hand proper a fleur-de-lys sable, a mascle of the last;* motto: *'Alis volat proprius'* (BLG (1937) 686). Gr. *c.* 1875 to W.T. Eley of Oxhey Grange, Herts., great-grandson of George, of Scropton (b. 1717). Lysons (302) imply that this family is related to that of Alport.

Elton. Elton. *Barry wavy of eight argent and azure on a bend or three mullets gules* (*Rel.* V (1865) 231). These appear to be the arms of Alport of Cannock, Staffs., but intended by Sleigh (on what evidence does not appear) for the above; John Elton of Elton, sen. and jun., living 1433, appear on the list of Derbys. 'gentlemen' (Glover, I. App. 59).

Erewash Borough Council. *Argent three bends wavy azure on a chevron overall gules* *between as many astronomical signs of Mars a fleur-de-lys or on a chief dovetailed of the third a garb between two hanks of yarn of the fourth* crest: *issuant from a mural crown or masoned gules charged with four annulets sable a stag rampant of the second attired and unguled of the first collared with lace proper between two torches issuing azure enflamed of the last*; motto: *'Per sapientiam constantiam que victoria'* (displayed in the borough). Gr. 1983.

Errington. Ashbourne; Hinchleywood Hall (Mapleton). *Argent two bars and in chief three escallops azure*; crest: *an unicorn's head erased per pale argent and gules* (BLG (1875) I.399). Conf. by RLS of 1895 and 1897 to Revd John Launcelot Errington of Hinchleywood (1828–1906); he took the name and quartered the arms of Turbutt (qv) 1895; his son, those of Gladwin-Errington 1897. Previously, George Errington of Ashbourne had used the above arms but crest: *a cock gules combed and wattled sable* (MI at Ashbourne church); plainly borrowed from Cockayne.

Etwall. Etwall. *Gules two bars argent between nine martlets* (Williamson's Notes, Box 57, allegedly from a tile from Welbeck Abbey). Ingram de Etwall was MP for Derbys. 1329; Hugh son of Nicholas de Etwall gave land there to Welbeck Abbey 1294. These arms resemble those Burke assigns to Ribeouf, which strengthens the supposition that they were of the same stock. One Richard Foliot of Etwall sealed with a *fleur-de-lys* with the legend RICHARD' ETEWE (Every Deeds in private hands, III.44, 1303). See also Riboef.

Evans. Caldwell Hall; Cromford Bridge House (Cromford); Darley Abbey; Derby etc. *Gyronny of eight argent and vert a lion rampant reguardant or*; crest: *on a charger a boar's head erased argent* (Glover, II.18). Gr. 1815 to Walter Evans of Parwich and Darley Abbey, quartering Ferne. Used by Samuel Evans (1785–1874), natural son of Thomas, father of the grantee, and his sons. Ald. Sir Thomas William Evans of Allestree Hall (mayor of Derby 1869–70) was cr. a bt 18 July 1887, and gr. arms with the tincture of the *lion* in the arms and the *boar's head* changed to *erminois*. Title ext. 1892.

Evans. Blackwall Hall (Kirk Ireton); Hulland. *Argent a chevron between three boars' heads erased sable*; crest: *on a ducal coronet or a boar's head erased fesseways gules* (BLG (1898) I.125). Borne by Revd Charles Evans of Hulland and *jure uxoris* of Blackwall, being conf. by RL 1871 as a quartering of Blackwall, which surname and arms he thereupon assumed.

Evershed. Albury House (Stapenhill). *Argent on a chief sable three mullets of six points pierced or*; crest: *a mullet of six points pierced or between a pair of wings displayed argent*; motto *'Sicitur ad astra'* (Pine, 118). Arms gr. 11 March 1697 to Thomas Evershed of Newdigate (Surrey) and Slinfold (Sussex) and borne by his brewer descendant Sydney (1825–1903) of Stapenhill. His grandson, Francis, was Master of the Rolls and was cr. 1956 Lord Evershed of Stapenhill (title ext. 1966) but appears to have had no grant of supporters.

Every. Egginton; Newton Solney; Derby. *Erminois two chevronels azure between two others gules*; crest: *a demi-unicorn argent goutée-de-sang crined or*; motto: *'Suum cuique'* (BP (1970) 964). Exemplified or conf. to Sir Henry Every Bt, 1805; to Edward Every-Clayton of Derby and Rowley (Burnley), Lancs., on assuming the additional surname and arms of Clayton of Rowley by RL 1835; and to Capt. Charles Every-Halstead of Essex when a similar situation arose 1886. Previously this family had borne *or four chevronels gules*; crest *an unicorn's head couped proper* (V. Somerset 1623). Gr. June 1604 to John Every of Wycroft Castle, Devon, a former Royal sergeant-at-arms, accepted as the arms of Simon Every of Egginton V. 1634 but 'not proved' to his son V. 1662. Simon was cr. a bt 26 May 1641. A Kent branch of the original Somerset family bore *or five chevronels sable*.

Eyam. Eyam. *Or a fesse sable issuant therefrom a demi-lion rampant gules* (Sleigh's MS, Local 6664). Attributed on the strength of a presumption of descent of Sir Henry de Eam, founder KG, from the C13 Eyams whose heiress marr. Stafford (qv).

D'Eyncourt. Park House (Pilsley); etc. The arms of the Deincourts of Blankney (Lincs.), of which Walter Deincourt, the Derbys. tenant-in-chief, was head, were: *Azure a fesse dancettée between ten billets or* (Burke). Those of the cadet (Derbys.) branch who lived at Park Hall were *sable a fesse dancettée between ten billets argent* (Lysons, lxi; Rel. V (1864) 231). The latter coat was quartered by Longford (see arms in Bakewell church, Cox

II.23), who marr. a coheiress of the Derbys. branch. The other coheiress marr. firstly Neville, whose heiress marr. Bussey of Hougham (Lincs.) (see Bushey); secondly Revell. As Cox (I.153n.) rightly says, this family 'were singularly capricious in their heraldic bearings' and the tinctures used varied considerably (as at Chesterfield, Cox loc.cit.).

Eyre. Bubnell; Highlow; Hope; Padley; Hassop; Rowter. *Argent on a chevron sable three quatrefoils or*; crest: *a man's leg erect in armour couped at the thigh quarterly argent and sable spurred or*; motto: *'Si je puis'* (Vv. 1569, Notts. 1662 (Bubnell)); V. 1569, 1611 (Highlow); V. 1569 (Hope) and V. 1662 (Hassop and Rowter); V. 1569 (Holme and Dunston and in glass once in Chesterfield church); Alfreton, V. 1611). Despite the famous legend, the crest derives directly from that of Foljambe (qv); the attribution of similar arms to Truelove (Somerset) rests on similarly incorrect ground, and the same coat as borne by Eyre of Wilts. and Ireland implies but does not represent kinship. Thomas Eyre of Highlow, 5th son of Sir Robert of Padley marr. the heiress of ap Gwilliam and bore: *argent a chevron between three cross crosslets fitchée sable within a bordure engrailed of the last thereon eight bezants* (quartering Payne; V. 1569). William Eyre, a descendant, assumed the surname and arms of Archer by RL 1730: *ermine a cross sable* (FD (1929) I.44); his brother, John, assumed in 1732, the surname and arms of Gell of Hopton (qv). The heiress of Archer marr. Houblon, and Charles Newton, formerly Houblon, assumed the surname and quarterly arms of Eyre by RL in 1831. John Lewis Eyre, of the Newbold and Dunston branch, was in 1815 made a Papal Count (ext. after 1902): his arms (quartering *argent two bars and in chief a lion passant gules*, Burnaby) were ensigned by the appropriate coronet; supporters: *on either side a knight in armour, visor open proper*; motto: *'Neminem mutue innocens'* (BP (1862) 1175). Harl.MS 6104 has, for Eyre of Hassop and Rowter (Castleton), V. 1662: *or on a chevron gules three quatrefoils argent* – an error.

Eyre. Hassop; Bradway (Norton). *Argent on a chevron sable three quatrefoils of the field*; crest: *as above* but *quarterly or and gules* (V. 1662). Some versions give the Hope variant with a *crescent for difference*, but it seems likely that a tincture change was allowed for the difference. Adam Eyre of Bradway, cadet of this branch, bore the same (V. 1662) but his descendants reverted to *quatrefoils or*. Francis Eyre of Hassop, owing to a misunderstanding of peerage law, assumed the earldom of Newburgh, viscountcy of Newburgh and Kinnaird and barony of Livingstone of Flacraig (Viscount Newburgh cr. 1647, the rest 1660, in the Scots' Peerage). They held this style until their line became ext. 1853, quartering Radclyffe of Derwentwater (Cumberland) and Livingstone, and assuming supporters: *dexter a wild man wreathed about the temples and loins with oak proper sinister a dapple grey horse bridled and saddled guled*; same crest and motto (E. Lodge, *Peerage* (1852) 412).

Eyre. Edale; Shatton. *Argent on a chevron sable three quatrefoils or and a bordure gules*; crest: as above but *quarterly argent and gules.* (V. 1662). Harl.MS 6104 gives the field or, the chevron *gules*: presumably an error conf. 14 Aug. 1662.

Eyre. Ashopton (Derwent); Booths (Hope Woodlands); Thorpe. *Argent on a chevron sable three quatrefoils or and a bordure gules*; crest: as above but *quarterly argent and azure* (V. 1662). Cadets of Eyre of Highlow; some MSS add 'sans proof', but gr. 14 Aug. 1662.

Eyre. Crookhill (Hope Woodlands); Hazelhead (Hathersage). *Or on a chevron gules three quatrefoils argent and a bordure* (V. 1662, Harl.MS 6104 version). Possibly a mistake for the blazon given for Edale or Ashopton; if not, this represents a new variant.

Fairclough. Bolsover. *Quarterly or and gules* (glass at Weston upon Trent church, V. 1611, Harl.MS 1093). Arms used by a family of minor gentry of Bolsover, mid-c15 and used on his memorial window by Hugh, vicar of Melbourne, 1482.

Fairholme. Hathersage; Eyam Dale House (Eyam). *Or an anchor gules quartering argent a boar's head erased sable armed or*; crest: *a dove with a branch of olive in its beak proper*; motto: *'Spero meliora'* (BLG (1937) 1739). Matric. (LO) 1751 to William Fairholme of Lugate, Midlothian, and borne by Frederick Charles, of Eyam and Hathersage (b. 1865).

Falcon. Shipley. *Gules three falcons or* (Rel. V (1865) 232). Used by Christopher Falcon, gent., of Heanor, 1595, and his son Henry, of

Shipley (1619–42).

Falconer (Fawconer). 'Co. Derby'. *Argent three martlets gules in chief three pellets* (as a quartering of Bradbourne on MI at Ashbourne church). Included by Sleigh (*Rel.* V (1865) 232) but actually the arms of William Faulconer (sic) of Thurcaston, Leics., whose heiress marr. Cotton of Ridware, Staffs., whence the quartering passed to Bradbourne. Fitzherbert of Norbury also quartered a coat of Falconer, as above, but omitting the *pellets*.

Fallowes. Alvaston; Derby. *Vert a camel or* (Burke). Believed to have been the arms used by William son of William Fallowes, solicitor of Friargate, Derby, and of Cheshire. Ince's pedigree of Fallowes of Alvaston, purporting to be another branch of the same family, gives for Roger, 5th son of John Fallowes of Fallowes, Cheshire, settled at Alvaston: *gules a fret ermine* (Box 57). The arms should be *sable a fret ermine on a chief or three escallops azure* (gr. 1771).

Fanshawe. Fanshawe Gate (Holmesfield). *Or a chevron between three fleurs-de-lys sable;* crest: *a dragon's head erased or flames of fire issuant from the mouth proper;* motto: *'Dux vitae ratio'* (seal of Dronfield Grammar School, Add.MS 6705; Harl.MS 6592). Gr. 1566 to Henry Fanshawe of Essex son of Henry of Fanshawe Gate. His descendant, Sir Thomas Fanshawe, was cr. 1661 Viscount Fanshawe in the Irish Peerage, being gr. supporters: *on either side a dragon or flames of fire issuant from its mouth proper,* crest: *argent* in lieu of *or* and motto: *'Dux vitae ratio in cruce victoria'* (which is an expanded version of that given above, and not new at all). He also was gr. an augmentation of honour in 1649 to be borne quarterly with his paternal arms: *chequy argent and azure a cross gules* (Burke). Col. Henry Fanshawe of Dengie Hall, Essex (1756–1828) was cr. a baron of the Russian Empire by Empress Catherine II; his family still bear the augmentation, but the viscounty became ext. 1716.

Fanshawe. Dronfield. *Or two chevrons ermine between three fleur-de-lys sable;* crest: *a dragon's head erased or thereon two chevrons ermines* (Burke). Gr. to John Fanshawe of Fanshawe Gate and Dronfield, Queen's Remembrancer, 14 Jan. 1571.

Le Fanu. Repton. *Azure a swan argent on a chief or three roses gules barbed vert seeded of the third;* crest: *a greyhound's head argent;* motto: *'Dat pretium candor'* (Burke, IFR 708). Gr. 1595 by Henri IV of France to Pierre son of Michael le Fanu of Caen, whom he cr. Seigneur de Montbenard, with supporters (not used in UK) *on either side a greyhound proper.* Borne (as conf. 1929) by John Lewen Le Fanu of Repton.

Fauvell. Wilsthorpe (Sawley). *Sable a chevron or between three escallops argent.* Probably borne by Sir William Fa(u)vell of Wilsthorpe, lord of a moiety of Alvaston and MP for Derbys., d. 1322. Heiress marr. Gryffin.

Fawkes. Quarndon Hall. *Ermine a mascle sable;* crest: *a falcon proper charged on the breast with a mascle sable;* motto: *'A deo et rege'* (BLG (1878) I.261). Gr. under RL of 1792 whereby Walter Hawkesworth of Farnley, Yorks., assumed the surname and arms of Fawkes. Borne by Maj. Francis Fawkes of Quarndon and his son, who sold. 1926.

Feilden. Burnaston Old Hall; Doveridge; Kirk Langley. *Argent on a fesse cotised azure between two martlets in chief sable and in base a rose gules three lozenges or;* crest: *a nuthatch perched on a branch of hazel holding in the beak a red rose slipped all proper;* motto: *'Virtus praemium honor'* (BLG (1937) 760). Gr. to Joseph Feilden of Witton, Lancs., with remainder to his grandfather, Joseph, 23 Nov. 1856, and borne by H. St C. Feilden (1856–87) of Langley and Richard Feilden of Burnaston C20. Before succeeding in 1946, Sir William Feilden, 5th bt, lived from 1919 at Doveridge. Title cr. 21 July 1846. Before the grant the arms used were: *argent on a fesse azure three lozenges or;* crest: *a nuthatch feeding on a hazel branch all proper* (Thompson, IV.70).

Fenton. North Lees Hall (Outseats). *Argent a cross between four fleurs-de-lys sable;* crest: *a cubit arm erect grasping an oak branch acorned proper* (arms: seal in Sheffield Record Office, FEN J.7281; crest: ceilings at North Lees). Borne by Richard Fenton of North Lees (1532–1601), a Catholic, alderman, and former mayor of Doncaster.

Ferne. Parwich. *Per bend indented or and gules;* crest: *a garb or between two wings expanded per pale indented or and gules* (V. 1611). Arms conf. and crest gr. 1585 to William son of William Ferne of Temple Belwood, Lincs., grandson of John, of Parwich. The arms were originally gr. 2 Feb. 1579 to the same. John, the yr brother of the grantee, received a grant as above, but *argent* in lieu of *or*, July 1583: he was of Crakemarsh, Staffs. (Vv. Staffs. 1583; London 1634).

Ferne. Bonsall; Snitterton. *Per bend indented argent and gules two lions' heads erased and counterchanged crowned or*; crest: *a mount of fern proper thereon a garb or banded gules* (Lysons, cxxvii). Gr. 10 Oct. 1707 to Robert Fern of Bonsall, son of Henry of Snitterton.

Ferne. Alderwasley. Arms as Parwich. 'Usurper' V. 1611.

Ferne. Hognaston. Arms as Parwich. 'Mr Jno Ferne of Hognaston promised to come to London', V. 1611.

Ferranti: see Ziani di Ferranti.

Ferrers. Duffield etc. *Argent six horseshoes sable nailholes or* (Lysons, lvii). Apparently the earliest coat of Ferrers, canting, and because of the plethora of horseshoe-scattered coats borne by their subtenants, undoubtedly right, although the tinctures are surely retrospective and probably speculative. William, 3rd Earl of Derby (cr. by charter 1138), added, from the arms of Peverel (qv): *vairé or and gules*, placing the *horseshoes semée argent* on a *bordure azure* (ibid.; cf. seal, 1249, PRO, P.1385). The bordure tinctures may represent the original ones of the earliest Ferrers coats, the 5th earl adopted the *Vairé or and gules* alone (FitzWilliam Roll, cf. seal of 1261, PRO, P.1378), but he marr. the heiress of the de Quincy and his successor bore thus on occasion: *gules seven mascles conjoined or three three and one* (seal, PRO, P.1377). William, yr brother of the last (attainted) Earl of Derby, bore, prior to 1268: *Vairé or and gules on a bordure sable eleven* (sometimes nine) *horseshoes argent* (FitzWilliam Roll). After the attainder, when Ferrers heraldry was being discarded with unseemly haste all over the county, he bore de Quincy (as impaled by Babington, MI at Ashover church). His son was summoned to Parliament by writ as Lord Ferrers of Groby, Leics., 1297. Ferrers of Baddesley Clinton, Warw., their cadets, bore de Quincy and a *canton ermine*; crest: *an unicorn passant ermine*; motto: *'Splendeo tritus'* (V. Warw. 1682).

Ferrers. Brassington. *Vair* (Glover's Roll, 1st version, 143). Borne, perhaps as a mark of cadency, by Hugh, a yr son of William, 4th Earl of Derby. He left a dau. and heiress.

Ferrers

Ferrers. Breadsall. *Vairé or and gules* (glass at Breadsall church, Local MS 6341). John, son of the attainted earl of Derby, was of Breadsall Nether Hall and was summoned to Parliament as Lord Ferrers of Chartley, Staffs., 1299.

Ferrers. Walton Old Hall (Walton on Trent); Bradbourne; Lea. *Vairé or and gules*; crest: *a unicorn passant ermine* (V. 1662) Borne with 48 quarterings by John Ferrers of Walton, a cadet of Ferrers of Tamworth, themselves cadets of Groby, Leics. Quartering Freville, Marmion, and de Quincy, and sometimes debruised by a *baston azure*.

Ffytche. Risley Hall. *Or a pellet between three cross crosslets fitchée sable* (Ffytche, ancient) *quartering vert a chevron between three leopards' faces or* (Ffytche, modern); crest: *a leopard passant proper holding an escutcheon vert thereon a leopard's face or*; motto: *'Esperance'* (Burke). Arms of John Lewis Ffytche of Risley Hall 1871 and his kinsman and heir R.J.L. Ffytche; the ancient arms can be seen in C19 glass at Wilne church with the expanded motto: *'Esperance in Dieu'*. See also Fitch.

Fiennes. Beighton. *Azure three lions rampant or*; crest: *a wolf sejant proper*; motto: *'Fortem posce animum'* (Burke). Hon. Sir John Fiennes, son of Richard, Lord Dacre of the South and great nephew of 1st Lord Saye and Sele (cr. by writ 3 March 1447), was *jure uxoris* of Beighton. 6th Baron Saye and Sele (supporters: *on either side a wolf argent gorged and chained or* (ibid.)) sold, 1570. Arms conf. quartered by Twistleton (qv) to 14th Baron by RL 26 Feb. 1825. See also Fynney.

Finderne (Findern). Stanton by Bridge; Potlock (Findern); Littleover etc. *Argent a chevron between three crosses formée fitchée sable*; crest: *an ox-yoke or descending therefrom a chain of the last ending in a hook gules*; motto: *'Vidi cheveronum cum ingralatione'* (V. 1569, Harl.MS 6592). The arms above are so shown as quartered by Harpur on a C16 MI at Swarkestone church, yet the chevron is frequently given as *engrailed*: e.g. as two MSS of V. 1569 and Local MS 6341. The seal of George Finderne of Findern 1529 went one further, with *an engrailed chevron thereon three crosses formée*: his son's arms were those at the head of the article.

Finney: see Fynney.

Firebrace. Derby; Duffield; Willington. *Azure on a bend or between two roses argent barbed and seeded proper three crescents sable*; crest: *an arm embowed in armour proper the hand supporting a portcullis or*; motto: *'Fideli quid obstat'* (*Rel.* XII (1872) 94). Gr. to Henry Firebrace of 'Derbys.' (actually Duffield), chief clerk of the kitchen to Charles II, 1 Dec. 1677. His son, Sir Basil, was cr. a bt 28 July 1698 (ext. 1759). The grantee's father was of Derby and the family originated in Willington C12.

Firebrace. Weston on Trent. *Sable an estoile of sixteen points argent* (hatched escutcheon on gravestone at Weston). Apparently used by William Firebrace of Weston, d. 1523 (Local MS 6341; D369).

Firth. Birchfield Lodge (Hope); Coal Aston; Norton Hall. *Or on a pile gules between two battleaxes erect in base sable a lion rampant of the field*; crest: *on a mount vert in front of a demi-lion rampant or two battleaxes in saltire sable*; motto: *'Deo non fortuna'* (BLG (1937) 789). Gr. to Mark Firth of Sheffield, 1868, builder of Birchfield Lodge, over the door of which he placed these arms.

Firebrace

Fisher. Foremark; Derby; Repton. *Argent a fesse wavy between three fleurs-de-lys sable*; crest: *a king's fisher proper holding in the dexter claw a like fleur-de-lys*; motto: *'Non sibi sed patriae'* (BP (1970) 1011; motto: FD (1905) 482). Conf. (arms being displayed on plate then 150 years old, but proof if any existed lost) and crest gr. 15 Sept. 1730 to John Fisher of Foremark and Repton. Reconf. 30 Nov. 1771 to his great nephew Thomas. His descendant, the Most Revd G.F. Fisher, Archbishop of Canterbury, was in 1961 cr. (for life only) Lord Fisher of Lambeth, but seems not to have had a grant of supporters.

Fisher. Littleover. *Azure a fesse embattled counter-embattled between three dolphins (naiant) or*; crest: *a king's fisher proper holding in the beak a fish or* (*Miscellanea Genealogica et Heraldica* 2nd series, II.229). Gr. 10 Nov. 1660 to William Fisher of London, merchant, 'son of William Fisher of Littleover ... where that family hathe lived in reputation and esteeme'.

Fitzaer (Fitzalcher): see Montgomery.

Fitch. Markeaton. *Vert a chevron between three leopards' heads or* (MI once in All Saints', Derby, Cox IV.404). Borne or used by Thomas Fitch of Derby and Markeaton 1561; the family were minor gentry at the latter place from C15; also by Ralph, of London, 1598.

Fitchett. Chesterfield. *Gules a lion rampant or* (in glass at Chesterfield church, Local MS 6341). John Fitchett of Chesterfield, living 1440–48, used (or bore) these arms. A seal of 1367 (PRO, P.290) adds for crest: *a bull's head.*

FitzAlan Howard: see Howard.

FitzErcald: see Hopwell.

Fitzherbert. Etwall; Norbury; Padley; Somersal Herbert etc. *Argent a chief vairé or and gules overall a bend sable*; crest: *a dexter arm in armour erect the hand appearing clenched with the gauntlet all proper*; motto: *'Ung je serviray'* (V. 1569: Norbury, Somersall, Derby (without quartering), Padley). Borne late C12 by Sir Henry Fitzherbert (Camden Roll) and 1350 by John (seal in Local MS 6341), both of Norbury, the original branch of the family, whose earliest arms were as above but without the *bend* (Burke), having been subtenants of Ferrers, a chief of whose arms they bore. After the disgrace of the Ferrers, a coat: *gules three lions rampant or* seems to have been adopted (see below) but only occasionally borne alone (e.g. by Somersal branch, V. 1662) being more often quartered by the older coat. In 1826, Basil Fitzherbert of Norbury and Swynnerton, Staffs., had the abeyancy of the 1640 barony of Stafford terminated in his favour, and had the arms conf. to him with supporters: *dexter a lion rampant argent sinister a swan argent beaked and legged sable ducally gorged per pale gules and of the second.* In glass in Smisby church in 1569 were arms: *argent a fesse gules between in chief a fleur-de-lys enclosed by two cross crosslets fitchée and in base three ermine spots sable* (Cox, III.456), borne by Fitzherbert of Twycross, Leics., and seemingly inherited with that estate. The original arms were also conf. to the two families of Fitzherbert-Brockholes of Claughton, Lancs., by RL 1783 and 1875, quartering Brockholes.

FitzHerbert. Tissington; St Helen's (Old) House (Derby). *Gules three lions rampant or*; crest and motto as above. (Vv. 1569, 1611,

1662). Borne, really for difference, by the FitzHerberts of Tissington, which branch has enjoyed a btcy since 22 Jan. 1784. Alleyne FitzHerbert, a yr son and, by quirk of history, of Somersal Herbert, was cr. Lord St Helens (Irish Peerage) 1791 and with the same title in the peerage of the UK 1801, ext. 1839. He was gr. crest: *a hand couped at the wrist apaumée proper*; supporters: *on either side a unicorn reguardant argent collared, armed, crined and unguled or*; motto: *'Antiminatis non oribus'* (Debrett (1817) I pl.29). A related branch, Fitzherbert of Hints, Staffs., bore these arms with *a canton or* (V. Staffs. 1663).

FitzHubert: see FitzRalph.

FitzHugh. Beighton. *Azure three chevronels interlaced and a chief or* (Military and Willement Rolls). Borne by Sir Henry son of Hugh FitzHugh; his descendant, Henry FitzHugh, son of 1st Lord FitzHugh of Ravensworth, Durham (cr. by writ 1321), was of Beighton, and the heiress of 5th baron marr. Fiennes (qv).

FitzNicholas. Kirk Langley; Twyford. *Quarterly gules and or a bend argent* (*DAJ* LVIII (1937) 57; seal on J.1166) Borne by Ralph fitz Nicholas, who held half a knight's fee at Kirk Langley and d. 1257. Of the stock of Nigel de Stafford, as were the Gresleys, Longfords, Pipards, Staffords and Toenis (qqv). Note the Ferrers-ish tinctures in the arms; cf. Longford; Stafford.

FitzRalph. Crich; Stretton. *Azure two chevrons or* (glass at Crich church noted V. 1569). Borne by Hubert fitz Ralph (d. 1225), grandson through his mother of Ralph fitz Hubert, who held Crich in chief up to 1140. Undoubtedly kin to Rye (qv). See Cox I.342; *DAJ* XLVII (1925) 165–6.

FitzRalph. Ilkeston. *Gules a fesse vair* (Glover's Roll, 1st version 180). Hugh FitzRalph of Greasley, Notts., and Ilkeston was sheriff of Notts. and Derbys., 1236–7. Eustacia, his grand-dau. and heiress, brought the estates to Sir Nicholas de Cantilupe (qv), whose son combined these arms with those of Cantilupe.

FitzRandolph. Birchwood (Alfreton); Pinxton. *Argent a chief indented azure*; crest: *on a chapeau or turned up azure a wyvern of the last* (Vv. Notts. 1569, 1614). Christopher FitzRandolph of Langton Hall, Notts., and, according to Sir Anthony Wagner, of princely descent, also held Birchwood, 1542; his descendant Edward bore these arms and was settled there 1670. Senior branch of the family later emigrated to the USA (A.R. Wagner, *English ancestry* (Oxford, 1961), pp. 23, 122).

FitzWalkelin: see Walkelin.

Flackett. Derby; Doveridge; Hanson Grange (Newton Grange); Unstone. *Argent on a fesse between three foxes' heads erased gules as many lions' gambs of the field*; crest: *a fox's head erased gules shot through the neck fesseways with an arrow sable feathered argent* (Thompson IV.50; D369). Arms used by John Flackett of Hanson Grange who disclaimed V. 1611; also by his descendant Edmund, of Derby 1659.

Flamstead. Denby; Derby; Little Hallam (Ilkeston). *Azure three horse barnacles argent on a chief of the second a lion passant gules* (on Vertue's engraving of Gibson's portrait of the first Astronomer Royal in J. Flamstead *Atlas Coelestis* (1725), p. 1). Used by the Flamsteads of Little Hallam, e.g. John of Little Hallam living 1663. His cousin, the homonymous Astronomer Royal (1646–1719), has engraved under his portrait in Derby Museum: *or three bars and on a chief sable a lion passant of the field*; crest: *a talbot's head argent erased gules gorged with a bar gemel and eared or,* actually the arms gr. to John Flamstead of Rushton, Northants., 28 June 1576, whose relationship to him (if any) is unknown.

Fleetwood. Dovedale. *Per pale nebulée or and azure six martlets counterchanged*; crest: *a wolf passant reguardant argent vulned in the breast gules* (V. Staffs. 1663). Borne by Sir R. Fleetwood of Calwich Abbey, Staffs., and Rowland, who left estate valued at £29 1*s*. in Derbys. 1715.

Fletcher. Horsley; Stainsby House (Horsley Woodhouse). *Argent on a cross engrailed a compass dial between four pheons or on a chief gules a level staff between two double coalpicks of the third*; crest: *a horse's head couped argent gouté-de-sang* (MI at Horsley church 1766). Gr., replete with the emblems of the foundations of his wealth, to John Fletcher of Stainsby 8 March 1732; the heiress marr. Barber (qv).

Fletcher. Walton Hall. *Argent a cross engrailed sable between four pellets on each a pheon or on a canton azure a ducal coronet of the third* (seal in private collection). Arms of Fletcher of Cannock, Staffs., used by Thomas Fletcher of Walton 1568.

Fletcher. Derby. Arms used not known. 'Mr [Richard] Fletcher promised to come to London', at V. 1611. His father Richard (d. 1606) was thrice bailiff of Derby.

Flint. Matlock. Arms if used, not known. Thomas Flint of Matlock disclaimed 1611.

Flower. Derby. *Quarterly 1 & 4: argent two chevronels between three ravens each holding in the bill an ermine spot sable between the chevronels as many pellets,* for Flower, *2 & 3: gules three towers argent*; crest: *a raven proper holding in the beak an ermine spot sable;* motto: *'Mens conscia recti'* (FD (1929) I.690). Arthur Frederick Ashbrook Flower (b. 1869) was a Derby surgeon living in Green Lane, 1902. His father and grandfather, both named Henry, were local apothecaries, claiming to be cadets of Flower, Viscounts Ashbrook, Lords Castle Durrow, Co. Laois (Peerage of Ireland, cr. 30 Sept. 1751 and 27 Oct. 1733 respectively). The arms were conf. to Thomas Flower of Castle Durrow, Co. Kilkenny 1681 (UO). Family originally from Whitwell, Rutland, the arms of which appear as *ermines a cinquefoil ermine*; crest: *a flower ermine foliated vert* (V. Rutland, 1618). The only certain fact is that if the Derby branch were descended from this family, it was before the creation of the barony and, more likely, before the migration to Ireland.

Fogge. Hartington. *Argent on a fesse between three annulets sable as many mullets pierced of the field* (*Rel.* XII (1872) 94). The reason why Sleigh put these arms (of a Kent family of the name) into his list is not known; he gives no reference.

Fokerham. 'Co. Derby'. *Or a bend lozengy azure* (Parliament Roll). Borne by Sir Richard Fokerham of Berks. and Derbys., c14. In Burton on Trent church was recorded in glass, 1592: *or four fusils conjoined in bend sinister azure* ascribed to this name. Burke offers a crest for the Berks. family: *a long cross vert.*

Folcher (Folger, Foucher, Fulcher). Champeyne Park (Windley); Osmaston by Derby. *Ermine on a bend gules three bezants* (impaled by Bradshaw of Windley at Mugginton church 1611 (Local MS 6341)). In most MSS of V. 1569 on the relevant quartering of Bradshaw (which family marr. the heir of Robert Folcher of Osmaston and Champeyne, living 1357) the charges on the *bend* are given as *plates.*

Foliot: see Etwall.

Foljambe. Hassop; Tideswell; Wormhill; Darley. *Sable a bend between six escallops or;* crest: *a man's leg couped at the thigh quarterly or and sable spurred of the first* (V. 1569; crest: seal of 1367, PRO, P.1408). Borne by Godfrey Foljambe of Hassop, who d. 1376 and marr. Avine, dau. of Sir Thomas Ireland of Hartshorne; see the arms of Foljambe impaling Ireland on their monument in Bakewell church (Cox, II.15). The only surviving brass to the Foljambes in Tideswell church shows similar arms (Cox, II.299).

Foljambe. Walton Hall. *Sable a bend between six escallops or;* crest: *a calopus passant quarterly or and sable horns also quarterly in like manner;* motto: *'Soyez ferme'* (V. 1569). Arms conf. and crest gr. to Sir Godfrey Foljambe of Walton (1472–1541) 9 June 1513. In 1530 he received the grant of a further crest: *on a chapeau a tiger statant argent ducally gorged or* (V. 1569) – both perhaps attempts to get away from the leg motif by then being flaunted by the ubiquitous Eyres. A further confirmation came 28 May 1587. Foljambe of Norton Lees and of Barlborough bore the arms as Walton (V. 1569); the branch of Linacre Hall (Brampton) bore the leg crest: *wreathed about the knee with a chaplet argent and azure* (V. 1569). The heiress marr. Francis Ferrand Moore, who assumed the name and arms of Foljambe by Act of Parliament 1776 (16 Geo. III c. xxxviii). C.G.S. Foljambe was cr. Lord Hawkesbury 1893 and in 1905 advanced as Earl of Liverpool, Viscount Hawkesbury and Lord Foljambe of Aldwark, Yorks., receiving a complex grant of crests and supporters in the former year: BP (1970) 1632.

Ford. Ford Hall (Chapel en le Frith). *Azure three lions rampant argent crowned or;* crest: a demi-lion rampant crowned or (*Rel.* XII (1872) 94). Arms borne by Clement Ford of Ford, bailiff and receiver of the castle and honour of the High Peak c14 (seal as seen by Sleigh) and crest used by his descendants, the Fords of Leek, Staffs., 1677. The arms were conf. and crest gr. to a branch in London c17 (*DAJ* XXXI (1909) 167).

Ford. 'Co. Derby'. *Ermine a fesse wavy azure surmounted by a barrulet also wavy argent and charged with a pallet counterchanged between in chief two estoiles gules and in base*
a sprig of oak slipped with three acorns fructed vert; crest: *a sprig of oak with three acorns leaved and slipped and ensigned with an estoile gules;* motto: *'Fidelis'* (FD (1929) I.697). Gr. c. 1920 to Arthur Douglas Ford, mayor of Riccarton, New Zealand, grandson of John Ford 'of Co. Derby'.

Forester. Abbot's Hill House (Derby). *Argent a chevron vert between three buglehorns stringed of the second ferrelled or* quartering Pulter and Ley, Earls of Marlborough; crest: *a buck trippant* (Glover, II.589: seal on a deed of 21 Jan. 1840, Derbys. Health Authority Deeds, Packet 73). Arms borne by William Forester of Abbot's Hill c18, descended from John Forester of London, draper, to whose ancestors in Yorks. the arms had been allowed, V. Yorks. 1584.

Fosbrooke. Ravenstone Hall; Shardlow Hall; The Hagge (Staveley). *Azure a saltire between four cinquefoils argent;* crest: *two bears' gambs sable supporting a spear erect proper* (Lysons, lxxxiv). Used by Leonard Fosbrooke of Shardlow (d. 1762), descended from John, of Cranford, Northants., who bore the same but the *cinquefoils or* (V. Northants. 1564), and no crest.

Foster. Hazelhurst (Norton). *Argent a chevron vert between three buglehorns sable stringed gules;* crest: *an arm in armour embowed holding the head of a broken tilting spear all proper;* motto: *'Si fractus fortis'* (BLG (1898) I.542). Probably those arms gr. to George Foster of Barbados, 3 May 1703; borne by William Foster of Hazelhurst (1797–1829) son of Frederick son of William, of Jamaica.

Foster. Ilkeston. *Argent a heart gules between in chief two foxgloves leaved and slipped and in base a caduceus proper;* crest: *in front of a stag's head couped proper three hearts in fesse gules;* supporters: *on either side an elk reguardant proper pendant from its neck a buglehorn stringed gules;* motto: *'Labore et virtute'* (Pine, 155). Gr. in 1910 to Sir Balthezar Foster, MP for Ilkeston, on his elevation to the peerage as Lord Ilkeston. Title ext. 1952.

Foucher: see Folcher.

Foulion: see Foljambe.

Fowler. Norbriggs Hall (Staveley); Whittington; Woodthorpe Hall (Staveley). *Quarterly azure and sable three crosses patée between two chevronels in chief as many lions passant guardant or and in base an owl argent;* crest:

an owl argent collared and charged on the breast with a cross patée gules wreathed about the head with ivy vert and resting the dexter claw on a cross patée or; motto: 'Sapiens qui vigilat' (FD (1929) I.709). Gr. 1890 to Sir John Fowler of Braemore, Ross-shire, cr. a bt 17 April 1890 (title ext. 1933) and to the descendants of his father, one of whom was William (1820–77) of Woodthorpe, whose son was of Norbriggs.

Fowne. Alderwasley; Hollington; Yeaveley. *Argent a buglehorn between three crescents sable on each a bezant* (as quartered by Lowe on MI at Wirksworth, Cox, II.561, 569). Borne by Thomas Fowne of Alderwasley living 1451; heiress marr. Lowe.

Fox. Derby; Osmaston Hall (Osmaston by Derby). *Argent a chevron between three foxes' heads erased gules*; crest: *a fox passant gules*; motto: *'Fidelis esto'* (Glover, II.581; V. Warwicks. 1619). Borne by Samuel Fox (1676–1755) of Thorn Tree House, Derby, mayor 1741, and his son, who occupied Osmaston Hall.

Fox. Derby; Youlgreave. *Or a chevron gules between three foxes' heads erased azure*; crest: *a fox passant azure* (*DAJ* XXXII (1910) 63–4). Arms (but not crest) gr. 18 June 1664 to Henry Fox of Youlgreave, who had been respited for proof at V. 1662. A descendant, Sir Douglas Fox (grandson of Francis Fox of Greenhill, Derby, and a coheiress of Douglas, qv) was knighted 1886 and obtained a new grant in 1903: *per chevron azure and argent two foxes' heads erased in chief or and a human heart in base gules between four ermine spots in cross sable*; crest: *on a rock proper a fox sejant or resting the dexter foreleg on a human heart gules*; motto: *'Faire sans dire'* (FD (1910) 602).

Foxlowe. Staveley. *Gules two bars argent* (Tilley, I.57). Used by Samuel, son of William Foxlowe (formerly Foolow) of Staveley, whose son marr. the heiress of Murray, whose name and arms were assumed in 1782 (qv).

Francis. Barlow Woodseats. *Ermine on a canton sable a harp stringed or*; crest: *out of clouds a hand grasping by the attires a stag statant proper* (Lysons, civ). Borne by Sir John Francis of Barlow Woodseats, mayor of London 1400.

Francis (Franceys). Ticknall; Foremark; Allestree etc. *Argent a chevron azure between*

three eagles displayed gules; crest: *on a vinebranch slipped fructed proper an eagle wings elevated or* (Vv. 1569, 1611; Willement Roll). 'Robert Franceys' is alleged in the somewhat retrospective Willement Roll to have borne these arms – presumably Sir Robert, first of Foremark, *temp.* Edward III. His grandfather William marr. the heiress of Ticknall, whose arms these almost certainly were originally; previously the Franceys family seem to have borne *per bend azure and argent a lion rampant counterchanged* (apparently from a seal, cited by Sleigh (*Rel.* XII (1872) 94), but cf. arms of Adam Francis of Tibshelf, Great Stretton and Allestree in Foster's 'Richard II Roll' (J. Foster, *Some feudal coats of arms* (1902), 31): *per bend or and sable a lion rampant counterchanged*). The crest was gr. *c.* 1600 to a 'Richard Francis of Ticknall', a cadet. In some MSS of V. 1569 the Foremark and Ticknall branches are differenced by *chevron gules, eagles sable* and, *chevron azure, eagles gules* respectively. The crests also differ – Foremark: *an eagle holding in its beak a vinebranch vert fructed proper*; Ticknall: *a demieagle displayed gules armed or*. The arms at the head of this article were also used by the Derby gentleman apothecary, Henry Franceys: Bassano painted them on his funeral hatchment, 1717, and was probably responsible for the frescoed ceiling in his house. The Franceys family of Coxbench Hall used the arms of Franceys of Ticknall with whom they claimed kinship.

Franceys. Derby. *Per bend or and sable a lion rampant counterchanged*; crest: *an eagle displayed ermine beaked and membered or* (Burke). Gr. 4 May 1577 to Edward Franceys of Derby: basically a crest added to the 'ancient' arms of Franceys.

Franceys. Repton. Confirmation of crest 20 Jan. 1607 to Edward Franceys of Repton: possibly the same man as the above and thus of the same crest.

Franceys. 'Derbys.' *Argent on a chevron wavy between three eagles displayed gules as many estoiles of the field* (V. Herts. 1572). It is not known from where in the county this Herts. family came; allowed to William Franceys of Herts. and conf. 1634 to Henry.

Franceys. 'Derbys.' *Gules a saltire between four crosses formée or* (*Rel.* XII (1872) 94). Borne or used by an unidentified family of Franceys of Derbys. and Essex.

Frank. Ashbourne Hall. *Vert a saltire engrailed or* (*Rel.* XII (1972) 94). Used by Robert Hayston Frank of Ashbourne Hall (1818–83) and his son Robert John Frank. The arms were borne at the siege of Calais by Sir William Franks, knighted there 1348 (Jenyns' Ordinary); he is alleged to have had connections with Woodthorpe, near Ashbourne.

Frankland-Payne-Gallwey: see Payne.

Frecheville. Brimington; Crich; Palterton; Staveley. *Azure a bend between six escallops argent*; crest: *a demi-angel proper crined or on his head a cross formée of the last, vested in mail arms in armour also proper holding in both hands an arrow in bend of the second feathered and headed argent*; motto: *'In Domine confido'* (Vv. 1569, 1611; in glass at Staveley church); motto (V. 1662): *'Qui aime le Roy aime la patrie'*. Arms borne by Ralph de Frecheville, summoned by writ 1306 as Lord Frecheville of Staveley. His descendant, John Frecheville, was cr. Lord Frecheville in 1665, being gr. supporters 15 April 1665: *on either side an angel as in the crest each holding an arrow in like manner*; ext. 1682. In some versions of V. 1569 the *cross* on the head in the crest is *passion*.

Frecheville. Brimington. *Azure a bend between six escallops argent*; crest: *a gem ring or stoned gules* (seal on will of Arthur Frecheville of Brimington (d. 1512), a cadet of the Staveley family (*DAJ* LIII (1932) 54).

Freeman. Wheston Hall. *Azure three lozenges or* (*Rel.* XII (1872) 94). Quartered by Charlton of Wheston (MI at Tideswell), and borne or used by Robert Freeman of Wheston (d. 1763), allegedly a cadet of Freeman of Fawley, Oxon. His father, however, was from Sheffield.

French. Abbott's Hill House (Derby). *Sable a bend argent between two dolphins proper*; crest: *a wolf rampant* (seal of 1840, Derbys. Health Authority Deeds, Packet 73). Borne or used by Capt. Richard French (descended from French of Hempnall, Norfolk), who marr. the heiress of Forester, c18. His son assumed the surname of Forester.

Freshfield. 'Co. Derby'. *Azure a bend between six escallops or*; crest: *on a mount vert a stag lodged per fesse or and gules crined of the last* (Burke). Arms, possibly, of William Freshfield of Mugginton, d. 1623, perhaps a remote cadet of Frecheville.

Freshfield. Derby. *Per bend nebulée or and azure two bendlets between six escallops all counterchanged*; crest: *a demi-angel proper winged or vested argent arms in chain mail holding a lance in bend point downwards also proper charged on the breast with a cross botonée and on the head with a like cross gules*; motto: *'Nobilitatis virtus non stemma character'* (BLG (1898) I.55). Gr. 1885 to James William Freshfield of Moor Place, Betchworth, Surrey, 'a descendant of the ancient baronial family of Frecheville', which arms he and his family had previously used with the above motto. The arms appear in glass at St Michael's church, Derby.

Frith. Bank Hall (Chapel en le Frith); Whittington. *Azure in chief two garbs in saltire or in base a sickle fesseways argent handled of the second* (Tilley, III.270). Used by Samuel Frith of Bank Hall, 1781.

Froggat. Froggatt; Ashbourne; Staveley. *Quarterly azure and or in the first and fourth quarters a mullet argent*; crest: *a parrot feeding on a bunch of cherries proper* (*Rel.* XII (1872) 94; crest, Burke). Arms used on a ½d. token issued by William Froggat of Ashbourne, mercer; crest used by John Froggat of Staveley, a contemporary (seal in Local MS 7769); why Sleigh (*Rel.* loc.cit.) attributed the arms to the Froggats of Froggatt is unclear.

Fulcher: see Folcher.

Fulwood. Fulwood's Castle (Middleton & Smerrill); Hognaston. *Gules a chevron between three mullets argent*; crest: *a buck statant proper attired russet in the mouth an oak branch slipped proper*; (Vv. 1569, 1611). 'Seen and allowed' to George Fulwood of Holborn, London, and crest gr. 10 July 1579; he was son of John Fulwood of Middleton. Local MS 6341 gives numerous arms for other branches of the family settled elsewhere at an earlier period.

Le Fun: see Fowne.

Furneaux. Beighton; Turnditch. *On a chief a demi-lion rampant sable* (*Rel.* V (1865) 232). Borne by Sir Robert Furneaux of Beighton, 1328. His descendant, Richard, assumed the surname and arms of Roper, 1428 (qv) but the Ropers (V. 1662) quartered *gules a bend between six cross crosslets or* and *gules a pale fusilly argent* for Furneaux.

Furness. Eyam; 'Furness'; Stony Middleton. *Argent a talbot sejant sable in chief* three crescents gules; crest: *out of a ducal coronet a lion's gamb grasping a lance all proper*; motto: *'Animo et Fide'* (*Rel.* XII (1872) 94; crest: Burke). Sleigh's attribution of 'Furness' is inexplicable; the family which used these arms in Derbys. was Furness of Eyam, descended from Richard, living 1617.

Furnival. Eyam; Stony Middleton; Bamford etc. *Argent a bend between six martlets gules*; crest: *a horse's helmet argent with a plume of feathers or* (Parliament Roll). Borne by Thomas, 1st Lord Furnival of Sheffield, 1295, the year of his summons to Parliament. The family passed extensive Derbys. estates to the Earls of Shrewsbury.

Fynney. Cotes Park (Alfreton); Derby; Little Longstone; Stony Middleton. *Vert a chevron between three eagles displayed or armed and langued gules*; crest: *a staff raguly or*; motto: *'Fortem posce animum'* (MI at Stony Middleton church of 1748, cf. Burke). Used by Richard Fynney of Stony Middleton, C18, on presumption of descent from Fiennes (qv). A kinsman, Richard Fynney of Derby and Fynney Lane, Staffs., used them on a seal with supporters: *on either side a wolf dog argent ducally gorged and chained or* reading 'Ricardus Fiennes alias Fynney Derbiensis et de Fynney in Com. Staff.' in 1688 (private collection; found at Sheen). Edward Fynney of Cotes Park, who also employed like arms, was 'a very rich old bachelor or widower' in 1687.

Fytche: see Fitch; Ffytche.

Gallwey: see Payne-Gallwey.

Gand (Gant). Ilkeston; Stanton by Dale; West Hallam. *Barry of six or and azure a bend gules*; crest: *a millrind proper* (Burke). Borne by Gilbert de Gand, summoned to Parliament as a baron 1295, and 5th in descent from Gilbert de Gand (i.e. Ghent), who held Ilkeston, West Hallam and Stanton by Dale in chief in 1086. Lord Gand was greatnephew of Gilbert, Earl of Lincoln, and d. 1297 (CP IV.12–13).

Gardiner. Brailsford. *Gules a plain fesse cotised engrailed argent between four roses three in chief and one in base of the last*; crest: *a stag proper gorged with a collar argent charged with three lozenges conjoined gules and supporting with the dexter leg an escutcheon also argent charged with four lozenges conjoined in fesse of the third between two barrulets sable and in chief a rose also gules* (College of Arms, Grants LX.30). Gr. 11 Sept. 1877 to John Gardiner of Brailsford, son of Revd Dr John Gardiner of Bath, rector of Brailsford, grandson of William, of Kittisford and Brompton Regis, Somerset, and to the descendants of his uncle, Robert Gardiner. Previously he had used: *Per fesse argent and sable a pale between three griffins heads all counterchanged*; crest: *a griffin's head erased sable*; motto: *'Fide sed cui vide'* (Local MS 9555.85).

Gargrave

Gargrave. One Ash Grange (Monyash). *Lozengy argent and sable on a bend of the last three crescents of the first*; crest: *a falcon rising argent* (Tilley, I.269). Borne *c.* 1445 by Sir John Gargrave, Master of Ordnance to Henry VI in France (Military Roll), and by his descendant, Sir Thomas Gargrave of Nostell, Yorks., and One Ash, which he received at the Dissolution.

Garlick. Great Hayfield; Whitfield (Glossop). *Argent three heads of garlic proper*;

crest: *a dexter arm erect in armour holding in the hand proper a cutlass of the last also erect pommel and hilt or* (Burke; arms as quartered by Needham, V. 1569). The Suttons of Kingsmead (qv) impaled these arms with a field *or* (Cox, IV.89) and the charges were occasionally blazoned as *pineapples* (e.g. Bassano, interpreting the arms as carved in the church at Hayfield, 1710, Cox, II.211n.). Borne by John Garlick of Whitfield 1428.

Gaunt. Weston Underwood. *Barry of six or and azure a bend gules*; crest: *a wolf's head or gorged vair* (Burke). Used by Thomas Gaunt of Weston Underwood who disclaimed in 1662, but claiming descent from the baronial de Gands (qv): Gilbert, Lord Gand of Lindsey, Lincs., bore these arms 1295 (Nobility Roll).

Gell. Carsington; Hopton. *Per bend azure and or three mullets of six points pierced in bend and counterchanged*; crest: *a greyhound statant sable collared or*; motto: *'Diligentia et studio'* (Vv. 1569, 1611, 1662). Arms conf. and crest gr. 8 Feb. 1576 to Anthony Gell of Hopton. Btcy gr. 29 Jan. 1642, ext. 1710. The surname and arms were assumed by William Eyre of Highlow's third son by RL in 1730.

Gell. Hopton; Langley; Middleton by Wirksworth; Shottle; Wirksworth. *Per bend argent and gules a rose between two mullets of six points in bend counterchanged*; crest: *a greyhound pean about the neck a collar argent thereon a rose between two mullets of six points gules*; motto: *'Vocatus obedivi'* (BLG (1972) III.368). Gr. 6 March 1732 to David Gell of Westminster, 4th in descent from John of Shottle Park, a half-brother of the grantee of 1576 (qv above) and to descendants of his father and uncle. This branch repurchased Hopton early C20 and sold it 1989.

Gell (Chandos-Pole-Gell). Hopton. *Per bend azure and or three mullets of six points pierced in bend and counterchanged and on a canton argent a rose proper.* (Local MS 9555.131). Gr. 1863 to Henry Chandos-Pole when he assumed the additional surname of Gell, and quartered these arms, by RL. Later relinquished.

Gell. Middleton by Wirksworth. Arms as Gell of the 1732 grant, but the *mullets pierced*. No crest. Gr. 1631 to John Gell of London and Middleton, ancestor of David (qv).

Gent. Tideswell. *Ermine on a chief indented sable two eagles displayed or*; crest: *out of a ducal coronet an eagle issuant* (*Rel.* XII (1872) 94). Used by Gervase Gent of Tideswell, merchant, on the ½*d.* tokens he issued in the 1660s. He was a cadet of Gent of Leek, Staffs., who bore these arms (*Rel.* VII (1867) 159–60).

Gerard. Etwall; Dalbury Lees. *Argent a saltire gules*; crest: *a lion rampant ermine crowned or* (V. 1569). Borne by Sir Thomas Gerard of Bryn *jure uxoris* of Etwall; D369 gives the crest as *azure a lion rampant ermine ducally crowned or*.

Gernon. Bakewell; Moor Hall (Bakewell). *Paly wavy of six argent and gules* (Glover's Roll, 1st Version, 214). Borne by Sir John Gernon of Bakewell (d. 1383). The Parliament Roll, for Sir William Gernon of Essex (of this family), gives: *argent three piles undée in point gules, c.* 1310. A seal of 1334 (PRO, P.324) supplies a crest: *a bush*. James Robert Augustus Gernon of Athcarne Castle, Co. Meath, bore in 1929: *argent an eagle displayed with two heads sable ducally gorged or*; crest: *a horse passant argent*; motto: *'Parva Contemnimus'* (FD (1929), I.755). He claimed descent from Roger, brother of Ralph de Gernon of Bakewell, who is supposed to have gone to Ireland in the reign of Henry II. See also Chester, Earls of.

Gery. Derby. *Gules on two bars argent three mascles of the first on a canton or a leopard's head couped proper* (hatchment once on a S. wall of St Alkmund's church, Derby, Simpson, I.326). Used by Thomas Gery, town clerk of Derby from 1663, and his son, Thomas, mayor, 1717. Adapted from *Gules on two bars argent six mascles of the first on canton or a leopard's face azure* (Papworth, 34).

Geynes: see Kniveton (Youlgreave).

Gibbs. 'Derbys.'. *Argent three battleaxes in pale sable* (*Rel.* XII (1872) 94; cf. V. Suffolk, 1664–8). Allowed to William son of Henry Gibbs of Stoke by Nayland, Suffolk, of a Worcs. family, holding land in Derbys.; where is unclear.

Gibson. Parwich. *Azure a chevron or surmounted of another gules charged with three pheons of the second between as many storks' wings expanded proper*; crest: *out of an antique crown or a lion's gamb erect proper grasping a club gules spiked also or*; motto: *'Recte et Fideliter'* (Debrett (1976) 496). Arms of Hon.

Hugh M.T. Gibson of Parwich, gr. to his father, cr. a baron (for life) in 1975. Lord Gibson's supporters (non-transmissible) are: *on either side a nightingale holding in its beak a scroll of music all proper.*

Giffard. Cubley. *Azure three stirrups leathered or quartering gules three lions passant argent;* crest: *a tiger's head couped affrontée spotted various incensed proper;* motto: *'Prenez la leine tirez fort'* (V. Staffs., 1663). Borne by Sir Thomas Giffard of Chillington, Staffs., 1517, *jure uxoris* of Cubley; the crest was gr. 1523 (some sources, 1513) and another was gr. 1530: *a demi-archer bearded couped at the knees in armour proper from his middle a short coat paly argent and gules at his middle a quiver of arrows or in his hands a bow and arrow drawn to the head of the last* (as carved in Chillington Hall, Staffs.).

Gilbert: see Kniveton (Youlgreave).

Gilbert. Barrow on Trent; Locko (Spondon); Mickleover; Lullington. *Sable a man's leg armed in pale couped at the thigh between two upright spears erect and shivered handles crossed argent heads or;* crest: *a dexter arm in armour embowed proper the hand grasping a broken spear or the head also proper* (Vv. 1611, 1662). Conf. to William Gilbert of Mickleover and Barrow 4 Dec. 1576. A descendant, John Gilbert of Locko Park (d. 1737), assumed the surname and arms of Cooper on inheriting Thurgarton Priory, Notts.: *or a bend azure between two lions' heads erased gules;* crest: *on a mount vert a unicorn sejant argent armed and crined or supporting a broken tilting spear of the last* (V. Notts. 1662-4). Gr. to William Cooper of Thurgarton 1 Jan. 1550. John Gilbert Cooper of Thurgarton assumed the surname and arms of Gardiner by RL 1819, conf. 1823 and 1833.

Gilbert. Barrow on Trent; Croxall. *Gules a man's leg armed in pale couped at the thigh between two upright spears erect and shivered handles crossed heads or and a canton argent;* crest: *an arm embowed in armour gules holding in the hand proper a spear argent headed or* (King, 77). Allowed to Walter Gilbert of Croxall (1604–78), cadet of Gilbert of Barrow. Kin in Leics., bore as above but *sans canton* (V. Leics., 1619). Richard Gilbert of Doveridge 'did not appear', V. 1662.

Gill. Brimington; Oaks (Norton). *Per bend or and vert three mullets in bend counterchanged* (Lysons, cxxi). Used by Philip Gill of Lightwood (Norton), who disclaimed V. 1611, and Leonard Gill of Norton 1654. Some members of the family bore Gell of Hopton (original form) with *mullets of five-points,* unpierced.

Gillet. Chesterfield; Whittington; Beighton Grange. *Ermine on a bend sable three lucies' heads erased argent;* crest: *a lion rampant holding in the dexter paw a battleaxe proper* (*Rel.* XII (1872) 93). Borne by Richard Gillet of Chesterfield, who purchased Whittington Manor c18, and of a Notts. family. Also used by Cyrus Gillet of Beighton Grange 1850, of a Norfolk family.

Giradot. Allestree Hall. *Quarterly argent a lion rampant sable and gules a chevron of the first* (Lysons, lxxxv). Arms gr. by the Parlement of Dijon to this Jersey family, of which John Charles Giradot of Allestree Hall (1805) was a member. Authority for their use in England does not appear to have been obtained.

Gisborne. Allestree Hall; Holme Hall (Bakewell); Horwich House (Fernilee); St Helen's (Derby); Walton Hall (Walton on Trent). *Erminois a lion rampant sable collared argent on a canton vert a garb or;* crest: *out of a mural coronet argent a demi-lion rampant ermines collared dovetailed or* (Glover, II.216). Gr. 28 March 1742 to John Gisborne of Derby and Yoxall Lodge, Staffs. Cf. the London pewterers, John and James Gisburne (sic) *c.* 1700, who stamped their wares *ermine two bars and a lion rampant.*

Gladwin. Durrant Hall (Chesterfield); Eddlestow Hall (Ashover); Stubbing Court (Wingerworth); Tupton. *Ermine a chief azure overall a bend gules thereon a sword argent hilt and pommel or;* crest: *on a mount proper a lion sejant argent goutée-de-sang holding in the dexter paw a sword erect or* (Burke). Gr. 15 Jan. 1687 to Capt. Thomas Gladwin of Tupton, son of Thomas, of Eddlestow. He had disclaimed in 1662, as had his cousins at Ashover, against whose entry the herald wrote 'query if the same family' – they were. See also Errington; Goodwin.

Glapwell. Glapwell Hall. *Azure a bend between two martlets argent* (Local MS 6341). As quartered by Linacre; the heiress of Richard de Glapwell of Pleasley marr. Roger Linacre of Linacre *c.* 1338. Their ancestor, Sir Simon de Glapwell, was nephew to Serlo de Pleasley (qv).

Glossop Borough Council. *Argent a rose*

gules barbed and seeded and ensigned with a mural crown proper between three cross crosslets fitchée gules; motto: *'Virtue, Truth and Freedom'* (Scott-Giles, 99). Gr. 7 July 1919. The borough was absorbed into High Peak Borough 1974.

Godber. Derby. *Per chevron argent and gules in chief five martlets two, one and two of the last and in base a sprig of white may flowered and leaved proper*; crest: *a crane's head and neck erased or between two sprigs of pink may flowered and leaved proper*; supporters: *on either side a crane or gorged with a collar gemel gules*; motto: *'Ex Fide Virtus'*. Gr. 1956 to Edward Godber (1888–1976), cr. 1st Lord Godber of Mayfield, Sussex, 23 Jan. that year. He was 3rd son of Edward Godber of Derby (1851–1938) and the title became ext. on his death in 1976 (BP (1970) 1114).

Goddard. Stanton in Peak. *Gules a chevron vair(é) between three crescents argent* (Rel. XII (1872) 93). Borne by this family – who presumably were of Wiltshire stock – whose heiress marr. Mayhall of Berks., and passed the quartering to Blackwall of Dethick, *c.* 1621.

Goodall. Foremark; Milton; Repton. *Or a pile sable on a canton azure a saltire engrailed argent*; crest: *a boar's head erased and erect sable platée ducally gorged or* (MI at St Martin's church, Leicester). Used by Sampson Goodall of Earl Shilton, Leics., and his sons, John of Leicester (1637–1720) and Sampson, whose posterity removed to the Repton area and continued to use the arms of Goodall of Lincs. into C20.

Goodall-Copestake: see Copestake.

Goodman. Eccles House (Chapel en le Frith). *Per pale ermine and sable a double eagle displayed or on a canton azure a martlet of the third* (Rel. XII (1872) 93). Gr. 1572 to Goodman of Ruthyn, Denbs., and used (or borne?) by Thomas Goodman of Eccles House 1798; the estate was sold 1983.

Goodwin. The College (Derby); Plumbley Hall (Eckington). *Argent three boars' heads erased sable and a mullet gules (?for difference)* (Local MS 4556 and hatchment formerly at St Werburgh, Derby). Used by Thomas Goodwin of The College, early C18; heiress marr. Coke. Samuel Goodwin of Plumbley and Derby, Thomas's uncle, disclaimed V. 1662.

Goodwin. Hartington. *Or three pellets sable on a chief gules as many martlets of the field*; crest: *out of a ducal coronet argent a nag's head or maned and bridled of the first* (Rel. V. (1865) 232). The bearer of these arms (or user – they belong to an East Anglian family) identified by Sleigh has proved elusive.

Goodwin. Hinchleywood Hall (Mapleton); Ashbourne. *Or a fesse between six lions' heads erased gules*; crest: *a griffin statant wings expanded or*; motto: *'Fide et virtute'* (BLG (1875) I.518). Used by Henry John Goodwin of Hinchleywood (1803–63) but the arms were gr. as a quartering to his son R.H. Goodwin in 1889 who assumed the surname and arms of Gladwin in addition to his own by RL 1881. He inherited Stubbing Court (Wingerworth) from his great uncle C.D. Gladwin and sold the estate in 1890.

Gore. Milford House. *Gules a fesse between three cross crosslets fitchée or*; crest: *a wolf salient argent collared gules*; motto: *'Sola salus servire Deo'* (BP (1970) 108). Gr. 1629 (UO) to an ancestor of Capt. Hon. Edward Gore, brother-in-law of Joseph Strutt, of Milford House, C19. He was 7th son of 2nd Earl of Arran (cr. (I) 12 April 1762), Viscount Sudeley and Lord Saunders of Deeps (Crossabeg, Co. Waterford) (I, cr. 15 Aug. 1758), and a bt (I, cr. 10 April 1662).

Gorell-Barnes. Ashgate (Brampton); Glapwell Hall. *Azure two lions passant guardant ermine each holding a sprig of oak slipped or between three annulets in pale argent*; crest: *in front of a cubit arm in armour hand grasping a broken sword all proper the wrist encircled by a wreath of oak or five annulets interlaced fessewise argent*; motto: *'Frangas non flectes'* (BP 1970, 1129). Gr. to Alfred, son of John Gorell Barnes of Ashgate Lodge, 1897. Previously this family had used: *azure two lions passant guardant argent*; crest: *in front of a cubit arm in armour erect grasping a staff the rays of the sun issuant from clouds all proper*; same motto (Local MS 9555.26). In 1909 the grantee's nephew, Sir John, was cr. Lord Gorell of Brampton, at which time the arms were conf. and supporters gr.: *on either side a ram proper charged on the shoulder with two annulets interlaced azure*.

Goring. Hazlebarrow (Norton). *Argent a chevron between three annulets gules*; crest: *a lion rampant guardant sable*; motto: *'Renas centur'* (BP (1956) 930). Borne by Capt. Henry Goring (1648–87), *jure uxoris* of Haselbarrow and son of Sir Henry, cr. a bt 18 May 1678 as a revival of that of Bowyer of Leythorne (Westhampnett), Sussex, with the same precedence: 23 July 1627. Arms allowed V. Sussex, 1633.

Gorst: see Lowndes.

Gosselin-Grimshawe: see Grimshawe.

Gotham. Norton Lees. *Per fesse embattled or and sable three goats trippant counterchanged* (as quartered by Parker of Norton V. 1569 and Reresby of Eastwood Hall (Ashover), Cox, I.34). The heiress of the senior line of this family marr. Parker C15.

Gould. Hanson Grange (Newton Grange); Pilsbury House (Hartington). *Per saltire azure and or a lion rampant counterchanged*; crest: *a demi-lion rampant azure bezantée*; motto: *'Love God not Gould'* (*Rel.* V (1865) 232; XIII (1873) pl. vii). Used by Edmund Gould of Pilsbury House (1817–59) and his cousin, Thomas, of Sheffield. Tilley's account of the arms (I.269) is in error.

Goushill. Barlborough. *Barry of six or and gules a canton ermine* (in glass recorded in Staveley church 1611, Local MS 6341). Borne by Nicholas son of Nicholas de Goushill (Willement Roll) and by Robert, of Barlborough, 5th in descent from Walter *jure uxoris* of that place C13. Members of this family occasionally bore inherited arms of Hathersage (qv).

Grammar. Ashbourne; Bakewell. *Or billettée gules a lion rampant argent a chief azure* (*Rel.* XII (1872) 94). Used by John and Robert, sons of Robert Grammar of Bakewell, mercer, C18.

Gratton. Bonsall; Gratton; Stanton in Peak. *Gules a pale per saltire azure and or*; crest: *on a human heart proper an eagle's gamb* (*Rel.* XII (1872) 94). Borne by Sir William Gratton of Gratton and Bonsall 1331; crest is probably spurious. It was used by John Gratton of Monyash and Bonsall (1693–1742).

Graves: see Kniveton.

Great Northern Railway. *Dexter, an escutcheon of England (ancient), sinister, one of Scotland* (Dow, p. 74). Arms adopted and used from *c.* 1910 by this railway company which opened a line through Derbys. 1876. Absorbed by the LNER 1 Jan. 1923.

Greatrakes. Great Rocks (Wormhill); Hopton. *Per pale sable and gules three leopards' heads erased or pellettée langued azure*; crest: *a leopard's head erased or pellettée*; motto:

'Vivat Greatrakes semper virescant' (*Rel.* V (1865) 233; Tilley, I.77). Borne by Valentine Greatrakes of Affane, Co. Waterford (*Rel.* IV (1864) 220, quoting a Dublin Castle funeral entry, 1683), whose father William, of the Great Rocks branch, came over from Derbys.

Greatrakes

Greatorex. Carsington. *Per pale indented sable and gules three leopard's heads erased or pellettée*; crest: *a leopard sejant or gorged with a collar fleury-counter fleury sable supporting in the dexter paw a tilting spear proper* (College of Arms, Grants LVI.101). Gr. 5 April 1866 to William Greatorex of Ealing, Middlesex, formerly of Carsington.

Greaves. Aston Lodge; Greaves (Beeley); Ingleby Toft; Matlock; Stanton Woodhouse (Stanton in Peak). *Per bend vert and gules an eagle displayed or* ; crest: *a demi-eagle displayed or wings gules*; motto: *'Aquila non captat muscas'*; *'Suprema quaero'* and *'Dum spiro spero'* (V. 1662; mottoes: *Rel.* V. (1865) 233). Allowed to John Greaves of Greaves, whose ancestor had been declared a usurper, V. 1611. Harl.MS 6104 of V. 1662 seems to preserve the offending and previously disallowed ensigns: *gules an eagle displayed or crowned* *argent*; crest: *a demi-eagle displayed or crowned argent*. The Ingleby branch assumed the surname and arms of Ley (qv) in lieu of their own by RL 1820. Cf. Bagshawe, assuming the additional surname and arms by RL 1825.

Greaves. The Rocks (Matlock). *Quarterly gules and vert an eagle displayed holding in the beak a slip of oak fructed or*; crest: *on a mount vert a stag trippant or holding in the mouth a sprig of oak of the first*; motto: *'Deo non Fortuna'* (FD (1929) I.804). Gr. 2 July 1782 to George Greaves of Attercliffe, Yorks.). His descendant, John (1794–1859), was of The Rocks; it was his kinsman who succeeded to Ford Hall (see Bagshawe).

Greaves. Derbys. *Per saltire vert and gules an eagle displayed or holding in the beak a cross crosslet fitchée argent*; crest: *out of battlements proper a demi-eagle displayed or wings gules charged on the breast with a rose of the second and holding in its beak a cross crosslet fitchée argent*; motto: *'Spes mea in Deo'* (BLG (1833–8) IV.105–6). Gr. 1836 to John Greaves of Irlam Hall, Lancs., 5th in descent from John Greaves of Greaves (qv), living V. 1634. Plainly the heralds were unable to substantiate his pedigree, or he would have been allowed Greaves of Greaves with due difference. Burke says he owned lands in Derbys.

Green: see Cotton.

Greenhalgh. Mellor Hall. *Sable on a bend between two hunting horns argent stringed or three roses gules*; crest: *a dragon's head erased vert charged on the neck with a fylfot or*; motto: *'Virtus sola invicta'* (FD (1910) 689). Gr. early C20 to Charles son of Edmund Greenhalgh of Mellor (b. 1856).

Greensmith. Breadsall Priory; Darley; Steeple Grange (Wirksworth). *Vert on a fesse or between three doves close argent beaked and legged gules each with an ear of wheat in its bill of the second as many pigs of lead azure*; crest: *a like dove argent beaked and legged gules with an ear of wheat in its bill or standing on a pig of lead azure* (Lysons, clix; cf. Woolley, 197, where no tincture is given for the pigs, which were perhaps intended to be *proper*). Gr. 14 Jan. 1715 to Robert Greensmith of Steeple Grange, an opulent lead merchant.

Greenwood. Ashbourne; Bradley; Egginton; Hollington; Ticknall. *Sable a chevron ermine between three saltires argent*; crest: *a*

demi-lion or holding between the paws a saltire argent (V. 1662, D369). These arms were displayed 'sans proof' V. 1662 by former parliamentary captain Robert Greenwood of Bradley, Hollington and Ticknall, a skinner at Ashbourne.

Gregg. Derby; Ilkeston; Norton Lees Hall. *Or three trefoils slipped between two chevronels sable in dexter chief point an eagle reguardant wings expanded of the second*; crest: *out of a ducal coronet or an eagle's head and neck couped per pale argent goutée-de-sang and sable holding in the beak a trefoil slipped of the last*; motto: *'Pro Rege et grege'* (Lysons, cxxxi). Gr. 25 June 1725 to Foot Gregg of Babington House, Derby, and the descendants of his father Francis, of Ilkeston and Norton Lees Hall. John Gregg (1584–1657), Francis's grandfather, was 5th son of Ralph, of Bradley, Cheshire, and displayed the arms of the family V. 1611: *or three trefoils slipped between two chevronels sable*; crest: *out of a ducal coronet or an eagle's head and neck couped per pale argent and sable holding in the beak a trefoil slipped of the last* (MIS at Ilkeston church) but was labelled 'an usurper' for his pains, although they were allowed to his eldest brother (V. Cheshire 1613). Foot Gregg's next brother, Francis (1701–78) received a grant at the same time as his brother: as above (top) but *in the dexter chief point an eagle's gamb of the second* in lieu of the *eagle* (Burke).

Gregory. Eyam; Leam (Eyam Woodlands). *Gules on a chevron between ten cross crosslets or three like crosses of the field and a canton of the second* (BLG (1937) 64). Borne by Maj. Geoffrey Gregory of Eyam who took the surname of Rose-Innes (qv) 1911.

Gregson. Sharrowhall (Thurvaston); Turnditch Hall. *Argent a saltire gules a canton chequy or and azure*; crest: *a dexter cubit arm vested bendy wreathed around the wrist with a ribbon gules and argent holding a battleaxe or handled sable* (V. 1662). Borne by George son of George Gregson of Turnditch, attorney, and painted by Bassano for his funeral hatchment at Duffield, 15 Oct. 1716 (now lost), having been allowed to Henry Gregson of Sharrow Hall, V. 1634; in 1611 they were 'usurpers'.

Grendon. Boyleston; Bradley; Sturston. *Argent two chevronels gules a label vert* (Parliament Roll). Borne by Sir Robert de Grendon of Leics., one of the many descendants of Serlo de Grendon (C12); possibly borne by members of the family in Derbys., later C13. Burke suggests that this family bore C12 as above, but without a *label*. Sir Ralph de Grendon, who held Sturston, was summoned as a baron by writ 29 Dec. 1299; he too bore the arms without the *label* (ibid.).

Grenfell. Alton Manor (Idridgehay). *Gules on a fesse between three organ rests or a mural crown of the field*; supporters: *on either side a griffin or collared gules supporting a spear proper flowing threrefrom a banner of the second charged with an organ rest of the first* (FD (1929) I.818). Gr. 1905 to Rt. Hon. Sir William Henry Grenfell, cr. 30 Dec. 1905 Lord Desborough of Taplow, Bucks. His widow, who bore these arms (of which the supporters were gr. 1906), purchased Alton Manor 1920s.

Gresley. Drakelow Hall; Gresley. *Vairé ermine and gules*; crest: *a lion passant argent goutée de sang armed and collared gules*; motto: *'Meliore fide quam fortuna'* (arms: Parliament Roll; Vv. 1569, 1611, 1662). Borne by Sir Piers and Geoffrey de Gresley C14; crest in use by 1569, anciently it was *argent* and was so allowed V. 1662. The arms may derive from the Ferrers coat. Sir Robert Gresley was summoned to Parliament as a baron by writ of 1308, but it was not repeated. Sir George was cr. a bt 29 June 1611 (ext. 1976). The baron's arms were *vairé gules and ermine* (Burke); a branch seated in Staffordshire bore *vairé gules and argent goutée-de-poix*. A cadet of this family, Philip Gresley of High Park, Salwarpe, Worcs., d. 1829, leaving as his heir Robert Archibald Douglas, 2nd son of Revd Robert Douglas. R.A. Douglas was exemplified arms pursuant to a RL of 17 Dec. 1829 wherein he assumed the surname and arms of Gresley, originally gr. 30 Jan. 1820 to Philip Gresley: *vairé ermine and gules a canton vert*; crest: *a lion passant argent gorged with a collar vairé ermine and gules* (College of Arms, Grants, XXXVII.170).

Gresley Priory. *A cross patée impaling vairé ermine and (?) gules* (Papworth, 603). It is uncertain whether this represents the whole achievement of the house, or merely the dexter side impaled with a Gresley prior.

Gretton. Barton Blount; Bladon House (Newton Solney). *Quarterly per fesse indented or and gules in the second quarter an anchor in bend sinister of the first in the third an antique lamp also or fired proper*; crest:' *an arm embowed proper vested above the elbow argent holding erect a torch fired and a sickle in bend sinister all proper*; supporters: *dexter a bull sable sinister a chestnut horse both gorged with a chain pendent therefrom an anchor or*; motto: *'Stand fast'* (BP (1956) 966). Gr. to 'John Gretton of Stapleford Park son of John, of Barton, Co. Derby' 1899. Rt. Hon. John Gretton MP was raised to the peerage as Lord Gretton of Stapleford Park in 1944 when the supporters were gr.

Greville. Eaton Dovedale (Doveridge). *Sable on a cross within a bordure engrailed or five pellets*; crest: *a greyhound's head erased sable bezantée collared argent charged with three pellets*. (Burke). Arms of Sir Thomas Greville kt bt of Chipping Campden, Glos., who succeeded to Eaton Dovedale 1445.

Grey. Codnor Castle. *Barry of six argent and azure*; crest: *out of a ducal coronet or a demi-peacock displayed wings elevated argent*; motto: *'Foy est tout'* (FitzWilliam Roll; cf. seal of 1196–1208 in Local MS 6341. Sometime *a bendlet gules* is added to the shield). Borne by Sir John de Grey of Barton (Headington), Oxon., whose son was *jure uxoris* of Codnor; also with crest by Sir Richard de Grey of Codnor before 1271. Sir Henry Grey was summoned to Parliament by writ as Lord Grey of Codnor 1299, and his descendants are said to have borne as supporters: *two boars* (Burke). Title abeyant 1496–1989, when terminated in favour of Charles Legh Shuldam Cornwall-Legh of High Legh Hall (Cheshire) as 5th Baron Grey of Codnor (held to have been cr. 1397).

Grey. Shirland. *Barry of six argent and azure a label of five points gules*; crest as preceding (Dering Roll; see tomb of Henry, 5th Lord Grey (d. 1396), in Shirland church: G. Turbutt, *A History of Shirland and Higham* (Higham, 1978), 99–100). Borne by Sir Reginald de Grey of Shirland etc, 1297, having been summoned to Parliament by writ in 1299 as Lord Grey of Shirland, later of Wilton Castle (Ross), Herefords. As quartered by the Egertons, Earls of Wilton, since 1614 the heirs of the house, the arms were: *barry of six argent and azure the uppermost bar embattled* (Debrett, *Peerage* (1817) I.17). As barons, these Greys bore as supporters: *de-*

xter a wyvern or sinister a lion argent ducally crowned or. In 1325, Roger de Grey, half-brother of 3rd Lord Grey of Shirland, was summoned to Parliament by writ, as Lord Grey of Ruthyn, Denbs. His descendants were advanced: 1465, Earl of Kent; 1740 Earl of Harold, Marquess de Grey and Duke of Kent (ext. 1741). As Lords Grey of Ruthyn the arms were: *argent three bars azure and a label gules* (1st Lord) or *barry of six argent and azure a bend of six lozenges gules* (2nd Lord; FitzWilliam Roll).

Grey

Grey. Risley. *Argent three bars azure in chief three torteaux and a label of three points of the field a crescent for difference*; crest: *a unicorn passant ermine and behind it a sun in splendour rayed alternately or and argent and a crescent for difference* (V. Staffs. 1663). Arms of the Groby and Bradgate (Leics.) Greys (as borne by Sir John, and Adam de Grey; St George Roll) 1308. Sir Edward, a cadet of 3rd Lord Grey de Ruthyn, was summoned by writ to Parliament 1446 as Lord Ferrers (later Grey) of Groby, and his grandson was made Earl of Huntingdon 1471, Marquess of Dorset 1475, and his grandson

1551 became Duke of Suffolk. A nephew of the duke (attainted 1555) was cr. 1603 Lord Grey of Groby, Leics., and his son, Earl of Stamford, Lincs., 26 March 1628. Latterly their arms were, as Grey of Codnor: crest as Risley (above), supporters: *on either side an unicorn ermine armed crined tufted and unguled or*; motto: *'A ma puissance'* (BP (1956) 2053). Titles extinct 1977. The brother of the 1st Lord Stamford was of Risley. The V. 1662 labelled his arms 'sans proof'. When Bassano painted the funeral hatchment of Elizabeth Grey (4 March 1722) the points of the *label* were *ermine* (Local MS 3525).

Grey. Sandiacre; Sutton Scarsdale. *Barry of six argent and azure a label of three points gules bezantée* (in glass at Heanor church, now lost, Cox, IV.236). Borne 1334 by John Grey of Sandiacre and Richard of the same (MS Ashmole 804; Jenyns' Ordinary). The heir, Sir Henry Hilary, took the name of Grey but bore composite arms: *Barry of six argent and azure on a bend gules three leopards' faces jessant-de-lys or* (glass in Sutton church, V. 1611).

Griffin. Appleby Parva. *Sable a griffin segreant argent*; crest: *a talbot's head erased sable*; motto: *'Gardez la fine'* (V. Northants 1566, 1618). Borne by Sir Edward Griffin, who sold Appleby in 1630.

Griggs. Wigwell (Wirksworth). *Gules on a pale between two feathers argent two other feathers of the field*; crest: *in front of two feathers saltirewise gules a sword in pale enfiled with a leopard's face proper*; motto: *'Casu non mutatus'* (BLG (1937) 985, and in glass at Wigwell Hall). Gr. to Joseph Griggs, alderman of Loughborough, Leics., 1889, and borne by his descendants, who used Wigwell as a shooting-box. Previously the family had used: *gules three ostrich feathers argent*; crest: *a sword erect in pale enfiled with a leopard's face proper* (Burke).

Grimshawe. Errwood Hall (Hartington Upper Quarter). *Argent a griffin segreant sable beaked and membered or*; crest: *a griffin segreant sable* (formerly in glass at Errwood; crest: formerly over entrance). Used by Samuel Grimshawe (1768–1851). His son's heiress married H.R.H. Gosselin of Bengeo, Herts. (1849–1924), who assumed the surname of Grimshawe but continued to bear the arms of Gosselin: *gules a chevron between three crescents ermine*; crest: *a negro's head in* *profile proper.*

Grimston: see Wilmot.

Groves. Bank Hall (Chapel en le Frith). *Or a stone pine tree eradicated proper between two flaunches vert on each a squirrel sejant respectant of the field;* crest: *between two garbs or a stone pine tree eradicated proper;* motto: *'Labor ipse voluptas'* (FD (1910) 704). Gr. to James Grimble Groves (1854–1914) early C20.

Gruffydd ap Gwenwynwyn. Ashford; Blackwell in Peak. *Or a lion rampant gules armed and langued azure* (C13 seal, *DAJ* XXIV (1912) 61). Eldest son of Gwenwynwyn, King of Powys, who was mediatized 1274 having in 1241 been gr. these manors in Derbys. One son marr. an heiress of Somerville of Blackwell. The arms (above) were quartered by Curzon of Kedleston along with those of Powys: *or a lion's gamb erased in bend gules* (c. 1611, Local MS 6341).

Gryn (Grym, Gwyn): see le Wyne.

Hackenthorpe. Hackenthorpe Hall (Beighton); Mosborough (Eckington). *Vert a chevron between three escallops or* (*Rel.* V (1865) 233; Thompson, IV.24). Apparently borne by the Hackenthorpes who became extinct before 1384. Tilley (I.57) gives instead: *a chevron between three crescents*: his source is unknown.

Hacker. Duffield; Sawley; Shirebrook. *Azure a cross vairé or and of the first between four mullets pierced of the second;* crest: *on the trunk of a tree fesseways a moorcock proper* (V. Notts. 1662). Francis Hacker of Sawley was labelled 'an usurper' V. 1611, and 'promised to come to London'. Presumably this resulted in his father, John, of East Bridgford, Notts., being gr. (28 Nov. 1611) the arms above. And whilst some members of the family bore as above, others did not: cf. hatchment at All Saints', Derby of Hugh Bateman, who marr. the heiress of Samuel Hacker of Duffield: *sable a cross vair between four estoiles or* (C18). Samuel was a descendant of the attainted regicide Francis Hacker of East Bridgford, eldest son of the grantee. Presumably the right to the arms above was thereby (through the attainder) forfeited, and he assumed instead those shown on the Bateman hatchment at All Saints'. When eventually the heiress of this branch marr. Heath-

cote of Chesterfield, the authorized arms were quartered as gr. under RL 1819, 1840 and 1871.

Hacket. Dronfield; Newbold. *Argent two bendlets gules* (D369; Thompson, IV.24). Borne by Sir Walter Hacket 'of Derbys.' (Dronfield) at the first Dunstable Tournament 1308 (Dunstable Roll 1; Parliament Roll) and John Hacket, later (Jenyns' Roll); the latter had been bailiff of Derby 1359. Used by Sampson, son of John Hacket of Newbold and Derby 'gent.' (1788–1857). See also Flackett.

Haden. Derby. *Or a human leg embowed and couped at the thigh azure* (Burke). Used by Dr Thomas Haden, mayor of Derby 1811 and 1819, a cadet of Haden of Haden Hill, Staffs., whose arms were not gr. until 1877 and 1879.

Hall. Castleton; Edale. *Or on a bend between two lions passant sable three chevrons of the first* (*Rel.* V. (1865) 233). Borne or used (their emblems may go back to the earlier C15) by this family seated there from before 1318 to c. 1850, when Isaac son of Joseph Hall was still sealing with this device. See also Halley.

Hallam. Kirk Hallam. *Argent a lion rampant azure goutée or* (*Rel.* V (1865) 233). Apparently borne by this family, which flourished from c. 1200 to mid-C14.

Halley. Aston (Sudbury); Doveridge. *Or a saltire engrailed vert* (as quartered by Blount of Burton, Local MS 6341). Ellena, dau. and heiress of John Halley of Doveridge marr. John Blount of Burton on Trent, Staffs., c. 1600; what title Halley had to these arms is unknown. If borne by Oliver Halley of Aston 1433 (Glover, Appendix, 60) they might predate 1415; unfortunately the family escaped notice V. 1569.

Halley. Blackbrook (Chapel en le Frith); Shatton. *Azure a chevron between three annulets and overall a fesse or* (V. London 1634). Borne by Halley of London, descended from Oliver Halley of Shatton, gent. 1434.

Hallifax. Chesterfield. *Or on a pile engrailed sable between two fountains three cross crosslets of the field;* crest: *a moorcock wings expanded per bend sinister sable and gules combed and wattled of the last ducally gorged and charged on the breast with a cross crosslet or* (*Rel.* V. (1865) 233; crest: Burke). Gr. 1573 and 1788, and borne by Rt Revd Dr Samuel

Hallifax, Bishop of St Asaph, whose father, Robert (d. 1769) was of Chesterfield.

Halton. S. Wingfield Hall and Manor. *Per pale azure and gules a lion rampant argent* (Burke). Sometimes the field is given with the tinctures reversed; others (e.g. Lysons, lxxxvi) with the lion *or*. Earlier sources in the family's native Cumberland suggest that the arms as given are correct. Burke gives a crest *a lion sejant argent holding a broken lance proper*. They were apparently conf. to Immanuel Halton (1628–99) of Greenthwaite Hall (Greystoke), Cumb., astronomer and agent to the Duke of Norfolk, and to whom the latter gave the great house and one-third of the park at S. Wingfield in 1680. A collateral branch had a grant 25 April 1954: *per pale azure and gules a barrulet argent overall a lion rampant or*; crest: *out of a wreath of oak fructed or a lion sejant argent supporting with the dexter paw a broken spear proper* to Col. F.W. Halton (1872–1965) with remainder to the descendants of his father: this branch had inherited but sold S. Wingfield, 1875.

Hallowes. Derby; Dethick; Glapwell; Hallowes (Unstone); Norton. *Azure on a fesse between three crescents argent as many torteaux*; crest: *a demi-griffin segreant sable winged argent* (Lysons, lxxxvi). Gr. 6 Dec. 1647 to Nathaniel Hallowes but invalidated by a warrant of 4 Sept. 1660. Consequently disclaimed V. 1662. A new grant was obtained 14 April 1766 by Brabazon Hallowes of Dethick to the descendants of his father Thomas. It differed in that the *fesse* was *argent*, the *crescents or* and the crest was also *collared argent*.

Hancock. Barlow; Brampton; Staveley; Whittington. *Gules a cinquefoil* (*Rel.* XII (1872) 95). John Hancock of Whittington etc, living 1587, marr. the heiress of Timothy Newton of Duffield, and used these arms as did John, who purchased the Risley estate 1770; heiress marr. Capt. W.H. Hall.

Handley. Handley (Staveley). *Gules a fesse between six mascles or* (*Rel.* V (1865) 233). Gr. 1738 to William Handley of London, merchant, descended from Thomas Handley of Handley, living *c.* 1440.

Hardinge. King's Newton; Melbourne. *Gules on a chevron argent fimbriated or three escallops sable*; crest: *a mitre gules banded and stringed or thereon a chevron argent fimbriated of the second charged with three escallops sable*; motto: '*Audax omnia perpeti*' (Lysons, cxxxii). Gr. 3 July 1711 to John Hardinge of King's Newton, Gideon his brother, and Nicholas his first cousin. Sir Robert, their grandfather, used *gules a chevron argent* (D369, V. 1662). In J. Gwillim, *A Display of Heraldry* (ed. J. Bloom, 5th ed., 1679), I.363, however, Sir Robert is credited with having used this device with *three escallops sable* on the *chevron*; crest: *on a mitre gules a chevron argent thereon three escallops sable*: plainly overtones of Fitzhardinge and Berkeley (qv) and Melbourne of Melbourne (qv), from which latter family the Hardinges rather dubiously claimed descent. The 3rd son of the primary grantee was made a bt (Ireland) 4 Aug. 1801 with remainder to his elder brother's sons. The 2nd bt's brother Capt. G.N. Hardinge was killed in heroic circumstances and was gr. as honourable augmentations (actually to the descendants of his grandfather): *on a chief wavy argent a frigate wholly dismasted with the French flag flying beneath the British ensign towed towards the dexter by a frigate of apparently inferior force in a shattered state British colours hoisted all proper*; and as an extra crest: *a dexter hand couped above the wrist vested in the uniform of a British naval officer grasping a sword erect proper hilt and pommel or surmounted of the Dutch and French flags in saltire the former inscribed 'Atlanta' the latter 'Piedmontaise' the blade of the sword enfiled by a wreath of laurels near the point and a little below another of cypress all also proper*; motto: '*Postera laude recens*' (BP (1956) 1026): what more need one say? The next brother of the hero was in 1846 cr. Viscount Hardinge and was gr. supporters: *on either side a lion proper the dexter murally crowned or each holding a flagstaff proper, flag of the second, the sinister easternly crowned also or*; motto: '*Mens aequa rebus in arduis*' (ibid.). In 1910 the younger brother of the 3rd Viscount was cr. Lord Hardinge of Penshurst, Kent, being gr. supporters: *dexter a brown bear, sinister a Bengal tiger both proper*; motto: '*Pro rege et patria*' (ibid.).

Hardwick. Hardwick; Ault Hucknall. *Argent a saltire engrailed azure on a chief of the second three cinquefoils of the field*; crest: *on a mount vert a stag courant proper attired or gorged with a chaplet of roses argent between two bars azure* (V. 1569). Some MSS make the *cinquefoils pierced.* Allowed to John, brother of Bess of Hardwick.

Hardy. Foston Hall. *Argent on a bend invected plain cotised gules three Catherine wheels or on a chief of the second as many leopards' faces of the third;* crest: *a dexter arm embowed in armour proper garnished or entwined by a branch of oak vert charged with two Catherine wheels one on the forearm the other on the upper arm gules the hand grasping a dragon's head erased proper;* motto: *'Arme de foi hardi'* (BP (1956) 1030). Gr. 1876 to Sir John Hardy of Dunstall Hall, Staffs., cr. a bt 23 Feb. 1876, and borne by his third son, G.H. Hardy of Foston.

Hareston. Sutton Scarsdale. *Crusilly fitchée three leopards' faces jessant-de-lys* (Tilley, III.269). Borne by Peter de Hareston, who was gr. Sutton 1255. The heiress marr. Grey. Burke gives for Hilary the above arms with field *sable,* charges *argent.* In view of the fact that the Hilarys bore a coat compounded of elements of the above and Grey, it is probable that these arms are in reality the pre-Grey-heiress coat of Hilary (qv).

Harington. 'Co. Derby'. *Per chief gules and or on a bend azure on annulet of the second* (*Rel.* XII (1872) 95; Harl.MSS 1093, 1486). Sir John Harington was a knight entered under Derbys. *c.* 1315; the Parliament Roll gives the arms *sans annulet.*

Harland. Ashbourne; Bradley. *Or on a bend wavy between two sealions azure three stags' heads caboshed of the field* (MI at Ashbourne church; *Rel.* XII (1872) 95). Borne or used by Christopher Harland of Ashbourne (1754–1839).

Harley. Bolsover. *Or a bend cotised sable;* crest: *a castle triple towered argent out of the central tower a demi-lion issuant gules;* supporters: *on either side an angel proper habits and wings displayed or;* motto: *'Virtute et fide'* (Burke). The 2nd Earl of Oxford inherited Bolsover from Holles, early C18. Earldom of Oxford and Mortimer and Barony of Harley of Wigmore, Herefs., cr. 24 May 1711; ext. 1853.

Harpur. Breadsall, Calke, Littleover, Swarkestone etc. *Argent a lion rampant sable armed and langued gules within a bordure engrailed of the second;* crest: *a boar passant or bristled and ducally gorged gules;* motto: *'Degeneranti genus opprobrium'* (Vv. 1569, 1611, 1662). On 3 Jan. 1566 these arms were exemplified to Richard Harpur of Swarkestone quarterly with the ancient arms of Harpur: *Per bend sinister argent and sable a lion rampant counterchanged within a bordure compony or and gules* (as on MI of Richard at Swarkestone church). The arms were originally those of Rushall of Rushall, Staffs., the ultimate heiress of which family (via Bowles and Grobere) marr. Sir John Harpur of Chesterton, Warw. *c.* 1435. In the Harl.MS 6104 of V. 1662 the *boar* of the crest is described as *pierced through the neck with a dart in bend sinister;* V. 1662 adds *the back sable;* MS Ashmole 798 gives a different motto: *'Cogita mori'* which sounds more like one from a funeral hatchment. According to the old MS pedigrees (Harl.MS 2134, f. 99; Harl.MS 291, f. 97), the earliest arms of the Harpurs were borne C12 by Sir Roger le Harpur: *a plain cross* but this may only be a mis-interpretation of a Templar's shield. On a hatchment at Calke church four crests are displayed: Crewe (dexter); Harpur (sinister); in a garter, Findern and on the helm *out of an eastern crown or a cross calvary gules* which may be intended to accompany these early arms. The crest of the quartered ancient arms was almost certainly: *a lion's head erased quarterly or and gules* (in error for the 1566 grant, crest in Harl.MS 291, f. 97, V. 1569). In 1808 the 7th bt (title cr. 8 Sept. 1626; dormant 1924) assumed by RL the surname and quartered arms of Crewe (of Steane, Northants.): *azure a lion rampant argent langued gules.* These arms quartered by Harpur and the surname Harpur-Crewe have been twice asumed by RL (1961 and 1981) by the Harpur heirs, the Jenneys (qv). John Lewis Harpur of Llanfrynach, Brec., a descendant of William Harpur of Bilston, Staffs., youngest son of 1st bt., was 25 June 1973 granted arms. *Argent two hunting horns in saltire sable virolled or mouthpieces downwards between in pale two lions rampant and in fesse as many dragons passant respectant gules;* crest: *on a mount vert in front of a lance in bend sable point upwards or and a battleaxe in bend sinister of the second blade upwards of the third a boar passant gules armed and unguled also of the third;* motto: *'Degeneranti genus opprobrium'.* Subsequently his descent has been consolidated, thus making the above grant seem premature, as he is clearly entitled to Harpur of Calke with due difference.

Harpur. Littleover. *Argent a lion rampant sable armed and langued gules within a bordure engrailed of the second a canton of the third*; crest as previous (V. 1662; crest: MI at Littleover). Allowed to Richard Harpur of Littleover V. 1662.

Harpur. Twyford. *Argent a lion rampant sable armed and langued gules within a bordure engrailed and on a canton of the field a fret of the second*; crest: *a boar passant or, back gules murally gorged of the second* (V. 1662). Allowed to George Harpur of Twyford, whose mother was a Vernon of Sudbury, whose arms supplied the motif for the *canton*.

Harrison. 'Smythes'. *Gules an eagle displayed and a chief or*; crest: *a snake vert entwined around a broken column or* (Burke). Gr. 5 May 1575 to John Harrison of London, son of William, of 'Smythes', Co. Derby: the place may be Smithcote (Codnor), Smisby, Smith Hall (Hulland) or Smithy Hill (Bradwell).

Harrison

Harrison. Snelston. *Per pale nebulée azure and sable three demi-lions couped each holding a cross crosslet fitchée or*; crest: *on a mount vert a demi-lion couped or semée of lozenges azure holding between the paws a chaplet of roses proper* (Local MS 9555.232, 367). Gr. 1853 to John Harrison of Snelston and Derby. His kinsmen, from whom he inherited, used: *azure three demi-lions or a canton argent*; crest: *a demi-lion or supporting a chaplet of roses vert* (Tilley, IV.61).

Harthill. Harthill; Middleton by Wirksworth; Parwich; Winster; Repton; Ballidon. *Argent two bars vert*; crest *on a mount vert a hart courant* (as a quartering of, and used as a crest by, Cokayne, V. 1569). Borne by Sir Richard de Harthill (d. 1390, Cox, II.96) and by a cadet, William, 1312 (seal, Local MS 6341). This William also bore the arms with *a canton argent thereon a buck trippant sable* (seal, ibid.). The canton may well be an allusion to the 'ancient' arms: *argent three bucks trippant sable attired or* (also quartered by Cokayne, V. 1569 – usually between Edensor and Rossington, cf. MIS at Ashbourne church and *DAJ* LV (1934) 25 & n.2).

Harthill. Woodwall (Parwich). *Argent two bars vert overall a bendlet gules* (Local MS 6341). Borne by a cadet branch of Harthill seated *c.* 1480–1530.

Hartington. Hartington. *Or a stag's head caboshed gules between the attires a cross patée fitchée* (as quartered by Pole, V. 1569, Harl.MS 2113; hatchments at Radbourne church). Borne by Sir John Hartington of Hartington, mid-C14, whose heiress marr. Pole. The arms are sometimes found without the *cross* (as quartered by Pole, Sussex; Burke). At Croxall church the arms appear as *argent a buck's head caboshed a fleur-de-lys between the attires gules* – in reality intended for Horton (cf. Cox, III.359)? Local MS 4556 gives a completely different coat: *vert a fesse between three stags' heads caboshed or attired argent*. See also Pole.

Hartshorne. Ashbourne; Chaddesden; Hartshorne. *Argent a chevron gules between three bucks' heads caboshed sable* (D369; seal, PRO, P.1513). Borne by Roger son of William son of Bertram de Hartshorne C14, and John, 1418, who bore a crest: *a pair of stags' attires* (ibid).

Haslerton: see Heslerton.

Haslam. Breadsall Priory; Derby. *Argent two bars wavy azure on a chief angrailed gules a lamb statant between two hazel leaves proper*; crest: *an eagle rising reguardant holding in* *the beak a hazel leaf slipped proper and pendent from the neck by a riband argent an escutcheon gules thereon a lamb statant proper*; motto: *'Agnus Dei salvator meus'* (FD (1905) 640). Gr. 1891 to Sir Arthur Seale Haslam of Breadsall, knighted that year, being mayor of Derby at the time of a royal visit, with remainder to the heirs male of the grantee's father, William.

Hastings. Dale Abbey; Melbourne. *Argent a maunch sable*; crest: *a bull's head erased sable armed and ducally gorged or*; supporters: *on either side a mantygre proper horned argent*; mottoes: *'Honorantes me honorabo', 'In veritate victoria', 'Post proelia praemia'* (V. 1569). Arms borne by Sir Ralph Hastings 1348 (MS Ashmole 804); earlier generations had borne field *or* (Caerlaverock Roll), e.g., 1st Lord Hastings, summoned to Parliament by writ 1299. The earldom of Huntingdon was cr. 1529, and the earls began to acquire Derbys. property from that time. Dale was acquired from Porte by 4th earl. A grant exists, dated *c.* 1536, to Sir Robert Hastings of Derby and Notts.: *or a maunch 'mawtallée' gules*. Exactly who this Robert was is unclear.

Hastings. Willesley. *Argent a maunch and a bordure engrailed sable*; crest: *a bull's head erased erminois attired and ducally gorged argent* (Lysons, lxvii) Gr. 1806 to Gen. Sir Charles Hastings, natural son of Francis, Earl of Huntington, cr. a bt 28 Feb. that year. The 2nd bt was gr. these arms quarterly with Abney, and assumed that name before his own by RL 1823. Ext. 1858.

Hatfeild. Glossopdale (Glossop); Hope; Norton Lees. *Ermine on a chevron engrailed sable three cinquefoils or*; crest: *a dexter cubit arm vested sable cuffed argent hand proper holding a cinquefoil slipped or*; motto: *'Pax'* (Harl.MS 4630). Apparently a late C17 confirmation to John Hatfeild (sic) of Hatfield (Shiregreen), Yorks., and his cousin John, of Laughton en le Morthen, Yorks., both 4th in descent from Nicholas, of Glossop, whose family had held land in Glossopdale over the six preceding generations. A branch was at Hope C15 and another member was of Norton Lees late C18: see also Rodes.

Hathersage. Hathersage; Barlborough; Killamarsh. *Paly of six argent and gules on a chief azure a barrulet dancettée or* (as a quartering of Longford, V. 1569 and Local MS 6341). Borne by Sir Matthew de Hathersage,

d. 1259, and grandson of William de Withington of Withington, Lancs. Heiresses marr. Longford and Goushill. Glover's Roll, 1st version, 175, gives the simpler *paly of six or and gules a chief argent* for this Matthew.

Hawe. Derby; Elton. *Sable a fesse humettée between three griffins' heads erased ermine*; crest: *a griffin's head erased ermine collared and lined or* (MI at Wilne impaled by Willoughby; crest: Burke). Borne by Henry Hawe of Norfolk whose forebears had had an estate at Elton; his dau. Frances marr. Sir John Willoughby of Risley. Gr. 15 Nov. 1559.

Hawkins. Calke. *Sable a lion passant or and in chief three bezants* (on a funeral hatchment at Calke). Used by (or retrospectively attributed to) Isaac Hawkins of Calke, father of Anne, wife of Sir Henry Harpur, 7th bt, whom he marr. 1792. She had been a lady's maid and d. 21 March 1827. The arms are those of Hawkins of Kent.

Heacock. Buxton. *Erminois an elephant statant and on a chief azure a sun between two beehives or*; crest: *a hind sejant reguardant erminois collared gules the dexter foot resting on a beehive or* (MI at St John's, Buxton). Gr. to Thomas son of Thomas Heacock of Stoke Newington, Middlesex, 1746 and used by Philip Heacock of Buxton, agent to the Dukes of Devonshire in the early C19, who appears to have come from a yeoman family of Etwall.

Heald. Alsop Manor (Eaton & Alsop). *Quarterly gules and azure in the first and fourth quarters an eagle wings elevated or in the second and third a fret of the last overall a fesse argent thereon between two crosses patée a rose of the first barbed and seeded proper*; crest: *on a mount vert a bundle of arrows fesseways points towards the dexter proper bound gules thereon an eagle wings elevated erminois in the beak a sprig of holly also proper the dexter claw resting on a cross patée as in the arms*; motto: *'Mea gloria Crux'* (FD (1910) 763). Gr. to James Heald of Portwood, Stockport, Cheshire, 1829 and borne by his descendant, John Norris Heald of Alsop Manor, at the turn of the century and into the 1930s.

Heanor: see Heynoure.

Heanor Urban District Council. *A Tudor rose proper*; motto: *'Labore progredimus'*. In use on a seal dated 1895. Authority abolished 1974.

Heath. Derby; Duffield; Makeney. *Argent a chevron sable between three heathcocks proper* (seal on deed in private hands, Derby). Used by the Makeney-born Derby bankers John, Isaac and Christopher Heath, who went bankrupt, March 1779.

Heathcote. Chesterfield. *Ermine three pommes on each a cross or*; crest: *out of a mural crown azure between a pair wings conjoined ermine a pomme as in the arms* (Lysons, lxxxvii). Gr. 20 Dec. 1709 to Gilbert Heathcote of Chesterfield and London, Lord Mayor 1711, cr. a bt 17 Jan. 1733, with remainder to his brothers. The 5th bt was cr. 1856 Lord Aveland, receiving then a grant of supporters: *dexter a friar vested in russet proper staff and rosary or sinister a savage wreathed about the loins and temples with oak proper*; motto: *'Loyauté me oblige'* (BP (1956) 60). His son, who was also 24th Lord Willoughby d'Eresby, *jure matris* (see Bec), assumed the additional surname and arms of Drummond-Willoughby after his own by RL of 1872, and in 1892 he was raised to the earldom of Ancaster, Lincs. (ext., with barony of Aveland, 1983). Samuel, 3rd brother of Sir Gilbert, had a son William, of Hursley, Hants., cr. a bt also 1733 (16 Aug.) with the same arms, but motto: *'Et Dieu mon Appui'*.

Heathcote. Chesterfield; Cutthorpe (Brampton); Derby; Littleover etc. *Argent three pommes on each a cross or*; crest as preceding (seal in local collection). Arms used by Geoffrey Heathcote of Cutthorpe Hall, who disclaimed V. 1662. His descendants, the Heathcotes of Barlborough, had the arms as gr. to Sir Gilbert (qv) conf. as a quartering 1776. Samuel Unwin of Sutton in Ashfield, Notts., marr. an heiress of this branch and was gr., on assuming the surname and arms of Heathcote in 1815: *ermine three hurts each charged with a cross engrailed argent*; crest: *issuant from a palisado crown or a hurt as in the arms between two wings erected ermine* (Heathcote, 203). Sir John Edensor Heathcote of Longton Hall, Staffs. (d. 1822) emblazoned his plate with the original arms gr. to Sir Gilbert (qv above) and supporters: *on either side a horse sable ducally gorged and charged on the shoulder with a horseshoe or* (ibid.): his ancestors were of Hartington, and the horseshoes represented a descent from the Edensors (qv). George Heathcote of Brampton, of this family, disclaimed, V. 1611.

Heathcote. Blackwell in Peak; Stancliffe Hall (Darley). *Per saltire erminois and ermine three pommes on each a cross argent and in fesse point a cross crosslet gules*; crest: *out of a vallary crown or a pomme as in the arms between two wings conjoined gules on each an estoile argent* (Heathcote, 206). Gr. to Arthur Shepley of Stancliffe Hall 1821 when he assumed the surname and arms of Heathcote by RSM. Heiress marr. Brailsford (qv).

Heathcote. Bakewell. *Per pale gules and azure three plates on each a cross engrailed vert between four ermine spots sable*; crest: *a plate as in the arms between two wings azure* (Heathcote, 211). Gr. 1819 to William Heathcote of Bakewell and Cundall, Yorks. (1798–1844), natural son of John son of Daniel Heathcote of Bakewell.

Heathcote. Duffield. *Vert three piles one reversed in base between two others issuant from chief or on each a pomme thereon a cross of the second*; crest: *on a mount vert between two roses springing therefrom gules stalked and leaved proper a pomme thereon a cross or* (quartered by Amory, BP (1956) 55). Gr. 1824 to John Heathcote, of Bolham, Devon, whose father was of Duffield. Heiress marr. Samuel Amory, and their son was cr. a bt 1874, taking the additional surname and arms of Heathcote.

Heather. Heather (Killamarsh). *Paly of six azure and or on a chief of the second a barrulet dancettée gules*; crest: *a lion's gamb erect sable holding a human heart gules*; motto: *'Vigilantia non cade'* (noted V. 1611 at Bakewell church). Gr. 1646–60 to Samuel Heather of London, but the shield at least probably borne by John Heather of Heather late C14 or used by a descendant. The motifs are strongly reminiscent of Hathersage (qv), once lords of Killamarsh.

Helyon. Bakewell. *Gules fretty argent a fesse or* (Lysons, cv). Borne by John Helyon of Bakewell C14.

Henderson. Nether Hayes (Etwall). *Argent three piles issuant from the sinister sable on a chief invected gules a pale of the field thereon an ermine spot between two cushions or*; crest: *two shepherd's crooks in saltire proper*; motto: *'Gratia gratiam parit'* (pers. comm.) Gr. (LO) 1970 to J.B. Henderson of Etwall.

Henley. The Friary (Derby). *Azure a lion rampant argent supporting a rudder or on a chief of the second an anchor sable between* *two trefoils slipped proper*; crest: *an eagle reguardant wings displayed or holding in the dexter claw an anchor erect cabled sable and in the beak a trefoil slipped proper*; motto: '*Perseverando*' (FD (1929) II.919). A C20 grant to Rear-Adm. J.C.W. Henley, descended from Michael (1732–1813), of the Friary.

Henniker. Allestree; Callow Hall (Mapleton). *Or on a chevron gules three estoiles argent in chief two crescents azure and in base an escallop of the last*; crest: *an escallop or charged with an estoile gules*; mottoes: '*Deus maior columna*' and '*Toy apiet yein eneka*' (bookplate; cf. BP (1956) 1084). Gr. 1765, quarterly with Major (1 & 4: *azure three Corinthian columns on each a ball or*: also gr. 1765) to Sir John Henniker, who inherited through his wife the btcy conferred 15 July 1765 on John Major, her father. Borne by Capt. Frederick Henniker of Callow Hall *c.* 1873–1908, descended from 1st Lord Henniker (Irish peerage, cr. 31 July 1800), and his grandson, A.T.M. Henniker of Allestree.

Henshaw. 'Co. Derby'. *Argent a chevron between three heronshaws sable*; crest: *a hawk close or preying on a mallard's wing of the first erased gules* (Burke, DFUSA). Used or borne by William W. Henshaw of Washington DC 1939, claiming descent from Sir Thomas Henshaw 'of Co. Derby' late C16, who has not been identified.

Henstock. Slaley Hall (Bonsall); Wirksworth. *Sable three chevronels between two lions rampant in chief and in base a waterbouget argent*; crest: *in front of a demi-lion argent holding in its paws a waterbouget a half Catherine wheel sable*; motto: '*Nil sine magno labore*' (BLG 1952, Supplement, 166). Gr. 1877 to Jesse Henstock of Slaley Hall, with remainder to the male descendants of his father, John, of a Bonsall family.

Herberjour. Chaddesden; Darley; Rodsley. *Gules a fesse between three horseshoes or* (seal, Local MS 6341). Borne by William de Herberjour of Chaddesden 1310. Replete with allusions to Ferrers.

Herbert. Bretby Hall. *Per pale azure and gules three lions rampant argent*; crest: *a wyvern wings elevated vert holding in the mouth a sinister hand couped at the wrist gules*; supporters: *dexter a panther guardant argent semée of torteaux and hurts incensed proper sinister a lion argent each ducally gorged per pale azure and gules chained or and charged on*

their shoulders with an ermine spot sable; motto: '*Ung je serviray*' (BP (1970) 486). Borne by Henry Herbert, 4th Earl of Carnarvon (cr. 1793), who inherited Bretby in 1866. Supporters gr. 1780.

Herbert Strutt School. Belper. *Argent in front of rays of the sun proper a cubit arm erect vested bendy of six or and sable cuffed of the field in the hand an escroll of paper also proper on a chief sable two Tudor roses proper* (R. Sutton, *The Herbert Strutt School* (Belper, 1959), title-page). Unauthorised achievement used by this school from its foundation in 1909, being the crest of Strutt of Bridge Hill (qv), with a 'Derbyshire' chief.

Heriz. S. Wingfield; Tibshelf; etc. *Azure three hedgehogs or* (as a quartering of Harpur, V. 1569). Borne by John de Heriz (d. 1330), although his grandfather sealed with *two lions rampant* (1275, *DAJ* XVI (1894) 43). John son of William Heriz of Withcote, Leics., adopted the prosaic surname of Smith and bore arms (gr. 8 Feb. 1500): *gules on a chevron or between three bezants as many crosses patée fitchée sable*; he claimed to be a cadet of Heriz of Derbys. His son Roger was gr. a crest 16 May 1565: *an arm couped sleeve per pale or and gules holding in the hand a griffin's head erased azure beaked or langued eyed and eared gules* (Vv. Leics. 1619; Northants. 1618–19; London 1568). A descendant was cr. a bt 20 Mar. 1661, title ext. 1721.

Heselerton (Haselton). Norton Lees(?). *Gules six lioncels rampant argent crowned or*; crest: *a flag azure thereon a cross argent* (Thompson, IV.20). Included in several local collections of arms, always with the locale 'Great Grimsby': presumably the Haseltons of that place claimed a descent out of Derbys., where the name is elusive. John Haselerton of Norton Lees 1785 might be the connection.

Hewitt. Beighton Fields (Barlborough); Killamarsh. *Azure on a chevron flory between three lions passant or as many lapwings proper* (*Rel.* V (1865) 233). Borne by Nicholas Hewitt of Wales, Yorks. and Barlborough 1518, and by William, of Killamarsh Netherthorpe 1505.

Heygate. The College (Derby); Mickleover. *Gules two bars argent on a bend overall or a torteau between two leopards' faces azure*; crest: *a wolf's head erased gules*; motto: '*Boulogne et Cadiz*' (*Rel.* XII (1872) 95).

Borne by Dr James Heygate of the College and Mickleover (1801–72), conf. to Reginald, of Feering, Essex, 9 Nov. 1549, and allowed with a *torteau for distinction* V. London 1634. Dr Heygate's first cousin, William, was cr. a bt 30 Sept. 1831.

Heynoure. Heanor. *Sable a pile azure* (sic; identified in church glass at Heanor by Ashmole, V. 1662). Borne probably (if the attribution is correct) by Robert son of Nicholas son of Thomas de Heanor of Heanor, *temp.* Henry III.

Heywood. Brimington. *Argent three torteaux in bend between two cotises gules* (as quartered by Coke of Brookhill (Pinxton), e.g. FD (1929) I.399). Used by George Heywood of Brimington (1714–84), whose dau. and ultimate heiress marr. Revd d'Ewes Coke of Brookhill, and whose descendants occasionally quartered the arms, although authority for their use by the Heywoods or their subsequent quartering appears to be lacking.

Heywood. Duffield Bank (Duffield). *Argent three torteaux in bend between two bendlets gules on a canton of the last a cross patée or*; crest: *on a mount vert a trunk of a tree entwined by ivy thereon a falcon perched wings displayed proper*; motto: '*Alte velo*' (BP (1956) 1100). Borne by Arthur Percival Heywood, later 3rd bt, a title cr. 9 Aug. 1838.

Heyworth. Belper; Makeney Lodge (Milford). *Ermine two barrulets wavy azure between three bats sable*; crest: *a crescent azure issuant therefrom flames of fire proper between two bats' wings sable*; motto: '*Nil Dimidum Est*' (Burke, AA 61; FD (1929) I.935). Borne by Lawrence Heyworth of Liverpool, Lancs., MP for Derby (1786–1872), whose grandson, Dr G.A.F. Heyworth, settled at Belper. His grandson, A.J. Heyworth, was of Makeney Lodge.

Hibbert-Ware. Slack Hall (Chapel en le Frith). *Quarterly 1 & 4: or two lions passant azure armed and langued gules within a bordure of the second thereon twelve escallops of the field* (Ware), *2 & 3: barry of eight or and vert a pale counterchanged* (Hibbert); crest: *a dragon's head or pierced through the neck with a broken tilting spear proper* (Ware), and *a hand holding a millrind proper* (Hibbert); motto: '*Sola salus sevire Deo*' (Burke). The son of Dr Samuel Hibbert-Ware (who bore these arms under a grant made when he adopted the surname and arms of Hibbert-

Ware by RSM 1837) inherited Slack Hall in 1905 from the Slackes (qv).

Higginson. Sandiacre. *Vert a chevron quarterly or and gules between two garbs in chief and a sun in base of the second*; crest: *a dexter hand erect between two stalks of wheat flexed in saltire issuant from a human heart all proper in the hand a book shut sable garnished or* (arms: Tilley, IV. 157; crest: Burke). Gr. to Joseph Higginson of Bridge Row, London, and Mile End, Middlesex, 1764, whose descendant Francis Higginson inherited at Sandiacre from Molyneux before 1816.

Hilary. Sandiacre; Sutton Scarsdale. *Sable crusilly fitchée three leopards' faces jessant-de-lys argent* (MS Ashmole 804; Willement Roll). Borne by Roger Hilary, *temp.* Edward III, whose kinsman marr. the heiress of Sir William Grey. His son, Sir John, adopted the surname of Grey and the arms: *barry of six argent and azure on a bend gules three leopards' faces jessant-de-lys or* (see Grey; Hareston), and d. 1392.

Hill. Ashbourne. *Per chevron argent and sable three cinquefoils counterchanged* (*Rel.* V (1865) 233; Thompson, IV.20). Gr. Nov. 1615 to Revd Robert Hill DD, son of Ralph, of Ashbourne.

Hill-Wood: see Wood.

Hilton. Alton Manor (Idridgehay). *Argent two bars azure with suitable difference*; crests: (i) *on a close helm Moses' head in profile glorified adorned with a rich diapered mantle proper*; (ii) *a stag couchant ducally gorged and chained or*; motto: '*Invicte stat anima*' (allowed to Hilton of Hilton Castle, Co. Durham, Vv. North 1552 and Westmorland 1530). Borne by Col. Peter Hilton, Lord Lieutenant of Derbys., by virtue of descent from Hilton of Hilton via those of Pennington, N. Lancs. (pers. comm.).

Hilton-Barber: see Barber.

Hinton. Derby. *Vert a bend or* (Thompson, IV.20; Bassano's MS, Local 3525). Used by Charles Hinton of Derby and Lichfield, Staffs., 1709. A relative, Christopher, was of Etwall and Burnaston 1627. Sleigh (*Rel.* V (1865) 233) makes the *bend argent*.

Hives. Derby; Duffield. *Or on a chevron sable three beehives of the field*; crest: *in front of a sun in splendour or an eagle rising proper*; supporters: *dexter a mechanic proper overalls azure holding in the exterior hand a micrometer sinister a draughtsman also proper coat* *argent holding under the exterior arm a set-and T-square also proper*; motto: *'Sic vos vobis mellificatis aes'* (BP (1970) 1345). Gr. 1950 when E.W. Hives of Rolls-Royce was cr. Lord Hives of Duffield.

Hoare. Ashe Hall (Ash). *Sable a double eagle displayed argent charged on the breast with an ermine spot all within a bordure engrailed of the second*; crest: *an eagle's head erased argent charged with an ermine spot*; motto: *'In ardua'* (FD (1929) I.949). Gr. 17 Dec. 1766, and borne by Seymour Hoare of Ash Hall *c.* 1900 and before.

Hodges. Rock House (Cromford). *Or three crescents and on a canton sable a ducal coronet of the field*; crest: *out of a ducal coronet or an heraldic antelope's head argent attired and tufted or* (Burke). Used by Thomas Hallet Hodges, who built Rock House and who was there 1782, but properly the arms of Hodges of Dorset.

Hodgkinson. Clattercotes and Overton (Ashover); Matlock. *Or on a cross humettée between four cinquefoils vert a like cinquefoil of the first*; crest: *a garb or between two dragon's wings vert* (Lysons, cxxxii). Used by the family from at least 1687. Ann dau. and heiress of William Hodgkinson of Overton (d. 1731) marr. Joseph Banks of Revesby Abbey (Lincs.). Their second son William took the name of Hodgkinson but his own son Joseph (cr. bt 1781) reverted to Banks (qv).

Holbrook. Bladon Castle (Newton Solney); Derby; Repton Grange. *A chevron between three martlets* (Rel. XII (1872) 95). Used by Joseph Holbrook of Repton Grange 1703, a former London alderman, and his descendants, but possibly borne by Walter de Holbrook, C14.

Holden. Aston on Trent. *Sable a fesse engrailed erminois between two chevrons ermine*; crest: *on a mount vert a moorcock rising sable winged or*; motto: *'Teneo et teneor'* (quartering Shuttleworth; FD (1929) I.957). Gr. under RL of 1791 to James Shuttleworth who assumed the surname and arms of Holden of Aston, with the remainder to his parents' heirs male. Later members of the family bore the meaningless (and less clever) motto: *'Holdene'* (e.g. bookplate of W.H. Holden, early C20). Previous to the grant the arms used had been: *sable a fesse between two chevrons ermine* (Lysons, lxxxvii.n.); crest: *a moorcock with a branch of heath in his bill* (V. 1662 –

respited for proof).

Holden. Darley Abbey. *Per pale sable and ermine a fesse between two chevrons all counterchanged*; crest: *a moorcock close sable semée of trefoils or*; motto: *'Holdene'* (Glover, II.351). Gr. 1853 to Robert Holden, son of Robert Holden of Darley Abbey, and kin to the above, whose unauthorised coat this family also used prior to this date. William, in the same year, assumed the additional surname and arms of Drury (qv) by RL, his son further assuming the surname and arms of Drury-Lowe (qv) in the same manner 1884.

Holland. Caldwell. Used arms but disclaimed 1662; they have not been identified.

Holland. Chesterfield; Dalbury; Dalbury Lees; Richmond Manor (Wirksworth). *Azure semée-de-lys and a lion rampant argent* (as quartered by Foljambe, V. 1569). Borne by Robert de Holland who was gr. Dalbury and Lees out of the Ferrers estates 1281, by Nicholas Holland of Lye (i.e Lees) and of Richmond Manor, 1433, and by Sir Thomas de Holland, also of Chesterfield, summoned to Parliament as a baron 1352. Anne, Duchess of Exeter, was the final Holland to hold all but Lees and the Wirksworth property, and bore *gules three lions passant guardant or a bordure azure semée-de-lys of the second* (Willement Roll); the duchy was cr. 1443. Her kinsman, Thomas Holland, cr. Earl of Kent 1376, bore *England and a bordure argent* (seal, 1371, Local MS 6341). The arms at the head of the entry were also used by the Hollands of Lea Hall, Glossop, *c.* 1500 (Rel. XII (1872) 95). Interestingly, Sir Thomas de Holland KG, Earl of Kent, bore *sable*; crest: *a plume of peacock's feathers proper*, from a desire to imitate the Black Knight of legend (British Library, Seal cxcvii.2).

Holland. Ford House (Stretton). *Argent semée-de-lys a lion rampant argent quartering barry bendy of eight gules and or*; crest: *a cubit arm erect proper issuant out of rays or and grasping a lion's gamb erased of the last* (seal in local collection). Used by Thomas Holland of Ford prior to 1729, and his son; the quartered coat is of Holland of Lincs.

Holles. Barlborough; Blackwell [Scarsdale]. *Sable on a bend argent between a talbot courant in chief and a dolphin embowed in base of the second three torteaux*; crest: *an arm embowed vested bendy of six argent and sable cuffed or holding in the hand proper a bunch of* *holly vert fructed gules* (Burke; Harl.MS 1093). Gr. 1539 when Sir William Holles became lord mayor of London. He purchased an estate at Barlborough, and was grandson of William, of Blackwell.

Holles. Bolsover Castle. *Ermine two piles in point sable*; crest: *on a chapeau a boar passant azure bristled hoofed and armed or*; supporters: *dexter a lion or sinister a tiger also or*; motto: *'Spes audaces adjuvat'* (V. Notts. 1614; supporters: Burke). John Holles, 4th Earl of Clare (cr. 1624; also Lord Houghton, 1616) inherited Bolsover from Cavendish and was in 1694 cr. Duke of Newcastle and Marquess of Clare, all extinct 1711. Glover (II.123) gives the tincture of the dexter supporter as *azure* and describes the sinister one as a *wolf*.

Hollins. Pleasley Vale. *Argent a chevron in chief two crosses formée fitchée and in base a cinquefoil azure*; crest: *a dexter hand couped at the wrist in the act of benediction azure issuant from a wreath of holly proper*; motto: *'Macte virtute'* (BLG (1969) II.241). Gr. C20 to Robert Hollins with remainder to the descendants of his father, Richard, of Pleasley Vale.

Holme. Derby. Crest: *a griffin's head and neck erased between two wings elevated* (on billhead *c.* 1891). Assumed by Ald. George Holme (1813–91), silk elastic manufacturer, from the arms of Holme of Up Holland House, Lancs., cadets of Hulme of Hulme, Lancs. Tinctures thus, head: *azure*; wings: *or* (Burke).

Holmes. Alfreton. *On a cross five mullets*; crest: a stag's head couped (Glover, 2nd ed., II.11). Used by Christopher son of Christopher Holmes of Alfreton d. 1779 (MI at Alfreton church).

Holt. Little Hallam (Ilkeston); Stanton by Dale. Arms used not known; 'an usurper', **V.** 1611.

Holy. Norton House (Norton). *Vert on a saltire between two annulets in pale and as many swans in fesse argent a cross crosslet gules*; crest: *an antelope's head couped holding in the mouth a branch of holly all proper*; motto: *'Suivez moi'* (FD (1910) 807). Authority unclear; ascribed to Thomas Beard Holy (1798–1867, formerly Hawley) of Norton House by Hunter (FMG II.705).

Hope. Burnaston; Derby; Grangefields (Trusley); Little Chester (Derby); Sutton on the Hill. *Argent a chevron engrailed sable between three Cornish choughs proper*; crest: *a* *Cornish chough rising proper* (Glover II.563; glass at St Alkmund's, Derby, transferred 1970, destroyed 1976). Mr Hope of Burnaston was 'an usurper', V. 1611; Capt. Charles Hope of Little Chester 'did not appear', V. 1662, and a note of 1687 adds that he 'died a beggar'. The family went on to municipal eminence and some members used the arms with a *plain chevron*, e.g., as painted by Bassano 1710 for the hatchment of Dr John Hope, impaling Bainbrigge (Local MS 3525). This was the family of Sir W.H. St John Hope.

Hopkinson. Bonsall; Wirksworth. *Azure on a chevron argent between three estoiles or as many lozenges gules all within a bordure of the third* (V. 1662). Some MSS show these arms as allowed to Henry Hopkinson of Bonsall, most declare them to be respited for proof, or not proved. On balance, one is inclined towards the latter.

Hopton. Hopton. *Gules crusilly fitchée and a lion rampant or* (as quartered by Rollesley and Kniveton of Mercaston, V. 1569). Known to have been borne by Sir Walter Hopton of Gloucs. C14 (presumably unrelated; MS Ashmole 804). Sleigh (*Rel.* V. (1865) 233; XII (1872) 95) gives further coats under the heading: *argent a chevron azure* (repeated by Thompson (II.19)), and *on two bars three mullets pierced an annulet for difference*, the latter recorded for a Robert de Hopton (no locale) early C14 (Jenyns' Ordinary). Nicholas de Rollesley marr. the heiress 1350.

Hopwell. Hopwell. *Argent three conies playing on the bagpipes gules* (as a quartering of Sacheverell, V. 1569, and on MI at Morley, cf. Cox, IV.233). Frequently assigned to FitzErcald, but this theory is untenable on several grounds: the FitzErcalds flourished too early (C12); the heiress marr. Longford, who did not quarter these arms; and they are plainly canting – the *conies* are *hopping well* to their own music. The Sacheverells inherited Hopwell C14 from Roger son of Roger de Hopwell, whose uncle, Henry, marr. Matilda, dau. of Richard Curzon of Breadsall: see Cox, IV.333n.

Hopwell Hall School. Hopwell. *Argent three conies playing on the pipes umbrated vert* (current letterhead). Arms used from 1987 by this Notts. C.C. school, based on those of Hopwell (qv).

Horne. Butterley Hall (Ripley). *Argent*

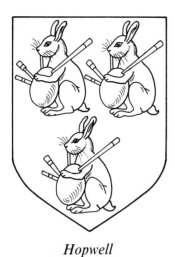

Hopwell

three buglehorns sable garnished or stringed gules each enclosing an estoile azure; crest: *a buglehorn enclosing an estoile azure* (Lysons, cxxiii). Used prior to 1784 without the *estoiles*, e.g. by William Horne of Butterley, described 1687 as 'another cole merchant ... tho' he was a poor collier's boy, yet now proud and ambitious and exalts his *horne* as high as any of his neighbours.' After the execution of William's son for incest and infanticide, the estate eventually passed to E.T. Warren (qv) who assumed the surname and arms of Horne by RSM 1784, when the heraldic situation was regularised.

Horpey: see Shepey.

Horsley. Alfreton; Horsleygate (Holmesfield). *Sable three cinquefoils or* (*Rel.* XII (1872) 95). Perhaps intended by Sleigh for the arms borne by Adam de Horsley of Horsleygate, 1388; the Willement Roll gives these arms with the *cinquefoils pierced argent* for a Robert de Horsley of the same period. Alternatively, the Horsleys, Alfreton industrialists flourishing C19, may have been intended.

Horton. Catton Hall. *Sable a buck's head caboshed argent attired or*; crest: *a demi-hart

salient argent attired or issuant from leaves vert* (V. 1569, and on MI at Croxall church: Cox, III.361). William, son of Roger, first of Catton (d. 1423), left a younger son John of Ilford (Ilminster), Somerset, whose posterity bore: *argent on a fesse azure between two wolves passant in chief and a crossbow in base gules three martlets or* (*DAJ* III (1881) pedigree facing p. 67). The heiress of Catton marr. Wilmot of Osmaston bt, and Sir Robert Wilmot, 2nd bt, assumed the additional surname and arms of Horton by RL 8 May 1823, the above arms acquiring *a canton ermine*. The shift of the btcy to a Wilmot cousin caused a further assumption of these arms and surname 1871, when the *canton* was omitted (J. Foster, *Baronetage* (1882), 664). The crest seems to have been acquired from the St Piers but V. 1662 gives: *A dolphin argent finned or pierced with a javelin or pointed of the first and standing on a wave also argent* (qv) which was the usual one used subsequently. See also Anson; Wilmot.

Hoskins. Bladon Castle and Newton Park (Newton Solney); *Per pale azure and gules a chevron between three lions rampant or*; crest: *a lion's head erased or incensed proper and crowned of the first* (M.J. Sayer, pers.comm.). Used by Abraham Hoskins of Newton Park, and usurped from Hoskyns of Llanwarne, Herefs., bt. Hoskins, a brewer, built Bladon Castle *c.* 1801.

Houghton. Long Eaton. *Or issuant from a barrulet wavy azure a stone bridge of three arches throughout proper in chief a rose gules barbed and slipped with two sprigs leaved proper charged with another rose argent seeded proper in base a barn owl statant also proper*; crest: *on a cap of maintenance a representation of the ruins of the church of St Thomas of Canterbury, Heptonstall, proper*; supporters: *on either side a badger proper gorged with a collar or charged with a barrulet wavy azure*; motto: *'Bear no base mind'* (Debrett, *Peerage* (1980), 616–17). Gr. 1974 to Arthur Houghton MP (b. 1898) on his elevation to a life barony as Lord Houghton of Sowerby, Yorks., which he represented in Parliament (Labour) from 1949. He was the son of John Houghton of Long Eaton of a family long associated with that place and with Stapleford, Notts.

Hounsfield. Brimington; Hackenthorpe Hall (Beighton). *Quarterly or and gules on the second and third quarters three plates*; crest: *in* *front of an oak tree a greyhound all proper*; motto: *'Fors et Fidelitas'* (Hunter, *Hallamshire*, Suppl. xlvi). Borne by Bartholomew Hounsfield of Brimington (d. 1680) and by James Hounsfield, *jure uxoris* of Hackenthorpe Hall from *c*. 1845, descended from the above via Bartholomew, of Rotherham, Yorks. (1704–52). The arms are, apparently, indexed at the College of Arms, and may pertain to the later medieval family of Holmesfield of Holmesfield. The crest is quite made up.

Howard. Derwent Hall; Glossop Hall; South Wingfield etc. *Gules on a bend between six cross crosslets fitchée argent an escutcheon thereon a demi-lion rampant pierced through the mouth by an arrow within a tressure flory counter flory of the first* (usually quartering FitzAlan (qv), England, *ancient* and de Warenne); crests: *on a chapeau a lion statant guardant tail extended or ducally crowned argent gorged with a label of three points of the last* ; and *issuant from a ducal coronet or a pair of wings gules each charged with a bend between six cross crosslets fitchée argent*; and *on a mount vert a horse passant argent holding in the mouth a slip of oak fructed proper*; supporters: *dexter a lion sinister a horse both argent the latter holding in the mouth a slip of oak fructed proper*; notto: *'Sola virtus invicta'* (BP (1956) 1134). Arms borne from C13, e.g. Sir William Howard, 1297 (Nobility Roll) and augmentation (*escutcheon on bend*) gr. 1 Feb. 1514 by letters patent to Thomas, 2nd Duke of Norfolk (cr. 1483) to mark his killing of the Scots' king at the battle of Flodden (Northumberland).

Howard. Glossop. Arms as above, but quartering *England, ancient and a label argent*, Warenne, and *gules a lion rampant·or* for FitzAlan; crests: as previous; supporters: as Duke of Norfolk, but *each charged with a crescent gules*; same motto. (FD (1929) I.676). Borne by Lord Edward FitzAlan-Howard (2nd son of 13th Duke of Norfolk), cr. Lord Howard of Glossop 1869. Title now merged with dukedom.

Howard (FitzAlan-Howard). Derwent Hall. Arms as previous; crest and supporters likewise, but each of the latter *charged on the shoulder with an escutcheon argent thereon a chief azure*; same motto (ibid.). Gr. by RL 9 June 1921 to Rt. Hon. Sir Edmund FitzAlan-Howard KG, PC, GCVO, DSO (3rd son of

14th Duke) on creation as Viscount FitzAlan of Derwent (ext. 1962). He had assumed the surname and arms of Talbot (qv) by RL 10 July 1876, but re-assumed those of FitzAlan-Howard 1921.

Howard. Cubley. *Gules on a bend indented argent between six crosses botonée fitchée or three escallops azure*; crest: *a lion's face or surmounted of a cross botonée fitchée gules between two wings of the last the dexter charged with a bend sinister indented the sinister with a bend also indented argent*; motto: *'Virtus sine metu'* (Local MS 9555.118, and inn sign at Cubley). Gr. late C19 to Robert Howard of Broughton Hall, Cheshire; the family had 2,344 acres in the county in 1883.

Howe. Edale. *Argent a fesse engrailed between three wolves' heads couped sable*; crest: *out of a ducal coronet a demi-wolf rampant sable* (Vincent's MS 154, College of Arms). Gr. to Roger Howe of London, merchant, *c*. 1634 a member of the family of Howe of Edale.

Hoyle. Holme Hall (Bakewell). *Ermine on a pale engrailed or between two pellets in fesse a pellet between two roses gules barbed and seeded proper*; crest: *an eagle's head erased sable charged with three plates in pale between two branches each bearing three roses gules stalked and leaved proper*; motto: *'Accedat Virtus Fidei'* (FD (1929) I.988). Gr. 11 June 1886 to Isaac Hoyle of Longsight, Lancs., whose elder son, E.L. Hoyle, was of Holme Hall between the two World Wars.

Huband. Long Eaton; Twyford. *Sable three leopards' faces jessant-de-lys argent*; crest: *a wolf passant or* (*Rel.* V (1865) 234). Ralph Huband, of Ipsley, Worcs., and Twyford marr. the heiress of Tevery of Long Eaton; he sold Twyford to Bristowe and their son John was cr. a bt 2 Feb. 1660 (ext. 1730).

Hubbersty (Cantrell-Hubbersty). Alvaston; Burbage Hall (Hartington Upper Quarter); Wirksworth. *Vert two bars engrailed between as many moles erect in chief and in base a griffin's head erased all or*; crest: *in front of a griffin's head erased argent charged with a fesse engrailed vert a mole fesseways or*; motto: *'Propositi tenax'* (FD (1905) 217). Gr. under RL of 1894 wherein Col. Albert Cantrell Hubbersty assumed the additional surname and arms of Cantrell (qv). Previously they had used: *vert a fesse or between three moles sable* (sic; *Rel.* XII (1872) 95). See also

Cantrell.

Huishe. Derby; Kirk Hallam; Smalley. *Argent on a bend sable three lucies of the field finned and tailed or*; crest: *an elephant's head couped argent crowned and tusked or* (arms: tea-cup from Smalley Hall; crest: livery button in local collection; cf. BLG (1875) II. Suppl. 44). As conf. 1589 to William Huysh of Doniford, Somerset, the crest was blazoned *an elephant's head couped azure bezantée crowned or* (V. Somerset 1623). The arms were borne as above by his descendant, Francis Darwin Huishe of Kirk Hallam Hall, and his uncle, John, of Smalley, both living 1875.

Humble-Burkitt. Stubbing Court (Wingerworth); Sutton Scarsdale; Walton House. *Argent on a chevron gules between three mullets pierced sable as many owls of the field in centre chief point a cross crosslet azure for difference* (Burkitt) *quartering sable a stag trippant and on a chief dovetailed argent a cross patée between two owls of the field* (Humble); crests: *a dexter arm embowed proper charged below the elbow with three bars or the hand grasping a club proper* (Burkitt) and *a morion proper thereon an owl's wings elevated sable* (Humble); motto: *'Decrevi'* (BLG (1937) 287). Gr. under RL of 1921 to Bernard Maynard Humble of Stubbing Court, whereby he assumed the additional surname and arms of Burkitt.

Hunloke. Egstow Hall (Tupton); Wingerworth. *Azure on a fesse between three tigers' heads erased or as many mullets of the field*; crest: *on a chapeau azure turned up ermine a cockatrice wings expanded proper combed beaked and wattled or* (V. 1611). Gr. 14 Dec. 1587 to Henry Hunloke of Wingerworth and London. His grandson, Henry Hunloke (1618–48) was on 28 Feb. 1643 cr. a bt, and the latter's son, Sir Henry had a grant of arms wherein the *mullets* were removed, 19 Dec. 1674, perhaps to distinguish his branch from that of some other kinsman. The crest probably reflects the association of the Curzons with Wingerworth prior to the Hunlokes. A further grant was made 14 June 1688. Title ext. 1856, when the representation of the family devolved on Capt. Hon. Frederick FitzClarence (son of George, 1st Earl of Munster) who adopted the surname and arms of Hunloke by RL 19 Dec. 1863. On his widow's death in 1904 her heir, Capt. Philip Perceval, did likewise.

Hunt. Ashover; Aston on Trent. *Argent a buglehorn sable stringed vert on a chief gules three mullets pierced of the field*; crest: *a buglehorn as in the arms* (Vv. 1569, 1611). Borne by Thomas Hunt of Aston 1569, grandson of John, of Ashover. In *Rel.* XII (1872) 95, Sleigh gives *roses or* on the chief in lieu of *mullets*: perhaps the arms as borne by Stevenson Hunt of Somersall near Chesterfield, *c.* 1500.

Le Hunte. Ashbourne; Derby. *Azure a bend between six leopards' faces or on a canton of the first a gauntlet of the second*; crest: *on a mount vert a goat sable collared horned and unguled argent*; motto: *'Deus mihi providebit'* (V. Rutland 1618). Gr. quarterly with Bainbrigge and Parker by RL 1833 to Peter Bainbrigge who thereupon assumed the additional surname of Le Hunte. He was heir of Revd John Le Hunte of Derby, rector of Radbourne. Arms previously used as above but without the *canton*.

Hunter. Kilburn Hall. *Three greyhounds courant two and one on a chief as many buglehorns*; crest: *a greyhound's head couped*; motto: *'Spero dum Spiro'* (MI at Kilburn church). Used or borne by William Hunter of Kilburn (d. 1757) of a family seated there from *c.* 1678 by virtue of marriage with the heiress of Grace (FMG I.224). The arms exactly match those of Hunter of Croyland, Lincs., cadets of those of Hunterston, Ayrshire, and the possibility exists of a genuine descent. If so, the tinctures would restore as: field *vert*; greyhounds, chief and crest *argent*; buglehorns *sable stringed gules* (Burke).

Hurd. Stydd Hall (Yeaveley). *Argent on a chief or a bird sable* (sic; as quartered by Brooks, at All Saints', Derby, Cox & Hope 147). Used by Christopher Hurd of London, Ashbourne and Stydd Hall C18, whose heiress marr. C18 Thomas Brooks of Derby. His ancestor in 1687, a 'person for a grant' (which he seems never to have taken), was described as 'a rich, proud clowne'.

Hurt. Alderwasley; Ashbourne; Kniveton; Wirksworth. *Sable a fesse between three cinquefoils or*; crest: *a hart passant proper attired or hurt in the haunch with an arrow of the second feathered argent*; motto: *'Mane predam vesperi spolium'* (Vv. 1569; 1611; Staffs. 1663). Arms conf. and crest gr. 4 Sept. 1565 to Thomas Hurt of Ashbourne. A possible cadet of the family was Jonathan Hurt of Sheffield,

Yorks., who marr. the heiress of Sitwell (qv); he assumed the Sitwell surname and arms by RL 1777. James Thomas Hurt of Wirksworth assumed the surname and arms of Edge of Strelley, Notts., 1848 and another scion of the family assumed the surname and arms of Wolley of Allenhill (Matlock) by RL 1827. The present seat of the family is Castern Hall, Staffs. See also Conway; Edge; Sitwell; Wolley.

Hussey. Kedleston; Long Eaton. *Or on a fesse sable a lion passant argent* (Burke). Borne by the Husseys of Long Eaton, *c.* 1430, most of whose property was in Notts., to which county Burke ascribes the arms; Sir Hugh Hussey held a moiety of Kedleston in 1411.

Hutchinson. Carsington; Derby. *Per pale gules and azure a lion rampant argent between eight cross crosslets or* (*Rel.* V (1865) 95). Used by Edward Hutchinson of Carsington and his sons Philip and John, 1712. Their nephew, Sir Francis, of Castle Sallagh, Co. Wicklow, was on 11 Dec. 1782 made a bt of Ireland with remainder to the issue of his brother and to the issue male of his nephew Samuel Synge, being gr. arms: (UO) *per pale azure and gules a lion rampant ermine between nine cross crosslets or*; crest: *out of a ducal coronet a cockatrice all proper*; mottoes: *'Non sibi sed toti'* and *'Coelestria canimus'* (J. Foster *Baronetage* (1882), 604); ext. 3 Nov. 1906. Note that Revd Dr Michael Hutchinson, the rebuilder of All Saints', Derby, used (or bore): *per pale azure and gules a lion rampant argent between nine cross crosslets or,* impaling Whitehall (qv; on MI at Packington, Leics., 1730).

Hutton. Derby. *Argent on a fesse sable three stags' heads caboshed or*; crest: *a ducal coronet or pierced with three broad arrows two in saltire one in pale* (*Rel.* XII (1872) 95). Attributed by Llewellyn Jewitt to William Hutton, the Derby historian (1723–1815); they are the arms of Hutton of Yorkshire and Cumberland (cf. Jewitt (1872), 6; the historian, although born in Derby of poor parents, claimed descent from the latter family).

Hyde. Long Lee Hall (Hayfield). *Azure a chevron between three lozenges or*; crest: *a raven volant sable (Gents. Mag.* (1764) ii.221). Gr. to John and Edward Hyde of London, brothers, sons of Edward son of Edward son of Jenkin son of Robert, of Norbury, Chesh-ire, 2 Apr. 1571. The *Gents. Mag.* comments: 'Robert Hide of Norbury Co. Chester the common ancestor of the Earls of Clarendon and Hyde of Long Lee'. As there were Hydes at Long Lee as early as Robert, 1415, this seems an unlikely statement. Tilley gives, no authority stated, *azure a saltire or between four bezants a chief ermine*; crest: *a nag's head couped argent* (cf. V. London 1634).

Ible: see Shirley; Snitterton.

Ilkeston Borough Council. *Argent on a saltire sable between in pale two cotton hanks in fesse as many dexter gauntlets all proper the astronomical symbol of Mars on a chief azure a piece of Maltese lace of the field*; crest: *a bear's head holding in the mouth a miner's lamp proper and charged on the neck with the astronomical symbol of Mars sable*; motto: *'Labor omnia vincit'* (Scott-Giles, 99). Gr. 24 Aug. 1887; the borough was absorbed in Erewash DC 1974.

Ince. Spinkhill (Eckington). *Argent three torteaux in bend between two cotises sable* (*Rel.* V (1865) 95). Arms of Ince of Ince Blundell, Lancs., borne or used by Richard Ince of Spinkhill, which he inherited from John de Spinkhill, 1462.

Inglefield. Parwich Hall; Windley Hall. *Barry gules and argent on a pile azure a naval crown and on a chief or a lion passant guardant of the third*; crest: *out of a naval crown or a double headed eagle displayed per pale gules and azure on the breast a representation of the Inglefield anchor behind the eagle's heads a sun in splendour or*; motto: *'The sun my compass'* (arms: BLG (1875) I.409; crest and motto on livery button in local collection). Apparently granted to Rear-Adm. S.H. Inglefield CB (1783–1848) *c.* 1829, but as shown in BLG (1952) 1343 for his descendant J.F. Crompton-Inglefield (surname by deed poll, 1930) and his brother, of Holbrook, they are: *gules three bars argent on a chief arched or a lion passant guardant or*; crest: *issuant from a naval crown or a double eagle displayed per pale gules and azure*; same motto, which looks like a later grant.

Ingleby. Bakewell. *Sable an estoile of six points argent*; crest: *A boar's head couped erect proper tusked or* motto: *'Non immemor beneficii'* (BLG (1898) I.792). Used by Thomas son of Richard Ingleby of Bakewell and his descendants, the Inglebys of Sedgeford Hall, Norfolk.

Ingleby. Weston on Trent. *Sable an estoile gules* (sic; on an MI at Weston church, V. 1611 (Harl.MS 1093)). Used by a family of this name living C16–17 in the Weston area.

Ingram. Darley; Walton. *Ermine on a fesse gules three escallops argent*; crest: *a cock or* (seal, Local MS 6341). Borne by Sir Arthur Ingram, who purchased Walton Hall 1633. See also Meynell.

Ingwardby. Willesley. *Or on a chief gules a lion passant argent* (Lysons, cvi). Borne by William Ingwardby of Willesley, *c.* 1410; heiress marr. Abney.

Inkersall. Brampton; Chesterfield; Duckmanton. *Gules a fesse dancettée ermine between six trefoils slipped or*; crest: *a griffin's head gules gorged with a fesse dancettée ermine between two wings displayed or* (College of Arms, C.28). Recorded as arms of Inkersall of Herts. and Middlesex, a family believed to have been descended from Roger de Inkersall of Duckmanton, 1311.

Inman. Chesterfield. *Vert on a chevron or three roses proper*; crest: *a wyvern wings elevated vert ducally gorged and chained or* (arms borne in pretence by Ray, MI formerly in Heanor church; crest: Burke). Used by John Inman of Chesterfield, *c.* 1800; heiress married John Ray.

Innes-Smith. Derby; Totley; Wirksworth. *Azure a burning cup or between in chief two chess rooks and on a chief argent three mullets of the field*; crest: *an arm embowed vested in red Innes tartan cuffed argent the hand proper grasping a key ward to the sinister and hanging downwards or*; motto: *'Stet fortuna nostra'* (pers.comm.). Gr. (LO) 14 Nov. 1977 to Robert Stuart Innes-Smith, formerly of The Old Manse, Wirksworth, as descendant of Sir James Innes, 12th of that Ilk, and the Smyths of Braco, Perthshire. His grandfather was of Totley (BLG III (1972) 836). See also Rose-Innes.

De Insula: see Ireland; L'Isle; Vernon.

Ireland. Hartshorne; Yeldersley. *Gules six fleurs-de-lys argent* (V. 1634 as quartering of Foljambe; Ballard's Book). Borne by John de Ireland, *c.* 1475, of Yeldersley and, if the Foljambe quartering is correct, by Sir Thomas de Ireland of Hartshorne *c.* 1300, whose dau. and heiress, Avena (by Avena dau. of Payn Villiers of Newbold, Notts.), marr. Sir God-frey Foljambe of Tideswell. Avena, if the foregoing is tenable, can only have been the heiress of a moiety of Hartshorne, for John de Ireland was holding Nether Hall there under the Earl of Shrewsbury *c.* 1500. Also borne or used by Tobias Ireland of Marston Montgomery, gent., *c.* 1631–50, claiming descent from the Irelands of Yeldersley. See also Monjoye.

Ireton. Little Ireton (Weston Underwood). *Ermine two bendlets gules*; crest: *a squirrel sejant cracking a nut proper*; motto: *'Fay ce que doy advienne que pourra'* (Vv. 1569, 1611). Allowed to William Ireton of Attenborough, Notts., and Little Ireton 1611; some MSS omit the *nut* in the crest. Motto often abridged to the first four words given above. Sir John Ireton, his descendant, and brother of Gen. Henry Ireton, was Lord Mayor of London 1658 and Burke gives his arms as *argent two bendlets gules*. Local MS 6341 (under Eyrton) gives the arms incorrectly as: *argent a fesse and in chief three lozenges gules*; Local MS 6341.4v has *argent on a bend sable three martlets or*, also an error and given correctly elsewhere in the MS.

Ironville, Codnor Park & Swanwick Church of England Primary School. *Sable on a chevron argent between in chief two garbs or and in base as many bars wavy of the second and azure a unicorn's head between four coalpicks in saltire or on a chief also of the second an open book proper all impaling the Bishopric of Southwell (qv). On a Reward of Merit medalet issued jointly in 1908; example in Derby Museum. No authority.*

Jackson. Brampton; Bubnell; Hassop. *Argent a lion passant and on a chief gules three battleaxes of the field*; crest: *a dexter arm in armour holding a battleaxe all proper* (V. Staffs. 1663). John Jackson of Bubnell Hall was respited for proof V. 1662, but his kinsmen, who were of Stanshope, Staffs. since *c.* 1475, were allowed arms then. However, the crest of the Stanshope branch was: *a dexter arm in armour holding a sword in bend sinister proper* (ibid.).

Jackson. Clay Cross; Stubben Edge (Ashover); Tupton. *Azure a fesse between two goats' heads couped in chief and a fleur-de-lys in base all between two flaunches argent*; crest: *on a ragged staff sable a goat's head couped argent semée of trefoils vert*; motto: *'Fortiter,* *fideliter, feliciter'* (BP (1970) 1435). Gr. 1869 to Sir William Jackson of Birkenhead, cr. a bt 4 Nov. that year, and borne by Brig. G.M. Jackson of Clay Cross and Stubben Edge.

Jackson. Sapperton (Church Broughton). *Or a chevron indented gules between three eagles' heads erased sable*; crest: *two lions' gambs erased or holding a double-headed eagle argent* (D369). Entered without explanation other than they were 'out of Yorkshire'. The arms undoubtedly refer to Robert Jackson of Sapperton (1526–1614). Burke ascribes the same arms to John Jackson of Harraton, Durham, a Royalist colonel.

Jacson. Ashbourne; Derby; Shallcross Hall (Fernilee). *Gules a fesse between three sheldrakes argent*; crest: *a sheldrake rising proper* (BLG (1875) I.694). Arms confirmed and crest granted c. 1536 to George or Roger Jacson of Ashbourne and Notts., and borne by Roger, of Derby, MP, who marr. the heiress of the Shalcross family of Shallcross. A confirmation was obtained by FitzHerbert Jacson of Newton, near Macclesfield, Cheshire, 1856, when he assumed the surname and quartered the arms of Widdington by RL.

Jardine. Oaker End (Wensley & Snitterton). *Argent a saltire couped and in chief three mullets pierced gules*; crest: *three mullets as in the arms each pierced by an arrow palewise and feathered vert*; motto: *'Faciam hercle sedulo'* (BP (1956) 1183). Gr. 8 March 1920 to Sir Ernest Jardine, cr. a bt 22 May 1919, and borne by his son, Sir John, of Oaker End.

Jebb. Walton Lodge. *Quarterly vert and or in the first quarter a falcon close argent belled of the second and in the fourth quarter a hawk's lure of the third*; crest: *on a hawk's lure lying fesseways argent a falcon rising wings expanded argent*; motto: *'Spe et labore'* (Lysons, lxxxviii). Gr. 20 Dec. 1728 to Samuel Jebb of Stratford-by-Bow, Essex, and Mansfield, Notts., whose father, Avery, was of Chesterfield. Dr Richard Jebb was cr. a bt 4 Sept. 1778 (ext. 1787). Sir Gladwyn Jebb was in 1960 cr. Lord Gladwyn of Bramfield, Suffolk, and was gr. supporters: *dexter a brown bear proper sinister a unicorn argent armed maned tufted unguled and charged on the shoulder with a cross patriarchal botonée or* (BP (1970) 1100).

Jelf. Offcote Hurst. *Per chevron engrailed azure and ermine in chief a plate between two doves argent and in base three cinquefoils*

gules; crest: *a stork wings elevated argent beaked and legged gules charged on the breast with a cross patée of the second resting the dexter claw on a fleur-de-lys or in its beak a trefoil slipped vert*; motto: *'Per fidem tutus'* (MI at Ashbourne church). Gr. to Jelf of Glos., 1809, and borne by Maj.Gen. Richard Jelf (1844–1913) of Offcote Hurst.

Jenkinson. Walton Hall. *Azure two barrulets or in chief three suns in splendour proper*; crest: *a sea horse's head couped azure finned and gorged with two barrulets or* (Lysons, lxxiv). Gr. 14 Apr. 1687 to Sir Paul Jenkinson of Walton, cr. a bt 17 Dec. 1685, ext. 1739.

Jenney. Calke Abbey; Ticknall Priory. *Ermine a bend gules cotised or*; crest: *on a glove in fesse argent a falcon close or belled of the last* (BLG (1937) 1246). Gr. (but with *cotises sable*) to Sir Robert Jenney of Knodishall, Suffolk, between 1604 and 1633 and borne (according to Burke (qv) but inaccurately) by Arthur William Jenney who married the ultimate heiress of the Harpur-Crewes of Calke. His sons successively assumed the surname and arms of that family (qv). Sleigh (*Rel.* V (1865) 233) gives the arms differently: *ermine a bend cotised gules*; crest: *on a glove fesseways argent a hawk proper belled or*; motto: *'Deus providebit'*, assigning them to 'Gyney of Frisby Hall, Co. Derby'.

Jervis. Quarndon Hall. *Sable a chevron ermine between three martlets or*; crest: *out of a naval crown or encircled by an oak wreath proper a demi pegasus argent wings azure thereon a fleur-de-lys or*; motto: *'Thus'* (BP (1970) 2362). Gr. by RL to 2nd Viscount St Vincent 7 May 1823, when he assumed the surname and arms of Jervis (allowed V. Staffs. 1664) in lieu of Ricketts, all under a special remainder when the viscountcy was cr. 27 April 1801 for Earl St Vincent (cr. 23 June 1797, ext. 1823). Borne by Hon. W.M. Jervis of Quarndon Hall (1827–1909), who was allowed the style of a younger son of viscount by RL May 1860.

Jessop. Derby; North Lees (Outseats). *Barry of six argent and azure nine mullets gules three, three, three*; crest: *a turtle dove standing on an olive branch proper* (V. Yorks. 1575). Gr. 13 July 1575 to Richard Jessop of Broom Hall (Sheffield), Yorks. (d. 1580), whose son, William, was of Norton Lees. The grant seems not to have included the crest, which Sleigh (*Rel.* XII (1872) 95) gives with the *olive branch in the dove's mouth*. A descendant, William, marr. the heiress of James D'Arcy of Sedbury Park (Richmond), Yorks., cr. 1721 (I) Lord D'Arcy of Navan, Co. Meath, with remainder to their issue male; ext. 1733. 2nd Lord D'Arcy bore the above arms quartering D'Arcy with their crest (qv). Supporters: *dexter a tiger argent armed gules sinister a bull sable hoofed maned and tufted or*; motto: *'Un Dieu, un roi'* (Clay, 45–50). Francis Jessopp of Derby (mayor 1840) sealed with the arms of Jessop of Broom Hall.

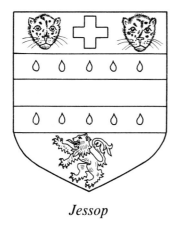

Jessop

Jessop. Butterley Hall (Ripley); East Lodge (Doveridge); Overton Hall (Ashover). *Or two bars gules goutée of the field in chief a cross couped of the second between two leopards' faces and in base a lion rampant sable*; crest: *a cockatrice's head couped proper combed beaked and wattled gules thereon two barrulets argent holding in the beak a trefoil slipped vert all between two wings of the first on each a cross couped of the third*; motto: *'Pax et amor'* (FD (1929) II.1055). Gr. to William de Burgh Jessop (1852–94). Previously the family had used *or two bars and in chief three leopards'*

faces gules; crest: *a cockatrice's head erased purpure combed gules winged proper* (Burke), the arms of Jessop of Doory Hall (Ballymahon), Co. Longford, Ireland (who bore the crest as Jessop of North Lees, qv (UO)), from whom William Jessop claimed descent.

Jewitt. Derby; Winster Hall. *Azure a three masted galley sails furled or flags at mast heads gules* (*Rel.* V. (1865) 234). Used by Llewellyn Jewitt (1816–86), the antiquary.

Jodrell. Duffield etc. *Ermines three round buckles tongues pendent argent in fesse point a trefoil slipped or*; crest: *a demi-cock wings erect or combed and wattled issuant out of a wreath of roses all gules seeded of the first*; motto: *'Non sibi sed patriae natus'* (J. Foster, *Baronetage* (1882), 345). Gr. 10 July 1707 to Paul Jodrell of Duffield (also of Staffs. and Cheshire, claiming to be a cadet of those of Yeardsley). In 1817 a descendant inherited under a remainder the btcy of Lombe of Sall Park, Norfolk (cr. 22 Jan 1784), ext. 1929. Thomas Jodrell of The Moor House (Congleton), Staffs., a kinsman of the grantee, was allowed arms as above, but with a *canton or* instead of the *trefoil*, V. Staffs. 1663.

Jodrell. Shallcross Hall (Fernilee); Yeardsley Hall (Whaley Bridge). *Sable three round buckles argent*; crest: *a cock's head and neck couped or wings elevated argent combed and jelloped gules*; motto: *'Vigilando'* (V. Cheshire 1612). Regrants under RL have been frequent since the male line of the family failed C18: surname and arms of Jodrell from Bower, 5 Apr. 1775; added to Philipps, 1868; added to Cotton 1890; and to Marsden, 15 Mar. 1920. On the final occasion, the *centre point* of the shield and the *neck* of the crest were *charged with a cross crosslet or* and *sable* respectively.

Johnson. Allestree Hall; Ambergate (Heage); Farnah Hall (Windley); Foston. *Or three pheons in fesse within two flaunches azure on each a like pheon of the field*; crest: *in front of a dexter arm embowed in armour proper the hand grasping a javelin in bend sinister pheoned or and enfiled with a chaplet of roses gules two branches of oak in saltire vert*; motto: *'Virtus patienta veritas'* (FD (1910) 884). Gr. C20 to Herbert Alfred Johnson (1866–1923), wire manufacturer.

Johnson. Ashford. *Or a water bouget sable on a chief gules three annulets of the first gemmed sapphire*; crest: *issuant out of a crown vallary gules two wings elevated and addorsed* *or*; motto: *'Onus sub honore'* (BLG (1952) 1388). Borne by W.H. Johnson of Ashford 1985, and granted to Walter Johnson of Arncliffe Hall (Ingleby Arncliffe), Yorks. (d. 1915).

Johnson. Aston on Trent. *Argent two chevronels between as many griffins' heads erased in chief and a palmer's scrip in base gules*; crest: *a griffin's head erased per fesse argent and gules holding in the beak a palmer's scrip of the last* (Burke). Borne by Nathaniel Palmer Johnson of Aston mid-C19; his heir George Lillingston of Aston and Burleigh Field (Loughborough), Leics., assumed the surname and arms of Johnson by RL 1859.

Johnson. Horsley; Kilburn. *Azure a woolpack argent* (Harl.MS 1537; Egerton MS 996). William Johnson of Kilburn, who used these arms, 'promised to come to London' at V. 1611, but seems never to have done so. Arms also used (although the tinctures are unclear) by Joseph Johnson of Duffield, 1761 (descended out of Callow), and his posterity at Coxbench (*Rel.* V (1865) 234).

Jolley (Joliffe). Cartledge Grange (Holmesfield); Elton. *Argent on a pile vert three dexter hands couped of the field*; crest: *a cubit arm habited vert charged with a pile argent holding in the hand proper a sword of the second hilt and pommel or* (ascribed to Jolley of Cartledge by Tilley (III.272), to Jolley of Elton by G. King (*Staffs. Peds.*, 144)). Gr. 27 Aug. 1614 to William Jollye of Leek, Staffs., and to 'all the descendants of John his grandfather'. Borne by Hylton Joliffe MP (1773–1843) who inherited a moiety of Elton (from Stevenson via Holden) from his grandfather John. His nephew was cr. a bt 20 Aug. 1821 and raised to the peerage as Lord Hylton 19 July 1866, receiving a grant of supporters: *on either side a lion guardant azure each charged on the shoulder with three annulets two and one or*; motto: *'Tant que je puis'* (BP (1956) 1156). The entitlement of the C16–17 Jolleys of Cartledge Grange to bear these arms is dubious.

Jones. Bowerhill (Repton). *Argent a cross indented gules between four spear heads azure each between two laurel branches proper*; crest: *in front of a spear between two laurel branches proper a cross patée gules*; motto: *'Esto fidelis usque ad mortem'* (Burke). Gr. 1871 to Hanry Cadman Jones of Bower Hill, Repton.

Joyce. Thorntree House (Bretby). *Barry of four ermine and gules on a bend between two*

leopards' faces or three water bougets sable*; crest: *in front of a lion rampant proper collared nebulée with a chain reflexed over the back or three water bougets fesseways sable*; motto: *'Nec temere nec timide'* (BLG (1952) 1405). Gr. 1901 to William Joyce of Ashby de la Zouch, Leics., and to the descendants of his father John (1803–79). Borne by Francis Joyce of Newhall, 1952.

Kay. Ashover. *Per pale gules and or two bendlets dovetailed between a key ward upwards and to the dexter in chief and a mascle in base all counterchanged*; crest: *an eagle's head argent erased gules holding in the beak a key in bend ward downwards azure with a chain in arch or*; motto: *'Clavis felicitatis labor'* (FD (1910) 902). An early C20 grant to Thomas Kay (mayor of Stockport, Cheshire, 1912) who had a home and estate at Ashover for some forty years from *c.* 1895.

Kaye: see Lister-Kaye.

Kelly. Somersal Herbert Grange. *Azure a tower triple towered supported on either side by a lion rampant argent chained or*; crest: *an enfield passant vert*; motto: *'Turris fortis mihi Deus'* (Burke, IFR 917; BLG (1972) III.501). Conf. (UO) 22 Jan. 1757 and borne by Dermot Lindsay Patrick Kelly of Somersal Grange, who was MFH of the Meynell Hunt in the 1970s.

Kendal. Darley. *Argent a bend vert* (as a quartering of Rooper of Abbot's Ripton, FD (1929) II.1678). No ancient authority for these arms appears to be forthcoming, and the quartering may well have been employed without specific authority by the descendants of the Ropers (qv).

Kendall. Smisby. *Gules a fesse chequy or and azure between three eagles displayed of the second* (Vv. 1569, 1611; 1662; Warw. 1619; FD (1929) II.1086). Exemplified 22 Aug. 1443 to John Kendall of Shepshed, Leics., whose grandson Bartholomew was first of Smisby. His brother, of Twycross, Leics., seems to have borne, by inheritance, *argent a fesse gules between in chief a fleur-de-lys between two cross crosslets fitchée sable and in base three ermine spots* (Cox, III.456; see also Fitzherbert).

Kenning. Clay Cross; Great Longstone Hall; Eastwood Grange and Stubben Edge (Ashover). *Azure on a fesse between two escallops argent as many winged wheels gules*;

crest: *between two escallops argent a cubit arm holding a propellor proper* motto: *'Work and pray'* (*Register of the Imperial Society of Knights Bachelor, 1939–46,* 216). Gr. 1944 to Sir George Kenning, who was knighted 9 Feb. that year.

Kenyon. Coxbench Hall; Holbrook. *Sable a chevron engrailed or between three crosses flory argent*; crest: *a lion sejant proper resting the dexter paw on a cross flory argent*; motto: *'Magnanimiter Crucem sustine'* (BP (1970) 475). Gr. 1656 to Roger Kenyon of Peel Hall (Little Hulton), Lancs., and borne by Hon. Edward Kenyon (2nd son of George, 2nd Lord Kenyon, cr. 1788) of Coxbench and Holbrook from *c.* 1846.

Kerr. Melbourne Hall; Over Haddon. *Azure a sun in splendour or,* for Lothian, quartering *gules on a chevron argent three mullets of the field,* for Kerr; crests: *a sun in splendour or,* for Lothian and a *stag's head erased proper* for Kerr; supporters: *dexter an angel proper habited per fesse vert and gules hair fair winged and with an astral crown or sinister a unicorn argent armed maned tufted and unguled or,* mottoes: *'Sero sed serio'* and *'Forward in the Name of God'* (BP (1970) 1652). Borne without supporters by Lord Walter Talbot Kerr, who inherited Melbourne Hall 1905, and matriculated his arms (LO) 10 Mar. 1913, grandfather of the present (12th) Marquis of Lothian (creations: Marquis 1701; Earl 1606; Earl of Ancram 1633; Lord Jedburgh 1622; Lord Newbottle 1591 (all Scotland) and Lord Ker of Kersheugh (UK) 1821).

Kevelioc: see Chester, Earls of.

Keys. Hopwell Hall; Horsley; Kilburn Hall. *Gules a chevron ermine between three leopards' heads or*; crest: *a griffin's head between two wings proper* (Local MS 9555). Used, apparently, by Henry Keys or Kayes of Hopwell, who sold up in 1731.

Killamarsh. Killamarsh. *Per fesse argent and sable a lion rampant counterchanged* (*Rel.* XII (1872) 95). Also recorded in glass at Willesley church (Cox, III.521), which arouses the suspicion that Sleigh mis-attributed them. The family are well-attested at Killamarsh for over 200 years to 1511.

Kinardsley. Alsop en le Dale; Brailsford; Derby; Lea; Sutton Scarsdale. *Argent a fesse vairé or and gules between three eagles displayed of the last*; crest: *on a mount vert a*

greyhound sejant argent collared or under a holly tree proper fructed gules (Vv. 1569, 1611). The Ferrers fesse may derive from the acquisition of Loxley, Staffs., by this family from a branch of Ferrers c13. Any change in arms was not universal within the family, however, for the senior (Loxley, Staffs.) line bore, nevertheless, *azure crusilly and a lion rampant argent* (with crest as above) as impaled by Bradshaw at Mugginton church V. 1611 (Local MS 6341). Of the senior line of the family (which the Brailsford branch recorded V. 1611 were not), Thomas Sneyd-Kynnersley of Loxley and Sutton Hall (Sutton Scarsdale) was granted the *lion rampant* version quartering his paternal arms of Sneyd in 1815; he had a house in St Peter's parish, Derby.

Kinder. Brampton; Great Hayfield. *Or on a fesse between three bells gules clappers sable as many cross crosslets of the field* (on c17 portrait). The above are the arms of Oxspring (the heiress of which family married John Kinder of Doncaster, Yorks., *c.* 1490) used by Philip Kinder, the antiquary (1597–1656). Most of his close kin used: *gules a chevron between ten crosses patée argent* (*Rel.* XV (1875) 167, 253), but his nephew William, son of Robert, of Cotgrave, Notts., was gr. 10 Feb. 1615 *Or a column gules between three Cornish choughs proper*; crest: *on a column or a Cornish chough sable beaked and legged gules* (Local MS 8022). Godfrey Kinder of Brampton was labelled a usurper V. 1611.

Kingdon. Ednaston Lodge. *Argent a chevron sable between three magpies proper* quartering *sable three crescents or for* Boughton; crest: *a double-headed eagle displayed sable*; motto: *'Regis donum gratum bonum'* (Burke). Clement Boughton Kingdon, a Cornishman, of Ednaston Lodge 1873, bore these arms.

Kingsmead Priory (St Mary de Pratis), Derby. *Barry of six or and azure on a bend argent three escallops gules* (Williamson's Notes, Director's Room, Derby Museum). This attribution should be treated with caution, not only because no local corroboration has been forthcoming but also because these appear to be the arms of Sir Walter Kingsmead of Salop., *c.* 1315 (Parliament Roll).

Kingston (Kingesson). Chesterfield. *Azure three swords fesseways in pale argent* (*Rel.* XII (1872) 95). Swords given as *or* in Burke; arms attributed by Sleigh to William, Roger and

Henry Kingston of Chesterfield, 1430–1598, of whom the former appears on the 'list of Derbyshire Gentlemen' of 1433 (T. Fuller, *The History of the Worthies of England* (1811 ed.), I.407).

Kirby. Doveridge Old Hall. *Argent two bars gemelles indented and on a canton gules a greyhound's head couped of the field collared or*; crest: *a greyhound's head couped argent gorged with a chaplet of roses proper* (Tilley, II.312). Gr. to Thomas Kirby of Lutterworth, Leics., 23 Aug. 1729, who was also tenant of Doveridge Old Hall in the earlier C18. Sleigh (*Rel.* XII (1872) 95) erroneously enters these arms under Kirkeby.

Kirke: see Kyrke.

Kirkeby. Derby. *Argent on a fesse vert three crescents or* (*Rel.* XII (1872) 95). Borne or used by Edward Kirkeby of Irongate, Derby, 1675.

Kirkeby: see Kirby.

Kitchin: see Kytchyn.

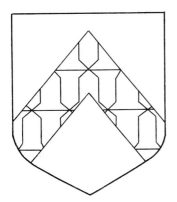

Kniveton

Kniveton. Bradley; Kniveton; Mercaston etc. *Gules a chevron vairé argent and sable*; crest: *a demi-eagle issuant or wings expanded sable*; motto: *'In Domino confido'* (Vv. 1569, 1611). Eventually borne by both main bran-ches of this most complex family. The arms developed through several stages after this family of former Ferrers sub-tenants did so well out of their overlord's ruin, and display obvious affinities with the Ferrers' arms. Local MS 6341 gives examples of arms and arms on seals: Matthew de Kniveton of Bradley, late C13: *gules a bend vairé argent and sable* (in glass at Norbury Manor of medieval date, however, *gules a bend vairé sable and or*); *gules a chevron vairé between three knives erect* was borne by his son, Sir Henry; this Sir Henry's grandson bore: *gules a bend vairé (or vair) between six crosses patée*, 1331; and his son John was the first to bear arms as at the head of this entry. Nicholas Kniveton, bore similar arms but the chevron *between three mullets* 1375: he was of the Mercaston branch, and his descendant, Sir Nicholas, 1490, bore for crest: *a fox* (surely, though, *a tiger?*) looking at its own reflection in a mirror proper (brass at Mugginton church). His descendant, Sir William, of Mercaston, was cr. a bt 29 June 1611; title ext. 1706.

Kniveton. Mugginton. *gules goutée d'or a chevron vairé argent and sable between two eagles' heads couped in pale of the second*; crest: *an eagle's head couped or goutée-de-sang holding in the beak an eagle's gamb erased proper between two wings vairé argent and sable*; motto: *'In Domino confido'* (BLG (1937 1307). Gr. 1895 to Maj. Reginald Knyfton, formerly Graves, of Uphill Castle, Somerset, who assumed the surname and arms of Knyfton in lieu of his own by RL. Previously, the ancestors of Thomas Tutton Knyfton (d. 1887), whose heir he was, had borne Kniveton (as previous entry) with due difference.

Kniveton. Youlgreave. *Gules a bend vairé argent and sable*; crest: *out of a ducal coronet or a griffin's head gules beaked of the first* (Vv. 1569, 1611, quartering Rossington and Statham. Arms known from a seal of 1405 (Local MS 6341)). John son of William de Kniveton inherited an estate at Youlgreave from Robert Gilbert, which surname his posterity used in lieu of, and occasionally with, their own. Thereafter, following marriage with the heiress of Rossington of Youlgreave, the Rossington arms were sometimes used alone as well (MI at Youlgreave). Sleigh (*Rel.* XII (1872) 95) inexplicably enters the name as 'Geynes'.

Knowles. Ednaston Lodge. *Gules on a chev-*

ron cotised between in chief two crescents and in base a cross crosslet argent three roses of the field; crest: in front of a ram's head couped argent armed or three roses gules; motto: 'Nec Diu nec Frustra' (FD (1910) 933). Gr. to Andrew Knowles of Swinton Old Hall 1889, whose son Robert settled at Ednaston, where his family remained, despite having subsequently sold Ednaston Lodge.

Kynnersley: see Kinardsley.

Kyrke. Greenhill Hall (Norton); Whitehough Hall (Chapel en le Frith). Per fesse or and gules a lozenge counterchanged on a canton azure a lion rampant of the first supporting a cutlass argent; crest: an arm armed proper purfled or holding a cutlass hilted of the last (DAJ XXXI (1909) 26). On 1 Dec. 1631 the arms were conf., crest and an augmentation of honour gr. to Capt. Sir David Kyrke and to 'his brothers Capt. Lewis (governor of a fort in Canada capt. from the French), Vice Admiral Thomas, John and James land lubbers by sea and land'. The augmentation consisted of the canton which alluded to the arms of the French Admiral de Rougemont whom Sir David defeated at sea. Presumably the brothers' ancestors, of Norton and Whitehough, were deemed to have borne the arms without the canton.

Kyrke. Eaves Hall, Martinside (Chapel en le Frith); Eckington. Argent a chevron between three boars' heads erased sable; crest: a wild boar passant sable (Burke). Used by Richard Kirke of Martinside and Gwersyllt, Denbs., d. 1839, descended ultimately from the Whitehough branch.

Kytchyn. Belper. Argent on a pile in point azure between two cross crosslets gules a dove volant of the field membered of the second; crest: a pelican's head erased azure vulned in the breast beaked gold (MS Ashmole 834.13b.) Gr. 12 Feb. 1579 to John Kytchyn of Islington, Middlesex, from Belper. They were also used by Anthony Kitchin alias Dunston, Bishop of Llandaff 1545–65; their relationship, if any, is unclear.

Lake. Hopwell Hall. gules a dexter arm embowed in armour issuant from the sinister holding in the hand a sword erect all proper thereto affixed a banner argent thereon a cross between sixteen escutcheons of the field charged with a lion passant guardant or quartering

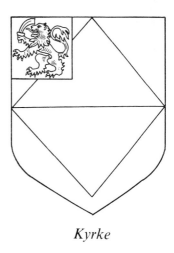

Kyrke

sable a bend between six cross crosslets argent for Lake, and Wardell (3rd), Bibye (4th); crests: a cavalier in complete armour on a horse courant argent bridled and trapped all proper in the dexter hand a sword embrued holding the bridle in his mouth sinister arm hanging useless round his body a scarf in bend gules, and: a sea horse's head argent finned or gorged with a fesse cotised gules; motto: 'Un Dieu un roy un coeur' (BP (1970) 1527). Original arms of Lake (as quartered above) and crest (2nd above) gr. 30 Dec. 1643 to Edward Lake, chancellor of the diocese of Lincoln, and the augmentations of honour (first quartering and first crest) to Col. Sir Edward Lake of Carnew, Co. Wicklow (severely wounded, as depicted, in the Civil War), 12 June 1661, who was cr. a bt of Ireland, 10 July 1661. Borne in Derbys. by Sir Bibye Lake Bt, who purchased Hopwell Hall. His title (GB) dated from 17 Oct. 1711, the previous honour having expired with the grantee 1674. These arms were re-gr. 7 Apr. 1713.

Lamb. Melbourne Hall. Sable on a fesse erminois between three cinquefoils argent two mullets of the field; crest: a demi-lion rampant *gules holding a mullet sable*; motto: *'Virtue et Fide'* (Burke). Gr. to Sir Peniston Lamb Bt 9 March 1774, who inherited Melbourne from the Cokes. His father was cr. a bt 17 Jan. 1755. Peniston was in 1772 raised to the peerage of Ireland as Lord Melbourne of Kilmore, and Viscount Melbourne a decade later. 2nd Viscount Melbourne was given a seat in the Lords through his creation in 1815 (UK) as Lord Melbourne and his brother, 3rd Viscount (the Prime Minister), was likewise honoured as Lord Beauvale in 1839; all ext. 1853. The supporters (conf. 1828) were: *on either side a lion gules collared and chained or on each collar two mullets sable* (Debrett, *Peerage* (1817), II, pl. 54).

Large. Chesterfield; Derby. *Argent a bend azure between three mullets gules* (seal on foundation deed of Large's Hospital, Derby Local Studies Library). Used by Edward Large of Derby (bailiff 1628; mayor 1640, 1649, 1658); his kinsman, Thomas Large of Chesterfield, used *six mullets* and disclaimed V. 1662.

Latham. Alfreton. *Or on a chief dancettée azure three bezants* (MS Ashmole 804). Borne by Sir Thomas Latham of Lathom, Lancs., 1345 and his kinsman, who inherited a moiety of Alfreton a century earlier. The arms as quartered by Stanley sported *plates* in lieu of *bezants* (as Calais Roll).

Latham. Hallowes (Unstone); Unstone. *Or on a chief indented azure three plates overall a bendlet gules*; crest: *an eagle reguardant or* (Tilley, III.272; Harl.MS 1437; cf. Ballard's Book). Borne by John Latham of Whiston, Lancs., and the Hallowes, who was *jure uxoris* of Unstone, C17. Another branch sporting these arms held in the C18 Park, Beard and Ollersett Halls (Hayfield and New Mills).

Lathbury. Holme (Egginton); Hargate (Hilton). *Argent two bars and on a canton azure a martlet or* (V. 1611 (Holme) and as a quartering of Leigh, Vv. 1569, 1611). Borne by Thomas Lathbury of Egginton, whose heiress marr. Leigh. At an earlier period the arms seem to have been as above but with *three bars* (as noted in the church *c.* 1611, Local MS 6341), and the arms borne by Ralph Lathbury, 1st of Egginton, 1324, appear to have been *paly of six argent and azure* with the same *canton* (glass at Egginton church, V. 1611). This man was chamberlain to Ralph

Pipard (qv) the charges of whose arms may have influenced the change. One of the cadets, seated at Hargate Manor, seems to have borne the *paly* coat and *on a canton or a crescent sable.*

De la Launde. Boyleston; Callow. *Gules a fesse or between three bezants* (as quartered by Sacheverell, V. 1569). Borne by William de la Launde who left a dau., heiress to her uncle, Sir John, of Callow Hall, who marr. Richard de Morley mid-C14. The family held a moiety of Boyleston *c.* 1254.

De la Launde. Clifton. *Gules a fesse argent between three bezants* (glass at Ashbourne church, noted by Wyrley 1596). Borne by William de la Launde of Clifton C13.

Lawton. Radbourne. *Argent on a fesse between three crosses crosslet fitchée sable as many cinquefoils of the field* (Papworth). Borne by Sir John Lawton, who marr. the sister and heiress of Sir John Chandos, *c.* 1365, and whose heiress marr. Pole.

Lax: see Maynard.

Leacroft. Breadsall; S. Wingfield; Wilderslow (Derby); Wirksworth. *Ermine a cross gules*; crest: *a cubit arm in the hand a wreath of laurel proper* (*Rel.* VI (1865–6) 38; XII (1872) 95; seal of E.B. Leacroft, 1775). Used by Capt. Richard Becher Leacroft of Wilderslow early C19, and most of his ancestors, who were descended from Thomas Leacroft of Walton (Stone), Staffs. The latter disclaimed, V. Staffs. 1663, but used *a cross patonce.* His grandson, Thomas (1665–1721), who settled at Wirksworth, used the arms as given at the head of the article, but field *or* (Tilley III.272). Glover's Ordinary gives: *ermine a cross patée throughout gules* for a Thomas Leycroft.

Leake. Hasland; Sutton Scarsdale. *Argent on a saltire engrailed sable nine annulets or*; crest: *two hawks rising argent supporting a peacock's tail erect proper*; motto: *'Gloria Deo in Excelsis'* (Vv. 1569, 1611). Borne by John de Leeke, late C14 (Willement Roll). Francis Leeke, 4th in descent from John of Sutton (1489), was on 22 May 1611 cr. a bt (being advanced to the peerage (1624) as Lord Deincourt of Sutton, and made Earl of Scarsdale in 1645 (all ext. 1736). The 1st earl was gr. supporters 14 Nov. 1627: *on either side an angel proper upper garments purpure lower ones wings and hair or* (Burke). His kinsman Sir Francis Leake of Newark, Notts., was cr.

a bt 15 Dec. 1663 (ext. 1689).

Leake. Williamthorpe (N. Wingfield). *Argent on a saltire engrailed sable five annulets or* (V. Notts. 1614; V. Norfolk 1612). Borne by Thomas Leake of Williamthorpe and his great-grandson, William, of Diss, Norf., 1605.

Leake. Hasland. *Argent on a saltire engrailed sable nine annulets or a crescent for difference* (MI at Ault Hucknall, impaled by Hardwick). Borne by Thomas Leake of Hasland, C16.

many mullets of the field; crest: *a demi-lion rampant guardant (? proper)* (Glover, II.592). Used by Ald. William Leaper of Derby (1754–1819), mayor 1776. His father, John, marr. the ultimate heiress of Newton of Mickleover and his son of the same name assumed the name and arms of Newton by 1789. The latter's brother assumed the name and arms of Spell likewise in the 1820s.

Leatt. Horsley. *Argent on a fesse gules between three fireballs sable fired proper a lion passant or*; crest: *on a mural crown or a fire*

Leake

Leatt

Leam. Leam (Eyam Woodlands). *Or a saltire engrailed vert* (addition to Parliament Roll). Thought to relate to Le Moyne, although written Leam, and refers to a person living *c.* 1307–27. Perhaps the arms of Eustace de Leam, whose mother was an heiress of a cadet Stafford of Eyam (qv) and whose family were almost certainly cadets of Morteyne (qv), who had held Eyam (including Leam) in chief.

Lealt: see Leatt.

Leaper. Derby; Leylands (Darley Abbey); Mickleover; Osmaston by Derby. *Sable on a bend between three leopards' faces argent as*

beacon sable fire proper between two wings azure (Rel. VI (1866) 38). Gr. to Nicholas Leatt of London, son of Nicholas of Horsley, 13 Dec. 1616. Entered in most references as 'Lealt'.

Leche. Barlow Lees; Bonsall; Chatsworth; Chesterfield; Shipley. *Ermine on a chief dancettée gules three ducal coronets or*; crest: *on a ducal coronet or a cubit arm erect proper hand grasping a leech environed about the arm vert*; motto: *'Alla corona fidissimo'* (V. 1569, Local MS 6341). The present Leches of Carden, Cheshire, cadets of this family, bear the arms with the *chief indented* and have added the motto (FD (1929) II.1148).

Leche. Belper. *Vair on a chief indented three crowns* (*DAJ* III (1881) 91; XI (1889) 23). Borne by Sir Roger Leche of Belper, Lord Treasurer of England 1415; the field might have been *vairé*, e.g. *vairé or and gules*, implying the usual Ferrers affinities, and may have been the original version of this family's arms.

Lee. Lady Hole Hall (Yeldersley); Postern Park (Shottle). *Azure three ducal coronets or within a bordure argent*; crest: *an arm in armour bent proper bandaged or gauntlet azure holding a battleaxe proper staff of the second.* (V. 1662). In most MSS of V. 1662 these arms are respited for proof; Harl.MS 6104 gives the field as *gules* and an MI at Ashbourne church (1713) omits the *bordure*. Humphrey son of Henry son of William Lee of Postern entered his pedigree (claiming descent from Leigh of Adlington, Cheshire) and these arms, V. London 1634, wherein a note says, 'Fee paid back again and no proof made of arms'.

Lee. Lea Hurst. *Azure two bars erminois overall a bend countercompony of the second and gules*; crest: *a bear passant argent muzzled collared and chained or*; motto: '*Partitur qui vincit*' (Burke, FR 380). Arms used by Sir Joseph Cocksey Lee (1832–94), tenant of Lea Hurst and property in Derby, late C19. Within a decade or so of his death, his son, L.B. Lee of How Caple Court, Herefs., obtained a grant: *azure three bars or a bend invected chequy of the last and gules plain cotised and in sinister chief point a bear's head erased at the neck ermine*; crest: *a bear passant argent collared and chained on the body two cinquefoils of the last resting dexter forepaw on an escutcheon or thereon a fleur-de-lys also azure*; same motto.

Lees. Ashford. *Argent two bars raguly between three cross crosslets fitchée in chief and a falcon belled in base gules*; crest: *a mount thereon amidst wheat a mower in his hand a scythe in the attitude of mowing all proper*; motto: '*Ein doe and spare nought*' (FD (1910) 974). Gr. 1885 to Joseph Lees of Alkrington Hall, Lancs., whose son Frederick (1856–1929) settled first at the Rookery, Ashford and later, as tenant, at the Hall.

Lees. Chapel en le Frith. *Sable two bars and on a chief argent a garb or between two roses gules barbed and seeded proper*; crest: *on a*

rock proper a lion rampant gules supporting a flagstaff proper flowing therefrom a banner sable thereon a garb or; motto: '*Perge sed caute*' (BP (1956) 1295). Gr. 12 May 1924 to Sir William Clare Lees (1874–1951) cr. a bt 2 Mar. 1937; the 2nd bt lived at 'Ardevin', Chapel en le Frith.

Leete: see Leatt.

Le Fanu: see under F.

Legh. Blackbrook (Chapel en le Frith); Fernilee. *Gules a cross engrailed argent*; crest: *out of a ducal coronet or a ram's head argent attired of the first in the mouth a laurel sprig vert* (Burke). A cadet branch of Legh of Lyme Park (Cheshire, but with some estate in Derbys.) was of Blackbrook; Raynold Legh being of Blackbrook 1498; another branch held at Fernilee *c.* 1430.

Legh. Cubley. *Gules a cross engrailed argent in the chief point on an escutcheon sable semée of estoiles an arm in armour embowed of the second the hand proper holding a pennon also of the second all within a bordure wavy or*; crest: *out of a ducal coronet or a ram's head argent armed of the first in the mouth a slip of laurel proper overall a pallet wavy azure*; motto: '*En Dieu est ma foi*' (BP (1956) 1613). Gr. *c.* 1892 when William John Legh of Lyme, Cheshire, was cr. Lord Newton (1892) and was further gr. supporters: *on either side a mastiff dog proper collared sable* (ibid.). Hon. David Legh, 2nd son of 4th Lord Newton, had an estate at Cubley, 1981.

Le Hunte: see under H.

Leigh. Egginton; Newton Solney. *Azure a plate between three ducal coronets or all within a bordure argent and a crescent for difference*; crest: *a unicorn's head couped argent armed and crined or charged with a crescent for difference* (V. 1569). Arms as borne by Thomas Leigh of Adlington, Cheshire, *c.* 1475 (Ballard's Book), from which family the Egginton Leighs derived. Lysons (cxxxv) give a different crest: *an arm couped at the shoulder or scarf azure grasping an halberd proper.* Arms also used (or borne) by William Leigh of Caldwell (1597–1668) and his sons.

Leigh. Egginton. *Gules a cross engrailed argent in the first quarter a lion rampant or in the second a lozenge of the second*; crest: *a lozenge gules charged with a unicorn's head couped argent crined or*; motto: '*Leges juraque servo*' (MI at Egginton church). Borne by Revd Joseph Leigh, rector of Egginton, whose brother lived locally and whose family held a turn of the advowson of the church; these Leighs consistently claimed descent from cadets of the earlier Leighs of Egginton: plainly the heralds, when the above arms were granted (6 Mar. 1811), did not agree. See also Legh.

Leslie. Hassop Hall. *Azure three crosses patée argent,* for Duguid, and quartering *argent on a fesse azure three buckles or,* for Leslie; crest: *a demi-griffin proper langued gules;* supporters: *on either side a griffin proper;* motto: *'Grip fast'* (hatchment in Bakewell church, *Bakewell Miscellany,* 11, Jan. 1978, 32). Borne (or used) by Col. Charles Leslie, 26th of Balquhain (Inverurie), Aberdeen (1785–1869), who showed supporters, perhaps as a result of being a kt of the Hanoverian Guelphic Order. Balquhain was elevated into a (minor) barony by charter 1340. Col. Leslie's son, C.S. Leslie-Duguid, matric. his arms (LO) 1889, which resulted in a change of crest and motto: *a dove holding an olive branch in her beak proper;* motto: *'Patienta et spe'* (FD (1929) II.1169).

Le Vavasour: see Vavasour.

Levett. Little Longstone. *Argent a fesse embattled counterembattled between three leopards' faces sable* (as a quartering of Shakerley V. 1569). Borne by Roger Levett of Little Longstone, *c.* 1485.

Levett-Prinsep: see Prinsep.

Levinge. Parwich; Sturston; Tissington. *Vert a chevron or and in chief three escallops argent;* crest: *an escallop argent within a garland proper;* motto: *'Vestigia nulla retrorsum'* (arms: V. 1611; crest: Lysons, lxxiv; motto: Burke). Allowed to Thomas son of Thomas Levinge of Parwich V. 1611 and crest gr. 10 Sept. the same year, and to Thomas Levinge of Sturston, V. 1611. Sir Richard Levinge, recorder of Derby and Speaker of the Irish House of Commons (1656–1724), was cr. a bt of Ireland 26 Oct. 1704.

Lewes. 'Derbys'. *Sable a bend ermine between six owls argent* (Thompson, IV.6, 50). Appears in Glover's roll of Derbys. and Notts. knights of *c.* 1300 (App. 55) and may refer to the family of Lewes of Headon, Notts. Note Richard Lewes gent., of Heanor, 1625.

Lewis. Parwich Hall. *Sable a chevron cotised between three trefoils slipped in pairle or;* crest: *issuant out of an Eastern crown or a plume of five ostrich feathers sable the centre*

one charged with a mascle of the first; motto: *'Spe tutiores armis'* (BLG (1952) 1518). Borne by Samuel Lewis (1838–86) and his son and grandson, of Parwich.

Le Wyne: see Wyne, Le.

Ley. Barrow on Trent; Brailsford; Catton; Shirley; Winshill. *Argent a bend lozengy between two broken tilting spears erect gules;* crest: *in front of a cubit arm in armour holding in the hand a broken tilting spear in bend sinister proper four lozenges conjoined fesseways gules;* motto: *'Post mortem spero vita'.* (BP (1956) 1326). Gr. 1888 to Francis Ley, a Derby ironfounder, of Epperstone, Notts., and Barrow Manor, cr. a bt 27 Dec. 1905.

Ley. Ingleby; Aston on Trent. *Argent a bend lozengy gules* (Papworth). Assumed with the surname of Ley by Robert Greaves, who marr. the heiress of the senior (Staffs.) line of Ley, 1820 (qv).

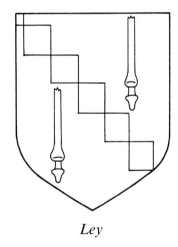

Ley

Lichfield, Bishopric of. *Per pale gules and argent a cross potent quadrate in the centre per pale of the last and or between four crosses patée those to the dexter of the second those to the sinister of the third* (Briggs, 234). Arms derived from those of the Kingdom of Jerusalem; the diocese of Lichfield (and, for some centuries, Coventry) included most of Derbys. prior to the formation of the diocese of Southwell in 1884.

Lillingston. Aston on Trent; Elvaston Castle. *Per pale argent and or a buglehorn sable garnished of the second stringed gules between three crescents of the third each charged with an ermine spot of the first;* crest: *a demi-wyvern issuant tail nowed sable wings expanded and elevated or charged with an ermine spot of the first and on the breast with two annulets conjoined in pale or* (BLG (1937) 1376). Gr. by 1797 when Abraham Spooner assumed the surname and arms of his father-in-law, Luke Lillingston. A descendant assumed the surname and arms of Johnson of Aston (qv) and another, by virtue of marriage with a dowager countess of Harrington, was of Elvaston C20.

Linacre

Linacre. Hasland; Linacre Hall (Brampton). *Sable a chevron between three escallops argent on a chief or as many greyhounds' heads erased of the field;* crest: *a greyhound's head erased quarterly argent and sable charged with four escallops counterchanged* (V. 1569). Arms

conf. and crest gr. between 1526 and 1549 to George son of Robert Linacre of Linacre.

Linacre. Plumbley Hall (Eckington). *Sable a chevron between three escallops argent and a chief or* (Burke). Borne by Gilbert Linacre of Plumbley C17, but shown in Local MS 6341 as 'Plumbley of Plumbley', which seems unlikely, as the arms are plainly an earlier form of Linacre. Or did the Linacres adapt their arms from the obscure Plumbleys?

Lindley: see Sleigh; Wilkinson.

Linford. Monyash. *Quarterly gules and or the first and fourth quarters charged with an escallop argent;* crest: *a talbot passant argent* (Burke). Probably the arms of Sir Laurence de Lynford of Monyash, knighted 1364 and his descendants, who held there until at least 1455.

L'Isle. Hartington; 'The Peak'. *Or a fesse between two chevrons sable* (carved above door of Hartington church). Arms of Brian son of William de L'Isle who was warden of the royal forests of England, constable of the Castle of the Peak, forester in fee of the Forest of the Peak and sheriff of Yorks., 1232; d. same year. Arms as those borne by John de L'Isle 1299 (Willement Roll). Sir Robert son of John de L'Isle (1368) bore as above and crest: *on a chapeau a millstone with a millrind* (seal, PRO, P.477).

Lister. Little Chester (Derby). *Ermine on a fesse sable three mullets argent;* crest: *a stag's head erased proper* (Vv. 1569, 1611; MI at present church of St Alkmund, Derby). Although seemingly allowed V. 1611 to Richard Lister of Little Chester, the arms were blank in 1569 and entered 'sans proof' V. 1662.

Lister. Barton Blount. *Ermine on a fesse sable three mullets or;* crest: *a stag's head proper erased or attired sable;* motto: *'Retinens vestigia famae'* (BLG (1965) I.53). Allowed to Lister of Arnoldsbigging (Rimington), Yorks., at the V. and borne by Nathaniel Lister of Armitage Park, Staffs., who purchased Barton *c.* 1776; they were unrelated to Lister of Little Chester.

Lister-Kaye. Morley Manor (Smalley). *Argent two bendlets sable* quartering Lister (as of Barton); crest: *a goldfinch proper charged on the breast with a rose gules,* for Kaye, and *a buck's head proper erased wavy or attired sable in the mouth a bird bold bendwise of the second flighted argent;* motto: *'Kynd Kynn*

Knawne Kepe' (FD (1929) II.1185). Borne by Cdr Russell Lister-Kaye, who marr. Mrs Bateman of Morley Manor and lived there first quarter of c20. Gr. by 22 Jan. 1806; a btcy was gr. 28 Dec. 1812.

Litton: see Lytton.

Liversage Charity. Derby. *A cross between in the first and fourth quarters on a bend between two crescents three mascles and in second and third quarters three mullets of seven points one and two*; crest: *in front of two swords in saltire points upwards a leopard's face*; motto: *'Juste et droit'* (on terracotta plaque set into building of c. 1904, Nottingham Old Road, Derby). Used by the charity set up by the will of Robert Liversage, a c16 dyer.

Locker-Lampson. Barlborough Hall. *Per pale argent and sable on a chevron nebulée between three dragons' heads erased as many padlocks all counterchanged*; crest: *in front of a stag's head erased proper attired two keys in saltire or* (FD (1929) II.1200). Gr. 1885 to Frederick Locker, later Locker-Lampson (1821–95), and borne by Godfrey Locker-Lampson MP, of Barlborough c20, who marr. the heiress of de Rodes (qv).

Lockett. Derby. *Or a chevron engrailed gules between two stags' heads couped proper in chief and a rose of the second in base barbed and seeded of the third two padlocks of the field*; crest: *on a rock a stag's head proper gorged engrailed vair in the mouth a padlock gules*; motto: *'Non nobis solum'* (FD (1929) II.1200). Gr. 1893 to R.R. Lockett of Sefton Park, Lancs., and Clonterbrook, near Swetenham, Cheshire. Previously the family had used arms *or a chevron gules between three stags' heads couped proper*; crest: *a stag's head proper* (Glover, II.585), including William Jeffrey Lockett of Derby, and his c19 successors there.

Lockhart. Barlborough. *Azure three boars' heads erased argent armed and langued gules*; crest: *a boar's head erased argent armed and langued gules*; motto: *'Sine labe fides'* (BLG (1898) I.918). At V. 1662 Alan Lockhart of Barlborough (where he paid tax on 12 hearths 1670), 'did not appear'. He marr. the widow of Sir Francis Rodes, 1st bt, and was 2nd son of Alexander Lockhart, 6th of Cleghorn, Lanark.

Lomas (Lomax). Foolow; Hartington. *Argent between two pallets gules three fleur-delys in pale sable a chief azure*; crest: *on a chapeau a pelican vulning herself proper* (*Rel.* VI (1865–6) 36; crest: Burke). Intended by Sleigh for the arms of George Lomas of Strangeways Hall, Lancs., and his father, John, of Upper Foolow, descended from William Lomas of Haslin House, Hartington (d. 1743).

Lombe. Derby. *Azure two combs in fesse between a broken lance fessewise or one piece in chief head to the dexter the other bendwise towards the dexter base point*; crest: *two tilting spears in saltire or on each a pennant gules*; motto: *'Justitiae tenax'* (arms: Burke; crest: on iron gates, Derby Silk Mill). Painted for the funeral hatchment of John Lombe of Derby, initiator of the Silk Mill, by Bassano, 16 Nov. 1722, and gr. (with remainders) to Edward Lombe of Weston Longville, Norfolk, 11 Feb. 1700. Arms assumed with the surname 1750 by Sir John Hase Bt. They were further and similarly assumed by Henry Evans of North Tuddenham, Norfolk, 1862. Btcy of Hase cr. 22 Jan. 1784; ext. 1929 (see Jodrell).

Long Eaton, Borough of. *Barry wavy of six azure and argent on a chevron or two bars gemelles sable in base a Tudor rose barbed and seeded proper and on a chief of the third a representation of a piece of lace fessewise of the fourth*; crest: *issuant from the battlements of a tower azure charged with three grenades in fesse fired proper a demi-lion or holding a torch sable enfiled with a celestial crown of the third*; motto: *'Progress by endeavour'* (Briggs, 244). Gr. 8 Apr. 1954 to replace: *a hart lodged within park pales* (Scott-Giles, 100) which too closely resembled the arms of Derby. Merged into Erewash DC (qv) 1974.

Longdon. Ashbourne. *Argent on a bend engrailed azure between two stags' heads caboshed proper an eagle's head erased*; crest: *an eagle displayed proper charged on the breast and each wing with an escallop azure supporting a stag's head caboshed proper*; motto: *'Crux scutum'* (Burke). The above arms were granted as quarterings and additional crest of Gregory of Harlaxton, Lincs., by 1860. They represent John Sherwin Longdon (1803–69), grandson of John of Ashbourne, by Martha, heiress of John Sherwin of Bramcote, Notts.

Longford. Longford etc. *Paly of six or and gules overall a bend argent*; crest: *an antelope queue fourchee gules crined or*; motto: *'En bon* *an'* (Parliament Roll; V. 1569). Borne by Sir John de Longford of Longford, C14, and conf. early C17 to Miss Longford on her marriage to John Miles of Cassiobury (Watford), Herts. The tinctures are thought to be redolent of Ferrers. V. 1569 (Local MS 6341) gives another crest: *a plume of pheasant's feathers therefrom three chebules lozengy or and argent stalked vert, feathers of the first, gules and azure.* Arms also borne by Roger Langford (sic) of Mansfield, Notts., 4th in descent from Sir Nicholas Longford, 1431 (V. Notts 1569).

Longsdon. Little Longstone. *Purpure a double-headed eagle displayed holding in each claw a fleur-de-lys or;* crest: *a double-headed eagle displayed purpure holding in each claw a fleur-de-lys and charged on the breast with a cross potent or;* motto: '*In modo suaviter fortiter in re*' (BLG III (1972) 550). Gr. within the last 30 years to Anthony Longsdon, of Little Longstone, whose family had previously used *purpure an eagle displayed with two heads or* (*DAJ* XXVIII (1906) 86; cf. Lysons, lxxxix). Stephen Longsdon of Little Longstone disclaimed 1611; his successor in 1662 did not appear. Alfred Longsdon of Wellesbourne, Warw., of a cadet branch, also obtained a grant, early C20: *purpure a double eagle displayed and on a chief or three lozenges barry of six azure and argent;* crest: *in front of a demi-double-headed eagle displayed purpure seven holly leaves erect proper;* motto: '*Recte et suaviter*' (BLG (1937) 1409).

Lord. Tupton Hall. *Argent on a fesse between three cinquefoils azure two pheons of the field;* crest: *a hand emerging proper from a maunch azure lined or* (Tilley, III.221). Used (or borne: the arms are those of a London family) by William Allwood Lord, senior and junior, of Tupton, late C18 and early C19.

Loudham. Walton; Whitwell. *Argent a bend azure crusilly or* (as a quartering of Foljambe, V. 1569). Borne by Sir John Loudham, of Lowdham, Notts., and Walton, late C14. Later generations of the family in Notts. bore on the bend only three *cross crosslets* (V. Notts. 1614).

Lovell. Elmton; Holmesfield. *Barry nebulée of six or and gules* (glass once at Chesterfield, Local MS 6341) Borne (but blazoned *undée*) by John Lovell of Titchmarsh (Northants.), kt bt, who was summoned to Parliament by writ as Lord Lovell 1299 (Parliament Roll)

and in Derbys. by William, 7th Lord Lovell. His grandson, Lord Lovell, Holland, Grey of Rotherfield and Deincourt (qqv) was cr. Viscount Lovell 4 Jan. 1483 but all the honours fell under attainder 1485.

Lovett. Codnor Park. *Argent three wolves passant in pale sable, a mullet for difference* (V. 1611). Allowed to Henry Lovett of Codnor 1611, a cadet of Lovett of Nottingham.

Lovett. Derby. *Argent three wolves passant in pale gules;* crest: *a wolf's head erased sable* (V. 1634). Allowed to John Lovett of Derby, 1634, but recorded as for Codnor, *an annulet for difference* V. 1662. Descended out of Northants.

Lowe. Alderwasley; Hasland; Hazelwood; Aldgreave (Heanor). *Gules a wolf passant argent;* crest: *a wolf's head erased* (sometimes *couped*) *argent collared or ringed gules* (Vv. 1569, 1611, 1662). Allowed to the Lowes of Alderwasley and Hazlewood V. 1662, but 'sans proof' for Lowe of Hasland (oddly, for a variant was allowed V. 1634, with a wolf *statant* with *three bezants on the collar*). Thomas Lowe, 1st of Alderwasley, was one of the Lowes of Macclesfield, Cheshire, of which family Nicholas le Low bore: *gules two wolves passant argent* (*temp.* Henry III, Dering Roll). A celebrated Derbys. armorial anomaly appears on Thomas's tomb in Wirksworth church: his arms (as above) are shown quartering Rosell, the heiress who brought Denby to his younger brother. The simple explanation, that this solecism is the result of inexact research on the part of the person responsible for the carving, is the most likely. See Cox, II.560n. and IV.252n.

Lowe. Park Hall (Denby); Stanton by Bridge; Locko (Spondon). *Azure a hart trippant argent;* crest: *a wolf statant 'okerish'* (Vv. 1611, 1662) The hart is described as *statant* in some MSS (e.g. V. 1662); Harl.MS 6104 gives (inaccurately) the field *gules* and the crest *passant.* V. 1569 enters the arms 'with a dubit'. The heiress of the Locko branch marr. Drury, and William Drury assumed by RL in 1791 the additional surname and arms of Lowe, those of Drury being: *argent on a chief vert two mullets each charged with an annulet azure;* crest: *a greyhound courant sable gorged with a plain collar charged with two mullets or* (Burke). Two more failures in the male line caused similar changes of name and arms: William Holden (qv) to Drury-Holden 1849 and his son to Drury-Lowe (arms quartered with both crests) 1884, and the grandson of this man added the surname and arms of Pack also by RL 1947 after his 2nd marriage.

Lowe. Derby. *Gules a hart trippant argent*; crest: *a wolf passant argent* (seal; tinctures, pers.comm). Used by Thomas son of Richard Lowe of Derby, maltster, mayor of Derby 1791, 1802, 1812, 1822, and his son, Revd Henry Lowe, mayor 1821. This family may have been entitled to the arms of Lowe of Alderwasley with due difference.

Lowndes. Palterton (Scarcliffe). *Argent fretty azure on a canton gules a lion's head erased or*; crest: *a leopard's head erased or gorged with a wreath of laurel proper* (Burke). Arms conf. and crest gr. to John Lowndes of Overton, Cheshire, 18 June 1612, whose descendant Robert, son of Robert of Lea, near Wybunbury, Cheshire, marr. the heiress of Milnes of Palterton. Their heiress marr. R.C. Gorst of Preston, Lancs., and his grandson inherited, assuming the surname and arms of Lowndes by RL 1853, quartering Gorst 1 & 4: *ermine on a pile per pale sable and azure three pheons or*; crest: *a lion's head erased or with a wreath of laurel proper*; originally gr. 2 Dec. 1652 under the Commonwealth but annulled 1660.

Lubbock. Melbourne. *Argent on a mount vert a stork close ermine on a chief gules three estoiles of the field*; crest: *a stork wings elevated ermine resting the dexter claw on an antique shield azure bordered or charged with a lion rampant guardant argent*; motto: *'Auctor pretiosa facit'* (BP (1956) 116). Prior to his election to Parliament as Liberal MP for Orpington, Kent, the present (4th) Lord Avebury (cr. 22 Jan. 1900) lived for some years at Penn Lane House, Melbourne. He also succ. to a baronetage, cr. 9 Apr. 1806, when the arms were gr. The barony carries supporters: *on either side a stork wings elevated ermine gorged with a chain or suspended therefrom an escutcheon gules charged with an estoile argent* (ibid.).

Lucas. Hasland; Brimington. *Ermine a chevron engrailed gules between three annulets sable on a chief azure a moorcock enclosed by two cross crosslets or*; crest: *out of the battlements of a tower a dexter arm embowed proper charged on the elbow with five annulets in cross sable holding in the hand a cross crosslet gules* (*Rel.* VI (1865–6) 38, crest: Burke). Gr. early

C19 to Lucas of Chesterfield, whose family had previously used: *argent a chevron gules between three pellets on a chief azure a moorcock between two cross crosslets or*; crest: *an arm embowed sable bezantée cuffed argent grasping in the hand proper a cross crosslet gules* (Glover, II.289).

Lucas. Middleton (by Wirksworth?). *Argent a fesse between six annulets gules* (Local MS 4556). Located by Sleigh (*Rel.* VI (1866) 38; date appears to be early C19. The arms are those of Lucas, Glam.: a connection is not known.

Lumbe: see Lombe.

Lygon: see Duffield; Pyndar.

Lytton. Litton. *Ermine on a chief indented azure three ducal coronets or*; crest: V. Herts. 1634). Probably borne by Sir Robert Lytton of Litton and Knebworth, Herts., Under-Treasurer of England, d. 1488. Allowed to Roland Lytton of Litton, who sold his Derbys. property 1569. Representation of the family passed to the Warburtons and the dau. and heiress of Richard Warburton-Lytton marr. William Earle Bulwer, who assumed the additional surname and arms of Lytton by RL 1811. His 3rd son was cr. bt 18 July 1838 and advanced to the peerage 1866 as Lord Lytton of Knebworth, his son becoming Viscount Knebworth and Earl of Lytton 1880. In 1811 the arms were differenced by *a canton argent thereon a rose gules*, and supporters were gr. 1866: *on either side an angel proper holding in the exterior hand an eastern crown or*; motto: *'Hoc virtutis opus'* (BP (1970) 1679). Note also that Edward de l'Establière Litton of Ardavilling (Cloyne), Co. Cork, claimed descent from this family. He bore arms as at the head of this entry, with the addition of *a crescent gules*, and crest: *out of a ducal coronet or an ermine's head proper*; motto: *'Prudentia Gloriam Acquirit'* (UO; Burke, LGI (1898), 264). It is also worth noting that his first Irish ancestor, Thomas (1657–1741), of Dublin, displayed the ancient arms of Lytton on his funeral certificate (Burke, LGI (1898) 263).

Lytton (Litton). Ashbourne. *Per fesse dancettée gules and or in chief three ducal crowns of the last and in base a pale ermine*; crest: *a stork standing in its nest all proper*; motto: *'Occulta peto'* (BLG (1937) 1385). Gr. 31 May 1910 to W.R.U. Litton of Woolmer

Lodge (Bramshott), Hants., 4th in descent from John Lytton of Ashbourne (1738–73), claiming cadetship with Lytton of Litton.

M'Connell. Cressbrook Hall (Litton). *Or a lion rampant in dexter chief a dexter arm couped gules holding a cross crosslet sable in the sinister chief a galley oars in action of the last flagged on a chief of the 2nd three trefoils slipped of the field*; crest: *a stag's head erased gules charged on the neck with a trefoil slipped or*; motto: *'Victor in arduis'* (FD (1905) 885). Matric. (LO) 1860 to Henry M'Connell of Cressbrook Hall.

M'Creagh: see Thornhill.

MacDonald. Crich. *Grand quarterly 1 & 4: quarterly, (i) argent a lion rampant gules, (ii) or an armed arm fessewise holding a cross crosslet fitchée gules, (iii) argent a lymphad sails furled oars in action sable, (iv) vert a salmon naiant in fesse proper*, for MacDonald: *grand quarters 2 & 3: as Bosville (qv)*; crests: *a dexter arm in armour fessewise hand holding a cross crosslet fitchée gules*, for MacDonald; *and as Bosville (qv)*; motto: *'Per mare per terras'* (Over entrance to his house at Crich; FD (1929) II.1252). Gr. under RL of 11 Apr. 1814 and borne by George Godfrey MacDonald, son of Hon. James William Bosville-MacDonald and grandson of 3rd Lord MacDonald of Slate, Co. Antrim (Peerage of Ireland, cr. 1776). The arms were also matric. (LO) 30 June 1910. Dr MacDonald lived at Crich from 1890.

Macklin. Derby. *Azure three swords points upwards argent pommels and hilts or on a chief of the 2nd a lion rampant between two crescents sable (quartering Audouin and Lamb)*; crest: *an eagle's head issuant from rays of the sun proper* (Local MS 9555). Gr. to Revd Wilson Macklin of Derby, son of Thomas, whose son was 1st vicar of Christ Church, Derby, 1836.

Mackworth. Mackworth; Ash. *Per pale indented sable and ermine a chevron gules fretty or*; crest: *a dexter wing per pale dancettée sable and ermine* (arms: seal 1463, Local MS 6341; crest: Lysons, cxxxvi, cf. V. Rutland, 1618). These arms represent the earliest grant in Derbys. known with an exact date (1 Aug. 1404), by John Touchet, Lord Audley, with 'a

parcel' of that nobleman's arms 'by consent', to Thomas de Mackworth of Mackworth and Ash and his brother, Dr John Mackworth, Dean of Lincoln, for 'ancestral services' – the family were hereditary stewards to the Touchets. Sir Thomas Mackworth of Empingham, Rutland, was cr. a bt 4 June 1619 (ext. 1803). Sir Herbert Mackworth, of a cadet branch, was cr. a bt 16 Sept. 1776 and received a grant of arms: *per pale indented sable and ermine on a chevron gules five crosses patée or*; crest: *a cock proper*; motto: *'Gwell angau na cywilydd'* (BP (1970) 1709). Although kin to the Mackworths of Gnoll (Neath), Glam. (the 1776 grant), the Mackworth-Praed family bore the arms of Mackworth of Mackworth as conf. by RL 1715, and certified by William Courthope, Somerset Herald, 26 Oct. 1864. Sir Herbert Bulkeley Mackworth-Praed was also cr. a bt 28 Dec. 1905 (ext. 1920). In Ashbourne church there was once an escutcheon of Mackworth impaling Thornhill wherein the *field* was *sable* throughout (*DAJ* III (1881) 92); Papworth also gives: *per pale indented or and sable a chevron chequy of the 1st and gules*.

Mackworth

Maesmor: see Masemore.

Malcolm. Spondon. *Or a saltire azure between four stags' heads couped within a bordure indented gules*; crest: *a pyramid encircled by a laurel wreath proper*; motto: *'Ardua tendo'* (over) and *'Dei dono sum quod sum'* (below) (BP (1956) 1431). Borne by Sir John Malcolm of Balbedie, Fife, 7th bt (title cr., Nova Scotia, 25 July 1665), whom the 1851 census reveals as then living at Stoney Cross House, Spondon.

Malebar (Mallabar). Coton in the Elms; Derby; Rosliston. *Or two axes erect and endorsed handles azure blades sable on a chief gules a lion passant guardant of the first*) (*Rel.* VI (1866) 38). Sleigh probably intended these arms for those used by Walter Malebar, citizen and vintner of London, 1698, whose family were anciently of Coton and Rosliston. Sleigh says that they were 'originally from France'; if so, it was before mid-C16, which seems unlikely.

Mallet. Horsley. *Gules a fesse between six mallets or* (*Rel.* XII (1872) 95). From Harl.MS 6137.19b, intended by Sleigh to represent the arms of Walter Mallet, lord of Horsley C14. The Parliament Roll, *c.* 1385, gives: *gules a fesse ermine between six buckles or* for a Sir Thomas Mallet of 'Cos. Derby and Notts'. *Rel.* VI (1866) 39 also adds: *gules a fesse dancettée between six round buckles argent*: there were Mallets with incomes above the £20 level, qualifying a man to become a knight, holding at Ballidon and Parwich C13, but not later.

Man. 'The Peak'. *Per fesse embattled argent and gules three goats passant counterchanged* (V. Lincs., 1564). Borne by John Man of Old Bolingbroke, Lincs., 5th in descent from John Man 'of the Peake'.

Mander. Bakewell; Derby; Wigwell Grange (Wirksworth). *Ermine three annulets interlaced in triangle gules* (seal in private collection). Used by John Mander of Bakewell and Derby, attorney, who sold Wigwell Grange in 1774 (FMG II.656).

Manley. Sandiacre; Carsington. *Argent a dexter hand couped and erect within a bordure engrailed sable*; crest: *a Saracen's head affrontée proper wreathed about the temples argent and sable*; motto: *'Manus haec inimica tyrannis'* (V. Staffs. 1663). Borne by Willoughby Manley of Hanbury, Staffs., in right of his mother, of Sandiacre (MI in church there, 1658, Cox, IV.373) and of his wife, of Carsington. Painted by Holmes & Co. on his carriage for A.E. Manley C19 (Local MS 9555, 209).

Manlove. Ashbourne; Church Broughton; Derby; Wirksworth. *Azure a chevron between three anchors ermine*; crest: *out of a mural coronet gules a cubit arm erect habited erminois cuffed argent hand proper holding a flaming sword wavy of the 3rd hilted or* (V. Staffs. 1663). Gr. between 1623 and 1635 to Rowland Manlove of Kynaston, Salop., later of Ashbourne. However, in the Derbys. V. 1662, he was respited for proof, and this was established 'by an attestacion of R. St George, Norroy 1614', which is odd, because when St George was Norroy, the Manloves lived in the territory of Clarenceux and, anyway, we know that St George made the grant *as Clarenceux* – i.e. between 1623 and his death in 1635.

Manlovel (Maulovel). Ravenstone; Rosliston. *Vert three wolves passant in pale or*; crest: *five bellflowers erect proper leaved vert* (Burke; quartered by Stanhope, V. 1662). Borne by the Manlovels of Rampton, Notts., of which family held Robert held Ravenstone from his nephew of the same name in 1226, the latter being of Rampton and Rosliston. It is unclear for how long they held estates in Derbys.

Mann. Hazlebrow (Duffield); Sandybrook Hall (Offcote). *Sable on a fesse counterembattled between three goats passant argent as many pellets*; crest: *a demi-dragon wings endorsed sable goutée-de-l'eau insides of the wings and talons proper*; motto: *'Per ardua stabilis'* (Burke). Gr. to Mann of Linton, Kent, 1692, and borne by Lucius Mann of Sandybrook, 1841, and his son Lucius Edward Mann of Hazlebrow (Duffield) a decade later.

Manners. Bakewell; Haddon Hall etc. *Or two bars azure on a chief quarterly of the 2nd and gules in the 1st and 4th quarters two fleur-de-lys and in the 2nd and 3rd a lion passant guardant of the field*; crest: *on a chapeau a peacock displayed proper*; supporters: *on either side a unicorn argent armed crined tailed and unguled or*; motto: *'Pour y parvenir'* (Vv. 1569, 1611, 1662). As originally borne, e.g. by John and Sir Robert Manners of Etal, Northumberland, the arms were: *or two bars azure and a chief gules*; crest: *a bull's head erased gules ducally gorged and chained or* (Jenyns' Ordinary). In 1526, when Sir Thomas Manners of Belvoir, Leics., 13th Lord Roos of Hamlake (now Helmsley), Yorks., was cr. Earl of Rutland, the chief was honourably augmented and the crest changed (barony of Roos by writ, nominal precedence, 1264). In 1679 the 9th earl was, in his father's lifetime, summoned to Parliament by writ as Lord Manners of Haddon (the barony of Roos having passed through an heiress 1587 and a re-creation of it, of 1616, having become ext. 1632). He was advanced 1703 to Marquess of Granby, Notts., and Duke of Rutland. The 7th duke, when a yr son, was cr. 1896 Lord Roos of Belvoir, Leics. Other, junior, descendants were cr. Lord Manners of Foston (1807) (whose arms were as above but the *dexter* supporter *charged on the shoulder with a cross flory azure*, the *sinister* one *with a portcullis sable* (BP (1956) 1442)) and Viscount Canterbury, Kent (1835, ext. 1941), whose arms were Manners quartered by Sutton of Laxton, Notts. (*argent a canton sable*) with the same supporters again, differenced on the *dexter* by *pendent from a chain or on an escutcheon azure a mace erect of the 2nd* and *sinister a similar escutcheon charged with a mitre, tinctures as before*: dates of grants, as creations). The supporters of the Duke of Rutland were conf. to 9th duke 1882.

Mansfield. Chesterfield. *An escallop within an orle of eight roundels*; crest: *a tree eradicated* (RBC 27). Quasi-heraldic seal employed by John de Mansfield, 1392.

Marbury. Darley. Sable a cross engrailed between four pheons argent crest: *on a chapeau gules charged with three bezants turned up argent a saracen's head in profile couped proper lined sable wreathed about the temples or and azure* (MI in Darley church as impaled by Columbell, Cox, I.161). Gr. to Sir Anthony Marbury of Lambeth, Surrey: 'testification of Knighthood, arms with quarterings and descent', 10 May 1616. Borne by William Marbury of Marbury, Cheshire, who inherited Darley 1673. On a hatchment for his sister and heiress, who marr. Gilbert Thacker of Repton, Bassano (7 June 1721, Local MS 3525) painted the *cross plain*. V. Cheshire 1580 calls the pheons *nails* and gives a quartering *or on a fesse engrailed azure three garbs of the field* for Marbury ancient (quoting a seal of 1336).

Marchington. Ashbourne; Cubley; Rodsley. *Argent a fret sable and a canton gules* (as

quartered by Curzon, Kedleston church, noted *c.* 1611, Local MS 6341). Borne by Sir Thomas de Marchington of Marchington, Staffs., also of Rodsley, Wyaston and Snelston *c.* 1397 (Willement Roll). An ancestor, Sir Roger son of Ralph de Marchington, was knighted 1281; his father was a Montgomery of Cubley; see Cubley, Montgomery; Vernon.

Markham. Brimington; Hasland; Stuffynwood (Shirebrook); Tapton. *Azure on a pale argent three lozenges sable issuant from a chief engrailed or a demi-lion rampant gules*; crest: *a lion of St Mark passant guardant or resting the dexter forepaw on a lozenge as in the arms, halo gules*; motto: '*Tenax propositi*' (BP (1970) 1760). Gr. 1911 to Arthur Basil Markham of Stuffynwood Hall and Beachborough Park, Hythe, Kent, when he was cr. a bt 10 July same year. His father, Charles Paxton Markham of Hasland and Tapton, used: *azure issuant from a chief or a demi-lion rampant gules*; crest: *a lion of St Mark winged or haloed argent supporting a lyre of the first*, the arms of Markham of Markham, Notts. (Sir Robert son of Sir John, *c.* 1315, Harl.MS 1481.84), from which family he claimed descent via the Markhams of Ollerton, Notts., Great Creaton (Northants.) and Northampton.

Marple(s). Bonsall; Edensor. *Sable crusilly fitchée argent a griffin segreant or*; crest: *a pegasus' head couped with two wings argent crined or* (MS Ashmole 844.70b). Attributed to (Richard) Marple of 'Edenstow Co. Derby' in the MS, but these arms conf. and crest gr. on 20 Sept. 1574 to Richard Marple senior, who was probably of Edensor. The College of Arms copy of the grant (Oxford Grants II.207–9) omits the *fitchée*. A previous crest was 'something of a griffin', but bore no authority. The family also lived for many generations at Bonsall.

Marples. Thornbridge Hall (Ashford). *Quarterly per fesse nebulée sable and ermine in the 1st and 4th quarters a griffin segreant or*; crest: *a griffin segreant or between two wings sable*; motto: '*Tenax Justitiae*' (MI at Ashford church). Gr. 1884 to George Jobson Marples of Thornbridge Hall (1845–1929). His father was George, of Brincliffe Tower, Sheffield, Yorks.

Marriott. Chesterfield. *Barry of six or and sable* (*Rel.* VI (1865–6) 42). A Thomas Marriott was added to the 1687 resumé of Derbys. Visitations (V. 1569 section) in a later hand. These were probably the arms he used.

Marsden. Chelmorton. *Gules on a bend argent three bald coots sable beaked and legged of the field in chief a unicorn's head erased of the 2nd*; crest: *a unicorn's head erased argent goutée-de-sang ducally gorged azure*; motto: *'Mars denique victor est'* (Burke). Gr. 10 Dec. 1733 to 'James Marsden of Chelmorton and Manchester', although the christian name should be Richard (son of Edmund) (1680–1751). William Marsden of Townend, Chelmorton, yr son of William, the grantee's 3rd son, obtained a further grant, 3 July 1804, which added to the arms, *in base a key fessewise ward downwards and to the dexter surmounted of a trefoil or* and *on a canton ermine an anchor sable*; behind the crest, in the mouth of which appeared a *trefoil slipped vert*, was *an anchor erect sable*; Motto: *'Mars dentalia tutatur'* (FD (1929) II.1311). John Bertram Marsden, son of Thomas, of a branch of this prolific family, was heir of the hydro magnate John Smedley; he assumed the additional surname of Smedley and, apparently without authority, quartered the arms Smedley used (qv).

Marshall. Sedsall (Doveridge). *Barry nebulée argent and gules a canton ermine* (once in glass at Doveridge church, noted V. 1611). Borne by John Marshall of Upton, Leics., and Sedsall (d. 1432), whose heiresses marr. FitzHerbert and Draycott. As quartered by the latter (V. 1569) the *nebulée* element is omitted, and as quartered by FitzHerbert on one MI seen by Bassano in Norbury church they are shown similarly, but with a colour change from *gules* to *sable* (Cox, I.32; III.238).

Martel: see Mallet.

Martin: see Stapleton-Martin.

Masemore. 'Co. Derby'. *Argent a lion rampant sable armed and langued gules* (*Rel.* VI (1866) 38). Sleigh provides this entry (spelt Maesmor) but no candidate for these arms (borne by Maesmor, Denbighs.) suggests himself; perhaps he misread 'Denbs.' for 'Derbys.'. A grant to Masemor was made 1794.

Massey. Morley. *Argent a fesse between three lozenges sable* (quartered by Sacheverell, V. 1569). Roger Massey of Sale, Cheshire, held Morley between the tenure of the Risleys and the Stathams C14.

Massingberd: see Mundy.

Master. Codnor Castle; Newhall; Stanley Grange. *Azure a fesse embattled between three griffins' heads erased or*; crest: *out of a mural crown or a unicorn's head erased argent crined and armed gules*; motto: *'Non minor est virtus quam quaere perta tueri'* (V. Kent 1619). Gr. 2 May 1608 to James Master of East Langdon, Kent. Sir Streynsham Master, one of his great-grandsons, purchased Codnor, 1692.

Matlock, Town of. *Vairé or and gules a cross patonce between five doves surmounted of a horseshoe and an headsman's axe all ensigned by a lion bicorporate issuant from a ducal coronet holding an escutcheon argent thereon a cross gules and in the dexter chief point a dragon's wing extended*; motto: *'Aquae salubritas usu'* (Scott-Giles, 100). The tinctures are mostly local.

Matlock College of Education. *Gules a lion bicorporate rampant counter-rampant or in fesse point on a plate fimbriated sable a Tudor rose barbed and seeded proper* (Briggs, 260). Gr. 18 Dec. 1953 to Derbys. County Council for use by the college, which was amalgamated with Derby Lonsdale College (now Derbyshire College of Higher Education), 1983, when their currency lapsed.

Maulovell: see Manlovell.

Mawbey. Ravenstone. *Or a cross gules fretty of the field between four eagles displayed azure on each a bezant*; crest: *an eagle displayed azure on its breast a bezant*; motto: *'Auriga virtutum prudentia'* (Burke). Gr. 15 Sept. 1757 to Sir Joseph Mawbey of Botleys (Chertsey), Surrey, son of John, of Ravenstone, cr. a bt 30 July 1765 (ext. 1817).

Maxwell, Clark-: see Clark.

Mayhall: see Marshall.

Mayhew. Overdale (Derby); Swanwick Hall (Alfreton). Crests: *a snake nowed attacked by an eagle wings elevated proper; a greyhound's head erased ermine* (livery button in local collection). Used by a Col. Mayhew, who was tenant of Swanwick Hall 1895, previously of Derby.

Maynard. Chesterfield; Nether Padley. *Argent on a chevron vert between three sinister hands erect couped gules five ermine spots or*; crest: *a stag trippant or gorged with a collar invected argent fimbriated sable*; motto: *'Manus justa nardus'* (Glover, II.291). Conf. to Anthony and John Lax of Chesterfield by RLS of 1812 and 1825 respectively, on assuming the surname and arms of Maynard, quartering Lax: *barry of six ermine and gules on a chief azure three Catharine Wheels or* (gr. to Anthony, senior, 23 Nov. 1775). The arms and crest were originally gr. under a previous RL to Sarah, dau. and heiress of John Jefferson, and heiress of Thomas Maynard of Kirklevington, Yorks., 1785, the crest to her male descendants. She marr. John, son of Anthony Lax of Eryholme, Yorks.

Measham (**Mesham**). Little Eaton; Measham; Repton. *A lion rampant and a label of four points* (as quartered by Lister of Little Chester, without tricks, Local MS 6341). Used (or borne?) by Nicholas Measham of Little Eaton c. 1433, whose heiress marr. Lister (qv). The family were also of Repton and Measham from C13, and the heiress of the Measham branch marr. Babington.

Medows: see Pierrepont.

Mee. Bretby. *Azure a chevron ermine between three roses or on a chief dancettée argent as many cross crosslets fitchée of the field*; crest: *between two sprigs of oak a stag's head erased (?) proper* (arms: Tilley IV.158; crest: Burke). Used or borne by John Mee, who was the devisee of the manor of Bretby for 41 years in 1569.

Melbourne. Melbourne. *Gules a chevron between three escallops argent* (MI in Melbourne church, cf. Cox, III.405f.). Borne by John de Melbourne of Melbourne c. 1435; his heiress marr. Edward Longford, a cadet of Longford of Longford who settled at Melbourne. George Melbourne was a Derbys. man whose great-grandson, Robert Milbourne (sic), was of Dunmow, Essex, and had these arms allowed to him V. Essex, 1612.

Melland. Bamford; Derby; Monyash; Youlgreave etc. *Paly of eight argent and gules a lion rampant sable* (*Rel.* VI (1866) 38). Used by many members of this widespread family. It occurs on the pewter of Stephen Melland of Youlgreave, who lived later C18, still owned by his heirs.

Mellor. Mellor. *Argent three woodpigeons proper*; crest: *a blackbird proper*; motto: '*Semper constans et fidelis*' (as quartered by Radclyffe, V. 1569; crest and motto: Burke). Borne by Roger de Mellor of Mellor c. 1430, whose family were cadets of de Staveley (qv). As the arms of the latter differed radically, it is possible that these arms belonged originally to the earlier homonymous C13 family from whom Simon de Mellor, son of Simon de

Staveley, inherited the manor. There were a whole group of families in the High Peak who bore three birds: Alsop, Tunstead, Columbell and Bakewell (qqv).

Mellor. Little Longstone. *Argent three blackbirds proper and a chief dancettée sable* (Cox, II.498n.). Conf. 3 July 1707 to John Mellor 'sometime of Little Longstone and London f. and heire of John grandson of John of the same' of Erddig Park, Denbs.; his heiress marr. Yorke. His ancestor Thomas, living 1415, has not been found a place on the main pedigree of the family.

Mellor. 'Derbys.'. *Argent three blackbirds proper*; crest: *a demi-leopard or supporting an anchor sable* (Burke). Conf. (and crest gr.?) to John Mellor of Cann, Dorset, son of John (by a dau. of John Wolley) of Derbys. 24 June 1586.

Mellor. Chaddesden; Derby; Idridgehay; Kirk Ireton. *Argent three blackbirds proper a chief indented sable*; crest: *a bull's head erased sable gorged with an eastern coronet holding in its mouth the upper end of a broken lance or*; motto: '*Melior virtus Fortuna*' (Local MS 9555.192). Gr. to John Mellor, 1719, but exhibited as Mellor of Mellor with crest as above V. 1662; Robert, of Idridgehay, disclaimed and Henry, of Derby, was respited for proof.

Mercaston. Mercaston. *Or three bars dancettée sable*. Borne by Robert de Shelford (probably Notts.), who marr. c. 1276, the heiress of Robert FitzWalkelin of Mercaston. Their descendants assumed the name of Mercaston. The heiress of Robert de Mercaston marr. Nicholas de Kniveton.

Merry. Barton Blount; Brizlincote; Kniveton; Radbourne; Stanton by Bridge. *Ermine three lions rampant gules ducally crowned or a canton of the 2nd*; crest: *a demi-lion rampant ermine ducally crowned and issuant from a ducal coronet or* (V. 1662; seen by Bassano on a banner in church at Sutton on the Hill 1710). Allowed (according to some MSS) in 1662 to John Merry of Barton and his cousin Valentine, of Radbourne. The arms eventually conf. to Capt. John Merry of Whitby, Yorks., Hatton Garden and Barton 'f. Robert formerly of Yarmouth, Co. Norfolk after of London' 2 June 1720. In 1611 Sir Henry Merry of Barton was branded a usurper and 'promised to come to London'; he was then using arms: *gules on a fesse engrailed* *argent between three water bougets or as many crosses patée sable* (Harl.MS 1093 and Local MS 6341) – in fact the arms of a family of the name from Hatfield, Herts.

Meschines: see Chester, Earls of.

Methuen. Stoneycroft (Kniveton). *Argent three wolves' heads erased proper the entire escutcheon charged on the breast of a double-headed eagle displayed sable*; motto: *'Virtus invidiae scopus'* (BP (1956) 1489). Borne by Hon. Robert Alexander Holt Methuen, of Kniveton, 3rd son of 5th Lord Methuen, cr. 13 July 1838.

Meverell. Edensor; Tideswell. *Argent a griffin segreant sable armed gules*; crest: *a dexter cubit arm armoured grasping a dagger all proper* (V. 1662; seal 1428, Belvoir MS IV.50). Borne by Sir Sampson Meverell 1428; the family were of Throwley, Staffs., and Tideswell. Sampson Meverell, 1611, is shown with a field *or* in Harl.MS 6592. On the tomb of Sir Sampson Meverell (1388–1462) – knighted by the Duke of Bedford – the crest is: *a griffin's head* (MI at Tideswell).

Meynell. Meynell Langley; Newhall; Tissington; Winster etc. *Paly of six argent and gules on a chevron azure three horseshoes or* (Cotgrave's Ordinary; as quartered by Franceys of Foremark, V. 1569). Borne by Gilbert de Meynell of Langley, *c.* 1360 and combining elements of the arms of the family's feudal overlords, the Ferrers. Stephen, son of Robert Meynell of Langley, Barlborough etc, *c.* 1190, was ancestor of the Yorks. Meynells, settled initially at Whorlton, who bore, probably through the heiress of de Malbis, *barry of six azure and or* (in glass at Eckington church, noted V. 1569; Cox, I.227). Descendants were summoned to Parliament as Lords Meynell of Whorlton 1295 (ext. 1322) and 1336 (subsequently abeyant). The arms of the Derbys. branch occasionally boasted *paly of eight* with *bend azure* (seal 1277), as Henry and William de Meynell, both yr sons, living *c.* 1330. This variant is also found with the *bend sable,* as on seal of William de Meynell of Langley, 1277 (Henry and William: Jenyns' Ordinary; William, *DAJ* XLVI (1924) 82). A cadet, William of Yeaveley, sealed with *paly of six a fesse a mullet for difference* (seal, 1285, PRO, P.534).

Meynell. Meynell Langley; Derby; Willington Ferry; Yeaveley. *Vairé argent and sable*; crest: *a horse's head argent*; motto: *'Virtute*

vici' (V. 1569 – Willington Ferry, Winster; 1611, Yeaveley). Early C14 Hugh Meynell of Langley etc, marr. Joanna, dau. and heiress of Robert de la Warde, Steward to the Household of Edward I, and adopted the arms of the Wardes (qv). One branch of these Meynells are now of Langley, another went C17 to Bradley, and later were also of Hoar Cross, Staffs., a scion of which house marr. the heiress of Ingram, Viscount Irvine. On adopting the additional surname and arms of Ingram, the arms of Meynell were differenced with a *canton or*, the crest with a *mullet sable* (RL 1842; MIs at Hoar Cross church). In 1905 representation of this family passed to the Hon. F.G.L. Wood, son of 1st Viscount Halifax (cr. 1886), who assumed the surname and additional arms of Meynell by RL 8 Feb. 1905. The arms of Meynell were recorded in Walton on Trent church in 1592 *within a bordure engrailed gules.*

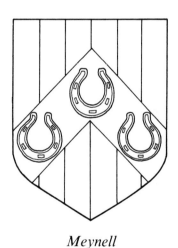

Meynell

Middleton. Eyam; Leam (Eyam Woodlands). *Ermine on a saltire engrailed sable an eagle's head erased or*; crest: *an eagle's head erased or charged with a saltire engrailed sable* (Burke). Gr. to Marmaduke Carver when he assumed the surname and arms of Middleton by RL 1795, which he relinquished in favour of those of Athorpe *(per pale nebulée argent and azure two mullets in fesse counterchanged)* in a similar manner 1822. The earlier Middletons, of whom he was heir, used arms: *argent a saltire engrailed sable* (Burke). According to J. Pym Yeatman (*Feudal history of Derbyshire*, IV.330–1), these arms were also used by John Middleton, town clerk of Chesterfield, C19, who belonged to an unrelated family.

Middleton

Middleton. Kedleston. *Or a saltire pean between two crosses patée in pale and as many annulets in fesse gules;* crest: *a falcon's head erased proper holding in the beak an annulet and charged on the neck with a cross patée gules.* Gr. 13 May 1814 to Rt Revd Dr Thomas Fanshaw Middleton, Bishop of Calcutta, son of Revd Thomas Middleton of Kedleston. The patent recites that the ancestors of the bishop 'had resided for many generations in the County of Derby and were by tradition descended from a family of that name in the County of York'.

Midland Counties Railway. Derby. *Quarterly: i, Leicester, ii, Nottingham; iii, Derbys. (qv); iv, Warwick* (painted cast-iron plaque in Derby Museum, cf. Dow, 36). Company founded 1832, line opened 1839; one the three railways which shared the station at Derby until amalgamated in 1844 to form the Midland Railway (qv).

Midland Railway. Derby. *Quarterly of six: i, Birmingham; ii, Derby (qv), iii, Bristol; iv, Nottingham; v, Lincoln; vi, Leeds;* crest: *a wyvern sans legs vert wings elevated or armed and langued gules;* supporters: *two dolphins or;* motto: *'Midland'* (painted panel in Derby Museum). Formed 1844, amalgamated with others to form London Midland & Scottish Railway 1 Jan. 1923; used above arms with variations throughout that period.

Miller. Shipley Hall. *Ermine a fesse wavy between three wolves' heads erased gules;* crest: *a wolf's head erased argent gorged with a collar wavy azure* (hatchment in church at Oxenhoath, Kent, *Coat of Arms*, XII.33, 85). Allowed V. Kent 1663 to Sir Humphrey Miller of Oxen Hoath, cr. a bt 13 Oct. 1660, and borne by his nephew, Col. Humphrey Miller, *jure uxoris* of Shipley. Heiress marr. Mundy. Btcy ext. 1714.

Milligan. Caldwell Hall. *Or in chief a dexter hand in base a heart between two spears staves rompu erect proper;* crest: *a merchant ship under sail colours flying proper;* motto: *'Just in time'* (BLG (1952) 1781). Borne by Col. Charles Milligan of Caldwell (1832–1902) and gr. 1774.

Millington: see Mylton.

Mills. Tapton Grove. *Barry of ten argent and vert overall six escutcheons gules three two and one;* crest: *a wing expanded barry of ten argent and vert* (Crest: Local MS 9555.173, thus arms, Burke). Borne or used by Mansfeldt Foster Mills of Tapton Grove from later C19 until 1930s. Gr. to Mills of Beds. and Herts. Nov. 1613.

Milner. Meersbrook (Norton); Totley Hall. *Sable a chevron between three snaffle-bits or;* crest: *a horse's head erased sable bridled and charged on the neck with a bezant* (arms, Burke; crest: livery button in local collection). Gr. c. 1674 to Peter Millner (sic) of Burton Grange, Yorks., and borne or used by William A. Milner of Totley Hall, late C19, who was descended from Peter's yr brother, William.

Milnes. Ashford. *Azure a chevron between three windmill sails or* (*Rel.* VI (1866) 38). Used by William Milnes of Ashford *c.* 1590.

Milnes. Aldercar Park (Codnor Park); Dunston. *Ermine a bear rampant sable muzzled and gorged with a collar or therefrom a line reflexed over the back gules*; crest: *on a mount vert in front of a bear's head couped sable muzzled a millrind or*; motto: *'Fortiter et recte'* (BLG (1937) 1600). Gr. under RL of 1816 to William Broughton Smith of Dunston who assumed the additional surname and arms of Milnes. Renewed 1932 to the Cravens (qv).

Milnes. Aldercar Park; Cromford. *Or a bear rampant sable muzzled collared and lined gules*; crest: *a bear's head couped sable thereon a millrind or* (Lysons, xci). Gr. to William Milnes, uncle of George, last of Dunston (qv), who was of Cromford, 1795, with an escutcheon of pretence of Soresby of Chesterfield (qv). Renewed by RL 1831 and 1873 to Revd William Smith and William Broughton Pegge-Burnell respectively.

Milnes. Holmesfield. *Gules three bars gamelles or on a canton argent five billets in saltire* (as impaled by Ince of Spinkhill, *Rel.* XII (1872) 95). Arms attributed to John Milnes of Holmesfield whose dau. marr. John Ince of Spinkhill C16.

Milnes. Brimington; Chesterfield; Palterton (Scarcliffe); Tapton. *Gules a fesse between three windmill sails saltirewise or*; crest: *a garb or banded dancettée azure thereon three mullets pierced of the first*; motto: *'Scio cui credidi'* (Glover, II.286; *Rel.* VI (1865–6) 39; Burke). An ancestor, William Milnes of Tapton, disclaimed the Ashford branch's arms 1662; his descendant Pemberton Milnes of Chesterfield and Wakefield, Yorks., was gr. those above 13 Mar. 1776. Robert, son of Jonathan Milnes of Wakefield, was 21 Mar. 1801 cr. a bt (ext. 1841). Richard Monckton Milnes was in 1863 cr. Lord Houghton of Great Houghton, Yorks., and was gr. supporters: *on either side a pegasus gorged dancettée azure thereon three mullets argent in the mouth a branch of laurel proper*; motto (extra): *'Sequor nec inferior'* (FD (1929) I.459). He marr. the heiress of 2nd Lord Crewe and his son assumed by RL the additional surname and quartered arms *(azure a lion rampant argent)* of Crewe 1894. The following year he was advanced to the Earl-dom of Crewe and in 1911 Earl of Madeley and Marquess of Crewe (all Cheshire and ext. 1945).

Milnes. The Butts (Ashover); Alton Manor (Idridgehay). *Ermine a millrind palewise between two flaunches sable*; crest: *a garb erminois between two trefoils slipped vert*; motto: *'Nil sine labore'* (FD (1929) II.1360). Gr. 12 Jan. 1853 to Henry Milnes of Alton and Hackneylane (Darley) and the descendants of his father. By RL of similar date he assumed the surname and arms of Walthall (qv). Previously, this branch of Milnes had used arms: *ermine a millrind sable*; crest: *a demi-lion holding between its paws a millrind sable* (Glover, II.57).

Milton: see Mylton.

Milward. Broadlowash (Thorpe); Doveridge; Eaton Dovedale (Doveridge); Snitterton; Sinfin; Thorpe. *Ermine on a fesse gules three bezants*; crest: *a lion's gamb sable grasping a sceptre or* (Eaton Dovedale, Vv. 1611, 1662; Snitterton, V. 1662). These arms were allowed to Sir William Milward of Eaton Dovedale and to John Milward of Thorpe and Broadlowash in 1611, the latter only with crest. The posterity of the latter branch were of Snitterton V. 1662 when they were 'sans proof', which seems odd. The earliest ancestor, Owen Milward (C14) is credited with having borne *argent a cross moline sable between three (sic) crescents gules* (sometimes, and surely correctly, *four crescents*: DAJ XL (1918) 90). Burke records the *cross* in this version as *quarter-pierced*. Sometimes the *bezants* are shown replaced by *plates*, as V. 1662.

Minshall. Derby; Shardlow. *Per chevron azure and ermine on a pale counterchanged a cross patée fitchée in chief of the 1st between two crescents argent between the horns an estoile radiated or and in base a like crescent between two like crosses*; crest: *out of flames of fire proper a crescent argent issuant therefrom a sword erect azure hilt and pommel or*; motto: *'Post funera virtus'* (ex inf. grantee). Gr. Oct. 1983 to A.F. Minshall, then of Derby, grandson of Dr H.B. Minshall of Shardlow (1867–1928), with remainder to father's issue male.

Mitford-Barberton: see Barber.

Mitton. Ashover. *Per pale gules and azure a double eagle displayed or within a bordure chequy of the 3rd and first*; crest: *a double headed eagle displayed azure legged gules charged on* each wing with a rose argent barbed and seeded proper; motto: 'Semper fidelis' (BLG (1952) 1798). Gr. 4 Feb. 1920 to A.D. Mitton and borne by Welbury Mytton Mitton of Dovecote, Ashover, 1952.

Molyneux. Newton (Blackwell). *Azure a cross moline quarter pierced or*; crest: *on a chapeau a plume of peacock's feathers proper* (V. Notts. 1663). Allowed to Sir Francis Molyneux of Flintham and Teversal, Notts., 1663 (2nd bt, title cr. 29 June 1611, ext. 1812), and borne by his C18 successors, who held Newton Manor.

Mompesson. Eyam. *Argent a lion rampant sable thereon a martlet or* (Parliament Roll). Borne by Sir Giles Mompesson, Norfolk, *c.* 1318, wherein the *martlet* is blazoned as a *pynzon*, and borne by his descendant, Revd William Mompesson, the vicar of Eyam who isolated the plague in the village 1666.

Monjoye. Yeldersley; Winster. *Azure three escutcheons or* (Dering Roll). Another family consanguineous with Shirley, Ireton, Edensor etc, of which Stephen de Monjoye (intended for Serlo, d. 1254) of Yeldersley bore these arms *c.* 1250. The heiress marr. de Ireland (qv) *c.* 1317, and Robert de Ireland of Winster assumed the surname and bore the arms of Monjoye.

Monsder (Mounser). Ashover. *Gules a chevron between three leopards' faces or* (*Rel.* VI (1865–6) 30). These arms were also in glass at Mugginton (Local MS 6341) and the attribution is Sleigh's. They are, however, identical with those of Parker of Norton (qv), although ensigns of Parker are unlikely to be found at Mugginton. Nothing is known of the family or their title to such arms.

Montgomery. Cubley; Marston Montgomery; Osleston; Snelston; Sudbury etc. *Or an eagle displayed azure* (MI at Trusley, Cox, III.96; Boroughbridge Roll; quartered by Stanhope V. 1662). Borne by Sir William de Montgomery of Cubley 1322, and by Sir John de Montgomery, Captain of Calais, 1345–48 (Calais Roll). The latter is something of a mystery, as he seems to have no place on the pedigree, or connections with Derbys. He was summoned to Parliament as a baron 1342 (ext. 1352). Before *c.* 1290 the arms borne were: *ermine a bordure gules semée of horseshoes argent* (seal of Nicholas de Montgomery *c.* 1390, but who usually quartered these with those above: as also quartered by

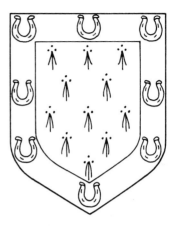

Montgomery

Stanhope. Vv. 1569, 1662; visible at Cubley church, Cox, II.322 & n.). The horseshoes are given as *or* in the arms of William de Montgomery *c.* 1242 (Glover's Roll, 1st Version, 212). Interestingly these arms are ascribed to the Marchingtons of Marchington, Staffs., in the D369 MS, who were probably cadets. Representation of the family passed sideways 1324, and the earlier coat with its Ferrers element might represent the arms of Montgomery, and the *eagle* coat may have been acquired by the cadet branch which inherited the estates of Rodsley (and later Cubley) therefrom. The Rodsleys of Rodsley were also remoter cadets of this family.

Montgomery. Derby. *Or an eagle displayed azure beaked and armed of the field a mullet for difference* (V. London, 1568). Borne by John Montgomery of London, son of Thomas, of Derby, probably to be identified with Thomas, 3rd son of Sir Nicholas, of Cubley (d. 1494).

Moore. Appleby Parva. *Ermine three greyhounds courant in pale sable collared and on a canton gules a lion passant guardant or*; crest: *a moorcock ermines wings displayed holding in*

the bill a heath-stalk (proper); motto: *'Non civium ardor'* (Glover, II.37; in churchyard and grammar school at Appleby). Gr. 25 Aug. 1683 to Sir John Moore, Lord Mayor of London 1682, and to the descendants of his father Charles, and conf. 1743, quartering Wilde and Townley, to George Moore of Appleby Parva Hall.

Moore. Bamford; Castleton. *Azure a swan argent wings elevated and a bordure nebulée or on a chief of the 2nd a lion passant of the field between two flowers of the cotton tree slipped proper*; crest: *a swan argent wings elevated barry of six or and azure holding in the beak a flower of the cotton tree slipped proper*; motto: *'More hoc mutati'* (FD (1905) 981). Gr. 1853 to William Cameron Moore of Bamford and Manchester, Lancs., *jure uxoris* of Castleton. Previously he had used *azure a swan proper on a chief argent a lion between two trefoils slipped all within a bordure engrailed (? or)*.

More. Dronfield. *Paly of six sable and argent a bend gules*; crest: *in a mural coronet a cockatrice sejant vert*; motto: *'Nefas flectere'* (Hunter, *Hallamshire*, 479). Borne by Edward, son of George More, *jure uxoris* of Dronfield mid-C16, whose posterity removed to Burghope, Herefs. (V. Herefs. 1634). Borne also by his ancestor Thomas de More of More Hall (Bradfield, Yorks.) 1380 (seal, cf. Hunter, loc.cit.).

More. Greenhill (Norton). *Argent a chevron between three moors' heads couped sable* (*Rel.* VI (1866) 30). Included by Sleigh and intended for the arms borne or used by Robert son of George More of Greenhill, gent., early C17.

More. Norton. *Azure on a cross argent five martlets sable*; crest: *on a ducal coronet an antelope argent* (V. Surrey 1623). Arms allowed to Sir George More of Loseley, Surrey (1553–1632), grandson of Sir Christopher More, formerly of Norton. Sir George's grandson, Sir Poynings More, was cr. a bt 18 May 1642 (ext. 24 July 1684).

Moreton. Derby. *Argent a chevron gules between three square buckles sable*; crest: *a demi-moorcock displayed sable combed and wattled gules* (D369). Borne by a member of this Staffs. family living in Derby early C17. Allowed to Moreton of Engleton (Brewood), V. Staffs. 1583.

Morewood. Alfreton; Oakes (Norton). *Vert an oak tree couped in base argent acorned or*;

crest: *two arms embowed proper supporting a chaplet of oak vert acorned or* (Lysons, xci). Gr. 23 June 1678 to Rowland (son of John) Morewood of Alfreton with remainder to the 'posterity' of his uncles, Francis, Joseph and Andrew. Previously the family had used: *argent an oak tree eradicated proper*; crest: *two hands and arms holding a chaplet vert* (Andrew Morewood of Hallowes (Unstone), V. 1662, 'no proof'). The arms were re-gr. 1793, 1797 and 1826, when successive indirect heirs succ. to the estate. The last was to William Palmer-Morewood, who, inheriting *jure uxoris* through the widow of the last Morewood, and thus enjoying no descent from his predecessors, quartered his original arms of Palmer of Ladbroke, Warw.: *argent on two bars sable each three trefoils of the field in chief a greyhound courant of the 2nd collared or*. The Morewood arms were differenced by *a trefoil in canton argent* and also on the crest (BLG (1937) 1627).

Morley. Callow; Morley. *Argent a lion rampant double queued sable crowned or* (as quartered by Sacheverell, V. 1569; Parliament Roll). Borne by Richard de Morley whose dau. and heiress marr. Hugh de Risley. The Parliament Roll shows Sir William Morley of Norfolk, summoned to Parliament by writ as a baron 1299, bearing the same arms: a connection between the two is not apparent. Hugh de Risley appears also to have assumed the name and arms of Morley C14.

Morley. Hollington; Mugginton. *Per pale gules and azure a leopard's head jessant-de-lys or*; crest: *out of a mural coronet or a griffin's head argent between a pair of wings the dexter azure the sinister gules* (College of Arms, Grants V.19). Gr. to Francis Morley of Hollington, 30 Oct. 1700, and used or borne (if the crest on his livery buttons is to be believed) by William Bateman Morley of Mugginton 1846.

Morris. Derby; Litchurch Grange (Derby). *Per saltire gules and sable goutée-de-l'eau a lion passant argent between four scaling ladders two in pale and as many in fesse or*; crest: *an heraldic antelope sejant argent goutée-de-sang resting the dexter foot on a scaling ladder or*; motto: *'Res non verbo quaeso'* (BLG (1937) 1633). Gr. 1883 to T. Henry Morris (1848–1927) of Halifax and Litchurch Grange; the family then had been of Derby for some three centuries.

Morteyne. Eyam; Park Hall (Mapperley); Risley. *Ermine a chief gules* (quartered by Willoughby on MI at Risley church 1514; Glover's Roll, 1st Version, 215). Borne by Robert and William de Morteyne (living 1272) and Roger de Morteyne, whose heiress marr. Willoughby. The MI at Risley also quarters *quarterly azure and argent four lions rampant counterchanged* which Cox (IV.403) also attributes to Morteyne but which are the arms of a branch of Pipard (qv). Glover calls William de Morteyne 'Breton', which conflicts with Statham's conjectural descent of him from Warner of Domesday (*DAJ* XLVIII (1926) 104–6) but which explains the field *ermine*, this tincture being the arms of the Breton royal house also alluded to in the 'ancient' arms of Montgomery.

Mortimer. Caldwell; Netherseal. *Or ten fleurs-de-lys sable, four three two and one and a chief azure*; crest: *a torteau between two wings or* (Tilley, IV.31). Gr. to John Mortimer of Cheshunt, Herts., 14 June 1688 and borne by his son Cromwell Mortimer of Caldwell (d. 1753).

Morton. Mugginton. *Quarterly gules and ermine 1st and 4th quarters charged with a goat's head argent* (*Rel.* VI (1866) 39). Arms of Sir Robert Morton of Morton, Notts., escheator of Derbys., 1370–77, but found in glass at Mugginton church 1611 (Local MS 6341) impaled with Kniveton. The marriage it reflects has not been traced.

Mosley. Breadsall; Burnaston House; Hulland Hall; Park Hill (Egginton); Thornhill (Derby). *Sable a chevron between three millpicks argent*; crest: *an eagle displayed ermine*; motto: *'Mos legem regit'* (BP (1970) 1893). Arms conf. and crest gr. 17 Feb. 1593 to Ald. Nicholas Mosley of London, son of Edward of Hough End (Salford), Lancs. Sir Edward Mosley (cr. bt 10 July 1640) was also of Breadsall, but on his son's death 1665 (title ext.) it passed to a cousin, Nicholas, whose grandson was made a bt, 18 June 1720 (ext. 1779). Another cousin, Sir John Parker Mosley, cr. a bt 8 June 1781, left posterity who lived at Burnaston House etc. Tonman Mosley, a son of 3rd bt, was cr. 1911 Lord Anslow of Iver, Bucks. (ext. 1933). He was gr. supporters 1911: *dexter a stork proper charged with a Stafford knot or sinister a swan wings inverted proper gorged with an antique crown or.* Sir Nicholas, 7th bt, is now 3rd

Lord Ravensdale (see Curzon).

Moss. Derby. *Ermine on a cross formée a bezant*; crest: *out of a mural coronet or a griffin's head ermine charged on the neck with a bezant* (hatchment in St Luke's church, Derby; cf. BLG (1852) 893). Used or borne by John Moss (1796–1860) of Holbrooke House, Derby, solicitor, mayor 1844 and 1852, and displayed on the hatchment of his widow, Frances Alice née Goodale (1813–80), a great benefactress to St Luke's, in which it still hangs. Whether Ald. Moss was a scion of the Mosses of Houghton Regis, Beds., whose arms these are, has not been ascertained.

Moubray (Mowbray). Bretby; Ible. *Gules a lion rampant argent*; crest: *a leopard or ducally gorged argent* (1st Dunstable Roll; crest in glass at Norbury church, Cox, III.245). Borne by Sir John de Moubray, kt bt, 1308, and by Thomas Mowbray, Duke of Norfolk and Earl Marshal 1398 quartered by *England with a label of five points argent* (Willement Roll). The crest was apparently gr. by the Crown 1394. John, 4th Lord Moubray of Thirsk, Yorks. (cr. by writ of summons, 1295), inherited Bretby. The 6th baron was cr. Earl Marshal (1386), Earl of Nottingham (1377) and Duke of Norfolk (1396), Earl of Warren and Surrey (1451; all ext. 1476). Heiress marr. Berkeley (qv).

Moult (Mold, de Montalt). Chapel en le Frith; Mellor Hall. *Azure a lion rampant argent*. Borne by Roger, 3rd son of Sir Roger de Montalt, who held of his father at Chapel en le Frith. His probable grandson Robert Mold (sic) held at Bowden Edge 1345, descendants of whom were of Bagshaw and Eccles Pike. William Moult, a descendant, was of Bridgefield, Tunstead Milton and Eccles, dying 1694. He was ancestor of J.D. de Montalt of Eastbourne, who claims arms as above with crest: *an arm embowed holding in fesse a dart point to the dexter proper barbed and flighted or;* motto: *'Deo Duce Christo Luce'* (pers. comm.). Amongst other descendants were Thomas and John Moult of Mellor Hall, 1846, to whom Tilley (I.149) erroneously ascribed *Azure three bars wavy argent in chief as many fleurs-de-lys or*; crest: *on a mount a pelican vulning herself proper.* These arms were gr. to the unrelated Francis Moult of Tollerton, Notts., 10 Feb. 1687.

Mount St Mary's College. Spinkhill (Eckington). *Or a chevron between three crescents*

azure on a canton of the last the Roman letters IHS between in chief a passion cross and in base three passion nails palewise all of the field; crest: *a lily flowered stalked and leaved proper between two wings displayed or*; motto: '*Sine macula*' (Briggs, 272). Gr. 1941; design reflects the arms of the recusant family of Pole of Spinkhill (qv).

Mousley. Etwall; Exeter House (Derby); Hilton Lodge. *Sable a chevron between three towers argent* (MI formerly at Etwall). Used by William Eaton Mousley of Derby, attorney, d. 1853, and his son Hardcastle Mousley of Etwall and Hilton Lodge. See also Mosley; Mozley.

Mowbray. Grangewood Hall (Netherseal). *Gules a lion rampant ermine between two flaunches or on each three billets in pale azure and in centre chief point a cross crosslet of the third*; crest: *an oak tree or therefrom pendant an escutcheon gules charged with a lion's head erased argent*; motto: '*Suo stat robore virtus*' (Burke, AA, 53–4). Gr. under RL 26 July 1847 to Rt. Hon. J.R. Cornish, who thereupon assumed the surname and arms of Mowbray of Co. Durham, his wife being dau. and heiress of George Isaac Mowbray of Bishopwearmouth. The latter's brother, Capt. Thomas Mowbray RN (1793–1864), built Grangewood Hall and he and his son, who dsp 1892, bore these arms. See also Moubray.

Mower. Barlow Woodseats; Chesterfield; Greenhill (Norton); Holmesfield. *Ermine on a chevron azure three roses argent* (Burke). George Mower of Greenhill disclaimed V. 1611, but the arms were allowed to Robert Mower of Barlow Woodseats Hall, V. 1634, although his son is reckoned to have disclaimed V. 1662. Since Robert Mower of Barlow Woodseats was considered by the heralds as 'a person for a grant' 1687, the inference must be that, as displayed in 1634, the arms were respited for proof, which was never obtained. Gr. 1815 by RL to Samuel Thorold of Welham, Notts., as a quartering.

Mozley. The Friary (Derby). Arms not known; crest: *a hand couped at the wrist holding erect a sunflower slipped with two leaves all proper* (Local MS 9555.193). Used by Ald. Henry Mozley of a C19 Derby family of printers originally from Lincs., who purchased The Friary.

Mucklowe. Derby. *On a saltire a lion rampant sable on a chief an escallop between two fleurs-de-lys* (MI at St Alkmund's church, Derby, Simpson, I.358). Used by Thomas Mucklowe of Derby, d. 1699. No connection has been found between these arms and a crest granted to a Mucklowe between 1536 and 1550.

Mundy

Mundy. Allestree; Markeaton; Quarndon; Shipley. *Per pale gules and sable on a cross engrailed argent five fusils purpure on a chief or three eagles' gambs erased à-la-quise azure*; crest: *a wolf's head erased sable bezantée incensed proper*; motto: '*Deus Providebit*' (Vv. 1569, 1611, 1662). Gr. before 1509 to Sir John Mundy of Checkendon, Oxon., lord mayor of London 1522, who purchased Markeaton etc 1516. Previously the family had used the arms with field *sable*, chief *argent* and cross *plain* (Burke). Other collaterals in Bucks. bore at this time: *per pale argent and sable on a cross gules five fusils or on a chief azure three eagles' gambs erased à-la-quise of the first* (ibid.). The Shipley branch are known to have varied their arms (without authority) with *lozenges azure* (ibid.). John, youngest son of Sir John, was of Rialton (St

Columb Minor), Cornwall, and his grandson Thomas bore: *quarterly gules and sable on a cross engrailed argent five lozenges azure on a chief or three eagle's gambs erased à-la-quise of the 4th* (V. Cornwall 1620). Charles Godfrey Mundy, of Burton Hall (Burton on the Wolds), Leics., of the Markeaton branch, assumed the additional surname and quarterly arms of Massingberd in 1863.

Murray. Ballidon. *Azure three mullets argent within a double tressure flory counterflory or* quartering Barclay: *gules three crosses patée argent*; crest: *a buck's head couped or a cross patée between the attires argent*; supporters: *on either side a lion gules armed or*; mottoes: *'Spero meliora'* and *'Uni aequus virtuti'* (BP (1956) 1446). In the 1770s the Earl of Mansfield was given an estate at Ballidon by Matthew Vernon of London, mercer, a fervent admirer. He was William Murray, 3rd son of 5th Viscount Stormont (Gospertie), Perthshire (cr. 1621), cr. Lord Mansfield, Co. Nottingham, 1756, and was at the same time gr. the supporters (above). In 1776 he was cr. Earl of Mansfield, Notts., and again of Caenwood (now Fenwood (Hampstead)), Middlesex, in 1792 but with different remainders; his barony became ext. on his death 1793. Lord Mansfield's father was cr. by Prince James Edward Stuart (as James III & VIII) Earl of Dunbar, E. Lothian, Viscount Drumcairn, Fife, and Lord Hadykes (now Halldykes (Lockerbie)), Dumfries, in 1721, with remainder to his brother and heirs male.

Murray. Staveley. *Paly of six or and sable* quartering *or a fesse chequy azure and argent* all quartering Murray (as preceding entry); crest: *a demi-savage proper holding in the dexter hand a dagger also proper hilt and pommel or in the sinister hand a key of the last*; motto: *'Furth fortune and fill the fetters'* (Burke). Gr. 1782 to William Foxlowe, whose seat was half of Staveley Hall, on his assumption by RL of the surname and arms of Murray, his wife being dau. and heiress of Gen. Lord John Murray of Banner Cross Hall, Sheffield, Yorks.

Musard. Staveley; Whitwell. *Or two chevrons azure* (Lysons, lxi; as quartered by Roper, V. 1662). Usually attributed to this family, at least in its later generations, C14. Previously they had borne *gules three plates* (Ralph de Musard, Dering Roll, mid-C13) and indeed, some heralds had gone so far as

to attribute (quite retrospectively) to Hasculf Musard, the Breton founder of the family, and tenant-in-chief of Staveley 1087–1101: *sable three plates* (*DAJ* XXXVI (1914) 58). These coats both are reminiscent of d'Abitot (qv), allied by marriage if not by blood. The heiress marr. Frecheville, her father having borne *Or two chevrons azure and a bordure engrailed sable* (sometimes *azure*) which is the version found V. 1569 quartered by that family – sometimes also sub-quartered with *sable three plates* (Harl.MS 6592, f. 5). See also Roper; Steynesby.

Muschamp. Horsley; Ilkeston; Stanley. *Or a chief azure* (as a quartering of Foljambe at Chesterfield church, Local MS 6341). Borne by Robert de Muschamp (Muskham) of Ilkeston, Constable of Horsley Castle *c.* 1200. The arms usually ascribed to Muskham, however, were *or three bars gules* (Burke), presumably borne by the Muschamps of Stanley and Stanton by Bridge. They were also borne by William de Muskham, Archdeacon of Derby and Bishop of Lincoln (early C13) and his uncle Geoffrey, Bishop of Lichfield.

Musters. Dove House (Ashbourne); Quarndon Hall. *Argent on a bend gules a lion passant guardant or within a bordure engrailed of the 2nd* for Musters, quartering *barry of ten argent and gules three martlets two and one sable within a bordure engrailed ermines* for Chaworth; crests: Musters: *a lion sejant guardant or supporting with the forepaws a shield of the arms,* and for Chaworth: *a tower argent charged with a bendlet wavy gules thereon a lion passant or issuant from the battlements an ostrich feather sable between four others of the first* (BLG (1937) 1660). Chaworth gr. under RL 1806, and Musters similarly conf. 1824. Arms above exemplified by RL 6 Oct 1888 to J.P. Chaworth-Musters, formerly Musters, and borne by Henry Chaworth-Musters of Dove House, *c.* 1895. John Musters of Colwich, Notts., who inherited Quarndon Hall 1677, bore the arms of Musters (as above) alone (V. Notts. 1614).

Mylton. Gratton. *Azure three millstones argent* (as quartered by Lowe of Denby, V. 1611). Borne by William Mylton *alias* Millington of Gratton of a Cheshire family, being allowed V. 1580 to Roger Millington of Millington, whose pedigree has no connection with that in Local MS 6341. His dau. and heiress marr. Laurence Lowe of Denby.

Mynors. Windle Hill (Osleston & Thurvaston). *Sable an eagle displayed or on a chief azure bordured argent a chevron between in chief two crescents and in base a rose of the 2nd;* crest: *a hand grasping a bear's gamb proper;* motto: *'Spero ut fidelis'* (arms: MI at Duffield church; crest and motto: BLG (1952) 1856). Borne by Sir Roger Mynors (d. 1536) of Treago Court (St Weonard's), Herefs., and Windle Hill, which he was gr. 1513 and where he built the house which was demolished in 1939. The replacement farmhouse erected nearby is now called Windlehill Farm.

Mynors. Rodsley. *Gules a fesse argent between three plates;* crest: *a hand erect grasping a lion's gamb erased in bend sinister proper* (V. Staffs. 1663). A Uttoxeter, Staffs., family who for many generations (*c.* 1270–1450) held Rodsley and settled cadet branches there.

Nadauld. Ashford; Derby; Kilburn. *Azure a sun in splendour proper* (*Rel.* VI (1866) 39). Gr. to the ancestors of Henri Nadauld in France, and borne by him in England, to which he came (working as a stone-carver at Chatsworth, 1703–5, as a result of having sculpted as a hobby), after the Edict of Nantes. His descendants were of Kilburn and Derby.

Needham. Cowley Hall (Wensley); High Needham (Hartington); Snitterton; Thornset (New Mills). *Argent a bend engrailed azure between two bucks' heads caboshed sable;* crest: *a phoenix rising in flames proper* (V. 1569). Borne by William Needham of Thornset and Cowley, marr. to the heiress of Garlick of Whitfield (Glossop), with *an annulet or on the bend,* and quartering *vert a broad arrow in pale head downwards argent,* thought by Cox (II.219) and others to be the arms of the office of the hereditary forester of the Peak, and Garlick. Some descendants bore Garlick alone (qv). The arms seem to have been acknowledged as of early origin, for they were also borne by Needham of Cheshire, the representative of which family in 1625 being cr. Viscount Kilmorey, Co. Laois, and gr. supporters: *dexter a bay horse maned and tufted sable sinister a stag proper;* motto: *'Nunc aut nunquam'* (V. Salop. 1663): this was in the Irish Peerage, as were the titles gr. to the 12th Viscount in 1822: Earl of Kilmorey, Viscount Newry and Mourne, Co. Down. In the windows at Hassop Hall is a representation of the so-called earliest arms of Needham; *the stag's head in base* is omitted. Another crest current in the family V. 1569 was *on a mount vert a stag lodged sable attired or* (*DAJ* XXXVI (1914) 70), and Sir Francis, of Melbourne bore: *out of a palisado coronet or a buck's head sable attired of the first* (Lysons, clxii). The Needhams of Kinoulton, Notts., bore the arms as at the head of the article, with *a canton or,* and the crest *charged on the breast with a trefoil slipped or* (V. Notts. 1664). The arms were conf. and a crest gr. 'for Browne to Needham of Wymondley' to 'John Needham of Wymondley, Herts., son of James son of Christopher son of John, 'called Black John Needham' of Needham Grange, Co. Derby' 18 Feb. 1587: *a dolphin naiant or* (Burke). The Needhams of Lenton, Notts., C19 used (or bore): *azure a bend engrailed argent between three bucks' heads caboshed sable;* same crest; motto: *'Soyez Ferme'* (Burke). The Needhams of Suffolk, descended from those of Melbourne, had the arms conf. as Cowley etc, V. Suffolk 1612, likewise those of Leics. The Suffolk branch also used the arms with an extra *buck's head* (Corder, 82–3).

Necsenche: see Newmarch.

Neile. Codnor Park. *Ermine a lion rampant between three dexter hands couped gules;* crest: *a dragon's head or vulned in the neck gules* (Tilley IV.159). Gr. by patent June 1614 to Dr Richard Neile, then Bishop of Lichfield, later Archbishop of York, who purchased Codnor 1634. Borne by his son Sir Philip, who sold Codnor to the Master family.

Nesfield. Castle Hill (Bakewell). *Argent a chevron between three mullets pierced sable within a bordure engrailed gules;* crest: an estoile (arms: *Rel.* VI (1866) 40; crest: Local MS 9555.203). Used by R.W.M. Nesfield of Castle Hill in the later C19, uncle of W.E. Nesfield, the architect.

Neville-Rolfe. The Knoll (Duffield). *Gyronny of eight or and azure on a chief sable three annulets argent,* for Rolfe, quartering *five fusils conjoined in fesse or on each an ermine spot sable within a bordure nebulée argent;* crest: *a lion's head erased argent fretty gules;* motto: *'Cresco Crescendo'* (BLG III (1972) 779). Gr. under RL of 1837 to Revd Strickland Neville who thereon assumed the additional surname and arms of Rolfe, and borne by Capt. Guy Neville-Rolfe of the Knoll, Duffield C20.

Newbold. Chesterfield; Newbold; Unstone. *Azure two bendlets and a chief argent* (as quartered by Revell of Carnfield, V. 1569).

Newbold. Hackenthorpe (Beighton). *Azure two bendlets wavy and a chief argent*; crest: *a cross patonce fitchée azure* (V. London, 1634). Allowed to William Newbold of London, descended from those of Hackenthorpe. Also borne by Michael, of Hackenthorpe (1623–93), who founded a dynasty in America.

Newdegate. Derby; Kirk Hallam. *Gules three lions' gambs erased argent*; crest: *a fleur-de-lys argent*; motto: *'Confide recte agens'* (Burke; Thompson, IV.50). Allowed to 1st bt, of Arbury, Warw. (cr. 24 July 1677, ext. 1806), and originally to Walter Newdigate of Newdigate, Surrey, between 1567 and 1592. Francis, 2nd son of 2nd bt, acquired Kirk Hallam. Christopher Parker, husband of his heiress, assumed the surname and arms of Newdigate by RL 10 June 1773. His descendant, Sir Francis Alexander Newdigate, assumed in 1902 the additional surname of Newdegate (sic) and was made GCMG 1925, being gr. supporters: *dexter a swan sable sinister a horse argent holding in the mouth a sprig of oak leaved fructed and slipped proper*; motto: *'Foyall Loyall'* (FD (1929) II.1430).

Newmarch. 'Co. Derby'. *Gules five fusils in fesse or* (as a quartering of Shirley, V. 1569; Parliament Roll). Borne by Sir Adam and Sir Roger de Newmarch. *c.* 1320, recorded as, *inter alia*, 'of Co. Derby' (Burke), an heiress of one of whom marr. Shirley. Another Adam, and Sir Thomas de Newmarch *c.* 1350, also recorded by some authorities for Derbys., bore *argent five fusils conjoined in fesse gules* (Parliament Roll). This Adam was a yr son of the family of Newmarch of Whatton, Notts., whose arms these are (Thoroton, *Notts.* (1793), I.270 with crest: *a demi-griffin crowned*). The heiress, *c.* 1400, marr. Ralph Newmarch of the Yorks. family of that name. Both arms are sometimes described as having a *fesse engrailed* due to misinterpretation of old rolls; sometimes it is shown as indented. Sleigh, Berry and Burke also enter *Gules a fesse engrailed or* (for Newmarch) as 'Neesench, Co. Derby'.

Newnes. Matlock. *Per fesse or and azure a pale with three boars' heads couped two and one and as many demi-otters also couped one and two all counterchanged*; crest: *a demi-otter couped sable holding in its mouth a roll of paper argent and resting the sinister paw on a boar's head couped or* (BP (1956) 1613) Gr. to Sir George Newnes, 1st bt (cr. 15 Feb. 1895) the publisher (1851–1910) in 1895. He was son of T.M. Newnes of Matlock. Ext. 1955.

Newton. Borrowash (Ockbrook); Chaddesden; Duffield; Horsley; Mickleover; Norton. *Sable two shin bones in saltire the sinister surmounting the dexter argent*; crest: *a heathen king kneeling on the sinister knee delivering his sword proper point downwards hilt and pommel or*; motto: *'Huic habeo non tibi'* (Vv. 1569, Horsley; 1611: Borrowash, Mickleover; 1662 Duffield). Allowed to several descendants of John Newton of Horsley, MP (Derbys.) 1477. The field is sometimes given, erroneously, as *gules* (e.g. Queen's Coll., Oxford, MS 97). John Leaper, the heir of Robert Newton of Mickleover and Norton, assumed the surname and arms of Newton by RL, 1789. John Newton of Barbados and King's Bromley, Staffs., purchased part of the Agards' estates in Derbys. and the heralds who reported for a planned V. 1688 say 'his father was a meane man borne in Derbys. (Col. Samuel Newton of S. Wingfield gent.) but not related to the Newtons of Mickleover' – nevertheless he used their arms, and d. 1706 (Bassano's MS, Local 3525).

Nightingale. Ashover; Lea Hurst; Matlock. *Ermine a rose gules*; crest: *a greyhound courant proper* (Local MS 9555.109). Used by Peter Nightingale (1736–1803). His heirs were the Shores (via the Evanses) and W.E. Shore, later Nightingale, father of Florence, bore arms of Shore (qv) but his heirs reverted to the Nightingale coat.

Noble. Littleover. *Ermine three leopards' faces sable on a chief indented gules as many annulets or*; crest: *issuant from a wreath of oak proper fructed or a leopard's head couped and affrontée sable collared or*; motto: *'Nomen et omen'* (FD (1910) 1202). Gr. to Lt-Col. John Noble of Littleover 1886 with remainders, and borne by his son W.J. Noble, Recorder of Newark, Notts.

Noel. Edale; Outwoods (Little Eaton). *Or fretty gules and a canton ermine*; crest: *a buck at gaze argent attired or* (BP (1956) 878). Borne by Edward Andrew Noel (1825–99) for many years of the Outwoods. He was a descendant of the 1st Earl of Gainsborough, Lincs., of the 2nd creation (1841, with Viscountcy of Campden (Chipping Campden), Glos., and Barony of Noel of Ridlington, Rutland, to Charles Noel, 3rd Lord Barham of Barham, Kent, the latter honour previously cr., with remainders, in favour of Adm. Sir Charles Middleton, 1805) and the arms were gr. under RL of 5 May 1798. Caroline Patricia, Mrs Gerard Noel, is ultimate heiress of Champion of Edale, and bears these arms (without crest) with Griffith Williams quartering Follet and Champion in pretence (BLG III (1972) 682).

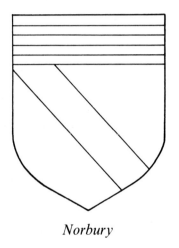

Norbury

Norbury. 'Co. Derby' *Argent a bend sable on a chief gules a barrulet or* (*Rel.* VI (1866) 40). William de Norbury, a justice in eyre 1277, sealed with these arms, and they were borne by Henry de Norbury who appears in a fine concerning the manors of Roston and Norbury (*DAJ* XI (1889) 102). His yr brother, Roger, Bishop of Lichfield (son of William) bore as above but with *two barrulets or* on the *chief* (ibid.); he held Sandiacre *ex officio*, and the arms once appeared in the church there (V. 1611). Another version gives these arms *within a bordure vairé or and gules*

– typical of Ferrers-connected families. The connection (with others) of Henry de Norbury with Norbury and the similarity in the arms suggests that this family were cadets of Fitzherbert.

Normanton. Derby; Horsley; Normanton by Derby; Repton. *Argent three cinquefoils gules and a label sable* (Burke; quartered by de Rodes, without the label, on pedigree of Robert Dale, Blanch Lion, 1695: Glover, II.81). Borne by the descendants of Engenulph de Normanton of Normanton, whose heiresses marr. de Aula and 'Grym' (i.e. Le Wyne) C13. William held in Horsley 1349; Roger in Repton, 1412.

North. Cubley. *Azure a lion passant and on a chief or three fleurs-de-lys of the field*; crest: *a swan proper gorged with a ducal coronet and chained gules* (*DAJ* XXXII (1910) 65; XL (1918) 90). Gr. 21 June 1676 to John North of Cubley. Thompson, (IV.50) gives the *lion* and *chief* as *argent*. 'Mr North' (no locale) disclaimed V. 1611.

North. Bubnell (Baslow). *Argent two chevronels between three mullets sable.* Quartered by Revell of Ogston, whose heiress they marr. On stained glass at Ogston and on Revell seal (1562).

Northedge. Northedge Hall (Ashover). *Sable a chevron engrailed ermine between three escallops argent* (as quartered by Hunt, formerly of Ashover; MI at Aston on Trent church, 1625). The heiress of this family marr. Hunt of Overton mid-C15.

North Midland Railway. Derby. *Per fesse azure and per pale argent and or in chief a fleece of the last ensigned by three mullets two and one of the 2nd in dexter base on a mount vert within park pales a buck couchant proper and in sinister base a Tudor rose ensigned by a Regal crown of the last enclosed by the Roman letters AR (for Adelaide Regina) gules*; crest: *an owl close proper* (painted iron plaque in Derby Museum; cf. Dow, 50). Company began operations 1840, amalgamated with Midland Railway 1844. The arms are an amalgam of those of Leeds, Derby and Derbys. No authority.

Nottingham, Diocese of. *Gules on a ragged cross vert* (sic) *a fleur-de-lys or* impaling *per fesse azure and or in chief three escallops of the last and in base an oak tree eradicated proper*; motto: *Sola salus servire Deo'* (Nottingham Cathedral). Gr. by the Vatican 23 Mar.

1972. The impalement is for the bishop of the time (still in office, 1989), James McGuinness. The diocese includes Derbys.

Nuttall. 'Co. Derby'. Gr. under RL of 1860 to Nuttall formerly Dixon.

Nutting. Brocksford Hall (Doveridge). *Chevronny of six gules and vert three griffins segreant and on a chief or as many nut branches slipped proper;* crest: *a demi-griffin segreant enclosed by two nut branches proper;* motto: *'Mors potior macula'* (BP (1970) 2012). Gr. 1903 to Sir John Nutting of Dublin, cr. a bt 12 Jan. 1903, and borne by Col. Sir Harold Nutting, 2nd bt, of Brocksford Hall 1925.

Oakes. Derby; Riddings House (Alfreton). *Gules on a chevron or between three acorns leaved and slipped proper as many crosses patée sable;* crest: *in front of an oak tree fructed proper two crosses patée fessewise or;* motto: *'Possunt qui posse videntur'* (FD (1929) II.1453). Gr. 1806 to James Oakes (1750–1828), then of Derby and Bury St Edmunds, who in 1818 bought the Riddings estate and developed its mineral resources.

Odingsells. Trusley. *Argent a fesse and in chief two mullets gules* (quartered by Coke on MI at Trusley church, cf. Cox, III.339). Borne by Thomas d'Odingsells *alias* de Trusley *c.* 1393 (cf. Jenyns' Ordinary) whose dau. and heiress marr. Thomas Coke of Trusley. The mullets are of six points on a C13 seal of William (PRO, P.585). Lysons (cviii) give the arms with *three mullets sable in chief.*

Offley. Ashgate (Brampton); Norton Hall. *Argent a cross flory azure between four Cornish choughs proper;* crest: *a demi-lion rampant or collared gules holding in its paws an olive branch leaved vert fructed of the first* (arms: Lysons, cxxxviii; crest: Burke). Gr. 5 Sept. 1588 to Ald. Hugh Offley of London, where it adds: 'the armes was otherwise; but now these confirmed' – a reference to the arms used by the lord mayor of London, 1556: *argent on a cross formée flory azure between four Cornish choughs proper beaked and legged gules a lion passant guardant or.* Robert Offley of Norwich, Norfolk, Hugh's descendant, marr. the heiress of Clarke, and the arms were conf. to Urith, Mrs Shore, née Offley, 1788.

O'Grady. Duffield Park. *Per pale gules and sable three lions passant guardant in pale per pale argent and or the centre one charged on the side with a portcullis azure;* crest: *a horse's head erased argent charged on the neck with a portcullis azure;* motto: *'Vulneratus non victus'* (Lodge, *Peerage* (1911), 913). Borne by Hon. Frederick Standish O'Grady of Duffield Park, son of 2nd Viscount Guillamore (Caher Guillamore, Co. Limerick), who succ. as 6th viscount 1918, when he left the county. From that date he bore supporters: *on either side a lion guardant per fesse argent and or charged on the shoulder with a portcullis azure* (FD (1929) II.1460) which were gr. (UO) 10 Jan. 1831, when the viscounty was cr. (peerage of Ireland). Title ext. 1955.

Ogston: see Walton.

Okeden. Longford; Marston Montgomery. *Sable on a fesse between six acorns or three oak leaves proper* (*Rel.* VI (1866) 40). Sleigh intended these for the arms used by Robert Okeden of Marston Montgomery 1855 (Local MS 4556), descended from Philip, of Longford.

Okedon. 'Co. Derby'. *Gyronny of eight argent and gules in the dexter chief point an oak branch fructed proper* (*Rel.* VI (1866) 40). It is unclear to whom Sleigh intended these arms to refer.

Okeover. Atlow; Osmaston by Ashbourne; Snelston. *Ermine on a chief gules three bezants;* crest: *out of a ducal coronet or a demi-wyvern ermine langued gules* (Vv. Staffs. 1583, 1663). Borne earlier by Philip de Okeover, *c.* 1265 (Willement Roll), and often shown quartering Atlow and 'Gryn' (i.e. Le Wyne) (qqv). The 3rd son of Philip Okeover (d. 1482) settled in London and arms were conf. to his descendant Philip, 6 Mar. 1585, as above with a *mullet for difference* and was gr. a crest: *an oak tree vert fructed or* (see V. London 1568). The senior line became ext. 1765, when the surname and arms were assumed by RL that year by Edward son of Moreton Walhouse of Hatherton, Staffs. On his death without issue in 1793 representation devolved on remoter Okeover cadets. This line became ext. in 1955; the heir, Sir Ian Walker (qv) of Osmaston Manor, 3rd bt, assumed the additional surname and arms of Okeover by RL in 1956.

Oldershaw. Derby. *Azure three annulets or;* crest: *a snake twisted between three arrows one erect and two in saltire;* motto: *'Certanti* *dabitur'* (Burke). Used by George Oldershaw, attorney of Derby, a 'person for a grant' in 1687.

Oldfield. Carsington; Upper Hall (Darley). *Or on a pile vert three garbs of the field*; crest: *on a garb or a dove argent beaked and legged gules holding in the beak an ear of wheat of the first* (Tilley, II.313). Borne or used by Revd John Oldfield, ejected minister of Carsington, b. at Chesterfield, d. at Alfreton 1682; also by another member of the family who lived until 1631 at Darley. Gr. to Anthony Oldfield of Spalding, Lincs., by patent Nov. 1616. A member of the family was cr. a bt 6 Aug. 1660; ext. 1706.

Oldfield. Derby; Doveridge. *Or on a pile engrailed azure three garbs of the field* (Local MS 3525). Painted by Bassano for the funeral of 'Mr Oldfield of Derby', marr. to a dau. of Cavendish of Doveridge, 12 Oct. 1722.

Oldknow. Derby; Mellor. Crest:*a cubit arm erect habited cuffed and holding in the hand an escroll in bend sinister all between two branches all proper* (livery button in local collection). Used by Samuel Oldknow of Mellor and Derby, high sheriff 1824, d. 1828; of a family from Heanor settled in Nottingham.

Oliver. Chellaston. *A hand and arm issuant from clouds from the dexter fesseways*; motto: *'Amor vincit omnia'* (C17 carving on pew once in Chellaston church, Cox, II.411). Used by John Oliver of Chellaston, gent., living 1633 and marr. to a Blackwall (qv) as impaled on the carving.

Olivier. Ashford Hall (Ashford). *Argent on a mount vert in base an olive tree proper*; crest: *an esquire's helm proper*; motto: *'Sicut oliva laetor in aede Dei'* (Papworth, 1113; Local MS 5555). Gr. by Louis XIV to Isaac Olivier of Nay, France, *c.* 1660, and used in Derbys. by William Olivier of Ashford Hall. Sir Sydney Olivier, an uncle, was cr. Lord Olivier of Ramsden (ext. 1943; no grant of arms) in 1924, and another uncle was father of the late Sir Laurence Olivier, cr. for life (1970) Lord Olivier of Brighton, Sussex.

Orby. Blackwell; Dronfield. *Gules two lions passant or.* John de Orby (Lincs.), constable of Gilbert of Ghent, marr. *c.* 1200 a coheiress of William FitzRannulph de Alfreton and acquired *jure uxoris* Blackwell. A junior branch held Dronfield 1285 of Tattershall.

Ord. Edgehill (Little Eaton). *Sable three fishes haurient argent a bordure ermine*; crest:

an elk's head proper (*Rel.* VI (1866) 40; crest: Burke). Gr. *c.* 1685 to John Ord of Fenham, Northumberland, ancestor of Revd James Ord, vicar of East and West Langton, Leics. (1759–1836), whose 3rd son James Pickering Ord (d. 1863) settled at Edge Hill. Collaterals varied the arms on becoming Blackett-Ord by RL 7 Dec. 1855.

Orme. Burnaston; Derby; Hoon. *Azure an eagle displayed between three poleaxes or*; crest: *a dolphin azure and a battleaxe or* (King, 182). Borne or used by John Orme of Burnaston, whose heiress marr. Bristow of Twyford, and gr. 18 Feb. 1663 to William, of Hanch Hall, Staffs.

Ormond. Alfreton. *Azure a chief indented or* (Harl.MS 1093; quartering Chaworth, MI at Alfreton, Cox, I.9). John Ormond (d. 1503) marr. the heiress of Chaworth of Alfreton. Sleigh misread and records the arms as: *sable a chief with sun's rays issuant therefrom or* (*Rel.* VI (1866) 40).

Osborne. Burrows Hall (Brailsford); Derby. *Or on a bend between two wolves' heads erased sable three dolphins embowed of the field*; crest: *a pelican in her piety or the nest sable* (Vv. 1634, 1662). Allowed to John Osborne of Derby, 5th son of William, of Nuthall, Notts., V. 1634 and to his nephew and heir, John (son of William of Brailsford) V. 1662. The magnificent wrought ironwork by Bakewell from his house in St Mary's Gate, Derby, is now at Derby Cathedral, where the tinctures have been restored reversed; within, the crest of a side gate remains, but the escutcheon was restored quite arbitrarily as *gules three escallops or*. Borne by the descendants of William, of Brailsford, and of Burrows Hall, Over Burrows, to the present.

Osborne. Ockbrook; Field House (Spondon). *Argent a bend sable between two lions rampant gules*; crest: *a demi-lion rampant gules* (bookplate in local collection; Burke). Richard Osborne of Ockbrook disclaimed these arms V. 1611; they were used by his descendants, of Field House, Spondon, e.g. Joseph (1745–1818).

Osmaston: see Wright.

Outram. Alfreton; Butterley Hall (Ripley). *Or on a chevron embattled between three crosses flory gules five escallops of the field*; crest: *issuant from an eastern crown a demilion or accolled with a wreath of laurel proper holding a cross flory gules*; supporters: *on* *either side a Royal Bengal tiger guardant accolled each with a wreath of laurel all proper and crowned with an eastern crown or*; motto: *'Mutare fidem nescio'* (BP (1970) 2054). Gr. 1858 to Gen. Sir James Outram, who was cr. a bt, 10 Nov. that year; son of Benjamin Outram of Butterley Hall. Supporters gr. 1859 to descend with the btcy.

Owen: see Coke.

Oxley. Derby; Wingfield Manor (S. Wingfield). *Argent a fesse gules between three oxen passant sable armed and unguled or*; crest: *an ox's head couped sable armed or and charged with three ermine spots*; motto: *'Tam aris quam aratis'* (BLG (1952) 1948). Gr. by RL to Christopher Braithwaite 1775 who assumed the surname and arms of Oxley, the estates of which family he inherited. The Oxleys were descended from Amor Oxley of Wingfield Manor (but from Bushbury, Staffs.), who d. at Morpeth, Northumberland, 1587. It is possible that the first two words of the motto are a deliberate canting juxtaposition; if so, why?

Oxspring: see Kinder.

D'Oyly. Litchurch (Derby). *Or two bendlets azure* (*Rel.* XII (1872) 94; cf. seal PRO, P.1305). Borne by Sir John d'Oyly of Raunton, Staffs., and Litchurch, early C13; his son, also of Litchurch, marr. the heiress of Sir William de Dunston of Dunston (now Duston), Northants., and bore Dunston in lieu of d'Oyly: *gules a buck's head caboshed argent* (ibid).

Page. Shirland. *Gules a chevron between three martlets argent* (Local MS 4556 cf. Burke). Possibly the arms used by Isaac Spencer Page of Shirland, *c.* 1786–1813.

Paget. Caldwell; Hanson Grange (Newton Grange); Stapenhill. *Sable on a cross engrailed between four eagles displayed argent five lions passant guardant of the field*; crest: *a demi-heraldic tiger sable maned ducally gorged and tufted argent*; supporters: *on either side an heraldic tiger as in the crest*; motto: *'Per il suo contrario'* (BP (1970) 75). Arms conf., crest and supporters gr., by letters patent 1552 to Sir William Paget of Beaudesert (Cannock), Staffs., summoned that year to Parliament by writ as Lord Paget, of Beaudesert. His descendant, 7th baron, was further cr. Lord Burton (Burton on Trent, Staffs.), 1712 and

Earl of Uxbridge, Middlesex, 1715; ext. 1769, except the original barony, which passed to his heir Henry Bayley, who assumed the arms and surname of Paget by RL 1770. He was son of Sir Nicholas, 2nd bt (cr. 4 July 1730, Irish), and was cr. in 1784 Earl of Uxbridge. His son was advanced to be Marquess of Anglesey 1815.

Paget. Darley House (Darley); King's Newton Hall (Melbourne); Stuffynwood Hall (Shirebrook). *Sable a cross engrailed between two escallops one in dexter chief the other in sinister base argent*; crest: *a lion rampant sable collared or supporting an antique escutcheon argent thereon an escallop sable*; motto: *'Espere et persevere'* (FD (1905) 1046). Gr. 1845 to William Paget of Loughborough, Leics., and the male descendants of his father, Joseph (d. 1842), and borne by Herbert Byng Paget of Darley House (1845–1914) and his 2nd cousin Joseph, of Stuffynwood (d. 1896). Another cousin, George Ernest, was cr. a bt, 25 Sept. 1897 and his son, Sir Cecil Paget, prominent in the Midland Railway, was of King's Newton, and d. 1936, when the title became ext. Previous to the grant, the family had used: *argent a cross engrailed sable fretty of the field between two escallops of the 2nd* charged as above, with the same crest, as still given as late as 1905, before the arms were exemplified (Debrett (1905) 481).

Palmer. West Hallam. Used arms, but disclaimed, V. 1611; what they were is unclear.

Palmer. West Broughton (Doveridge). *Argent a chevron gules between three bundles vert* (impaled by Lathbury at Egginton church V. 1611, Harl.MS 1093). One suspects that the *bundles* may have been intended for *palm branches*. Used or borne by William Palmer of West Broughton, whose dau. and heiress marr. Francis Lathbury of Holme (Egginton), C16. See also Morewood.

Pares. Hopwell Hall. *Sable a chevron in the dexter chief a cross crosslet argent*; crest: *a demi-griffin or*; motto: *'Pares cum paribus'* (Local MS 9555.114). Used by Thomas Pares (1716–1805) of a Leicester family who purchased Hopwell. The arms were borne by a medieval family called Parys.

Parker. Derby. *Argent three stags' heads caboshed sable* (D369). Shown quartering *sable a fesse between three bezants*, neither of which is in Papworth. Used by Ald. Joseph Parker (1590–1646) of St Michael's parish, bailiff of Derby 1634.

Parker. Derby; Little Eaton. *Argent a chevron between three mullets gules on a chief azure as many stags' heads caboshed or* (on silver given to All Saints' church, Derby, 1765). Arms disclaimed by Joseph Parker of Derby, 'son of a baker worth 8 or 10 thous. £', V. 1662. Used by Frances, dau. and heiress of Edmund Parker of St Michael's, Derby, and Little Eaton, before 1765.

Parker. Derby; Norton Lees; Parwich. *Gules a chevron between three leopards' faces or*; crest: *a leopard's face erased and affrontée or ducally gorged gules*; motto: *'Sapere aude'* (V. 1611). Arms conf. and crest gr. 1599 to John Parker of Norton Lees, the arms having been entered V. 1569 by his like-named father. William son of George Parker of Parwich, the yr John's nephew, was 'a usurper' V. 1611. His descendant, Thomas, of Derby, was cr. 1716 Lord Parker of Macclesfield (Cheshire), and Viscount Parker, and in 1721 Earl of Macclesfield, receiving on 10 Mar. 1716 conf. of the arms and a gr. of supporters: *on either side a leopard reguardant or ducally gorged gules* (BP (1956) 1396). His kinsman, Admiral Sir William Parker, was conf. in these arms 1797 and cr. a bt, 18 Dec. 1844, of Shenstone, Staffs. He adopted the motto: *'Sub liberate quietem'* (ibid. 1690).

Parker. Derby; Little Norton. *Argent a chevron pean between three mullets sable on a chief azure as many bucks' heads caboshed or*; crest: *a talbot's head couped argent eared and langued gules gorged pean* (*DAJ* V (1883) 30–1). Gr. 10 Nov. 1775 to John Parker of Greystones (Sheffield, Yorks.) (1700–79), b. at Little Norton. His forebears were kin to others of Little Norton (qv).

Parker. Little Norton. *Argent a chevron gules between three mullets pierced sable on a chief azure as many stags' heads caboshed or*; crest: *a stag's head erased quarterly sable and argent charged with four mullets counterchanged* (DAJ V (1883) 30–31). Allegedly gr. (no reference found) to a member of this family early C17. However, they were describing themselves as 'yeoman' until the father of John, gr. arms 1775 (see preceding entry), who used arms as Parker of Norton Lees, but the *chevron engrailed* (Burke). See also Newdigate.

Partington. Glossop. *Sable on a bend nebulée between four mullets of six points two in chief and as many in base argent three Cornish choughs proper*; crest: *out of the battlements of a tower a goat's head proper charged on the neck with a mullet of six points between two escallops sable* (FD (1929) II.1505). Gr. 1898 to Edward Partington of High Street East, Glossop. Knighted in that year and in 1917 cr. Lord Doverdale, of Westwood Park, Worcs., when he was gr. supporters: *on either side a sacred ibis proper*, and adopted as motto: *'Fortiter et recte'* (ibid). Title ext. 1949.

Patten. Baslow; Derby. *Fusilly ermine and sable a canton gules*; crest: *a griffin's head erased vert*; motto: *'Nulla pallescere culpa'* and *'Virtus sidera tollit'* (J. Foster, *Peerage* (1881), 705). Arms allegedly borne by John Patten of Baslow C15 (Shirley, 64). A descendant inherited part of the estates of the Wilsons, of Derby (qv), and assumed the surname and arms of Wilson additionally 1784. John Wilson-Patten was in 1874 cr. Lord Winmarleigh, of West Lancs., and was gr. supporters the same year: *dexter a griffin vert charged with a lozenge ermine sinister a wolf or charged with an estoile sable* (ibid.). Ext. 1896.

Paveley. S. Wingfield. *Or on a fesse azure three crosses recercelée of the field* (glass in N. Wingfield church, cf. Cox, I.431). Attributed to Roger son of Lawrence Paveley of S. Wingfield, 1284.

Payne-Gallwey. Castle Hill House (Bakewell). *Grand quarterly of four, I. quarterly i & iv per fesse or and gules in chief an eagle displayed sable and in base a castle argent, for Gallwey ii & iii gules a fesse between two lions passant argent, for Payne; II: Payne; III: Gallwey; IV: Frankland quartering Russell*; crest: *a cat-à-mountain passant guardant proper gorged with a collar gemel or, for Gallwey and a lion's gamb erased argent holding the lower part of a tilting spear in bend gules* (FD (1929) 1513). Borne by Albert Philip Payne-Gallwey (1871–1931) who succ. the Nesfields (qv) at Castle Hill. Arms of Payne gr. 1770; Frankland quartering Russell by RL 9 Feb. 1837; Payne quartering Gallwey gr. by RL 7 Mar. 1814 to Gen. Sir William Payne-Gallwey, cr. a bt, 8 Dec. 1812. The 3rd bt assumed the additional surname and arms of Frankland by RL 4 Apr. 1914.

Peach. Kirk Langley. *Gules three martlets between two chevronels argent*; crest: *a demi-*

lion rampant ducally crowned (Local MS 9555.129). Used by 'Dr (Thomas) Peach' of Langley Hall, *c.* 1846–83; the arms were gr. to the unrelated Peaches of Rooksmoor, Glos., 8 Nov. 1769 but with a different crest.

Peachey: see Peché.

Peacock. Marston Park (Marston Montgomery). *Argent three peacocks' heads and necks proper each ducally gorged or* (as quartered by Buckston of Bradbourne, Glover, 2nd ed., II.155). Used by this family, whose heiress marr. Stubbing, and the heiress of Richard Stubbing marr. *c.* 1710, George Buxton (sic), whose son quartered them.

Peacock. Rodsley. *Argent a chevron gules between three peacocks' heads and necks erased and ducally gorged or* (Glover, 2nd Ed., II.155). Confusingly, these arms, used by Richard Peacock of Rodsley *c.* 1718, were also quartered by the Buxtons of Bradbourne, one of whom marr. the heiress.

Pearce-Serocold: see Sorocold.

Pearson. Bradbourne Hall; Matlock; S. Wingfield; Wirksworth. *Argent on a pile azure a rose of the 1st barbed and seeded proper between three arrows points downwards or barbed and flighted also of the field*; crest: *an eagle's wing sable semée-de-lys or pierced by an arrow embrued in bend point upwards and vulned proper*; motto: *'Ne tentes aut perfice'* (BLG (1937) 1773). Gr. 1845 to John Pearson of S. Wingfield (1814–94).

Pearson. Brailsford. *Gules a cross or in the 1st and 4th quarters a sparrowhawk proper in the 2nd and 3rd a cross crosslet fitchée of the 2nd*; crest: *on the trunk of a tree in front of two sprigs of laurel in saltire a sparrowhawk supporting in the dexter claw all proper a cross crosslet fitchée in bend or*; motto: *'Sudore non sopore'* (FD (1929) II.1519). Gr. 12 Sept. 1923 to Sir Louis Frederick Pearson (b. 1863) of Lenton and Brailsford, son of John of Chilwell, Notts., and of Derbys. descent.

Pearson. Derby. *Per fesse embattled ermine and sable three suns in splendour or* (on a misericord in St Peter's church, Derby). Judging from the style of these arms, they probably represent those of Revd S. Pearson (1746–1811), incumbent of Osmaston; buried at St Peter's; he was brother of Revd J.B. Pearson, vicar of Croxall. Their father, John, a Derby burgess, was of London and Derby. Authority for arms unclear.

Peché. Sharrowhall (Thurvaston). *Azure a*

lion rampant double queued ermine crowned and on a canton or a mullet gules (*Rel.* VI (1866) 40). Allowed V. Leics. 1563 to William Peché, or Peachey of Kingsthorpe, Northants., grandson of John, of Sharrow Hall, Derbys. The arms are found, without *canton*, in the Willement Roll as borne by a John Peché, *c.* 1380. However, the above arms were conf. 'without variation and stated in Patent that descent from John (son of William Peachey) of Kingsthorpe was proved' and crest gr. to William Peachey of Sussex, 20 Feb. 1664. His son, Henry, was cr. a bt 21 Mar. 1736, with remainder to his brothers, the youngest of whom was further cr. Lord Selsey (Sussex), being gr. supporters: *on either side a maiden habited argent crowned or*; the crest gr. in 1663 was: *a demi-lion rampant double queued ermine in the dexter forepaw a sword erect argent hilt and pommel or*, but as borne by Lord Selsey lacked the *sword*, and in the arms had the tinctures of the *canton* changed to *argent*. Motto: *'Memor et fidelis'* (Debrett, *Peerage* (1817), I.27). Titles ext. 1838.

Pechell: see Peshall.

Pecke. Brampton. *Argent on a chevron gules three crosses formée of the field* (V. 1611). Thomas Pecke of Brampton was of a Yorks. family which bore the arms as above, but the chevron *engrailed* (V. Yorks. 1612). As quartered by Revell, however, in Local MS 6341, the crosses are given as *or*. In D369 the arms of this family are also given as: *sable semée-de-lys argent three crosses patée or*; these are in fact the arms gr. 13 Dec. 1598 to Pecke of Lutterworth, Leics.

Peckham. Stanley Grange (Dale Abbey). *Sable a chevron or between three crosses crosslet fitchée argent* (*DAJ* XL (1918) 91). Used by George Peckham of Stanley Grange and entered in some MSS of V. 1611. Most leave a blank shield: apparently, he 'promised to come to London'.

Pedder. Kilburn Hall. *Quarterly sable and gules on a bend argent between two escallops or a greyhound courant between two quatrefoils of the 2nd*; crest: *between two branches of olive proper as many lions' heads erased at the neck addorsed erminois gorged with a collar gules*; motto: *'Je dis la verité'* (FD (1910) 1262). Gr. 26 Mar. 1814 to Edward Pedder, mayor of Preston, Lancs., 1790, and borne by his grandson Col. Charles Denison Pedder

(1826–98) of Kilburn Hall.

Pegge. Ashbourne; Beauchief; Melbourne; Osmaston by Ashbourne; Shirley; Yeldersley. *Argent a chevron between three Passion nails sable*; crest: *a demi-sun issuant or rays alternately argent and sable* (V. 1662). Allowed to Edward Pegge of Beauchief, 1662 (the *Passion nails* therein blazoned as *pegges*), although the shield is left blank in some MSS. Conf. by RL 1836 when Benjamin Stead, the heir, assumed the surname and quarterly arms of Pegge-Burnell. Pegge of Yeldersley was labelled 'an usurper' V. 1611, and had his arms entered 'sans proof' V. 1662. Edward Pegge of Ashbourne, an attorney and father of Edward of Beauchief, was respited for proof on the same occasion, which suggests that, prior to 1836, the arms were used without authority.

Perryn. Charnock Hall (Eckington). *Argent on a chevron sable between three pineapples vert as many leopards' heads of the field*; crest: *a pineapple stalked and leaved or* (*Rel.* VI (1866) 40). Borne by Peter Perryn of Charnock Hall *c.* 1410 (the crest is probably anachronistic), whose son by a Parker of Norton Lees, John, was of Brockton, Salop.

Peshall. Eddlestow Hall (Ashover); Lea. *Argent a cross formée florettée sable on a canton gules a wolf's head erased of the field*; crest: *a boar's head couped at the neck gules armed and crined or* (V. Staffs., 1614). Conf. 1436 by Joan 'late wife of William Lee of Knightley' (Staffs.) to Richard son of Humphrey Peshale (W. Camden, *Remains concerning Britain* (1605), 220). A descendant of Humphrey's half-brother, Richard Peshall, was *jure uxoris* of Lea and Eddlestow C16. The family's original arms were: *argent a cross flory sable on a quarter gules a lion's head erased of the field crowned or* (Adam de Peshall of Weston under Lizard, Staffs., *c.* 1390, of the senior line; Willement Roll). Sir John, grandson of Richard, was cr. a bt 25 Nov. 1611; title ext. 1712.

Peveril. Castleton etc. *Vairé or and gules* (Lysons, lxi). Borne by William Peveril II (d. *c.* 1134) and adopted by the descendants of the heiress who marr. Ferrers (qv). Another coat frequently quoted for this man is: *quarterly gules and vairé or and azure a lion rampant argent* (although the *azure* is sometimes given as *vert*, in glass at St Mary's, Nottingham, cf. Thoroton, *Notts.* (1793), II.86). But

note that pre-1134 is a uniquely early date for hereditable arms, even if, as here, they seem to have been attributed on the strength of the Ferrers' sudden addiction to *vairé or and gules* from the mid C12, a factor which suggests that they were not merely retrospectively attributed.

Phelips. Stubben Edge Hall (Ashover). *Argent a chevron between three roses gules seeded and leaved proper*; crest: *a square beacon (or chest) on two wheels or filled with fire proper*; motto: *'Pro aris et focis'* (Burke). Borne by Sir John Phelips of Barrington, Somerset, 3rd bt, cr. 16 Feb. 1620, who was *jure uxoris* of Stubben Edge. Title ext. 1690. V. Somerset 1623 (Harl.MS 1141) gives the arms of the unrelated Phillips of Yeovil, at the head of the pedigree of Phelips of Barrington and Montacute: *argent a lion rampant sable collared and lined or*, which is demonstrably in error.

Philips. Alsop Hall (Eaton & Alsop). *Per pale azure and sable a lion rampant erminois ducally crowned and holding between the paws a mascle or within an orle of fleur-de-lys argent and a canton ermine*; crest: *a demi-lion rampant erminois collared sable ducally crowned or holding between the paws a fleur-de-lys within a mascle of the third*; motto: *'Simplex munditiis'* (FD (1929) II.1547). Gr. 22 July 1822 to John Philips of Heath House (Upper Tean), Staffs. (1759–1834) and borne by Edward Mark Philips of Alsop Hall in the 1920s and 1930s.

Pierrepont. Beighton; Calow; Owlcotes (Heath); Tibshelf etc. *Argent semée of cinquefoils gules a lion rampant sable*; crest: *a lion rampant sable between two wings erect argent*; supporters: *on either side a lion sable armed and langued gules*; motto: *'Pie repone te'* (V. Notts 1662). Arms conf., crest and supporters gr., 1623 to 1st Viscount Newark and Lord Pierrepont (creation of that year) who inherited Owlcotes and whose ancestors had acquired property in Derbys. from C13. At this earlier period the arms were: *argent a lion rampant sable and an orle of six cinquefoils gules* (Powell Roll), as borne by Thomas and Sir Edmund Pierrepont, *c.* 1360. Lord Newark was made Earl of Kingston, Yorks., 1628, and the family were later raised to the Marquessate of Dorchester, Dorset (1644, ext. 1680, and again, 1706) and Dukedom of Kingston upon Hull (1715, all ext. 1773). In

1773 the estates passed to Charles Medows, who in 1788 assumed the surname and arms of Pierrepont in lieu of his own and 23 July 1796 was cr. Lord Pierrepont of Holme Pierrepont, Notts. and Viscount Newark. He was further advanced 9 Apr. 1806 as Earl Manvers (all ext. 1955). In 1883 the Derbys. holdings of Lord Manvers amounted to 3,729 acres.

Piggin. Ockbrook. Robert Piggin of Ockbrook disclaimed V. 1611; the arms he used are not known.

Pigot. Hucklow; Eyam; Weston upon Trent. *Gules a bend fusilly between six martlets or* (V. Notts. 1664). Gr. 6 Dec. 1662 to Gervase Pigot of Thrumpton, Notts., 3rd in descent from Thomas Pygot of Weston. Similar arms were borne by Sir Peter Pygot, sheriff of Notts. and Derbys. 1311–12, although they are also given as: *azure a bend engrailed* (in error, no doubt, for *fusilly*) *between six martlets or* (Walford Roll, *Archaeologia*, XXXIX).

Pilkington. Stanton by Dale. *Azure a cross patonce voided argent*; crest: *a mower holding a scythe proper* (Vv. 1569; 1611; MI at Stanton church and in glass in Chesterfield, 1611, Local MS 6341). Allowed to George Pilkington of Stanton 1569, 3rd in descent from Geoffrey, 1st of Stanton (d. 1494), yr son of Sir Thomas, of Pilkington, Lancs., who was heir of an Agnes Pilkington as lessor of the manor of Unstone. His arms were: *argent a cross patonce voided gules* (Burke).

Pim: see Pym.

Pinder: see Pyndar.

Pinon (Pinxton). 'Co. Derby'. *Vair two bars gules a canton or* (Burke). Gr. between 1727 and 1740. Nothing further known.

Pipard. Kirk Langley. *Argent two bars and on a canton azure a cinquefoil or*; crest: *a lion sejant proper supporting an inescutcheon of the arms* (Falkirk Roll, 1298 (*Rel.* XVI, 1875); seal of 1300, Egginton Charter 35 in Every Deeds in private hands). Assumed and borne by Sir Ralph Pipard of Rotherfield Peppard, Oxon., Kirk Langley and Twyford (Bucks.), son of Ralph FitzNicholas by Alice, dau. and heiress of William Pipard. In 1300 he was summoned to Parliament as a baron. Ralph Lathbury (qv) was his chamberlain; his similar arms may be the result of a grant by Lord Pipard. The earlier Pipards bore *argent two bars azure* (Nobility Roll).

Pipe. Barlborough; Hearthcote (Castle Gresley); Killamarsh; Netherseal; Stanton by Dale; Whitwell. *Azure crusilly and two organ pipes in chevron or* crest: *a leopard's head erased or*; motto: *'Qui sera sera'* (arms, as quartered by Vernon of Sudbury, V. 1569; achievement, V. Staffs. 1664). Borne by Pipe of Bilston, 1664, which family had for many years been of Hearthcote and were then holding in Stanton by Dale. Also by Sir Richard Pype, lord mayor of London 1578, who purchased Barlborough, Killamarsh and Whitwell (sold 1593). Samuel Pipe of Hearthcote etc was also of Statfold, Staffs., which he inherited from the Wolferstans, assuming the additional surname and quartering the arms of that family by RSM 15 June 1776: *sable a fesse wavy couped between three wolves' heads erased or*; crest: *a wolf statant in front of a tree or leaved vert* (BLG (1937) 2478).

Piro. Aldwark; Hilton. *Argent a boar passant sable* (Burke). Borne, apparently, by William son of Robert de Piro, who held half a knight's fee in Aldwark *c.* 1182–1200 in succession to his father.

Player. Ednaston Manor (Brailsford). *Argent a pale azure between two saffron-flowers leaved and slipped proper*; crest: *a cubit arm couped grasping in the hand three saffron-flowers in bend leaved and slipped all proper*; motto: *'Spes mea in Deo'* (FD (1929) II.1561). Gr., with remainders, C20 and borne by S.D. Player (d. 1982) of Ednaston Manor.

Pleasley (Plesley). Pleasley. *Argent on a fesse between two bars gemelles gules three fleurs-de-lys of the field* (Local MS 4556). Borne (apparently) by William de Pleasley 'alias Jameson', vicar of Tibshelf 1391–1424 (son of John son of James), allegedly cadets of the line of Serlo de Plesley; cf. Glapwell. Papworth only gives Normanvill for these arms.

Plumbley. Plumbley Hall (Eckington). *Sable a chevron between three escallops argent a chief or* (Local MS 6341). Surely an archaic form of the arms of Linacre (qv), who marr. the heiress. Perhaps descended from a common ancestor.

Plumpton. Darley. *Argent five fusils in fesse sable each charged with an escallop of the field* (as quartered by Eyre on MI at Hathersage church, Cox, II. 234). Borne by Sir William (yr son of Sir Robert Plumpton of Plumpton, Yorks.) who settled, in consequence of the marriage of his father to the heiress of Foljambe, at Darley. Heiress marr. Sotehill. Sir Robert bore as above but field *azure, fusils or, escallops gules* (Willement Roll).

Pochin. Normanton House. *Or a chevron gules between three horseshoes sable*; crest: *a harpy wings expanded proper full faced tail twisted around the leg* (V. Leics. 1619). Borne c18 by George Pochin of Bourne, Lincs., and Normanton *jure uxoris*. His wife was a dau. of Sir Wolstan Dixie, 4th bt. House sold *c.* 1819.

Poë (Poër). Poësfield and Wynn's Castle (Pinxton). *Or a fesse between three crescents azure issuant therefrom flames of fire proper.* Gr. 6 July 1599 to Leonard Poë of London, son of James son of Richard of Poësfield Co. Derby. He was a presumably a cadet of the family of Ranulph son of Ranulph le Poer of Temple Normanton and Pinxton, where he held a quarter of a knight's fee, *c.* 1275. The heiress marr. Le Wyne (qv), hence Wynn's Castle. Dering Roll (Robert le Poer): *quarterly ermine and azure two leopards' faces or.* Leonard's descendant, Col. William Hutchinson Poë, was cr. a bt 2 July 1912, and his son took the additional surname and arms of Domville and was gr. a crest (*a lion's head erased argent ducally crowned or*, BP (1956) 663) by Act of Parliament of the Irish Free State, 1936.

Pole. Bartonfields (Barton Blount); Hartington; Hopton; Radbourne Hall etc. *Argent a chevron between three crescents gules*; crest: *a falcon rising proper*; motto: *'Auxilum divinum maneat semper nobiscum'* (Vv. 1569, 1611, 1662). Borne by Sir John Pole of Newborough, Staffs., *jure uxoris* of Wakebridge (qv) *c.* 1370, and by his descendants of Radbourne. His father, also John, was of Hartington *jure uxoris* and bore the arms usually attributed to Hartington of Hartington: *or a stag's head caboshed between the attires a fleurs-de-lys gules* (Willement Roll). Unpublished research suggests that these Poles were descended from Poole of Cheshire, who bore *azure semée-de-lys or a lion rampant argent* (V. Cheshire 1580). A cadet branch of the Derbys. family were subsequently settled at Pool Hall, Hartington, who differenced with *an annulet or* (once in glass at Ashbourne church, cf. *DAJ* III (1881) 90). Sir Charles van Notten (cr. a bt 28 July 1791) marr. the heiress of a cadet, Charles, who had a confirmation of the arms 1742, and assumed the surname and arms of Pole in lieu of van Notten, by RSM 1787. He was gr. 1794 the supporters of HSH Wilhelm, Landgraf v. Hesse-Cassel: *on either side a lion reguardant proper on each a pale of three tinctures per pale gules and argent and azure*; motto: *'Pollet virtus'*. In 1853, by RL, their descendants added the surname and quartered the arms of van Notten. The Poles of Radbourne assumed the surname and quartered arms of Chandos-Pole by RL 1807, and a descendant assumed the additional surname and arms of Gell 1863 also by RL, the latter process was reversed in the same manner, 1918.

Pole. Park Hall (Barlborough); Spinkhill (Eckington); Wakebridge (Crich). *Argent a chevron between three crescents gules and a canton azure*; crest: *a falcon wings endorsed proper ducally gorged or* (Vv. 1569, 1611, 1662). Allowed with crest and canton 1569; crest modified V. 1662. Previously the arms had been borne as Radbourne with difference (seal of Peter de la Pole 1379, Local MS 6341).

Pole. Heage; Kirk Langley. *Argent a chevron between three crescents and a canton gules*; crest: *a falcon haggard volant proper* (Vv. 1611, 1662). Gr. quarterly with Dethick and Wakebridge and crest 1578 to Godfrey Pole of Heage, supplanting a grant of the same crest, but the original arms differenced with a *mullet*, to Philip Pole of Heage of 1525. V. 1662 omits the canton and calls the crest a *dove*.

Pole. Mercaston. *Gules a chevron between three crescents argent* (*Rel.* VI (1866) 40). Borne by Anthony Pole of Mercaston, 4th son of Ralph, of Radburne Hall, 1490.

Poole. Brailsford. *Or two bars azure* (*Rel.* VI (1866) 40). Used by John Poole of London, merchant (d. 1686), who claimed Derbys. ancestry. His son, Barnabas, was rector of Brailsford and d. 1698.

Port(e). Etwall. *Azure a fesse engrailed between three pigeons each holding in the beak a cross formée fitchée or*; motto: *'Intende prospere'* (MI at Etwall church). Gr. 27 June 1506 to Henry Port(e) of Chester, whose son, Sir John, was of Etwall.

Port(e). Culland Hall (Brailsford); Windle Hill (Osleston & Thurvaston). *Vert a fesse engrailed cotised argent between three pigeons each holding in the beak a cross formée fitchée*

Porte

or (V. Staffs. 1663). Gr. 1583 to John son of John son of Richard Port(e) of Ilam, Staffs., the latter being a brother of the grantee of 1506 (see previous entry). However, the field was sometimes given as *azure*, e.g. V. Staffs. 1614. Rowe, son of George Newall of Ilam and Windlehill, assumed the surname and arms of Port(e) by RL 1747, as did his sister's nephew, John Sparrow, also by RL, in 1761. See also Repton School; Sir John Port School.

Pott. Stancliffe Hall (Darley). *Barry of ten argent and sable on a bend azure three trefoils slipped or*; crest: *on a mount vert a greyhound couchant gules collared or* (V. 1611). Gr. 19 Nov. 1611 to John Pott of Stancliffe, son of John, of Cheshire, and who marr. the heiress of Columbell via Newsom. The senior line of the family, then seated at Pott Hall, near Bollington, was allowed (in the person of Edmund Pott): *or two bars and overall a bend azure*; crest: on a mount vert an ounce sejant proper collared and lined or (V. London 1634).

Potter. Heanor; Ilkeston; Shipley Wood; West Hallam. *Azure on a chevron argent between three lozenges or as many estoiles gules*

all within a bordure engrailed of the 2nd; crest: in front of three garbs or a sickle in bend sinister proper; motto: 'Claude os aperi oculos' (BLG (1952) 2060). Gr. 1942 to Col. William Allen Potter of Woodborough, Notts., of an Erewash valley family.

Pountain. Barrow Hall (Barrow on Trent); Derby. *Azure a bend between two demi-horses erased argent*; crest: *a demi-horse erased argent supporting a cross crosslet fitchée or gorged with a collar dovetailed azure*; motto: 'Fidelis usque ad mortem' (Local MS 9555.74). Borne or used by Capt. J.T. Pountain of Barrow, a Derby vintner (1842–87).

Powell. Ashbourne. *Gules a lion rampant within a bordure engrailed or*; crest: *a lion's head erased argent gorged with a collar flory gules*; motto: 'Anima in amicis una' (BLG (1937) 1837). Arms conf. and crest gr. to Thomas Powell of Whittington, Salop., 5 July 1574, and borne by his descendant, Capt. Henry Folliott Powell (1803–72) of The Mansion, Ashbourne, and his son, L.R. Powell.

Powerdon (Pourdon). 'Co. Derby.' *Ermine a chevron and on a chief sable three leopards' faces or* (Rel. VI (1866) 40). It is not clear to whom Sleigh was referring when he included this coat.

Powtrell. Breaston; West Hallam Hall. *Argent a fesse between three cinquefoils gules*; crest: *a porcupine passant gules spined collared and chain flexed over the back and terminating in a cinquefoil or* (V. 1611). Borne originally by Elias de Prestwold, whose heiress marr. Robert Powtrell of Thrumpton, Notts., *c.* 1275. At that time he bore: *or on a bend azure three fleurs-de-lys argent* (Parliament Roll), but by the end of C14 the Prestwold arms were borne exclusively. Thomas Powtrell of Thrumpton d. *c.* 1420, and his heiress marr. Thomas Smith of Breaston, who then assumed the surname and arms (as above) of Powtrell.

Powys: see Gruffydd ap Gwenwynwyn.

Prescott. Derby. *Ermine a chevron and on a chief sable two leopards' faces or*; crest: *out of a ducal coronet or a boar's head and neck argent bristled of the first* (V. Lincs. 1592). Borne by William son of John Prescott of Derby, who marr. there 1652. The arms are remarkably akin to those of Powerdon (qv).

Prime. Normanton. Maj. Philip Prime of Normanton, where he had 'a small estate', 'did not appear', V. 1662. The arms he used

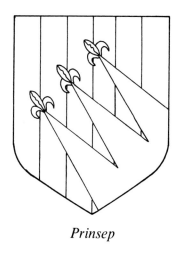

Prinsep

in bend flory at the points or; crest: *an eagle's head gules goutée d'or holding in the beak a bird-bolt sable* (FD (1910) 989). Gr. under RL of 1835 to Thomas Levett-Prinsep, formerly Levett, of Wychnor Park, Staffs., and Croxall, quartering Levett: *argent a lion rampant between three cross crosslets fitchée sable on a bordure engrailed azure four like crosses and as many fleur-de-lys alternately or*, with the motto: *'Non prodigus neque avarus'* (ibid). His father, Theophilus, of Wychnor, marr. the heiress of Thomas son of Thomas Prinsep of Croxall (d. 1814).

Pursglove. Tideswell. *Argent a cross fleury engrailed sable within a bordure also engrailed gules bezantée* (*Rel.* VI (1866) 40). Alleged by Sleigh to have been borne by Robert Pursglove of Tideswell, suffragan Bishop of Kingston upon Hull, Yorks., C15. Heiress marr. Eyre of Holme Hall (Newbold). The arms are usually associated with Purslow of Hawkstone, Salop.

Pye. Hoon. *Ermine a bend fusilly gules*; crest: *a cross crosslet fitchée gules between a pair of wings displayed argent*; motto: *'In Cruce glorior'* (Vv. Herefs. 1569, 1634). Conf. to brothers Sir Walter Pye (of The Mynde

are not known – perhaps, *argent a man's leg couped sable.* The family were also of Godmanchester, Hunts.

Prince. Repton. *Gules a saltire or surmounted of a cross engrailed ermine impaling a chevron between three cross crosslets*; crest: *out of a ducal coronet or a cubit arm habited gules cuffed ermine holding in the hand proper three pineapples of the 1st stalked and leaved vert* (Local MS 9555). Gr. to Prince, Salop, 1585, and borne or used by William Prince of Field Houses and Repton Villa (Repton) mid-C19.

Pringle. Darley. *Argent on a saltire engrailed sable five escallops or*; crest: *a heart gules winged or*; motto: *'Sursum'* (FD (1929) II.1598). Gr. (LO) 1673 and matric. with confirmation of crest (LO) 18 Nov. 1828 to Alexander Pringle of Whytbank, Roxburghshire, whose descendant, Robert Keith Pringle (1802–97), was of the Grove, Darley. His 5th son, William, was later 12th of Whytbank and matric. the arms (LO) including supporters: *on either side a palmer proper* (BLG (1952) 2083).

Prinsep. Croxall Hall. *Paly of six argent and gules three piles issuant from sinister base*

Pursglove

(Much Dewchurch) and Kilpeck, Herefs., 1571–1635) and Sir Robert (of Untons (Faringdon), Berks., 1584–1662) 11 Feb. 1633. The former's grandson was cr. by James II (between his flight from England and that from Ireland) Lord Kilpeck in 1689 (ext. 1690). Sir Robert was cr. a bt in 1645, but the patent did not pass the Great Seal. As his eldest son was a fanatical republican, the grant was renewed 13 Jan. 1665 to the 4th son, Sir John Pye of Hoon, a cavalier (title ext. 1734). One of the heirs left Hoon to a descendant of the eldest son of Sir Robert Pye of Untons in 1812: Henry John Pye of Clifton Campville, Staffs., *de jure* 8th bt (of Untons), who also bore these arms. Rice Pye of Derby (Poll Book for 1710 in Local Studies Library) was one of the descendants of the 'two and forty' sons and daus. left by John Pye of The Mynde (d. aged 106, c16: MI at Orcop, Herefs.) and bore *ermine a bend lozengy gules*.

Pym. Long Eaton. *Argent an annulet sable* (*Rel.* VI (1866) 40). Christopher Pym of Long Eaton gent. used these arms and was labelled 'an usurper' V. 1611; his son, Michael, was 'respited for proof' V. 1634: and his son, Christopher, disclaimed in 1662.

Pyndar. Derby; Duffield. *Azure a chevron argent between three lions' heads erased ermine ducally crowned or*; crest: *a lion's head erased ermine ducally crowned or* (V. 1662, D369). Used by Reginald Pyndar of Duffield, who disclaimed V. 1662. He claimed descent from Reginald Pyndar of Southwell, Notts., gr. these arms 1577. He eventually secured a grant 30 Sept. 1682; *gules a chevron argent between three lions' heads erased erminois crowned of the 2nd*; crest: *a lion's head erased erminois crowned argent* (Burke). His descendant, Reginald, of Kempley, Glos., marr. the heiress of Lygon of that place, and heir general of Lord Beauchamp of Powyke (now Powick, Worcs.), left a son, who assumed the surname of Lygon. William, his elder son, was cr. 1806, Lord Beauchamp of Powyke and in 1815, Viscount Elmley (Worcs.) and Earl Beauchamp. At first he bore: *Gules a chevron engrailed erminois between three lions' heads erased ermine ducally crowned or*; crest: *a lion's head as in the arms*; supporters: *dexter a bear proper muzzled collared and chained or, sinister, a swan argent wings elevated gules beaked and legged sable*

gorged with a ducal coronet and lined or on the breast of each suspended from the collar and coronet an escutcheon gules thereon a fesse between six martlets or; motto: *'Ex Fide fortis'* (ibid.). The supporters were gr. and arms conf. 1806, but a subsequent entry in *Grantees of Arms* (XXIII.332) gives a *grant* of arms and supporters in the same year. This must refer to the grant to Lord Beauchamp of the arms of Lygon: *argent two lions passant double queued gules*; crest: *a Saracen's head affrontée couped at the shoulders proper wreathed about the temples argent.* To which were added a new motto: *'Fortuna in bello campo'* (FD (1929) II.1232). Titles ext. 1979.

Pype: see Pipe.

Pyrot. Catton. *Azure a bend engrailed between six martlets or* (*Rel.* XII (1872) 96). Borne by Ralph son of Reginald de Pyrot of Harlington, Beds., who exchanged Harlington for Catton with Sir Almaric de St Amand in 1336.

De Quincy: see Ferrers.

Radclyffe. Mellor Hall. *Argent two bendlets engrailed sable overall a label of three points*; crest: *a bull's head erased sable horned or ducally gorged and chained charged with a pheon all argent*; motto: *'Caen, Crecy, Calais'* (Vv. 1569, 1611). Borne by Sir John Radclyffe of Ordsall (Salford), Lancs., *c.* 1360 (Harl.MS 1481.68), and the Derbys. branch the arms likewise, quartering Mellor, but without the motto which dates to a confirmation to Alexander Radcliffe of Ordsall 1707. The earliest form of the arms was *argent a bend engrailed sable* (glass in church in Ashbourne; also at Mellor, quartering Mellor, and *vert a broad arrow argent*; see Mellor; Needham; cf. Cox, II.218).

Radclyffe. King's Newton (Melbourne); Mugginton. *Argent a bend engrailed sable between three pellets* (Mugginton church, cf. Cox, III.220 & n.). Used by Ralph son of Robert Radclyffe of Mugginton and his brother, Hugh, haberdasher of London, 1685, descended from King's Newton and allegedly from 'Francis Radclyffe of Radclyffe' (Lancs.). See also Ratcliff.

Radford. Holbrook; Smalley Hall; Stanley; Carnfield Hall (South Normanton). *Argent a* *fesse engrailed azure fretty or between two chevrons vair*; crest: *a fret or thereon a partridge proper*; motto: *'Possunt quia posse videntur'* (FD (1929) II.1611). Gr. 1862 to Alexander William Radford-Norcop of Betton Hall (Berrington), Salop., with remainder to the sons of his father John, of Smalley. By RL of 19 July 1904 Alexander's cousin, John, of Smalley (and by bequest, of Betton) assumed the additional surname and arms of Norcop: *sable three ostrich feathers enclosed by two chevronels between three boars' heads erased or* (quartering Radford) and crest: *on a mount vert a boar's head erased sable in front of two ostrich feathers or* (ibid.). Previously the Radford family had used: *gules a fesse between two chevrons vair*; crest: *a partridge holding an ear of wheat in the beak proper*; same motto (Burke).

Raikes. Makeney Lodge (Milford). *Argent a chevron engrailed pean between three griffins' heads erased sable each charged with an ermine spot gules*; crest: *a griffin's head as in the arms*; motto: *'Futuri cautus'* (FD (1929) II.1612). Gr. to Thomas Raikes of London and the descendants of his grandfather, Timothy, 28 Aug. 1783, and borne by H. St J.D. Raikes of Makeney from 1889.

Raphael. Allestree Hall. *Azure three annulets in bend between two bendlets all between as many tulips leaved and slipped all or*; crest: *on a mount vert an eagle's head erased azure gorged with a collar gemel or all between two tulips as in the arms*; motto: *'Esse quam videri'* (FD (1910) 1344). Gr. 1897 to Henry Lewis Raphael, son of Henry, of London, and borne (by virtue of a remainder) by the grantee's eldest brother, Herbert Henry Raphael MP, of Allestree Hall (1859–1924), cr. a bt 10 Feb. 1911. Title ext. 1924.

Ratcliff. Newton Park (Newton Solney). *Argent a bend engrailed plain cotised sable between four pellets three in chief and one in base*; crest: *in front of a bull's head erased sable armed or gorged with a vallery crown a pheon argent*; motto: *'Virtus propter se'* (FD (1929) II.1622). A C20 grant borne by Robert Frederick Ratcliff MP (1867–1943).

Rawdon-Hastings. South Derbys. *Argent a fesse between three pheons sable* (quartering Hastings); crest: *on a mural coronet argent a pheon sable a branch of laurel issuant therefrom proper*; supporters: *on either side a bear argent supporting a staff muzzled and lined or*;

motto: 'Trust winneth truth' (Lodge, *Peerage* (1852), 287–8). The history of this family, which inherited the bulk of the Huntingdon estates in Derbyshire in 1789, is complex: see CP IV.186–9. The marquessate of Hastings became ext. in 1868 and in 1874 part of the depleted estates (consisting of 2,750 ac. in S. Derbys.) passed to the (10th) Countess of Loudoun, Co. Ayr (cr. Scotland 12 Mar. 1633), the heiress. Her husband, C.F. Clifton, was cr. Lord Donington (Leics.) and assumed and surname and arms of Abney-Hastings (qv) by Act of Parliament in 1859. The eldest son, Charles Edward, succ. as 11th Earl of Loudoun on his mother's death. The 2nd son, Paulyn, assumed the surname and arms of Rawdon-Hastings (as above, no supporters) by RL in 1887 as did the 3rd, Gilbert, who eventually succ. as 3rd Lord Donington in 1920. The latter's family had also assumed the surname and arms of Clifton-Hastings-Campbell (qv) by RL in 1896.

Ray. Heanor Hall. *Azure a chevron engrailed ermine between three scimitars proper on a chief or as many martlets gules*; crest: *an ostrich or in the beak an horseshoe azure*; motto: *'Et juste et vray'* (arms: *Rel.* VI (1866)

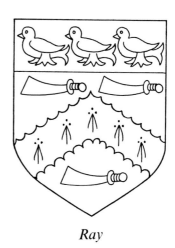

Ray

40; crest: Tilley IV.159). Used, with an inescutcheon of Inman quartering Sutton (qqv), by John Ray of Heanor Hall (Burke), and by his son, John, and grandson, F.G.C. Ray, all quartered: a classic example of the marshalling of unauthorised arms.

Rayner. Duffield. *Ermine on a chief indented azure two estoiles or* (Jewitt's Notes, Box 57). Used by Gervase Rayner, claiming descent from the Rayners of East Drayton, Notts., who disclaimed V. 1662.

Read. Derwent Hall; Norton House; Mickleover. *Gules a saltire between four garbs or*; crest: *on the stump of a tree vert a falcon rising proper belled and jessed gules*; motto: *'Cedant arma togae'* (*Rel.* XII (1872) 96). Borne by Sir William Read, who inherited a moiety of Mickleover, C16, and, used by John Read of Norton House, ironfounder, later of Derwent Hall, 1846: the attributions are Sleigh's.

Reaston. Barlborough Hall. *Argent on a chevron gules between three rudders azure as many cinquefoils of the field* (as quartered by Rodes, Glover, II.81). Gr. to Thomas Reaston of Hull, Yorks., 1796 and conf. to Revd Cornelius Heathcote Reaston-Rodes as a quartering by RL 1825. His father, Revd P.A. Reaston, who marr. the Rodes (Heathcote) heiress, bore Reaston with Rodes in pretence.

Renshawe. Bank Hall (Chapel en le Frith); Darley. *Per pale and per chevron three martlets all counterchanged*; crest: *a decrescent argent and an increscent adossé or* (*Rel.* XII (1872) 96). Used by John Renshawe of Darley C17 and by his descendant, Henry Constantine Renshawe of Bank Hall, C19.

Repton School. *Azure a fesse engrailed between three pigeons each holding in the beak a cross formée fitchée all or*; crest: *a pigeon holding in the beak a cross formée fitchée or*; motto: *'Porta vacat culpa'* (B. Thomas, *Repton, 1557–1957* (1959), 210). Arms and crest of Porte of Etwall – Sir John of that family being the founder of the school – used without authority (A.C. Fox-Davies, *Public Arms*, 650).

Reresby. Alkmonton; Eastwood Hall (Ashover). *Gules on a bend argent three crosses patée fitchée sable*; crest: *on a chapeau a goat argent* (V. Yorks. 1612). Sir Adam de Reresby of Thrybergh, Yorks., and Eastwood bore the arms (Jenyns' Roll); the *crosses* are also found *crosslet* (MI at Littleover church), *patonce* and *flory* (Burke). Sir John Reresby,

King's Governor of Hull, Yorks., was on 16 May 1642 cr. a bt. Title ext. or dormant 1748.

Revell. Ogston (Brackenfield). *Argent on a chevron gules three trefoils slipped ermine all within a bordure engrailed sable*; crest: *a dexter arm embowed in armour argent garnished or holding a dagger of the 1st point downward hilt and pommel of the 2nd point embrued between two dragons' wings gules membraned also or all issuant from clouds proper* (Vv. 1569, 1611; V. 1662 omits the *clouds*). Arms conf. and crest gr. 10 July 1545 to John Revell of Ogston, descended from Revell of Newbold Revel, Stretton under Fosse, Warw., and quartering Malory. William Revell of Newbold, from whose alleged 3rd son, Simon, this family was said to descend, and his ancestor, John, bore: *ermine a chevron gules within a bordure engrailed sable* (Powell Roll).

Revell. Carnfield (S. Normanton). *Ermine on a chevron gules three mullets or within a bordure engrailed sable*; crest: *a cubit arm proper holding in the hand a lion's gamb erased gules* (V. 1611). Conf. to Robert Revell, then of Norton, 1546. One MS of V. 1611 adds two other crests: *on a chapeau a boar's head*

Revell

argent and *out of a ducal coronet two garbs.*
Francis Revell (1602–56), natural son of Edward, succ. to the estates in 1639 and apparently obtained a grant of the arms *within a bordure compony or and sable,* conf. to his grandson, Robert, 25 Aug. 1712 (*DAJ* XCI (1971) 141f.).

Rhodes. Hadfield (Glossop); Tintwistle. *Azure on a bend between two lozenges or a leopard's face gules between two holly leaves vert;* crest: *two lions' gambs erased gules supporting a lozenge thereon a holly leaf as in the arms;* motto: *'Per vias bonas'* (BP (1970) 2249). Gr. 1919 when Sir George Wood Rhodes of Hollingworth, Cheshire was cr. a bt 29 May; his father, Thomas, was of Mersey Bank, Hadfield, and his grandfather, William, was of Tintwistle.

Rhodokanakis-Dukas. Littleover. *Azure a cross argent between four Imperial Byzantine diadems or caps proper each surmounted with an aureola of six estoiles or all within a bordure of the 2nd and all charged on the breast of a double-headed eagle also or Imperially crowned proper;* supporters: *on either side an Imperial Byzantine eagle or;* motto: *'Re Dei re regnante Dei regnante',* all charged on an Imperial pavilion purpure doubled ermine and ensigned with an Imperial crown proper* (blazon in *Genealogika della Casa Imperiale del Rhodokanakis di Scio* (1868)). Conf. by the Holy See 1839 to Prince Pantias Rhodocanakis-Dukas (1786–1846), and borne in Derbys. by the late Prince E. Rhodokanakis-Dukas of Littleover, a descendant of Peter, Prince Pantias's 3rd son. Pantias's uncle, Manuel, was recognized by the same authority as titular emperor of the East, as Manuel III, and the descendants of his father were gr. the style of Imperial Highness, bearing the above arms without the *bordure.* Originally the arms, as borne by Imperial Grand Constable Nicholaus Rhodokanakis (1351–1427), were *azure a cross argent.*

Riboef. Etwall; Stretton; Bradley; Ockbrook. *Argent a chevron gules between three torteaux* (Grimaldi Roll; Jenyns' Ordinary). Borne by Richard son of Richard de Riboef ('Riboo') of Newbiggin (Yorks.) and Etwall, earlier C14, the attribution supported by the sketch of a broken seal impression from an Etwall charter in the Every papers (in private hands). Burke gives another coat: *gules two bars between nine martlets argent,* which are the arms he attributes to Etwall of Etwall (qv). Robert, son of Ingram de Etwall (MP Derbys. 1329), marr. Richard de Riboef's heiress *c.* 1340, but the marriage produced no issue, and these arms (originally de Etwall?) may have passed into the Riboef family (Robert son of John being the heir) with the land.

Richardson. Derby; Smalley. *Argent three chaplets vert each with four roses gules* (*Rel.* XII (1872) 96). Used by Samuel Richardson of Smalley 1721, and by the possibly unrelated Henry Richardson of Derby, banker (1736–1815).

Richardson. Eckington. *Sable on a fesse engrailed or between in chief an open book proper bound gules edged of the 2nd between two mullets and in a base a swan argent a lion passant guardant of the 4th;* crest: *the head of a rhinoceros erased sable behind the horn an escroll argent thereon the words, 'Till time cease' gules;* motto: *'By friendship and by service'* (BP (1970) 2251). Gr. 1960 to Sir John Samuel Richardson of Sheffield, Yorks., and the descendants of his father, John. Sir John was cr. a bt 20 Nov. 1963. The grantee's great-grandfather removed from Little Norton to Ecclesall, Yorks., and was of an Eckington family.

Richardson. Thulston (Elvaston). John Richardson disclaimed V. 1611; arms, if used, not known.

Rickards. Baslow; Draycott; Hartshorne; Spondon. *Gules three garbs bendwise or between two bendlets argent all between as many lozenges vair;* crest: *on a tower a talbot couchant proper the former charged with three annulets conjoined in triangle gules;* motto: *'Vigilanti Salus'* (FD (1929) II.1650). Gr. 1834 to Revd T.A. Rickards, vicar of Cosby, Leics. (1790–1878), with remainder to the descendants of his grandfather, T.P. Rickards (d. 1821), whose heiress marr. a cousin, the issue therefore quartering the same arms. The family were descendants of a C17 rector of Hartshorne, who left descendants there and collaterals, some of whom settled at various times at Parwich, Baslow and Draycott House. The grantee's kinsman, Edward, was of Normanton House, *c.* 1900. Another kinsman, Benjamin, was of Spondon, and on his death 20 May 1721 Bassano painted the arms he used on a hatchment: *argent on a bend engrailed gules three garbs or* (Local MS 3525).

Ricketts: see Wilkinson.

Ridware. Boyleston. *Azure an eagle displayed argent armed gules*; crest: *an eagle displayed argent* (in glass at Chesterfield church noted V. 1569, Cox, I.158n., and Parliament Roll; crest: Burke). Borne by Sir Thomas de Ridware and Sir Walter son of Walter de Ridware who re-inherited the moiety of Boyleston early C14, held a century before by Roger son of Walter de Ridware. Heiress marr. Cotton (qv).

Ripley Urban District Council. *Vert a chevron or between in chief two stags' heads caboshed and in base a fleur-de-lys argent a chevronel sable surmounted by a Tudor rose barbed and seeded proper all within a bordure also argent thereon six horseshoes also sable*; crest: *out of a mural crown sable flames proper issuant therefrom a unicorn's head argent armed and crined or charged with three spearheads erect, one and two gules*; motto: *'Ingenium industria alitur'*. Gr. 8 April 1954; authority abolished 1974. Its successor, the Amber Valley District Council, uses the arms gr. to Belper RDC (qv) but without authority.

Risley. Risley. *Argent a fesse azure between three crescents gules* (as quartered by Sacheverell, MS Ashmole 854, and MI at Morley, 1656). Borne by Hugh de Risley of Risley who marr. the heiress of Risley and assumed that name early C15. V. 1569 (D369 version) gives the *fesse* as *gules* in the Sacheverell quartering. Glover (II.189), who takes them from a seal, gives the arms as quartered by Chadwick of Callow as: *argent a fesse (azure?) bezantée between three crescents gules*.

Rivett. Derby; King's Newton (Melbourne); Mapleton Manor; Repton. *Per pale argent and sable on a chevron between three lozenges as many martlets counterchanged*; crest: *a cubit arm erect vested bendy argent and sable cuffed of the last holding in the hand proper a broken sword of the 1st hilt and pommel or*; motto: *'Holde faste'* (BP (1970) 484). Gr. 8 May 1801 when James, 3rd son of Ald. Thomas Rivett of Derby and Mapleton, assumed the additional surname and arms (quartering Rivett with both crests) of Carnac, and conf. 1910. The Carnac arms are: *quarterly argent and azure two swords in saltire proper between three annulets one in chief and two in fesse a crescent in base all counter-*

changed; crest: *a sword erect proper issuant from a crescent ermine the internal part gules*; motto: *'Sic itur ad astra'* (ibid.) The grantee's eldest son, James, of Derby and Warborne, Hants., MP was cr. a bt 12 Mar. 1836. Prior to 1801 the family used *argent three bars and in chief as many trivets sable* with crest as above (MI once visible at All Saints', Derby, Cox & Hope, 133). The same were used by Francis Rivett of King's Somborne, Hants., MP (d. 1668) son of William, of King's Newton, and kin to the Repton branch from whom the Derby Rivetts are descended. The account in BP (1970) 484 describing them as a branch of Ryvett of Suffolk is unsubstantiated by the facts.

Rivington. Chesterfield. *Argent a boar's head couped sable transfixed by a sword in pale point downwards proper hilt and pommel or in chief two falcons close also proper belled of the 4th*; crest: *in a crown vallery or a mount vert thereon a falcon close as in the arms holding in the beak a hawk's lure reflexed over its back azure*; motto: *'Deum timete et regem favete'* (BLG (1898) I.xiii). Gr. 1892 to H.J. Rivington of London, publisher, descended from Charles Rivington of Chesterfield, b. 1688.

Robertson. Chilcote. *Gules three wolves' heads erased argent, langued azure under the escutcheon a wild man lying in chains proper*; crest: *a dexter hand holding an Imperial crown proper*; motto: *'Virtutis gloria merces'* (BLG (1875) II.1175). Borne (or used) by Francis Robertson of Chilcote (1765–1852), 2nd son of Robertson of Balconie (Kiltearn, Ross & Cromarty), cadets of Robertson of Kindeace (Invergordon, Ross & Cromarty), themselves cadets of Struan, Perth, by whom these arms were matric. (LO) 1672.

Robey. Denby Old Hall; Derby. *A chevron between three bucks trippant gules armed and unguled or*; crest: *a buck's head* (carved over entrance of Denby Old Hall; cf. Local MS 3525). Painted by Bassano on the hatchment of Edward Robey of Castle Donington, Leics., 1720, and carved for his grandfather Thomas at Denby Old Hall c. 1636. Oddly, Thomas's son, Robert, of Denby, who marr. Grace, dau. of Sir Thomas Gresley, 2nd bt, impaled Gresley with *or a roebuck trippant proper* (MI at Church Gresley). Neither of these coats seems to be authorised.

Robinson. Mammerton (Longford). *Sable a fret ermine on a chief or three escallops azure*

(Tilley's Notes, Box 57). The heiress marr. Roger Fallowes of Alvaston *c.* 1575.

Robinson. Derby. *On a chevron between three bucks' trippant as many cinquefoils slipped;* crest: *a unicorn's head erased ducally gorged and chained* (on a wrought iron gate from 22 Friar Gate, Derby, now at Derby Industrial Museum). Used or borne by Capt. James Robinson, of Derby, living at Ald. Chesshyre's former house in Friar Gate, 1791. The crest on this gate (by Robert Bakewell) almost certainly does not belong to the shield below it for the workmanship is infinitely superior to the inverted light-bulb-shaped escutcheon upon which the Robinson arms are charged. Presumably a previous achievement was removed (but what was it?) and the crest left.

Rodes. Derby. *Argent on a cross engrailed between four lions rampant gules five bezants* (D369). Entered without information. The arms are those of Rodes of Knaresborough, Yorks.

Rodes. Staveley Woodthorpe. *Sable a lion passant guardant in bend argent between two acorns or all between as many cotises ermine;* crest: *a dexter hand erect proper habited ar-*

Roe

gent holding a branch of oak vert acorns or cups azure; motto: *'Occident occidens'* (seal of 1381 (Local MS 6341) and V. 1569). Borne 1381 by William Rodes of Staveley Woodthorpe, who marr. the heiress of Cachehors, whose arms his descendants quartered.

Rodes. Barlborough Hall. *Argent between two cotises ermines a lion passant guardant gules between two acorns in bend azure;* crest: *a cubit arm erect grasping an oak branch acorned all proper;* motto: *'Robur meum Deus'* (Vv. 1611, 1662.) Allowed to Francis Rodes, a son of John, of Staveley Woodthorpe and Barlborough, in lieu of those given above (was there an irregularity in John's 3rd marriage, thus illegitimising Francis Rodes, and hence the fresh grant of arms?), V. 1611. He was cr. a bt 14 Aug. 1641; title dormant 1743. The arms were gr. under RLs of 1742, 1776 (to Heathcote), 1825 (to Reaston), 1844 (to Gossip) and 1884 (qqv).

Rodsley: see Montgomery.

Roe. Derby. *Argent a buck couchant proper on a chief vert a garb between two crosses patée or* (painted on wall of Prince Charlie Room, Derby Museum, 1879). Used by Thomas son of Thomas Roe of Litchurch House, Derby, MP, knighted in 1894 and raised to the peerage as Lord Roe of Derby 1917; title ext. 1923. However, on the gold loving cup presented to Sir Thomas Roe to mark the conclusion of his 2nd mayoralty of Derby (1897) on 30 March 1898, are emblazoned the arms of Rowe of Alport (qv).

Rogers. Cowley Hall (Wensley); Underhill Grange (Hartington Middle Quarter). *Azure on a chevron or between three stags trippant argent in centre chief point a fleur-de-lys of the 2nd a buglehorn sable garnished also of the 2nd stringed vert between two branches of oak chevronwise fructed and slipped all proper;* crest: *a stag's head erased proper suspended from the neck by a riband vert a buglehorn as in the arms all between two branches of oak fructed proper;* motto: *'Nos nostraque Deo'* (FD (1905) 1169). Gr. later C19 to Maj. Revd G.E. Rogers, vicar of Southwater, Sussex, with remainder to the descendants of his father, George, of Underhill and Forty Hill (Enfield), Middlesex. George's father, John, was 'close kin' to Joseph, of Cowley, both using *argent three stags sable* (see Harthill).

Roland. Eyam; Rowland; Priestcliffe (Taddington). *Sable a pile wavy argent issuant*

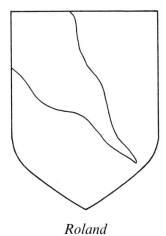

Roland

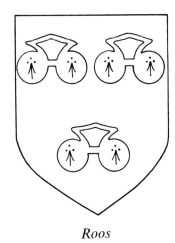

Roos

from the dexter chief towards the sinister base (seal noted in Add.MS 6672, ff. 54, 59; tinctures from Papworth, 1022). Borne by Roger de Roland (or Rowland) of Rowland, *c.* 1396. The heiress marr. Stafford of Eyam but, as quartered by Bowles (qv), these arms were borne with the pile plain (Tilley, I.83).

Rolfe: see Neville.

Rollesley. Rowsley. *Gules a fesse and a bordure ermine*; crest; *a demi-lion rampant per pale argent and gules holding a rose of the last stalked and leaved vert* (V. 1569; MI in Darley church, *DAJ* XXVII (1905) 25). Borne by this family, descended from one Peter who marr. Joan, dau. and heiress of Jordan de Rollesley, *c.* 1284. The previous line seem to have borne *two lions rampant* seen by Cox (II.164n.) on an old MI at Darley.

Rolleston. Derby; Lea; Stanton by Bridge; Swarkestone. *Argent a cinquefoil pierced azure on a chief gules a lion passant guardant or*; crest: *an eagle's head erased proper*; motto: *'Ainsi et Meillieur peust estre'* (V. 1569; V. Notts., 1662–64). Harl.MS. 886 gives the tinctures of the crest: *head gules, beaked or*. The C18 Rollestons of Derby (whose place on the

family pedigree is uncertain) bore or used the same arms (hatchment, All Saints', Derby). A descendant of the Lea branch (later settled at Watnall, Notts.), Sir Humphrey Davy Rolleston, was cr. a bt 24 June 1924 (title ext. 1944). He was allowed these arms, with the *cinquefoil unpierced* and *on a canton of the field a rod of Aesculapius proper* (FD (1929) II.1675).

Roo: see Rowe.

Rookhill. 'Co. Derby'. *Argent a chevron between three chessrooks sable* (*Rel.* XII (1872) 96). Quartered by Bradbury, Essex, through the marriage of William Bradbury of Braughing, Herts. (2nd son of Robert, of Ollersett (New Mills) (qv)) with the heiress of a family of this name. It is unclear from where in Derbys. they hailed.

Rooper: see Roper.

Roos. Worsop Wood (Pleasley). *Gules three water bougets ermine* (Willement and Parliament Rolls). Borne C14 by the sons (perhaps James and William) of John le Roos himself a son of Roger, and Agnes de Eyam, whose posterity were of Worsop Wood 'for several generations' (Lysons, 232). The heraldic evidence suggests that they were close kin to Sir Robert Roos of Gedney, Lincs., who bore the same arms with *a label azure* (Parliament Roll).

Roper. Heanor; Turnditch. *Sable an eagle close or*; crest: *on a chapeau sable turned up ermine a blazing star or*; motto: *'Lux Anglis crux Francis'* (Vv. 1634, 1662; motto: BLG (1937) 1947). Allowed to Thomas Roper of Turnditch and Heanor Old Hall, 1662. His ancestor, Richard Furneaux of Beighton, is said to have taken the arms and this name in lieu of his own 1428 on his marriage to the dau. and heiress of John Roper of Turnditch. He himself is said by some authorities (Lysons, clxii; Tilley IV.109) to have been descended in the male line from a cadet branch of Musard of Staveley. Sir Thomas Roper, allegedly (V. 1634 is sole authority) greatgreat grandson of Hugh Roper of Turnditch, was cr. 1627 (Peerage of Ireland) Viscount Baltinglass (Co. Wicklow) and Lord Bantry (Co. Cork), but bore quite different arms: *ermine two chevrons paly of six or and gules*; crest: *a boar's head couped in bend or langued and vulned gules*; motto: *'Deus veritatem protegit'* (arms: CP I.228 & n.(c); crest & motto: Fairburn, 480). Titles ext. 1676. In some sources, the *eagle* in the arms is replaced by a *stork* (Burke) and a *parrot* (V. 1662, Harl.MS 6104).

Roper. Weston Hall (Weston on Trent). *Per fesse azure and or on a pale counterchanged between two bucks' heads in chief a like buck's head in base or*; crest: *a lion rampant sable holding in the dexter paw a ducal coronet or*; motto: *'Spes Mea in Deo'* (BP (1970) 2626, cf. V. Kent 1619). Borne by Anthony Roper, son of Sir William, of Eltham, Kent, who inherited an estate at Weston, and commenced building a colossal house there 1633, but sold it unfinished 1647. His senior descendants assumed the surname and arms of Curzon (of Waterperry, Oxon.) by RL 1788 and reassumed the additional surname and quartered the arms of Roper similarly in 1813.

Rose. Ashbourne. *Per pale argent and gules three roses in fesse between two lions rampant in pale all counterchanged*; crest: *a lion rampant sable gorged vair holding a lyre or resting the dexter hind leg on a vase argent*; motto: *'Armat spina rosas'* (Burke, FR (1897) 515). Gr. C19 to William Rose of Carnsdale House, Barnston, Cheshire (1795–1875), grandson of

Mark Rose of Ashbourne. His elder brother was also of Ashbourne.

Rose. Hasland. *Sable on a chevron argent three roses gules seeded and barbed proper in the dexter chief point a close helm of the 2nd* (*Rel.* VI (1866) 41). Gr. 1781 to William Rose and his grandfather, Jacob, of Carshalton, Surrey, and Hasland.

Rose-Innes. Leam (Eyam Woodlands). *Quarterly of four: i, Athorpe (qv); ii, or a boar's head couped gules between three water bougets sable all within a bordure azure thereon three garbs and as many boars' heads alternately of the field, for Rose; iii, argent three mullets azure within a bordure chequy of the 2nd and first, for Innes; iv, Athorpe*; mottoes: *'Armat spina rosa'* and *'Ornatur radix fronde'* (BLG (1937) 1219). Borne by Lesley Clara, Mrs Geoffrey Gregory-Rose-Innes, who marr. 1911, when her husband assumed the additional surname of Rose-Innes by deed poll and she matric. the arms as above (LO). Arms of Rose gr. (LO) 1780. They were also matric. by George Rose-Innes 5 Feb. 1897 the heir male of her father, T.G. Rose-Innes, 4th of Netherdale, Turriff, Banffs. As matric. in 1897 the arms were: Rose quartering Innes, with crests: *a rose gules stalked and leaved proper*, for Rose, and *a palm branch slipped proper*, for Innes (ibid.). See also Gregory; Athorpe.

Rosell. Denby. *Argent three roses gules barbed and seeded proper* (as quartered by Lowe of Denby V. 1569). Borne by William Rosell of Denby *c.* 1311, who marr. an heiress called de Denby. The arms rendered: *sable three roses gules barbed vert seeded or* were seen by Cox (IV.252) in Denby church, probably due to inexpert restoration.

Rosell. Draycott. *Argent on a bend gules three roses or* (V. Notts. 1662-4). Allowed to the descendants of John son of William Rosell of Draycott (living 1539, father d. 1502) then of Ratcliffe on Soar, Notts., 1664. However, when Anne Rosell of Ratcliffe on Soar (widow of Gervase) d. 29 Dec. 1723, Bassano painted on her hatchment: *sable three roses or*, implying descent from Rosell of Denby (qv).

Rossington. Scropton; Youlgreave. *Argent a fesse between three crescents gules*; crest: *a griffin's head erased gules armed or* (V. 1662, Scropton; as quartered by Kniveton *alias* Gilbert of Youlgreave, V. 1569). Borne by Sir

John Rossington of Youlgreave, *c.* 1420. Dugdale (V. 1662) adduces the descent of the Rossingtons of Scropton from this man's yr brother and allowed them the same arms, although they were branded as usurpers, V. 1611.

Rotheram. Dronfield. *Vert three bucks trippant or* (Lysons, cxlii). Borne or used by Samuel Rotheram of Dronfield who d. 1785. The Lysons claim for him cadetship of the Rotherams of Rotherham, Yorks., but note John Blythe *alias* Rotheram (of the Norton Blythes, qv) 1633, and Thomas Rotheram, Bishop of Lincoln, gr. land at Dronfield 1474.

Routhe. Birley (Brampton); Romeley Hall (Clowne). *Gules on a chevron between three herons or as many ogresses* (seal in local collection, cf. Burke). Used (or borne) by William Routhe of Birley gent., 1601, of the family of Routhe of Romeley.

Rowe. Alport. *Gules on a bend between three garbs or as many crosses patée fitchée of the field;* crest: *a dexter arm in armour proper holding fessewise a sword argent hilt and pommel or supporting a chaplet vert* (MI Youlgreave, 1613). Borne by Roger Rowe of Alport (d. 1613) and allowed V. 1611, except that in most versions (D369 excepted) the *sword* is missing from the crest, but the *wrist* is *encircled with a scarf gules*. But, strange to say, the same man was gr. a completely different coat 9 June 1608 (or possibly 1605) ('to Roger Rowe of Alport, elder brother of Sir Francis Rowe and the heirs of his body'): *per pale or and gules semée of trefoils and a lion rampant all counterchanged;* crest: *an arm embowed vested gules holding a garb or* (Lysons, cxliii). Roger's cousin once removed, William Roo of London, used: *gules on a bend between two garbs or three crosses crosslet fitchée sable* (Papworth).

Rowe. Windlehill (Osleston & Thurvaston). *Or on a bend cotised azure between six trefoils slipped vert three escallops of the field;* crest: *an arm vested erminois the hand proper grasping a trefoil slipped vert* (Lysons, cxliii). Arms conf. and crest gr. 9 July 1612 to Robert Rowe of Windlehill, and his brother Roger, of London, sons of Henry of Windlehill, grandsons of William. Heiress marr. Newell *alias* Porte, of Ilam.

Rowland: see Roland.
Rowsley: see Rollesley.
Rowthorne. Rowthorne (Ault Hucknall).

Chequy argent and vert on a chief gules an ostrich issuant or; crest: *five ostrich feathers one in pale or the others argent and gules alternately* (Tilley, III.274). A medieval family holding a small estate at Rowthorne. The attribution is entirely Tilley's.

Royce. Derby. *Sable a griffin segreant and on a chief argent a rose gules barbed and seeded proper between two spearheads also proper;* crest: *in front of a demi-griffin segreant sable a millrind fessewise or;* motto: 'Fortis et prudens simul' (BP (1931) 2046). Gr. to Sir Frederick Henry Royce on his elevation to a btcy 26 June 1930, ext. on his death in 1933.

Royce

Ruding. Litchurch Lodge (Derby). *Argent on a bend between two lions rampant sable a wyvern wings overt of the field;* crest: *a dragon's head sable collared and chained or holding in the mouth a lion's gamb erased of the last* (V. Leics. 1681). Borne by Rogers Ruding of Litchurch Lodge early C19. He was 3rd son of John Clement Ruding, a cadet of Ruding of Westcotes, Leics.

Russell: see Cokesay.

Rye. Whitwell. *Gules on a bend ermine three ears of rye sable;* crest: *a cubit arm erect vested purpure cuffed argent in the hand proper three* ears of rye or (Harl.MSS 1093.81 and 1537.16, cf. Lysons, clxiii). Gr. 1575 to William Rye of Whitwell, according to *Grantees of Arms*, I.98, but 1653 according to Local MS 6341; allowed 1569 to Edward son of Brian Rye of Whitwell. His ancestor, Ralph, replied to a Quo Warranto of 1331 that 'he and his ancestors had held a park there (i.e. at Whitwell) from time immemorial' and sealed with *gules a bend ermine* – the arms of the Ryes of Gosberton, Lincs., of which he was the representative, descended from a common ancestor with Ralph fitz Hubert of Crich. His yr son, from whom the Whitwell branch descended, differenced as above.

Ryley. Eyam; Ripley. *Or a fesse between three crosses formée fitchée sable* (as quartered by Sleigh on MI at Etwall, Cox., III.329). Used by John Ryley of Broadmeadow Hall (Sheen), Staffs., whose dau. and heiress marr. Hugh Sleigh of Pilsbury *c.* 1565. Local MS. 6341 gives the field as *ermine* as quartered by Sleigh. The heiress of the Ripley branch marr. Eyre.

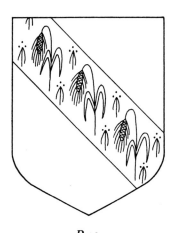

Rye

Sacheverell. Boulton; Hopwell; Morley. *Argent on a saltire azure five water bougets or*; crest: *a goat statant argent horned and bearded sable* (Vv. 1569, 1611). Allowed to John Sacheverell of Morley 1569 and entered in Jenyns' Ordinary referring back to an earlier period, although to some extent retrospectively. Arms usually quarter Hopwell (qv).

Sacheverell. Stanton by Bridge. *Argent on a saltire azure four water bougets or*; crest: *on a lure charged with a bouget or fretted gules cords of the 1st a falcon argent beaked and belled also of the first*; motto: '*En bonne joy*' (V. 1569). Allowed to Patrick Sacheverell, a cadet of Morley, of Stanton by Bridge.

Sacheverell. Ible; Snitterton. *Argent on a saltire azure five water bougets or a chief gules*; crest: *on a hawk's lure or a hawk close belled and jessed proper* (V. Notts., 1614). This branch were of Ible and Snitterton C15, and inherited Kirkby in Ashfield, Notts., the heiress ultimately carrying the property to Coke.

Sacheverell. Callow; Derby. *Argent on a saltire azure five water bougets or and a bordure gules*; crest: *a goat statant proper collared gules* (as quartered by Chadwick, Glover, II.189; crest: Burke). Gr. 11 May 1665 to George son of Valens Sacheverell of Callow, the father being 3rd natural son of Henry, of Morley. George was a great supporter of his unrelated namesake, Dr Henry Sacheverell, to whom he left his estate on his death in 1715, and who marr. his widow. Dr Sacheverell also used the arms as of Morley, without authority.

Sacheverell. Hopwell. *Argent on a saltire azure five water bougets or and a bordure wavy erminois* (Burke). Borne or used by Ferdinando Sacheverell of Hopwell, 2nd natural son of Henry, of Morley, d. without issue 1661; his dau. marrying (as his 1st wife) George Sacheverell of Callow (qv). The quartering was, however, conf. to a descendant of Zachary Sacheverell of Notts., who marr. a sister of Ferdinando in 1780.

Sackville. Croxall. *Quarterly or and gules a bend vair; crest: out of a coronet of fleurs-de-lys or an estoile argent;* supporters: *on either side a leopard (proper);* motto: '*Aut nunquam tentes aut perfice*' (Debrett, *Peerage,* (1817) I.54 & pl. VII). Borne by Sir Andrew Sackville 1308 (Willement Roll), and in Derbys. by Edward Sackville, 4th Earl of Dorset (cr. 1594; also Lord Buckhurst (Sussex), cr. 1567)

Sacheverell

who was *jure uxoris* of Croxall. The 7th earl was also cr. 1720, Duke of Dorset; his father had been cr. 1675 Earl of Middlesex and Lord Cranfield. The 3rd duke sold Croxall *c.* 1785; titles ext. 1843.

Sadler (Sadlier). Doveridge Old Hall; Snelston. *Or a lion rampant per fesse azure and gules*; crest: *a demi-lion rampant azure ducally crowned or*; motto: *'Servire Deo Sapere'* (Burke, IFR, 1138). Gr. to Sir Ralph Sadler kt 1575, in lieu of patent of 1544; he was in charge of Mary, Queen of Scots during some of her time in Derbys. Borne (or used) by M.T. Sadler, MP for Newark, Notts. (1780–1835), son of James Sadler of Snelston and Doveridge, claiming descent from Sir Ralph.

St Amand. Catton. *Or fretty and on a chief sable three bezants* (Glover's Roll, 1st Version, 180; cf. seals 1303, 1383, PRO, P.1983, P.1982). Sir Almaric de St Amand, later summoned to Parliament (1371) in his uncle's barony of St Amand (cr. 1299), was of Catton until he exchanged it for Harlington, Beds., with Ralph Pyrot (qv).

St Anselm's School. Bakewell. *Argent goutée-de-sang a cross patée gules* (displayed at school). It is unclear upon what authority these arms are displayed.

St Elphin's School. Darley. Three escutcheons conjoined: *dexter, or on a pale gules three mitres argent a canton barry bendy sinister of six of the 3rd and sable*; centre, *gules three mitres argent*; sinister, *argent an eagle displayed sable on a chief per pale azure and gules dexter an open book and sinister a ship with three masts proper*; crest: (over central escutcheon) *a mitre proper*; motto: *'Nisi Dominus Frustra'* (displayed in monochrome, but hatched, outside school). Authority unclear.

St James's Priory. Derby. *Per pale gules and azure and a bordure argent* (recorded by Williamson (Notes in Director's Room, Derby Museum) based on a (lost) encaustic tile; colours, no doubt, from Burke). A cell of Bermondsey Abbey, Surrey, a version of the arms of which these are.

St John. Derby. *Argent on a chief gules two mullets or*; crest: *on a mount vert a falcon rising or belled proper ducally gorged gules*; motto: *'Data fata secutus'* (FD (1929) II.1712). Borne by Winstan St Andrew St John MRCS, LRCP (1872–1962) of Derwent House, Derby, and his son, O.H. St A. St John. He was a descendant of Barons St John of Bletso (now Bletsoe, Beds.), cr. 1559. There was also a btcy cr. 28 June 1660.

St Loe. Chatsworth. *Argent on a bend sable three annulets of the field* (Local MS 6341.6r). Borne by Sir William St Loe MP (Derbys. 1563), 3rd husband of Bess of Hardwick.

St Maur. Seymour's Place and Hardwick (Egginton). *Argent two chevrons gules and a label azure* (Powell and Planché Rolls). Borne by Nicholas de St Maur of Egginton, *c.* 1245 (seal noted in Every papers in private hands).

St Pier. Catton; Walton on Trent. *Argent a bend sable a label of five points gules* (glass once at Walton church, noted by Wyrley 1592, Cox, III.513). Borne by Sir Urien de St Pier (d. 1311), who held the manor of Catton and land at Walton (Planché Roll). As quartered by Horton, the *label* is only of *three points* (MI at Croxall church 1659). A seal of Sir John, 1332, gives a crest: *a fish impaled on a trident* (PRO, P.689) – later adopted by Horton (qv).

Sale. Barrow Manor (Barrow on Trent); Derby; Swadlincote; Ticknall; Willington. *Argent on a bend engrailed sable three fleurs-de-*

lys of the field; crest: *a pheon sable* (V. 1662 and on MI at Weston on Trent church, Cox, IV.429). Exhibited 'sans proof' by William son of Richard Sale of Barrow, who left numerous posterity, one of whom seems to have had a grant of these arms.

Sale. Shardlow. *Or on a bend engrailed sable three fleurs-de-lys argent*; crest: *a pheon sable* (*DAJ* XLII (1920) 28). Most MSS of V. 1662 (except D369) give a blank shield for this branch of the family, Richard Sale, brother of William (above) being the sole representative.

Salford. Derby. *Argent on a fesse engrailed between three wolves passant sable collared or as many boars' heads couped close of the last* (Burke). Borne or used by John Salford of Burton on Trent, Staffs., whose elder son was of Derby, and whose yr son marr. the heiress of Welbeck of Compton. Descendants of both settled in Derby and London, where the arms and pedigree were recorded at the College of Arms Nov. 1571.

Sall: see Sale.

Sallow. Sawley; Stanton by Dale; Sandiacre; Risley. *Gules a chevron or between three escallops argent* (as a quartering of Pilkington on MI at Stanton church, Cox, IV.419). Borne by Sir George Sallow, or Sawley, of Risley and Stanton by Dale, living 1416, whose grand-dau. and heiress marr. Thomas Pilkington. The arms seem otherwise unrecorded and could thus be an early example of an invented coat.

Salmond. Longwood Hall (Pinxton). *Or three salmons haurient sable*; crest: *issuant from clouds a dexter arm embowed the hand all proper grasping a trident sable* (livery button in a local collection; cf. Burke). Arms used by Maj. Walter Salmond of Longwood Hall C19. The arms were recognised when his nephew, Marshal of the RAF Sir John Salmond, was gr., between the two World Wars, the arms as above with *a chief sable thereon two wings conjoined with a wreath of laurel or*.

Salvein: see Selioke.

Sanders (Sandars). Caldwell; Derby; Little Ireton (Weston Underwood); Lullington. *Sable on a chevron ermine between three bulls' heads caboshed argent a rose gules*; crest: *a demi-bull rampant and erased gules armed or charged with a rose argent*; motto: *'Non bos in lingua'* (V. Staffs. 1663). Some MSS of V. 1662 record these arms as borne by Col.

Thomas Sanders of Caldwell (1610–95) as 'sans proof', but not in those for Staffs. They were, indeed, gr. to his father Collingwood (1578–1653) in 1615, and vary those gr. to his 2nd cousin once removed, Sir Thomas Sanders of Charlwood, Surrey, 1 Mar. 1552: as above but without the rose; crest: *a demi-bull,* as above, but again without the *rose* (Burke).

Sandford. Blackwell. *Ermine on a chief dancettée sable three boars' heads or a crescent for difference* (V. 1611, Local MS 6341 version). Allowed to 'William Sandford de Bakewell (sic) haeres and possessor in terris de Tickhill' which seems strange, for the Sandfords of Tickhill, Yorks., bore *per chevron sable and ermine in chief two boars' heads or* (V. Yorks. 1584). This coat was also allowed to William's yr brother's family in Notts. at the V. 1614. Lawrance (*DAJ* XL (1918) 95 n.1) ventures that the Tickhill version is the correct coat. But if the former was allowed in V. 1611, that too must thereby have been endowed with a measure of correctitude.

Sapperton. Sapperton; Aston (Sudbury); Boyleston; Foston. *Argent a chevron gules between three boars' heads couped sable* (quartered by Montgomery, Local MS 6341). Borne by William son of Roger de Sapperton of Sapperton (Church Broughton), Boyleston and Foston mid-C14; the heiress marr. Montgomery. He was MP (Derbys.) 1328 and 1334. The arms are virtually identical to those of neighbouring Agards (qv) and there may have been a connection. Note also John de Sapperton, living at the same period, who bore *or an eagle displayed vert membered gules debruised by a baston compony argent and gules* (Jenyns' Ordinary) – conceivably of another family entirely, although the arms employ the symbolism of the later Montgomery coat (qv).

Du Sautoy. Derby. *Argent three Maltese crosses in chevron between as many towers azure that in the sinister chief charged with a bar gules on a chief sable a bezant* (letter to E. du Sautoy from Armorial de la Noblesse de France, 6 July 1855, in possession of family). Motto: *'Force et Foy'* (Burke). Borne by Edward du Sautoy of Derby (1820–74) and his posterity there, and gr. in France to Jacques Pierre de Sautoy, sieur de Melk, Alsace, his ancestor; it does not appear to have been confirmed by the College of Arms; Burke also gives a crest : *a hand holding a sickle proper.*

Savage. Stainsby (Ault Hucknall); Tissington. *Argent six lioncels rampant sable*; crest: *out of a ducal coronet or a lion's gamb erect sable* (Willement Roll; Lysons, cxlv). Borne by Sir Ernand de Savage 1334, and deriving from the achievement of William de Longespée via the Leybournes, much as Ferrers derivatives proliferated in Derbys. (Humphery-Smith, 14). Also quartered by the heirs of Edensor (V. 1569, passim). In 1415, by which time the Stainsby branch was normally seated in Cheshire, the Savages adopted the arms of Sir Thomas Daniel of Clifton (also called Rocksavage) whose heiress they had marr.: *argent a pale fusilly sable*; crest: *a unicorn's head erased argent*; motto: *'Ware the horn'* (Ballard's Book; noted in window at Chesterfield church, V. 1569). They had a grant or confirmation of this coat 1416. In 1639 Viscount Savage (cr. and a bt, cr. 29 June 1611) inherited the earldom of Rivers (cr. 1626) and the Viscounty of Colchester, Essex, (1621) under a special remainder from his father-in-law, Thomas Darcy of Chiche (now St Osyth), Essex, when he reverted to the ancient arms, with supporters: *dexter, a falcon belled or; sinister, a unicorn argent*; motto: *'A te pro te'* (Burke). Titles ext. 1728. The Savages of Ardkeen, Co. Down, were also descendants of the Derbys. Savages, and bore a different crest (with the ancient arms): *a mermaid rising from the sea all proper*; motto: *'Fortis et fidelis'* (UO; Burke, FR (1897) 534).

Savage. Castleton. *Argent a pale fusilly sable a crescent for difference*; crest: *a unicorn's head argent erased gules a crescent for difference* (V. 1611). Allowed to Humphrey Savage V. 1611, wherein there is the note, 'be it remembered that this Humphrey Savage sayeth his ancestors descended out of the house of Savage of Brindsley' (now Brindley, Cheshire). His kinsman, Godfrey, of Eckington disclaimed V. 1611. These arms were also borne by Arnold, 3rd son of the 1st Savage of Rocksavage, Cheshire, who settled at N. Wingfield *c.* 1480.

Savage. N. Wingfield. *Argent a pale fusilly sable debruised by a bend sinister gules* (note appended to D369 under Savage of Castleton). Borne or used by Ralph, natural son of Arnold Savage of N. Wingfield by Agnes Liversage.

Savile. Bakewell; Beeley Hill Top. *Argent*

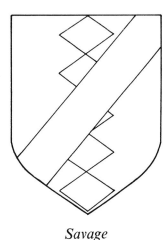

Savage

on a bend cotised sable three owls of the field; crest: *an owl argent charged with a trefoil slipped gules* (V. 1662). Allowed 1662 to William Savile of Bakewell, son of William, of Blaby, Leics. (who bore the arms without the *cotises*, V. Leics. 1634), descended from the Saviles of Howley, Yorks. Burke records the *cotises* as *gules*, doubtless from Harl.MS 610. The Saviles of Howley bore the arms without the *cotises* (Willement Roll).

Savile. Barlborough Old Hall. *Argent on a bend sable three owls of the field*; crest: *an owl argent*; motto: *'Be fast'* (impaling Garth, in plaster overmantel, Barlborough Old Hall). John Savile, elder son of Henry, of Bradley (Halifax), Yorks., was attached to the household of Sir John Rodes of Barlborough, and occupied the Old Hall early C17. His son, Sir Henry, of Methley, Yorks., was cr. a bt 29 June 1611 (ext. 1632).

Sawley: see Sallow.

Schwabe. Hinchleywood (Mapleton); Upwoods (Doveridge). *Vert an arrow point downwards in pale argent between two garbs or on a chief azure a cherub's face between two estoiles of the 2nd*; crest: *a falcon wings elevated proper charged on the breast with a* *cherub's head holding in its beak an arrow in bend sinister point downwards argent*; motto: *'Tenez le droit'* (Local MS 9555.164, from a bookplate). The achievement of Henry Thackeray Schwabe of Upwoods (1911) and Hinchleywood (1925), probably based on a grant made in the German state from which came the ancestors of his father, Louis, of Hart Hill, Lancs.

Schwind. Broomfield Hall (Morley). Crest: *a pegasus salient wings elevated proper* (livery button in local collection). Used by Charles Schwind (son of Charles, of Rio de Janeiro, Brazil) who built Broomfield Hall 1873, and his son, Lionel.

Scot: see Chester, Earls of.

Scott. Draycott House. *Or two mullets in chief and a crescent in base azure.* (Burke). Matriculated by the Scotts of Synton (Selkirk), (LO) 1672, ancestors of Scott of Raeburn, Dumfriesshire, to which family belonged William Hugh Scott, who settled at Draycott House in 1823.

Scott. Hartington Hall. *Argent on a fesse gules cotised azure between three Catherine wheels sable as many lambs passant of the field*; crest: *on a mount vert a beacon fired proper ladder or*; motto: *'Regi fidelis patriaeque'* (FD (1929) II.1736). Gr. to Sir Joseph Scott of Great Barr, Staffs., cr. a bt 30 Apr. 1806. The 3rd bt inherited as 2nd bt of Hartington from Sir Hugh Bateman (qv) 1824, which title passed out of the family in 1905.

Seely. Brookhill (Pinxton); Wingerworth. *Azure three ears of wheat banded or within a chaplet of roses argent*; crest: *on the trunk of a tree fessewise proper three ears of wheat banded or*; motto: *'I ripen and die, yet live'* (BP (1956) 1986). Gr. to Sir Charles Seely 1896 when cr. a bt 19 Feb. The family were previously of Brookhill, and the 2nd bt was of Wingerworth. The 3rd bt was in 1941 cr. Lord Sherwood (Notts), being gr. supporters: *on either side a pegasus argent winged or charged on the breast with a hurt thereon three ears of wheat banded or* (ext. 1970). The yr son of the 1st bt was also cr. a peer (in 1933) as Lord Mottistonelow. The arms were varied: *azure three ears of wheat banded or between in pale two martlets and in fesse as many chaplets argent*; same crest: supporters: *on either side a hippocampus azure gorged with a mural coronet and charged on the shoulder with a maple leaf or*; motto: *'In Deo spero'*

(BP (1970) 1564). Previously they had used *vert three ears of corn tied with a ribbon or* (*Rel.* VI (1866) 41).

Segrave. Bretby; Coton in the Elms; Rosliston; Staveley Woodthorpe. *Sable a lion rampant argent crowned or* (FitzWilliam Roll). Sir John de Segrave kt (whose grandfather first held land in Derbys.), who bore these arms 1300, was of Bretby. He had been summoned to Parliament as a baron in 1295. The Caerlaverock Roll has the lion *or* as well. Earlier in the C13 the family had borne *gules three garbs or* (Matthew Paris Shields, I.66), reflecting their subinfeudation to the Earls of Chester.

Selioke. Hazlebarrow (Norton); Hallowes (Unstone). *Argent three oak leaves vert*; crest: *out of a mural coronet or a cubit arm vested argent holding in the hand proper an oak branch vert fructed of the first* (V. 1569). Robert son of Thomas de Selioke of Hallowes marr. the heiress of Salvein (qv) *c.* 1335, and at first used the arms of Salvein alone. By V. 1569 they merely quartered them: *argent on a chief azure two mullets pierced or a bordure engrailed gules* (Local MS 6341). The chief was occasionally given as *sable.*

Serocold: see Sorocold.

Severne. Hoon Hall; Sudbury. *Argent on a chevron sable five bezants*; crest: *a cinquefoil or*; motto: *'Virtus praestantior auro'* (BLG (1952) 2289). Gr. 1788 to Thomas Severne of Sudbury, who marr. the heiress of Pye of Clifton Campville, and conf. to S.A. Severne 1843, who was also heir of the Pyes of Hoon.

Severn-Trent Water PLC. *Per fesse wavy argent and azure a fesse curling into a wave above and below counterchanged*; crest: *barry wavy of six azure and argent encircled by a chain of nine links or water splashing through them proper*; supporters: *on a compartment per pale barry wavy of six azure and argent and vert, dexter a trout haurient and sinister a heron both proper*; motto: *'Ruat Coelum'* (Annual Report, 1981).

Sevier. Derby; Hulland. *Tenné on a chevron engrailed azure between three martlets sable as many mullets pierced of the field*; crest: *a demi-moor proper holding in the hand a shrub stalked proper* (BLG II (1968) 557). Gr. to Richard Sevier of London (1816–93), HM Consul in St Petersburg, Russia, and borne by the Seviers of Hulland, Derby solicitors.

Seymour: see St Maur.

Shakerley. Calver; Heber Hill (Buxton);

Little Longstone. *Argent a chevron gules between three bundles of rushes vert banded or a mullet for difference*; crest: *a wing per fesse indented or and gules* (V. 1569; crest only given in Queen's Coll., Oxford, MS 97). Allowed to Robert Shakerley of Little Longstone and Rowland, of Heber Hill, as cadets of Shakerley of Shakerley, Lancs., 1569 quartering Levett.

Shakerley. Spital (Chesterfield). *Argent three molehills vert* (Burke). Borne or used by Henry Shakerley who occupied Spital House from *c*. 1545.

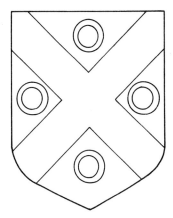

Shallcross

Shalcross. Shallcross (Fernilee). *Gules a saltire between four annulets argent*; crest: *a martlet or holding in the beak a cross patée fitchée gules* (Vv. 1569; 1634; 1662). The various MSS of V. 1611 mainly give the tincture of the *annulets* as *or* but this is corrected back in subsequent visitations. D369 has the *martlet* of the crest *holding in the bill a cross flory fitchée gules*. A probable descendant of this family, George Shawcross of Rivington, Lancs., was conf. arms 3 Feb. 1910: *gules a saltire between four annulets and a chief or fretty azure*; crest: *a martlet or holding in the*

bill *a cross patée fitchée gules between two annulets of the first*; motto: *'Verité sans peur'* (FD (1929) II.1759). Humphrey Shalcross of Faringdon Without, London, son of Humphrey, b. at Mayfield, Staffs., bore the same arms as Shalcross of Shalcross, but charged (on the *saltire*) with a *mullet* (V. London 1634), although a definite connection with the presumed parent stock has not been established. The latter arms are recorded in *Grantees of Arms* (I.151) as having been allowed 12 May 1621.

Shardlow Rural District Council. *Vert on a chevron between two garbs in chief or and in base a fountain four annulets sable*; crest: *a tower azure rising from a coronet of eight bezants or*; motto: *'Quanti est sapere'* (Briggs, 362; Scott-Giles, 100). Gr. 17 Mar. 1952; authority abolished 1974, having previously been renamed South East Derbys. RDC.

Shawcross: see Shalcross.

Shawe. Burnaston; Culland (Brailsford). *Argent a chevron invected pean between three eagles displayed sable*; crest: *a hind's head quarterly argent and or vulned through the neck with an arrow headed azure broken and dropping argent* (Tilley, II.61, 310). These arms are those of Shaw of Wood House (Cheadle), Staffs., and the connection with Thomas son of Thomas Shawe of Culland (d. 1498) is Tilley's.

Shawe. Hazlebarrow (Norton); Offerton. *Argent a chevron ermines and a canton gules*; crest: *a falcon volant argent* (V. Lancs. 1664). Allowed to Shawe of Preston, Lancs., 1664, and borne by Joseph Shawe of Liverpool, Lancs., who marr. Dorothy, dau. and coheiress of Wingfield of Hazlebarrow. A descendant, Henry Cunliffe Shawe (d. 1911), was also of Offerton Hall.

Shawe. Fern (Hartington); White Hall (Fernilee). *Sable a chevron between three lozenges ermine on a chief argent two stags' heads caboshed of the field*; crest: *a hind's head couped at the neck argent gorged with a wreath of roses and pierced through the nose with an arrow in pale or*; motto: *'Te ipsum nosce'* (FD (1905) 1325). Gr. C19 to either Henry Shawe of Ferne (1844–68) or his eldest son, A.P. Shawe of White Hall. See also Somersall.

Sheffield. Measham; South Normanton. *Argent a chevron between three garbs gules*; crest: *a boar's head erased at the neck or*; motto: *'Comiter sed fortiter'* (Burke). Borne by Edmund, 3rd Lord Sheffield of Butterwicke, Lincs. (cr. 1547), whose supporters were *on either side a boar or,* and who sold the Normanton estate which an ancestor had acquired C15. He was also in 1626 cr. Earl of Mulgrave, Yorks. The 3rd earl was cr. Marquess of Normanby, Yorks. (1694) and Duke of Buckingham and Normanby (1703); all ext. 1735. Charles, a natural son of the 1st duke, was cr. a bt 1 Mar. 1755. The arms, gr. 1904, are: *argent a chevron engrailed between two garbs in chief gules and in base a sheaf of five arrows proper banded of the 2nd;* crest: *a boar's head erased at the neck or between two arrows points downwards proper;* same motto (FD (1929) II.1761).

Sheldon. Monyash; Sheldon. *Argent on a bend gules three sheldrakes of the field;* crest: *a sheldrake argent* (Tilley, I.271). Respited for proof when exhibited by Richard son of Hugh Sheldon of Monyash, V. 1662.

Sheldon. Lea Hall (Lea); Sheldon. *Argent on a chevron gules three sheldrakes of the field;* crest: *a sheldrake argent beaked gules* (Burke). Gr. to Gilbert Sheldon, Bishop of London (later Archbishop of Canterbury 1663–77), 'out of Derbys.' (and a root of the Sheldons of Monyash) 4 Sept. 1660. On 26 Dec. 1681 the sons of Ralph son of Roger Sheldon, the elder brother of the archbishop, were gr. an augmentation: *on a canton gules a rose argent barbed vert seeded or;* the *sheldrake* of the crest *holding in the beak a rose gules seeded or slipped and leaved vert* (ibid.). A descendant of Ralph today lives at Lea Hall.

Shepey. Caldwell; Smisby. *Azure a cross or fretty gules* (Parliament Roll; Harl.MSS 6589, 6137). Borne by Sir John Shepey *c.* 1318, whose grandfather came to Smisby through marriage to the heiress of Comyn. *Rel.* VI (1866) 41 gives 'Horpey' for Shepey with arms *azure a cross or a fret gules.*

Shepherd *alias* **Thwaites.** Milnhay (Heanor). *Argent on a fesse sable between three fleurs-de-lys azure as many bezants;* crest: *a hind's head proper* (V. 1611). Allowed to Anthony Thwaites of Milnhay (Heanor) and Remerston, Notts., who through a marriage assumed, somewhat inconsistently, the surname of Shepherd. John Shepherd of Milnhay did not appear, V. 1662.

Shepley. Coal Aston; Holmesfield; Mytham Bridge (Bamford); Stancliffe (Darley). *Argent a mascle and a bordure engrailed sable;* crest: *a*

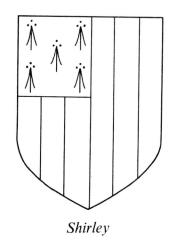

Shirley

buck's head erased proper (BLG (Suppl. 1954) 167). Arms allowed Vv. Lancs, 1567 and 1664 to the ancestors of John Thorpe Shepley of Woodthorpe Hall, Holmesfield (b. 1880), whose sons lived C20 at Coal Aston and Chesterfield. They were 5th in descent from James, of Chapel en le frith. The relationship with the Heathcotes of Stancliffe is unclear. Crest assumed 1763. See also Heathcote.

Sherbrook. Shirebrook; Tibshelf. *Vair a chief or on a bend overall gules three mullets pierced argent;* crest: *a horse's head couped argent charged with three bars gules;* motto: 'Vi si non consilio' (BLG (1898) II.1343). Gr. quarterly with Coape (qv) in 1810 to Maj. Gen. Sir John Sherbrook, with supporters to him only: his remote claimed ancestor, Thomas de Shirebrook son of John son of Nicholas of Bolsover, bore *vair a chief or and a bend gules* (St George Roll, Robert de Shirebrook, *c.* 1265).

Sherratt. Ashbourne; Tideswell. *Azure two boars passant in pale or a canton ermine* (MI at Ashbourne church). Used or borne by James son of John Sherratt of Tideswell, buried at Ashbourne, 1710. His father, John, of Basford, Staffs., claimed descent from Sherard of

Cheddleton, Staffs., whose arms these are.

Shirley. Shirley; Brailsford; Derby etc. *Paly of six or and azure a canton ermine*; crest: *a saracen's head in profile couped at the shoulders proper wreathed about the temples or and azure*; motto: *'Honor virtutis praemium'* (V. 1569). Anciently the arms differed slightly; William de Shirley of Shirley bore *c.* 1250: *paly of six or and azure a bend gules* (Charles Roll); Sir Ralph Shirley of Staunton and Ettington, Warwicks.: *paly of six or and sable, c.* 1318 (Parliament Roll); Hugh and Sir Ralph Shirley of Staunton Harold, Leics.: paly of six or and sable a canton ermine (Willement Roll). The *canton* is occasionally shown as a *quarter*. This family, like the Brailsfords, descend from a Saxon ancestor holding in Derbys. in 1066, and who was the ancestor of the families of Edensor, Ible, Ireton, Monjoye and Snitterton (qqv). On 22 May 1611 a btcy was conferred on George Shirley. The 7th bt had the abeyance of the baronies of Ferrers of Chartley, Staffs., Bourchier and Louvain terminated in his favour 1677. He was conf. in his arms, quartering Washington, and gr. supporters: *dexter a talbot ermine eared and langued gules ducally gorged or, sinister a reindeer gules billettée and charged on the shoulder with an horseshoe argent attired and ducally gorged or* (BP (1970) 998). He was further cr. 1711 Viscount Tamworth (Staffs.) and Earl Ferrers, the 5th earl obtaining a confirmation of his achievement 1777. Remoter cadets enjoyed baronetcies of Oat Hall (Haywards Heath), Sussex (27 June 1786, ext. 1815), and Preston, Sussex (6 Mar. 1666, ext. 1705), both bearing the arms as above (Vv. Sussex 1574, 1633).

Shore. Darley; Derby; Snitterton. *Argent a chevron sable between three holly leaves vert*; crest: *a stork reguardant holding in the dexter claw a pebble proper*; motto: *'Perimus licitis'* (V. 1662). Allowed to Sir John Shore MD of Derby, son of John, of Snitterton, 1662. Harl.MS 6104 gives *oak leaves* rather than *holly* and blazons the crest: *a crane holding in his right foot a mullet argent*. The grantee's great grandson, Sir John Shore, Governor-General of India, was cr. a bt 27 Oct. 1792 and was cr. Lord Teignmouth (Devon) in the Irish peerage 1797 (both titles ext. 1981). Supporters: *on either side a stork reguardant argent beaked and membered gules crowned with an eastern crown or* (Burke).

Shore

Shore. Derby. *Argent a bend between three bay leaves vert* (*Rel.* VI (1866) 41). Used by Thomas, brother of Sir John (qv above), who sold Snitterton, and his descendants, who were of Derby c18.

Shore. Mickleover; Norton Hall; Tapton. *Argent two chevronels sable between three holly leaves slipped vert*; crest: *a stork reguardant argent ducally crowned beaked and membered gules holding in the dexter claw a pebble proper gorged with a collar gemel sable in the beak a holly leaf slipped vert*; motto: *'Non dormit qui custodit'* (Burke). Gr. 1839 to Offley Shore of Norton and to the descendants of his grandfather, Samuel. Offley's 3rd son, O.B. Shore, was of Mickleover Old Hall. William, 4th son of Samuel Shore of Norton, marr. the ultimate heiress of Nightingale of Lea (via Evans) and his son W.E. Shore assumed the surname of Nightingale (qv), 1815, being father of Florence. Before 1839 the arms used were as Lord Teignmouth, but motto as above.

Shore. Heage Hall. *Argent two chevronels sable between three oak leaves vert* (*Rel.* VI (1866) 41). Used by Enoch, son of John Shore of Heage Hall, *c.* 1862, claiming descent from a common ancestor with Shore of Norton. See also Milnes; Nightingale.

Shuttleworth. Nether Hall (Hathersage). *Argent three weavers' shuttles sable tipped and furnished with quills of yarn thread pendent or;* crest: *a cubit arm in armour proper grasping in the gauntlet a shuttle as in the arms;* motto: *'In Domino confido'* (BLG (1968) II.560). Borne by Ashton Shuttleworth of Hathersage Hall (1754–1830) and his son who removed to Nether Hall in the parish, cadets of Shuttleworth of Gawthorpe (Burnley), Lancs. An uncle, James, marr. the heiress of Holden of Aston (qv) and assumed that surname and arms in lieu of his own by RL 1791.

Sidebottom. Glossop; Tintwistle. *Or on a chevron engrailed between three buglehorns sable stringed gules as many bees volant of the field;* crest: *on a mount vert a talbot reguardant sable gorged vair resting the dexter forepaw on an escutcheon argent thereon a bugle horn sable;* motto: *'Labor ipse voluptas'* (FD (1910) 1461). Gr. to William Sidebottom C19. His elder son Thomas was of Tintwistle and another was mayor of Glossop, where he lived, 1873; both were MPs.

Sidebottom. Glossop. *Sable on a mount a hurst of oaks issuant from the dexter and a square embattled tower issuant from the sinister all argent in the dexter chief a decrescent or;* crest: *On a mount in front of a hurst of oaks a square embattled tower all proper;* motto: *'Think and thank'* (FD (1929) II.1770). Gr. early C20 to Maj. R.B. Sidebottom, of Glossop in 1929, son of Edward, of Mottram, Cheshire.

Sikes. Derby. *Ermine a chevron paly of six or and sable between three fountains;* crest: *a bull proper resting the dexter foot on a fountain and charged with eight billets sable;* motto: *'Quod facio valde facio'* (BLG (1858) 1898). Gr. by RL 7 Jan. 1858 to Francis Sikes, formerly Baines, heir of Revd Joseph Sikes of Derby and Newark, Notts. (1781–1858). Previously the Sikes family used: *argent a chevron between three fountains proper* quartering Chambers (of Derby) and Burton (qqv); crest: *a bull passant proper;* mottoes: as above and *'Ferox inimicis'* (Burke).

Simpson. Derby; Stoke Hall. *Per bend or and sable a lion rampant counterchanged;* crest: *out of a tower azure a demi-lion rampant guardant per pale or and sable holding in the dexter paw a sword erect argent hilt and pom-*mel of the 2nd (Burke). Gr. under an Act of Parliament 1786 (25 Geo. III c. xxx) to Hon. John Simpson, formerly Bridgeman, 2nd son of Sir Henry, bt (cr. 7 June 1660), cr. 1794 Lord Bradford of Bradford, Salop., who marr. the heiress of Revd John Simpson of Stoke Hall.

Simpson. Derby; Wirksworth. *Per bend or and sable a lion rampant counterchanged;* crest: *a demi-lion rampant sable* (Printed pedigree of Simpson, Box 57; crest: bookplate, Derby Museum). Used by the Derby Simpsons, descended from Blythe Simpson (1731–92), governor of Derby gaol, and ancestor of a long line of local solicitors. The family came from Wirksworth C17.

Simpson. Barton Blount; Bonsall; Mellor Lodge. *Per bend nebulée or and sable a lion rampant counterchanged;* crest: *out of a mural coronet argent a demi-lion rampant guardant per pale or and sable holding in the dexter paw a sword erect proper* (BLG (1875) II.1265). Borne or used by Richard Simpson of Mellor Lodge 1846, grandson of Adam, of Bonsall. Also used by the Simpsons of Barton Blount, having been painted by Bassano for the hatchments of Alice, wife of Thomas Browne of Hungry Bentley, dau. of Richard Simpson, of Barton, in 1717, and for Merry Simpson of the same 22 Feb. 1718 (Local MS 3525).

Sir John Port School. Etwall. *Azure two barrulets wavy or between three pigeons argent.* Used without authority by this modern comprehensive school on the site of Etwall Hall.

Sitwell. Eckington; Renishaw Hall. *Barry of eight or and vert three lions rampant sable armed and langued gules;* crest: *a demi-lion rampant erased sable holding an escutcheon per pale or and vert* (V. 1662). Arms conf. and crest granted 1 Mar. 1661 to George Sitwell of Renishaw, confirming a Commonwealth grant of 15 Feb. 1648 and conf. by RSM 1777, whereby Francis, son of Jonathan Hurt (from Yorkshire and not provably related to those of Derbys., qv) assumed the surname and arms of Sitwell in lieu of his own. The son of the latter was cr. a bt 3 Oct. 1808. See also Wilmot.

Skinner. The Hill (Outseats). *Sable a chevron or between three griffins' heads erased argent* (D369). Used by Richard Skinner of The Hill (1569–1618), who was recorded as a usurper V. 1611. These are actually the arms of the Skinners of Hill (Walford, near Ross), Herefs.

Skrymshire. Durrant Hall (Chesterfield); Tapton. *Gules a lion rampant or and a bordure vair*; crest: *a demi-knight in armour arm embowed holding a crooked sword all proper hilt and pommel or a shield in the other hand gules* (V. Staffs. 1663). Crest gr. and arms conf. 13 Apr. 1584 to Thomas Scrymshire of Aqualate, Staffs., and borne by Sir Charles Scrymshire of Norbury, Staffs., *jure uxoris* of Durrant Hall and Tapton. Tilley (II.274) gives the crest differently: *a lion rampant or holding a crooked sword proper hilt and pommel of the first.*

Slack. Brownside (Chinley); Little Hayfield. *Azure on a cross formée throughout ermine between four crescents or a human heart gules*; crest: *in front of a crescent or a snail proper*; motto: *'Lente sed Certe'* (BLG (1898), II.1385). Probably gr. to Robert Slack (1822–93) and matric. (LO) 1894 by his son Dr Robert Slack of Derwent Hill (Keswick), Cumb., descended in the 7th generation from Nicholas Slack of Brownside and Chinley, living 1586. The latter's 4th son Thomas was ancestor, through his own 4th son, of the Slackes of Slack Hall (qv). Note that Sir Owen Slacke CB of Fane Valley (Dundalk), Co. Louth (1837–1910), claimed descent from one of three brothers, scions of the Slack Hall branch, who migrated to Ireland in 1693. He bore (UO): *Azure a cross patée throughout per bend sinister ermine and or charged with a quatrefoil counterchanged thereon a mullet gules*; crest: *a lion couchant proper resting the dexter forepaw on a quatrefoil as in the arms*; motto: *'Lente sed Certe'* (Burke, LGI (1898), 412–13).

Slacke. Slack Hall (Chapel en le Frith). *Per pale azure and ermine a saltire patée or thereon a cinquefoil counterchanged* (Tilley, I.271). Used by Thomas Slacke of Slack Hall 1846.

Slater. Barlborough; Durant Hall (Chesterfield); Tapton Hall. *Or a chevron gules between three trefoils slipped vert*; crest: *a dexter arm in armour couped below the wrist holding in the gauntlet a sword all proper hilt and pommel or*; motto: *'Crescit sub pondere virtus'* (Burke). Used by Dr Adam Slater of Chesterfield, who purchased Durrant Hall and Tapton 1746 and 1755 ordered a Chinese armorial service bearing these arms impaling

Warren of Stapleford, Notts. (Howard, M6).

Slaughter. Barlow Lees; Chatsworth; Chesterfield. *Argent a saltire azure*; crest: *out of ducal coronet a demi-eagle displayed sable* (V. 1611; Local MS 6341). George Slaughter disclaimed in 1611, but the arms are nevertheless entered in some MSS. His father Richard marr. the heiress of Ralph Leche (qv). Another member of the family marr. the ultimate heiress of Foljambe of Brimington. The disclaimer may have been because the arms were allowed in Vv. Herefs. 1634 and 1683; the family were descended from the Slaughters of Slaughter, Gloucs.

Sleigh. Ashe Hall (Ash); Derby; Etwall Hall. *Gules a chevron between three owls argent beaked and legged or*; crest: *a demi-lion rampant argent crowned or holding in the dexter paw a cross crosslet fitchée gules*; motto: *'Medio tutissimus'* (V. 1662; motto, Cox, III.330). Gr. 1600 to Gervase son of Hugh Sleigh of Derby, who purchased Etwall and Ash 1603, and conf. 2 May 1626 to the same man. In Dugdale's copy of V. 1662 (College of Arms, MS C.34) the crest is *azure*.

Sleigh. Chesterfield; Derby; Biggin and Pilsbury (Hartington). *Gules a chevron between three owls or* (*Rel.* VI (1866) 42). Used by Gervase Sleigh of Derby, who 'promised to come to London' V. 1611; most of his kinsmen, however, disclaimed: Edmund, of Derby; John, of Biggin (both V. 1611); Samuel, of Northead (Hartington) and Lawrence of Biggin (both V. 1662). Nevertheless, these arms were being used by Hugh Sleigh of Pilsbury, later c16 (Local MS 6341). Ald. Edmund Sleigh of London, was 'respited for proof', V. London 1634, but had a grant later (see next entry).

Sleigh. Pilsbury (Hartington). *Gules a chevron embattled between three owls argent beaked and legged or* (Burke). Gr. 1657 to Ald. Edmund Sleigh (see above), son of Richard, and great-grandson of Hugh, of Pilsbury, 'as on an achievement in Cheapside' – presumably his business premises. Of this family, John Sleigh assumed the surname of Lindley of Skegby, Notts., and in 1773 was gr. the arms of that family: *argent on a chevron sable three griffins' heads erased of the field*; crest: *out of a ducal coronet gules a demi-bear or* (Burke).

Smalley. Alvaston. *Sable on a bend argent three roses gules in chief a chessrook of the 2nd*

SMALLEY

(V. Leics. 1619). Anthony Smalley of Alvaston was a usurper V. 1611; the related Smalleys of Thorpe Arnold and Newbold (both Leics.) were, however, allowed these arms, V. Leics. 1619.

Smalley. Smalley. *Sable on a bend argent three roses gules in chief a like rose of the 2nd* (*Rel.* VI (1866) 42).

Smedley. Riber Castle (Matlock). *Ermine a chevron lozengy azure and or* (*Rel.* (VI (1866) 42). Used by John Smedley of Lea, Matlock and Riber, mid-c19. See also Marsden.

Smelter. Norton. *Gules a pale fusilly of four between two flaunches argent on each an oak tree eradicated proper fructed or*; crest: *a woodcock standing on a mount of bullrushes proper* (College of Arms, Grants XIX.303). Gr. 9 Sept. 1796 to John Smelter of Richmond (Sheffield, Yorks.), grandson of John Smelter of Norton (doubtless kin to Philip Smelter of Holmesfield Hall). He marr. Anne, dau. and heir to Thomas Wainwright of Finningley (Notts.); she was at the same time gr. the arms of Wainwright to herself, her descendants and those of her father.

Smith. Ashford Hall (Ashford); Hulland Ward. *Gules a bend engrailed argent between two salamanders incensed proper*; crest: *on a mount vert in front of a rock a chamois proper*; motto: *'Per saxa per ignes'* (FD (1929) II.1791). Gr. 1855 to Richard Smith of Dudley Priory, Worcs., and Worcester. His grandson Richard Clifford Smith was of Ashford Hall. On his death, the heiress marr. a cousin, R.F. Smith, who bore these arms under a further grant of 1887.

Smith. Brailsford; Quarndon. *Gules six lozenges in fesse between three maidens' heads couped at the shoulders argent crined or*; crest: *on a mount vert a tower triple towered or on the sinister side a laurel branch pendant over the edifice proper* (*Rel.* VI (1866) 42). Gr. 1585 to William Smith of the Inner Temple, son of William, of Brailsford. His cousin, William Smyth, was of Quarndon; his heiress marr. Mundy.

Smith. Denby; Padley Hall (Ripley); Whitemoor Hall (Belper). *Per chevron azure and or three escallops counterchanged*; crest: *an escallop per fesse or and azure* (Lysons, clxv). Gr. to Matthew Smith of Denby 10 Feb. 1685, whose father Henry had disclaimed V. 1662.

Smith. Derby; Spondon. *Azure a chevron between three leopards' heads erased or pelletée*; crest: *a ship gules* (V. 1634). Allowed to Thomas Smith of Derby 1634, descended from another Thomas, living 1553.

Smith. Coxbench; Derby; Duffield Hall; Wingfield Park (S. Wingfield). *Or a chevron cotised between three demi-griffins those in chief respectant sable*; crest: *an elephant's head erased or eared gules charged on the neck with three fleurs-de-lys two and one sable*; motto: *'Tenax et Fidelis'* (over porch of Duffield Hall; BLG (1952) 2331-7). Gr. 1718 to Thomas son of Thomas Smith of Broxtowe, Notts., and Gaddesby, Leics. Borne by his descendants Rowland Smith MP (1826–1901) and his posterity at Duffield Hall, also by Francis Nicholas Smith of Wingfield Park (1838–1929), and by Sir Gerard Smith KCMG of Derby, whose son, G.H. Smith, moved to Coxbench c. 1934. Smith's Bank, founded by a member of this family, had branches in Derbys. from c18; members of the Smith family worked therein from time to time, e.g. at Ilkeston as late as 1900.

Smith. Brocksford Hall (Doveridge); Clifton Hall. *Gules two bars wavy ermine on a chief or a demi-lion rampant issuant sable armed and langued gules*; crest: *an ostrich holding in the beak a horseshoe proper*; motto: *'Duriora Virtus'* (BLG (1898) II.1366). Allowed V. Staffs. 1614 to the Smiths of Newcastle under Lyme, Staffs., and borne by W.R. Smith of Clifton Hall and his kinsman C.W.J. Smith of Brocksford Hall, both there 1898.

Smith. Dunston Hall (Newbold). *Argent on a bend engrailed azure between two unicorns' heads erased gules three fleurs-de-lys or*; crest: *a unicorn's head erased per pale argent and azure armed and crined or gorged with a ducal coronet counterchanged*; motto: *'Fortiter et Recte'* (Lysons, xcvi; crest: Burke). Gr. 1816, impaling Mower quartering Milnes, with crest, to Elizabeth Mary, widow of Thomas Smith, and conf. to Smith-Milnes 1831, 1873.

Smith. Parkfields (Derby); Alvaston Fields. *Per fesse nebulée gules and argent a pale counterchanged three goats' heads erased two and one of the 2nd and as many chaplets of roses one and two of the first*; crest: *in front of a goat's head erased argent holding in the mouth a rose gules slipped and leaved proper two cross crosslets fitchée in saltire gules* (FD (1905) 1254). Gr. 1886 with remainders to

150

Ald. Sir John Smith, mayor of Derby 1872, and borne by W.J. Smith of Alvaston Fields.

Smith. Heanor. *Sable a dexter arm embowed and couped at the shoulder proper holding in the hand a lamp suspended by three chains between two ivy leaves in pale and on a chief or three mullets of six points gules*; crest: *two pickaxes in saltire sable thereon an eagle wings expanded or on each wing a mullet of six points gules*; motto: *'Quaerendo'* (FD (1910) 1478). Gr. 1895 to Sir Clarence Smith, MP for Hull, Yorks., son of Revd Dr Gervase Smith of Heanor. Sir Clarence left six sons and four daus., some of whom remained in Derbys. See also Craven; Heriz; Innes-Smith; Milnes; Powtrell.

Smithers. Little Longstone; Thornbridge Hall (Ashford). *Argent an eagle displayed vert* (*Rel.* VI (1866) 42). Used by Sydney Smithers of Thornbridge 1846 and by his forebears at Little Longstone a century earlier.

Smyth: see Smith.

Sneyd: see Kinnersley.

Snitterton. Ible; Snitterton. *Gules a snipe argent ducally gorged or* (as a quartering of Sacheverell, on MI at Morley church). Borne by Ralph de Snitterton of Ible 1304, of the stock of Shirley etc.

Solney. Church Broughton; Newton Solney. *Quarterly argent and gules* (as quartered by Longford, Local MS 6341). Borne by one of four successive Alureds de Solney C14 (Charles Roll) and by John, whose heirs quartered the arms.

Somersal. Somersal Herbert. *Argent on a bend sable three butterflies of the field* (in stained glass at Somersal Herbert Hall (C16) and as quartered by FitzHerbert and Draycott, V. 1569). Allegedly borne by the untraceable Somersals of Somersal, the heiress of whom is said to have marr. William son of Sir William Fitzherbert of Norbury, c. 1250. The alliance may be a figment of the imagination of Tudor genealogists and the arms inspired by those of Somersall of Somersall (qv).

Somersall. Somersall; Ashgate (both Brampton). *Or on a bend sable three butterflies argent* (V. 1611, some MSS only). Allowed (according to D369) to John Somersall of Ashgate V. 1611, whose dau. and heiress marr. Ralph Bullock of Unstone. Borne also by the Somersalls of Somersall and by their heirs, the Shawes of Somersall, to 1578, who often

Somersall

added 'alias Somersall' to their name.

Sorby. The Lodge (Darley). *Argent a chevron between three annulets azure*; crest: *a buck's head proper*; motto: *'Cara Patria carior libertus'* (bookplate, Local MS 7769). Used by Clement, yr son of John Sorby of Sheffield, Yorks., who settled at Darley Dale in 1852. Their son, R.A. Sorby, removed to Thorpe Salvin, Yorks. Arms originally borne by John Soureby C15 (Glover's Ordinary).

Soresby. Chesterfield; Cromford; Shardlow. *Quarterly ermine and gules in the 1st quarter a lion passant of the 2nd* (Glover, II.292; Tilley, III.275). Gr. as an inescutcheon of pretence to William Milnes of Cromford, who marr. the heiress of William son of Adam Soresby of Cromford and Chesterfield in 1795.

Sorocold. Hargate (Hilton); Derby. *Per chevron argent and sable in chief two fleurs-de-lys azure and in base a castle or*; crest: *a castle or issuant from the battlements a fleur-de-lys azure* (V. Lancs. 1664). Allowed to Thomas Sorocold, V. London 1634 (but said by Burke to have been gr. to him 1644) and to Thomas, of Lancs. 1664. Believed to have been borne (although there is an element of doubt in his

Sorocold

pedigree) by George Sorocold, water engineer, of Derby (b. 1668), whose grandfather George, of Ashton in Makerfield, Lancs., owned a small estate at Hargate 1641. Revd Edward Serocold (sic), whose mother was the ultimate heiress of the grantee, was gr. these arms quarterly with Pearce under RL 1842.

Sotehill. Darley. *Gules an eagle displayed argent* (Glover, II.360). Borne by Sir Henry de Sotehill 1322 (Boroughbridge Roll) and Sir John (Powell Roll), and thus by John de Sotehill of Stockerston, Leics., who marr. the heiress of Plumpton C15. As quartered by Frecheville of Staveley, however, their arms are given as *gules six cocks or* (Local MS 6341).

South Derbyshire District Council. *Vert on a chevron masoned or between three garbs proper as many annulets azure a chief vairé gules and ermine*; crest: *on a mount sable issuant flames of fire proper a tower also issuant with clouds argent*; supporters: *dexter a lion ermine gorged with a collar vairé gules and ermine sinister a wolf erminois gorged with a collar quarterly ermine and gules each charged on the shoulder with a Tudor rose proper barbed vert seeded or*; motto: *'The earth our wealth'*

(SDDC *Official Guide* (1978), 6). Gr. 1978, designed by H. Ellis Tomlinson.

South East Derbyshire RDC: see Shardlow.
Southwell-Wandesford, Butler-Clarke-: see Butler.

Southwell, Bishopric of. *Sable three fountains proper on a chief or a pale azure charged with a representation of the Blessed Virgin Mary seated bearing the infant Christ or between dexter a stag lodged proper and sinister two staves raguly crossed vert* (Briggs, 366). Diocese included Derbys. 1884–1927. Gr. 1884.

Sowler. King Sterndale. *Sable two pallets ermine over all three open sandals erect or*; crest: *a palmer's staff sable between two open sandals erect or*; motto: *'Per Orbem'* (FD (1929) II.1814). Gr. C20 to Sir Thomas Sowler of Rusholme, Lancs., and borne by his son, Col. Harry Sowler of King Sterndale.

Spateman. Derby; Lea; Roadnook Hall (Wessington); Tansley; Wirksworth. *Ermine on a fesse gules double cotised sable three griffins' heads erased or*; crest: *out of a mural coronet a griffin's head erminois*; motto: *'Et quae non fecimus ipsi'* (V. 1662). Gr. 2 Mar. 1664 to John Spateman of Roadnook. Previously they had used arms as above, but *ermine* instead of *erminois*.

Spencer. Hathersage. *Azure a fesse wavy ermine between six seamews' heads erased argent*; crest: *on a rock proper a seamew* (Hunter, *Hallamshire*, 416). The Spencers succ. the Ashtons at Hathersage for one life C18. The arms were gr. to William Spencer of Attercliffe, Yorks., 1648, to vary his use of the arms of Spencer of Northants. (gr. 1504) which he had previously borne (as above, but *fesse* plain) by descent and as quartered by Stanhope, who marr. the ultimate heiress.

Spencer. Edgemoor (Hartington Upper Quarter). *Quarterly argent and gules in the 2nd and 3rd quarters a fret or overall on a bend sable three escallops of the first*; crest: *out of a ducal coronet a griffin's head argent gorged with a bar gemel gules between two wings expanded of the 2nd*; motto: *'Dieu defend le droit'* (BLG (1937) 2104; cf. Vv. Northants. 1618, 1681). Allowed to Sir Robert Spencer, cr. (1603) Lord Spencer of Wormleighton, Warwicks. (V. Northants. 1618), who was gr. supporters: *dexter a griffin per fesse ermine and erminois gorged with a collar edged flory counter-flory and chained sable thereon three* escallops argent, sinister a wyvern erect on his tail ermine collared and chained as the griffin. The 3rd baron was advanced as Earl of Sunderland, Co. Durham (1643), and his descendant, John, was cr. Lord Spencer and Viscount Spencer 1761 and Earl Spencer and Viscount Althorp (Northants.) 1765. His descendant John Trevor Spencer, Bishop of Madras, India, settled at Edgemoor and d. 1866, and he and his descendants there bore arms as above.

Spendlove (Spindelowe). 'Co. Derby'. *Or five fleurs-de-lys in saltire sable*; crest: *a dolphin embowed gules* (D369). It is difficult to identify which family of this name bore or used these arms: perhaps Spindelow of Heage and Fernilee 1471, or the Spendloves of Shottle, Duffield and Dalbury Lees, C17–C19.

Spilsbury. Willington. *Argent three ducal coronets gules*; crest: *a garb or thereon a dove proper* (T.W. Stafford, *The Staffords of Botham* (1906), 3). Borne or used by Benjamin Spilsbury of Willington Hall (d. 1815) and his son, Revd F.W. Spilsbury.

Spigurnell. 'Derbys.' *Gules fretty ermine on a chief a lion passant guardant of the field* (*Rel.* XII (1872) 96). Attributed by Sleigh to a Derbys. family of this name, but borne by Sir John de Spygurnell of Bucks., 1318 (Parliament Roll). Perhaps intended to cover the Derbys. landholdings of the Spigurnells of Skegby, Notts., 1207–1315.

Spurrier. Cubley; Marston Hall (Marston on Dove); Wakelyn Old Hall (Hilton). *Azure a griffin segreant and on a chief arched or two spurs fessewise rowels inwards of the field*; crest: *a long cross or on three grieces sable argent and gules between dexter a rose argent and sinister a like rose gules both barbed and seeded proper*; motto: *'Stimulus adde'* (BLG (1968) II.580). Gr. to Sir Henry Spurrier of Marston Hall 1955, when he was knighted. Henry, his grandfather (founder of Leyland Motors), used: *azure a griffin segreant or*; crest: *a long cross or on three grieces*; same motto (Local MS 9555, 1881).

Stafford. Bottoms Hall (Mellor); Derby; Eyam; Stony Middleton etc. *Or a chevron gules between three martlets sable* (Bottoms, Vv. 1569, 1662; Eyam: as a quartering of Bradshaw etc, V. 1569). Borne by Humphrey Stafford of Eyam, and allowed, with *a mullet for difference*, to Tristram son of Thomas Stafford of Bottoms 1662. Also borne by

John Stafford of Shaw (Mellor) C17, cadet of Bottoms, themselves cadets of Eyam. Henry Stafford, later Strafford (which alteration this branch made before 1772) used a crest: *a swan rising proper* (T.W. Stafford, *The Staffords of Botham* (1906), 26), which some evidence suggests may have been in use from a much earlier period. George Strafford of Calcutta, India, a kinsman, usurped the crest of his mother's family, the Spilsburys (qv) (ibid.).

Stafford. Egginton. *Or on a chevron gules five plates* (glass noted in Egginton church, c. 1611, Local MS 6341). Borne by Sir Robert son of Sir William de Stafford of Egginton 1302; he sealed with a *a swan rising* (Egginton Charter 10, in private hands), probably a crest. Robert, son of Henry de Stafford (d. 1261) of the senior (Stafford) line, bore: *argent on a chevron gules three bezants* (Glover's Roll, 1st Version, 52), which emphasises likely kinship between these branches.

Stainrod. Dronfield. Gervase Stainrod of Dronfield disclaimed V. 1662.

Stainsby: see Steynsby.

Staley. Pindale (Castleton); Redseats (Castleton). *Argent a chevron azure between three fusils sable* (*Rel.* VI (1866) 42). Borne or used by Christopher Staley of Hope c. 1450, and by Elias, of Redseats, from 1536. This family were perhaps descendants of Sir Ralph Staveley (sic), whose son John was gr. land at Hope and Castleton (cf. Staveley).

Stamford. Derby. *Argent two bars azure on a canton gules a gauntlet grasping a broken sword erect proper hilt and pommel or* (ibid; Thompson, IV.50). Used on his seal by Ald. Thomas Stamford of Derby (d. 1785); this man's yr dau. marr. Wedgwood's partner, Thomas Bentley, and his horse was commandeered by Prince Charles Edward's vanguard in 1745.

Stanhope. Bretby; Cubley; Newton Solney. *Quarterly ermine and gules*; crest: *out of a tower azure a demi-lion or ducally crowned gules holding between its paws a grenade fired proper*; motto: *'A Deo et rege'* (V. 1569; FD (1929) II. 1826). In 1569 Sir Thomas Stanhope of Elvaston was allowed a shield as above, but the crest was merely *a lion holding an ogress*. His brother John was in 1605 cr. Lord Stanhope of Harrington, Northants (ext. 1675); He was gr. suporters: *on either side a wolf or*; motto: *'Quaere sic est'* (Burke).

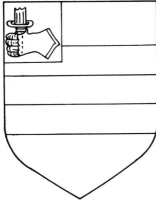

Stamford

Stanley

Sir Philip Stanhope (1585–1656) was cr. 1616 Lord Stanhope of Shelford, Notts., and 1628 Earl of Chesterfield, being gr. supporters at The Hague, Netherlands, 29 May 1660: *dexter a talbot guardant ermine sinister a wolf erminois each gorged with a chaplet of oak proper* (ibid.). Admiral Sir H.E. Stanhope, a descendant, was on 13 Nov. 1807 cr. a bt, being gr. supporters: *dexter a female figure representing Faith sinister a British sailor the interior hand supporting a flag and the exterior one an anchor all proper* (Burke). The 2nd bt assumed by RL the additional surname and quarterly arms of Scudamore 1827, and the 3rd bt inherited as 9th Earl Stanhope, Lord Stanhope of Elvaston (cr. 1718) and Viscount (Stanhope of) Mahon, Minorca, Spain (cr. 1717). Earl Stanhope differenced with *a crescent* and his supporters were: *dexter a talbot ermine sinister a lion or ducally crowned gules each charged on the shoulder with a mullet issuant out of a crescent azure* (BP (1956) 2055). All honours ext. 1967, except the viscountcy of Mahon which passed to the Earl of Harrington (qv).

Stanhope. Elvaston. Arms as above, but *a crescent within a crescent for difference;* sup-

porters: *dexter a talbot guardant argent gouttée-de-poix sinister a wolf erminois each gorged with a chaplet of oak proper* (BP (1970) 1260). William Stanhope was in 1729 cr. Lord Harrington of Harrington, Northants., and advanced 1742 as Viscount Petersham (Surrey) and Earl of Harrington, Northants. The 11th Earl succ. 1967 as (8th) Viscount (Stanhope of) Mahon. Supporters gr. 1730.

Stanley. Barlborough; Derby. *Argent on a bend azure three stags' heads caboshed or; crest: on a chapeau an eagle or preying on an infant in its cradle proper swathed gules;* motto: *'Sans changer'* (Burke). Borne by Sir Humphrey Stanley of Lancs. C15 (Ballard's Book), and assumed at an early date, being originally the arms of Bamville, the heiress of which marr. into this family. Borne in Derbys. by Hon. Sir Edward Stanley of Hornby Castle, Yorks., KG, son of 1st Earl of Derby (cr. 1485) and 2nd Lord Stanley (cr. by writ of summons 1456), who was, amongst other places, of Barlborough. He was cr. also by writ of summons Lord Monteagle (from his crest), 1514. In the later middle ages his kinswomen Elizabeth and Isabella de Stanley were successively prioresses of St Mary de

Pratis, Derby.

Stanley. Dronfield; Hassop; Stanley. *Or three eagles' legs erased à-la-quise gules on a chief indented azure as many bucks' heads caboshed of the field*; crest: *an eagle's head argent charged on the neck with three pellets one and two in the beak an eagle's leg as in the arms* (MI at Sutton Bonington of 1564; cf. Thoroton, *Notts* (1793), I.18). Allowed to Michael Stanley the yr of Sutton Bonington, Notts. (and emblazoned on his homonymous father's tomb in 1564), V. Notts. 1569, and to a kinsman of Hassop (V. 1611) and another of Chichester (V. Sussex 1633). Richard Stanley of Hassop House, London, C19 bore these arms and claimed descent from the Derbys. offshoot via antecedents at Stanley and Dronfield.

Stanton. Snelston Hall; Yeldersley Hall. *Vairé argent and sable on either side of the honour point an escutcheon gules thereon a cross patée fitchée or*; crest: *a lion passant or holding in the dexter paw a cross patée fitchée gules in front of two ears of wheat of the first*; motto: '*Exactavit me in petra*' (BLG (1968) II.582). Gr. C20 to Henry Stanton of Snelston Hall (1851–1922) with remainder to the heirs of his father Henry.

Stanton. Stanton by Bridge. *A fleur de lys* (seal on quitclaim of 1322, Cox, III.468). Borne by Sir Robert de Stanton of Stanton by Bridge, a descendant of Ernui, King's Thegn, 1086.

Stapleford. Sandiacre. *Argent on two bars azure three cinquefoils or* (*Rel.* VI (1866) 42). Borne by Adam son of Robert de Stapleford of Sandiacre c. 1240; his father, Robert son of William, however, sealed with *a knight on horseback* (ibid.).

Stapleton Martin. Norbury Hall. *Argent three talbots statant in pale within a bordure sable charged with as many fylfots or*; crest: *a talbot statant sable charged on the body with a fylfot or*; motto: '*Sure and Steadfast*' (FD (1929) II.1318). Gr. 8 Dec. 1913 to John Stapleton Martin (1846–1922), whose elder son, M.B.B. Stapleton Martin (d. 1988), settled at Norbury Hall 1968.

Starkey: see Barber.

Statham. Horsley; Morley; Tansley; Tideswell. *Gules a pale fusilly argent*; crest: *a greyhound's head erased gules*; motto: '*Adjutor meus Deus*' (as in Morley church, Cox, IV.326). Originally borne by the de Lymmes

of Lymm, Cheshire, allegedly before C12, cf. Chester Abbey, which bore *gules a pale fusilly or*, adapted from the ensigns of William de Lymme, son of Nigel, Viscomte de Contentin, Baron de St Sauveur, who had founded it by 1133 (*DAJ* XLV (1923) 76–90). Borne by Sir Ralph de Statham of Statham in Lymme, *jure uxoris* of Morley (d. 1380). His supposed descendant, Sir John Statham, bore the same (if his claims are accepted); he was of Tideswell, descended from a Statham of Horsley. His 2nd son d. 1770. A great uncle of Sir John, William, of London bore: *argent a pale fusilly gules*; crest: *a lion's head erased within a fetterlock proper* (Burke).

Staunton. Willington. *Vairé sable and argent a canton gules* (MI of 1458 at Castle Donington church; as quartered by Haselrigg, V. Notts. 1619). John, 2nd son of John Staunton of Staunton Harold, Leics., was of Willington and d. 1458, leaving an heiress who marr. Meynell of Yeaveley. Sir William and Ellis de Staunton bore *vairé argent and sable a canton gules* c. 1250 (Parliament Roll).

Staveley. Redseats (Castleton); Staveley. *Argent a fesse engrailed azure* (*Rel* VI (1866) 42). Borne, apparently, by Simon de Staveley, father of the first Mellor of Mellor (qv). A yr branch settled at Redseats (Castleton), represented by Ellis Staveley 1533, but see Staley (also of Redseats) credited with quite different arms, even if their surname is a contraction of Staveley. Harl.MS 1808, 18b, gives, however, 'Arma Adae de Staueley *barry of eight gules and argent a fleur-de-lys sable*'. According to Ford (pp. 278–80), an old seal found at Chesterfield of an Adam (de Staveley?) bore a crude *fleur-de-lys*.

Steade: see Pegge.

Steel: see Coke.

Stephenson. Hassop Hall. *Vair on a pale between two pallets gules three leopards' faces or all between two flaunches of the 2nd*; crest: *a rock thereon a falcon's head erased proper gorged vair pendent therefrom an escutcheon vert charged with two arrows saltirewise points downwards or* (FD (1905) 1283). Gr. with remainders to Sir Henry Stephenson of Sheffield, Yorks., typefounder and mayor there (knighted in 1887) in 1890. His son, Col. Sir Henry Stephenson, purchased Hassop from the Leslies and was cr. a bt 16 July 1936.

Stephenson. Tapton House. *Argent a chevron between two fleurs-de-lys in chief and a* *cross fleurettée in base gules on a chief azure three mullets of the field*; crest: *between two fleurs-de-lys argent a cubit arm vested azure cuffed also argent holding an escroll proper*; motto: *'Fidus in arcaniis'* (FD (1929) II.1839). Gr. 1838 to Robert Stephenson and the descendants of his father George, the celebrated engineer, who in later years lived at Tapton House.

Sterndale. Pool Hall (Hartington). *Or on a bend engrailed between two mullets of six points pierced azure three mascles of the field*; crest: *a mullet of six points pierced by three arrows two in saltire points downwards and one fesseways point to the sinister or barbed and flighted argent* (Burke). Gr. 1835 to W.H. Sterndale of Sheffield and Ottar, Hindustan, India, descended from the Sterndales of Pool Hall, who used arms as above, but without crest (as *Rel.* VI (1866) 42), e.g. Ralph Sterndale of Pool Hall, living 1749.

Sterndale. King Sterndale. *Argent fretty vert a lion rampant gules ducally crowned or all within a bordure of the 2nd bezantée*; crest: *a demi-lion rampant vert armed and langued gules* (*Rel.* XII (1872) 96). Used by the medieval Sterndales, also lords of Ilam, Staffs., according to Sleigh.

Stevenson. Elton; Rowsley; Stanton in Peak. *Azure on a bend argent between two lions passant or three leopards' faces gules* (Lysons, cxlvii). Gr. 14 June 1688 to John son of John Stevenson of Rowsley Hall, Elton and Stanton. He disclaimed V. 1662.

Stevenson. Unstone. *Gules on a bend argent three leopards' faces vert*; crest: *a garb or* (Vv. 1634, 1662). Exhibited V. 1662 by Roland son of Francis Stevenson of Unstone.

Stevenson. 'Weston'. *Gules on a bend argent three leopards' faces proper* (FMG II.835). Used by a relative of the Stevensons of Unstone, seated at the unidentified 'Weston' C17.

Stevenson. Tor House (Matlock). *Per chevron or and gules two clarions in chief of the last and a chaplet of roses in base also gules barbed and seeded proper leaved or*; crest: *a falcon wings elevated and addorsed belled and jessed or hooded between two lures gules*; motto: *'Impelle obstantia'* (FD (1929) II.1843). Gr. 11 Nov. 1902 to George Stevenson of Tor House.

Steynesby. Stainsby; Hardwick; Hardstoft (Ault Hucknall); Heath; Smalley. *Azure on a fesse between three falcons belled argent as many millrinds sable* (Tilley, II.275). Intended by Tilley for the arms of Jocelyn de Steynesby of Stainsby etc, 1263, but they appear to be part of the arms gr. far more recently to the Stainsby-Conant family.

Stockdale. Baslow Hall. *Ermine on a bend sable three pheons argent in sinister chief an escallop gules*; crest: *a talbot passant proper* (Burke). Gr. under RSM 19 Feb. 1695 to Christopher Stockdale of Bilton Park, Yorks., and borne by Revd Jeremiah Stockdale, who built Baslow Hall in 1907, placing the crest on the gable ends. This was originally gr. and the arms conf. to Robert Stockdale 28 June 1582; the subsequent grant was the result of a change of the surname and arms from Walters by RSM.

Stone. Carsington. *Sable a fesse between three lozenges or* (Local MS 6341). Used by Robert Stone of Carsington, a usurper V. 1611. Note, however, that Local MS 4556 attributes to this family *argent a lion passant guardant sable*.

Stones. Mosborough; Bradway Hall (Norton); Norton; The Hill (Outseats). *Vert on a bend counter-embattled or between six doves argent three crosses humettée sable*; crest: *a demi-dragon pean holding a cross vert gorged argent collar charged with three roses gules* (Lysons, cxlviii, and carved over former entrance at Mosborough Hall). Gr. 21 July 1693 to Joseph Stones of Mosborough.

Stones. Norton. *Vert on a bend counter-embattled or between six doves argent three cross crosslets fitchée sable* (MI at Norton 1676). Used by Nicholas Stones, a close kinsman of the above, of Norton and Hemsworth (Norton), who in fact disclaimed V. 1662.

Storer. Kirk Ireton. *Per fesse argent and gules on a pale counterchanged in chief a crane close between two others in base argent*; crest: *a crane argent* (MS pedigree by Isaac Heard, later Garter, 1764 at Blackwall Hall). Gr. to Storer of Jamaica, and attributed on Heard's pedigree (of the Blackwalls of Kirk Ireton, (qv)) to the father of Elizabeth Storer of Kirk Ireton. The inclusion of the attribution on this document, which records the Blackwalls' pedigree and confirms their arms, must accord to this family arms previously of dubious status.

Strafford: see Stafford.

Street. Glossop. *Vert a fesse between three horses courant argent*; crest: *a friar habited* *proper holding in the dexter hand a cinquefoil and in the sinister pendent from a ribbon a cross patée and from the neck a cinquefoil* (arms: *Rel.* XII (1872) 96; crest: livery button in local collection). Gr. to J.F.D. Street of Mottram Hall, Mottram in Longdendale, Cheshire, son of Col. Street of Glossop, 1865. The same year he assumed the surname and arms of Wright of Mottram Hall, the arms quartering Street: *argent a cross parted and fretty gules between in the 1st and 4th quarters three martlets and in the 2nd and 3rd as many annulets sable*; crest: *a demi-man in armour proper breastplate charged with a cross as in the arms supporting within the dexter hand a flagstaff therefrom flowing to the dexter a banner gules charged with an annulet or*; motto: *'Quo virtus vocat'* (Burke). These Wrights were formerly of Offerton Hall, Cheshire, and were patrons of St Peter's, Derby, where they owned a considerable estate C18–19.

Strelley. Beauchief; Brough; Castleton; Hazlebadge; Shipley. *Paly of six argent and azure*; crest: *a saracen's head affrontée couped at the shoulders wearing a wreath gules of hawks' bells or* (arms: Jenyns' Ordinary; whole, V. 1611; Vv. Notts. 1614, 1662–64). Allowed to Strelley of Beauchief 1611, and, if the *Stranley* of early MSS is, in fact, Strelley, borne by the Strelleys of Brough (there from *c.* 1199). Also borne by Sir Sampson de Strelley of Strelley, Notts., and Shipley *c.* 1355 (Jenyns). Arms conf. with due difference to Strelley of Great Bowden, Leics., 1512 (with *a bordure indented ermine*) and London, 1555, as cadets of Shipley.

Strelley. Oakerthorpe (S. Wingfield); Woolley (Brackenfield). *Paly of six argent and azure a cinquefoil gules*; crest: *a cock's head argent combed and wattled gules gorged with two bars nebulée azure* (*DAJ* XIV (1892) 72–109). Gr. to the Strelleys of Woodborough, Notts., who were later of Oakerthorpe until early C20.

Stretton. Unstone. *Argent a bend engrailed sable* (Tilley I.184). Hervey de Stretton of Stretton, Staffs., inherited a moiety of Unstone from the Brailsfords *c.* 1200; the arms were thought by Tilley to have been borne by his descendant, Richard *c.* 1293.

Stringer. Norton. *Sable three eagles displayed erminois*; crest: *an eagle's head erased erminois* (V. Yorks. 1664–5; *DAJ* XL (1918) 92). Thomas Stringer of Norton was allowed

these arms (with difference) V. 1611 and was 2nd son of Thomas, of Whiston, Yorks.; some MSS give the field incorrectly as *or.*

Strode: see Chetham.

Strutt. Belper; Milford House; Makency House; St Helen's House (Derby). *Per pale sable and azure two chevronels engrailed between three cross crosslets fitchée or*; crest: *in front of rays of the sun proper a cubit arm erect vested bendy of six or and sable cuffed argent in the hand an escroll also proper*; supporters: *on either side a leopard proper gorged with a collar gemel azure therefrom pendent an escutcheon of the last charged with a cross crosslet or*; motto: *'Propositi tenax'* (BP (1970) 242). Gr. with supporters 1856 to Edward Strutt MP, cr. the same year Lord Belper, the arms remaindered to the heirs of Jedidiah Strutt (1726–97) and thus borne also by the Strutts of Milford House and Makeney House. Previously the family had used: *sable a chevron ermine between three cross crosslets fitchée or*; crest: *a cubit arm erect vested sable cuffed erminois thereon a cross crosslet fitchée or hand proper holding an escroll also proper*; same motto (as painted on wall of Prince Charlie Room, Derby Museum, 1879; crest: livery button in local collection).

Stubbing. Marston Montgomery; Somersal Herbert; Stubbing (Wingerworth); West Broughton (Doveridge); Whittington. *Quarterly azure and argent overall five bezants in bend*; crest: *a lamb sejant proper collared gules the dexter foot on a trefoil slipped vert* (Lysons, cxlviii). Gr. 1712 to Thomas Stubbing of West Broughton, whose father Richard and uncle Thomas (of Marston) disclaimed V. 1662. They claimed descent from Godfrey Stubbing of Stubbing 1319, also ancestor of Stubbing of Whittington Manor (FMG III.1008).

Stuteville. Eckington; Stretton. *Barry of ten argent and gules overall a lion rampant sable* (FitzWilliam Roll, 557, 598; as quartered by Vernon of Sudbury, V. 1569). Borne C13 by Robert son of Robert de Stuteville of Eckington; a descendant, Robert son of Henry, was attainted 1340. A cousin, another Robert, was of Stretton. The arms of the Stuteville vassals – Goushill, Hathersage and perhaps Longford – seem to derive from those of Stuteville: see ASP II.149, 154.

Styrchlegh. 'Co. Derby'. *Argent an eagle*

displayed sable membered gules (*Rel.* VI (1866) 43). It is by no means clear who Sleigh intended when he included this coat; probably Walter de Stokesley, constable of Horsley Castle 1274–91, a kinsman of Sir John de Strechley (sic) of Notts., who bore arms as above (Parliament Roll, Jenyns' Ordinary).

Sudbury: see Montgomery.

Suligny: see Solney.

Sumner. Beard (New Mills); Ollersett (New Mills); Park Hall (Hayfield). *Ermine two chevrons gules*; crest: *a lion's head erased argent ducally gorged or*; motto: *'Surmonte toi'* (Burke, FR (1897) 567). Used by John and Francis Sumner, owners of the above estates from 1807 into C20.

Sutton. Heanor; King's Mead (Derby); Over Haddon. *Or a lion rampant queue fourché vert*; crest: *out of a ducal coronet or a demi-lion rampant queue fourché vert*; motto: *'Fraudem fuge'* (V. 1569). Arms (borne by Sir Richard de Sutton of Sutton, Cheshire, kt. *c.* 1318, Parliament Roll) conf. and crest gr. 26 Nov. 1550 to his descendant Alan Sutton of Over Haddon and King's Mead. He was gr. a further crest 24 Oct. 1566: *three annulets interlaced two in base and one above or*; an explanation of the two crests as a poem is to be found Harl.MS 886. These arms were used (or, conceivably, borne) by John Sutton of Heanor Hall *c.* 1800.

Sutton. Shardlow. *Argent a wolf passant sable on a chief arched azure an annulet between two crosses flory of the field*; crest: *three annulets interlaced one and two argent between two wings sable each charged with a cross flory of the first.* (BLG III (1972) 912). Gr. 1906 with remainders to Henry Sutton, 3rd son of James of Shardlow.

Swadlincote Urban District Council. *Quarterly ermine and gules a cross quarterly counterchanged between in the 1st and 4th quarters a Tudor rose proper and in the 2nd and 3rd a fleur-de-lys argent all within a bordure vairé of the 1st and 2nd*; crest: *issuant from flames proper rising from a mount sable a cubit arm also proper holding a billet fessewise or*; motto: *'E terra divitiae'* (Scott-Giles, 100). Gr. 14 May 1947; authority abolished 1974.

Swann. Hurdlow (Hartington); Lea Hall. *Azure a chevron ermine between three swans argent holding in their beaks a mascle* (*Rel.* VI (1866) 43). Impaled by Bullock on MI as Ashford and used by Samuel son of Samuel

Swann of Hurdlow late C18. Presumably they claimed descent from a Kent family who bore these arms.

Swanwick Church of England School. *Quarterly i, argent three miners' axes sable; ii, sable a garb or; iii, sable a swan naiant proper; iv, sable three shuttles or overall on a cross gules a book open argent* (on a medallion of 1906 in Derby Museum, DBYMU 1936-12). Other examples known from 1902, 1903. No authority; amateurishly conceived.

Swift: see Swyfte.

Swillington. Crich; S. Wingfield; Tibshelf. *Argent a chevron azure a label of three points ermine* (window glass in Eckington church, noted V. 1569). Borne by Adam, Lord Swillington (cr. by writ of summons 1326) without the label 1326 (Jenyns' Ordinary) and in this form by Robert, 2nd son of Adam, who was of Crich etc (Willement Roll; seal, PRO, P.769). Apart from his legitimate successors at Crich, he left a natural son, Thomas de Hopton; whether this man had any connection with the de Hoptons (qv) is unclear.

Swinborne. Bakewell. *Per chief gules and argent three cinquefoils counterchanged* (Jenyns' Ordinary). Borne by William de Swinborne of Haighton, Lancs., *c.* 1350. Sir Richard, of the same, inherited Bakewell from Botetourt. His heiress marr. Helyon. The arms are more usually given with the field *per fesse* as borne by the bts of the name, descended from a brother of the above, and gr. 26 Sept. 1660.

Swindell. Brailsford; Burnaston; Repton. *Argent two swords in saltire azure hilted or in chief a boar's head erased proper*; crest: *a boar's head erased proper*; motto: *'Suaviter in modo, fortiter in re'* (Arms: *Rel.* VI (1866) 43; Tilley IV.61; crest: Local MS 9555.35). Used by John Swindell of Brailsford early C19; Messrs Holmes painted the arms, uniquely with crest and motto, for George Swindell a generation or two later.

Swingler. Derby; Edgehill Tower (Little Eaton); Smalley. Crest: *a crescent on a garb*; motto: *'Surgere tento'* (livery button in a local collection). Used on buttons by Henry son of Thomas Swingler, a Derby industrialist, of Edge Hill, and his brother Alfred, of Smalley, early C20.

Swinnerton. Hilton; Repton. *Argent a cross patée fleurettée sable* (Dunstable Roll). Borne at the Dunstable tournament by Sir Roger de

Swinnerton joint lord of Repton and of Swynnerton, Staffs., who also held an estate at Hilton. He was cr. by writ of summons Lord Swinnerton 1337. The forebears of Giles, of Hilton, a junior descendant (d. 1439) bore: *argent a cross fleurée sable* (Jenyns' Ordinary); a seal of 1322 adds crest: *a crescent between two horns* (PRO, P.2102).

Swyfte. Dore; North Lees Hall (Outseats). *Or a chevron vair between three bucks in full course proper*; crest: *a sinister arm embowed vested vert cuffed argent holding in the hand proper a sheaf of five arrows or feathered proper barbed azure* (MI St Peter's, Sheffield, Hunter, *Hallamshire*, 254). Gr. 10 May 1562 to Sir Robert Swifte of Rotherham, Yorks., whose uncle, Robert, was *jure uxoris* of North Lees and Dore. His yr son, Barnham, was in 1627 cr. in the Irish peerage Viscount Carlingford, Co. Louth (ext. 1635). It is unclear what Lord Carlingford's supporters were; his crest was *a demi-buck rampant holding in its mouth a honeysuckle all proper stalked and leaved vert* (UO) and mottoes: *'Festina Lente'* and *'Cum magnis vixisse'* (Burke).

Sykes. Ollerenshaw Hall (Chapel en le Frith). *Argent on a chevron sable goutée-de-l'eau between three tufts of grass vert as many fountains proper*; crest: *on the trunk of a tree eradicated fessewise and sprouting to the dexter proper a swan wings addorsed argent beaked and legged sable charged on the breast with a fountain*; motto: *'Puritas fons honoris'* (FD (1905) 1321). Gr. 1881 to Edward H. Sykes of Edgeley Fold (Stockport), Cheshire, and borne by Arthur Henry Sykes (1841–1926) who was, amongst other places, of Ollerenshaw Hall. His kinsman, Alan Sykes, was cr. a bt 17 July 1917 (ext. 1947). See also Sikes.

Talbot. Eyam; S. Wingfield; Stony Middleton etc. *Gules a lion rampant within a bordure engrailed or* quartering: *azure a lion rampant within a bordure or*; *argent two lions passant gules,* for Strange, and Furnival (qv); crest: *on a chapeau a lion statant tail extended or*; supporters: *on either side a talbot argent*; motto: *'Prest d'accomplir'* (quarterings: Garter stall plate, St George's Chapel, Windsor; MI in All Saints', Derby, and at Mugginton, Cox III.220). Anciently, the arms of Talbot

were: *or five bendlets gules* as borne by Richard de Talbot *c.* 1250 (St George Roll; FitzWilliam Roll). His son Gilbert marr. Princess Gwenllian ferch Rhys Ieuornc, son of Gruffydd ap the Lord Rhys ap Gruffydd ap Rhys ap Tewdwr Mawr, King of Deheubarth, and adopted his father-in-law's 'Bardic' arms (quartering 1 above), and so borne by him 1308 (Dunstable Roll; cf. *Dict. Welsh Biog.*, p. 319). John, 2nd son of 4th Lord Talbot (cr. by writ of summons 1331), marr. the heiress of Furnival and inherited huge Derbys. estates, broken up on the death of Gilbert, 7th Earl of Shrewsbury in 1616 (title cr. 1442, also Earl of Waterford in the Irish peerage, 1446 to this same John). See also Howard.

Tatham. Ilkeston. *Gyronny of six azure and argent three doves of the first*; crest: *out of a ducal coronet or a plume of ostrich feathers proper* (Tilley, IV.160). Used by Messrs Edward, Walter and William Tatham of Ilkeston, needle and lace manufacturers, *c.* 1887.

Taylor. Ashbourne; Chesterfield; Durrant Hall (Chesterfield). *Ermine on a chevron gules between three anchors azure as many escallops argent*; crest: *a stork argent resting the dexter foot on an anchor azure* (V. 1662). Gr. 6 Dec. 1662 to George Taylor of Chesterfield and Durrant Hall, merchant, son of Thomas, of Ashbourne.

Taylor. The Mansion (Ashbourne). *Ermine on a chevron between three anchors sable as many escallops argent* (Rel. VI (1866) 43). Used by Revd Dr John Taylor, Dr Johnson's friend, for whom Joseph Pickford of Derby rebuilt the Mansion, 1763. He was kin to Taylor of Ashbourne and Chesterfield above.

Taylor. Bolsover. *Argent on a chevron gules between three anchors azure as many escallops of the field* (quartered by White of Tuxford, Notts., FD (1929) II.2074). Borne or used by Thomas Taylor of Bolsover (living 1670) whose dau. and heiress marr. a White of Tuxford, the descendants of which family included these arms in their total of 27 quarterings (for which the only authority given in FD is V. Notts. 1614).

Taylor. Derby. *Azure a saltire voided between four stags' heads caboshed or* (Rel. VI (1866) 43). Gr. 1610 to a family of this name from Cheshire, and borne or used by John Taylor of All Saints', Derby, living 1670, and by his great-grandson, Josiah, 1741.

Taylor. Derby. Crest: *on a ducal coronet an heraldic tiger passant*; motto: *'Toi le ciel t'aidera'* (seal impression on deed of 1824, Derbys. Health Authority, Deeds 10/68B). Used by William and Thomas Taylor, proprietors of the Old Silk Mill, Derby, when buying the land on which they built Wilderslow House, Derby.

Taylor. Hulland. *Quarterly ermine and or in the 1st quarter a wolf's head couped sable on a chief invected gules three escallops argent*; crest: *in front of a dexter arm embowed in armour the hand in a gauntlet grasping a flaming sword all proper a shield ermine charged with a wolf's head couped sable*; motto: *'Pro Deo patria et rege'* (BLG (1952) 2475). Gr. to F.H. Taylor (1822–98), a descendant of John Tayleur of Hulland (b. 1590), whose son Richard was also of Derby.

Taylor. Walton Hall (Walton on Trent). *Per pale azure and or a chevron between three bucks' heads all counterchanged on a chief gules two greyhounds courant respectant argent collared of the 2nd* (Lysons, cxlix). Allowed V. Surrey 1623 to this family, whose respresentative, Richard, was of Walton Hall and d. 1692. The heiress marr. Disbrowe *c.* 1733.

Taylor-Whitehead. Burton Closes (Bakewell). *Argent a fesse dancettée azure between in chief two crosses tau and in base a pheon gules*; crest: *in front of a tau cross gules a pheon argent*; motto: *'Cruce non hasta'* (FD (1905) 1333). Gr. to Smith Taylor-Whitehead 1873 and borne by Samuel Taylor of Burton Closes, who had assumed the additional surname of Whitehead 1865.

Tennant. Darley Abbey. *Ermine two bars each per pale gules and sable charged with three bezants two and one*; crest: *between two wings gules on each a bezant a sword erect proper hilt and pommel or point downwards transpiercing a human heart of the first*; motto: *'Tenax et fidelis'* (BLG (1937) 2217). Borne by Robert Hugh Tennant of Arncliffe Cote, Yorks., chairman of the Westminster Bank 1927–31, who lived at Highfields, Darley Abbey.

Tetlow. Unstone. *Argent a bend engrailed sable cotised gules* (Tilley, III.276). Richard Tetlow of Unstone marr. the heiress of Newbold of Unstone *c.* 1355; their son d. without issue and so the attribution of the arms of this Lancastrian family looks like an anachronism on Tilley's part.

Tevery. Long Eaton; Twyford. *Azure a lion rampant argent a bordure engrailed or* (Thoroton, *Notts.* (1793), III.195). These arms were entered V. 1611 by Gervase Tevery of Long Eaton, Twyford and Stapleford (Notts.), although on his father's MI at Stapleford appears *argent on two bars azure three cinquefoils or*; crest: *a wolf's head erased argent muzzled azure*, which Thoroton (loc.cit.) claims was the achievement of the Staplefords of Stapleford, an heiress of which family marr. a John Tevery *c.* 1350. It was this coat which was ultimately conf. to the same Gervase Tevery in 1639 but with *cinquefoils argent* (ibid.).

Thacker. Thacker Hall (Heage); Repton. *Gules on a fesse or between three mascles each charged with as many gouttes sable a trefoil slipped azure between two bitterns' heads erased of the field beaked proper gorged with a leash argent*; crest: *a bittern sitting amongst reeds proper gorged with a leash gules purfled and tassled or* (V. 1662). Gr. 1 May 1538 to Thomas Thacker of Thacker Hall and Repton, merchant of the Staple, and allowed to Thomas Thacker of Heage V. 1662: 'This grante of arms was exhibited unto William Dugdale, Esqre. Norroy at his visitacon for the Co. Derby 7 Aug: 1662'.

Thacker. Darley Hall (Darley); Repton. *Gules on a fesse or between three lozenges ermine a trefoil slipped azure between two eagles' heads erased of the field beaked and gorged with a leash argent*; crest: *a bittern russet standing amongst reeds vert* (Vv. 1569, 1611, 1662). This coat must represent an error for that above, for it was allowed to Gilbert son of Thomas Thacker of Repton and Heage, before the Heage and Repton branches of the family split, and was thus not merely a differenced coat. Nevertheless, it functioned as one thereafter, for Godfrey, elder son of Gilbert, founded the Repton branch and his brother Thomas that of Heage *c.* 1615.

Thornewell. Eyam. *Argent a bend between two crosses crosslet sable* (*Rel.* XII (1872) 96). The arms seem to belong to a family called Burnam (Burke); the name and connection seem elusive.

Thornhill. Stanton Hall (Stanton in Peak); Thornhill; Wharnebrook (Hope). *Gules two bars gemelles and on a chief argent a mascle*

Thacker

sable; crest: *on a mount vert a thorntree proper charged on the trunk with a mascle or*; motto: *'Amantes ardua domos'* (Burke). Gr. to John Thornhill *jure uxoris* of Stanton 9 July 1730. Only the *mascle* and the crest distinguish these arms from those of the quite unrelated Thornhills of Fixby, Yorks., John thereof being gr. arms 29 Mar. 1734, inexplicably as of 'Stanton Co. Derby & Fixby & Thornhill Co. York'. John of Stanton was in fact a descendant of a Castleton innkeeper. The male line failed 1875, and the ultimate heiress carried Stanton to Henry Hurlock who assumed the surname and arms of Thornhill by RL 1880, but d. a year later, which resulted in the hext heir, Maj. Michael M'Creagh, assuming in the same manner the additional surname and arms of Thornhill (differenced by a *cross crosslet sable* in the crest) in 1881. IIis son d. without issue and the surname and arms were again assumed by RL additionally to his own by Humphrey Davie in 1959. The arms of M'Creagh were: *or on a fesse embattled between in chief three estoiles and in base a lion rampant gules a sword proper point to the dexter hilt and pommel of the first*; crest: *a demilion rampant gules collared gemel charged on* the shoulder with two estoiles or holding a bezant thereon two mascles interlaced sable; motto: *'Mors ante dedecora'* (quartered with both crests and motto, cf. FD (1929) II.1251). Those of Davie are: *azure an ancient ship with two masts or sails furled argent flags also argent charged with a cross gules on a chief of the 2nd three cinquefoils pierced of the third* (quartered by Thornhill, BLG III (1972) 895).

Thornhill. Ollerenshaw Hall (Chapel en le Frith); Wardlow. *Or two tilting spears in saltire sable surmounted of a stag browsing proper on a chief azure a crescent between two pheons of the field*; crest: *out of a mural coronet gules a demi-eagle displayed or pendent from the neck by a riband a buglehorn stringed sable* (*Rel.* VI (1866) 43). Gr. to William son of Joseph Thornhill of Wardlow and Ollerenshaw Hall 1841.

Thorold. Unstone; Barlow Woodseats (Barlow). *Sable three goats salient argent*; crest: *a roebuck passant argent attired or*; motto: *'Cervus non servus'* (BLG (1937) 2242). Allowed to William Thorold of Marston, Lincs. (Vv. Lincs. 1564, Oxon. 1566). His descendant William was cr. a bt 24 Aug. 1642 (the only btcy of four in this family to survive) and Samuel Thorold, son of Samuel, of Welham, Notts., was *jure uxoris* of Unstone and Barlow Woodseats from 1843. Arms gr. 9 Apr. 1574 to Thomas Thorold, quarterly of four.

Thoroton. Swanwick Hall (Alfreton). *Argent a fesse between three buglehorns stringed sable*; crest: *a roebuck proper* (RL 1815; BLG (1937) 1114). Thomas Thoroton of Screveton and Flintham, Notts., was of Swanwick Hall 1754–91.

Thwaites: see Shepherd.

Tickhill. Chaddesden; Dale Abbey; Stanley Grange (Dale Abbey). *A maunch* (from a seal, Local MS 6341). Borne by Robert de Tickhill of Chaddesden 1458, who then held it *jure uxoris*, being succ. by his son. The heiress marr. Quarmby. Note also Robert Tickhill of Dale and Stanley Grange, gent., 1507, and Robert, of Dale, 1596, who were probably close kinsmen. The tinctures should restore as: *gules a maunch argent* (Tickhill of Tickhill, Yorks.: see Burke, who also gives an earlier *argent a maunch tenné* with no locale).

Ticknall. Ticknall. *Argent a chevron between three eagles displayed gules*. Borne, it would appear almost certainly, by Ralph son of Ralph de Ticknall whose heiress marr.

Franceys and carried to them these arms at the beginning of C14, for the Franceys (qv) family had previously borne *a lion rampant* on their arms.

Tideswell

Tideswell. Kingswood (Bradley); Tideswell. *Azure a bend or between six escallops argent* (*Rel.* VI (1866) 43). The heiress of Hamelin son of Thomas de Tideswell marr. de Paunton (qv); Henry de Tideswell still held an estate there 1392. The arms are those of one of these men. Note their similarity to Foljambe, Frecheville and, most importantly, Daniel, the ultimate heirs of de Tideswell. Hugh son of Alexander de Tideswell was gr. considerable lands at Tideswell by Sir Richard Daniel, *temp.* Edward II.

Tillot. Repton. *Gules a lion rampant argent overall a bend azure* (Burke). Robert Tillot, of a Yorks. family, was gr. Fynderne's moiety of the manor of Repton 1413.

Timporley. Tideswell? *Gules three inescutcheons argent* (Calais Roll; *Rel.* VI (1866) 43). For whom Sleigh intended these arms is unclear; they are assigned to a knight of this name in 1348: J.G. Nichols (ed.), *Herald and genealogist* (1863), III.420. There were Tim-

perleys at Tideswell throughout the C17 and C18, although none reached the status expected of even a user of arms.

Tindal-Carill-Worsley. Highfields (Chaddesden); Winster Hall. *Argent on a chief gules a mural coronet or quartering* Carill: *argent three bars and in chief as many martlets sable a cross crosslet for difference,* and Tindal: *argent a fesse dancettée in chief a fleur-de-lys azure between two crescents and in base a like crescent of the 2nd between two fleurs-de-lys of the third*; crest: *on a mural crown or a wyvern wings expanded gules charged with a cross crosslet for difference,* for Worsley; *on a mount vert a stag lodged reguardant or with similar difference,* for Carill, and *in front of five ostrich feathers argent a fleur-de-lys azure between two crescents gules*; mottoes: *'Quod adest gratum juvat'* for Worsley; *'Per castra ad astra'* for Carill and *'Nosce te ipsum'* (FD (1929) II.1939). Gr. under RL 1878 to Nicholas Tindal-Carill-Worsley of Winster Hall, whose son, Ralph, was of Highfields on his assumption of the additional surname and arms of Tindal (gr. 1875). John Lees of Manchester had assumed likewise the surname and arms of Carill-Worsley 1775; his son inherited Winster Hall.

Toeni. Crich. *Argent a maunch gules* (Matthew Paris Shields I.57). Senior line of an Anglo-Norman family, cadets of which were Stafford, Gresley and Longford in this county. Hasculf de Toeni marr. a co-heiress of Ralph son of Hubert of Crich *c.* 1175, but there is no reason to think that either he, or his son by this marriage, Graelent, bore these arms at so early a date, although they were borne by his kinsmen, the brothers Ralph and Sir Roger, before 1227, and by Sir Robert de Toeni of Clifford Castle, Herefs., etc, summoned to Parliament 1299 as a baron (ext. 1309).

Toke (Tolka, Touk). Arleston; Hilton; Potlock (Findern); Sinfin; Willington. *Barry of six argent and sable* (seal, Local MS 6341). Borne by Toke of Hatton (and Hilton) 1394. The Willington and Potlock families were almost certainly of the same stock. On an early seal of this family (in the Every papers in private hands) is *a cross raguly*.

Toplis. Wirksworth. *Vert on a chevron argent between two beehives in chief or and in base a talbot passant of the 2nd langued proper a rose barbed of the field between two crescents* *gules* (*Rel.* VI (1866) 43). Gr. 1816 to John son of John Toplis of Wirksworth (1747–1826). Previously the family had used: *Vert on a chevron argent a rose barbed of the field between two crescents gules* (Tilley, II.314).

Touchet. Allestree; Derby; Mackworth; Markeaton; Quarndon. *Ermine a chevron gules*; crest: *out of a ducal coronet or a swan naiant argent wings elevated beaked gules ducally crowned or*; motto: *'Je le tiens'* (Lysons, lix; V. Cheshire 1580; crest and motto: Burke). Borne, according to Jenyns' Ordinary, by Robert de Touchet of Markeaton *c.* 1318.

Touchet. Chesterfield? *Ermine a chevron and a canton gules* (noted by Wyrley in glass at Chesterfield church 1592). Impaled by Meverell, date unknown. The match seems not to have been recorded.

Took: see Toke.

Towle. Twyford. *Argent on a chevron between two doves sable each holding in the beak a sprig of olive proper a dove or holding in the beak a like sprig between two escallops also or*; crest: *between two wings argent an escallop charged with a cinquefoil sable*; motto: *'Amo pacem'* (FD (1929) II.1952). Gr. 1919 or 1920 to William Towle of Twyford and London (son of Edward, the Twyford blacksmith), who was knighted in the latter year, and his son Francis William a year earlier. William's brother was of Twyford Hall early C20, but what remainders were included in the grant is unclear.

Townrowe (Townrawe). Alton Hall (Idridgehay); Chesterfield; Hassop. *Gules on a cross argent between four bezants a cinquefoil azure pierced or*; crest: *a tiger sejant per pale ermine and sable* (Vv. Lincs. 1564, 1592). Gr. to William Townrowe of Alton 20 May 1562.

Trent River Authority. *Barry wavy of eight azure and argent a saltire couped gules in chief an ancient crown or*; crest: *a heron statant proper collared or on a fishwheel of the last*; supporters: *dexter a lion rampant sable supporting between the paws a ditching spade proper blade downwards and sinister a stag likewise supporting a pipette proper*; motto: *'Pax fiat per fluminis aquas'* (Briggs, 388). Gr. 1 Aug. 1967; authority absorbed into Severn Trent Water PLC (qv).

Treves. Wirksworth. *Argent on a cross couped gules between in the 1st and 4th quar-* ters *a dexter hand couped and erect proper and the 2nd and 3rd a tent purpure pole garnished or a tower triple towered of the last on a chief of 2nd a lion passant guardant of the 5th*; crest: *an opinicus statant or wings elevated and addorsed purpure resting the dexter paw on a fleam fesseways argent*; motto: *'Fortiter, fideliter, feliciter'* (E. Lodge, *Peerage* (1912), 1867). Gr. 1902 to Sir Frederick Treves, cr. a bt 30 July that year in honour of his having performed an appendectomy on Edward VII; he was further rewarded, by RL of 1906, with an augmentation of honour, being the chief on the arms. Title ext. 1923. He lived and practised at Wirksworth for most of his professional life, where he founded the Cottage Hospital.

Treys. Horsley. *Argent a chevron gules* (as quartered by Kniveton of Bradley, Local MS 6341). John Kniveton of Bradley marr. the dau. and heiress of John Treys of Horsley C15 or early C16. Burke gives these arms, without locale, and adds a crest: *two hands couped conjoined in fesse issuing therefrom a scimitar proper*.

Tristram. Chesterfield; Wingfield Hall (S. Wingfield). *Argent three torteaux and a label azure*; crest: *on a chapeau a martlet wings addorsed sable* (Burke; crest: livery button in local collection). Gr. 1467 to Matthew Tristram by v. Romeryck, 'King of Arms of the Holy Roman Empire', and borne (although whether recognised by the College of Arms is unclear) by Capt. W.H. Tristram *c.* 1900. Most of this family had for a crest: *a wolf's head erased sable* (BLG (1952) 2549).

Trott. Ballidon; Little Chester (Derby); Mapleton Manor; Parwich. *Paly of six or and gules on a quarter argent a bear rampant sable*; crest: *on a chapeau a unicorn's head erased* (Vv. 1634 Derbys. and London). Gr. 1574 to John Trott of London and borne by Baptist Trott of Mapleton etc, 1610, although the authority for the crest, if not the whole achievement, is suspect, since his descendant Josiah Trott of Mapleton Manor was a 'person for a grant' in 1687. However, as 'He thinks his father was a physitian' (he was), his account of his relationship to the grantee might have been confused by ignorance.

Trubshawe. Thurvaston. *Argent a bend sable* (impaled by Lister on MI at St Alkmund's, Derby). Used by William Trubshawe of Thurvaston, living *c.* 1575.

Trusley. Trusley. *Azure three bendlets or* (Tilley, II.310; *Rel.* VI (1866) 43). Borne by Robert de Trusley, who sold Trusley to Oliver de Odingsells in 1253.

Trussell. Seymour's Place (Egginton). *Argent fretty sable bezantée at the joints* (glass formerly in the church at Walton on Trent; Jenyns' Ordinary). Borne by William Trussell of Noteworth, Northants., *jure uxoris* of Seymour's Place 1346, and his kinsman, Sir Theobald. William bore these arms at Calais, 1345–8 (Calais Roll), although the colour is sometimes given as *gules* (e.g. V. Cheshire 1580, which adds for crest: *out of a ducal coronet a unicorn's head proper armed of the first*). In a window at Barrow on Trent church the arms are given as *or a fret gules on each joint a plate* (Bassano's Notes, 1710, quoted by Cox, IV.24).

Tufton. Clay Cross; Crich; Stretton; Shirland. *Sable an eagle displayed ermine and a bordure argent*; crest: *a sea lion sejant proper*; supporters: *on either side an eagle wings expanded ermine*; motto: *'Ales volat propriis'* (Debrett, *Peerage* (1817), I.167; Burke). Conf. with 5 quarterings and grant of supporters 22 Oct. 1628 to Sir Nicholas Tufton, 2nd bt (cr. 18 Jan. 1623), who was cr. Lord Tufton 1626 and Earl of Thanet, Kent, 1628. The 7th earl inherited the Derbys. estates from Talbot via Herbert and Savile C18; titles ext. 1849, although the line is represented by Lord Hothfield (cr. a bt 16 Jan. 1851 and a peer 1881), whose family inherited the Thanet estates, the 1st bt having been a natural son of the last Earl of Thanet. The arms (gr. by RL 5 May 1850) were differenced by replacing the *bordure* with another, *wavy or*; the crest was tinctured *argent charged with a bendlet wavy sable* and the supporters embellished with *a collar gules pendent therefrom an escutcheon of the arms*; same motto: (BP (1956) 1137).

Tunstead. Tunstead (Wormhill); Stodhart (Chapel en le Frith). *Sable three falcons reclaimed argent* (Vv. 1569, 1611). Allowed to Anthony Tunsted of Tunsted, bailiff of the Forest of the Peak, 1569 (in some MSS *sable three doves argent*). A cadet, James, also bailiff of Peak Forest, did not appear at V. 1662, at which another Tunstead family disclaimed.

Turbutt. Ogston (Brackenfield). *Azure three turbots naiant argent finned or*; crest: *a naked arm proper holding a trident or armed and headed argent* (BLG (1937) 608). Gr. 20 Mar. 1628 to William (d. without issue 1648), son of Richard Turbutt of York, and used by the descendants of his heir, another William son of Richard, for there appear to have been no remainders to the grant of 1628. However, they were conf. 1909 to Maj. William Gladwyn Turbutt of Ogston (1853–1932). This man's brother assumed the surname and arms of Duppa de Uphaugh: *gules a lion's gamb couped in fesse between two chains or a chief nebulée of the last thereon two roses of the first barbed and seeded proper* quartering Turbutt: *per fesse azure and sable a trident fessewise or between three turbots argent*; crests: *in front of a dexter arm embowed in armour hand in a gauntlet proper grasping a lion's gamb in bend sinister couped a rose between two annulets gules*, for Duppa and, as above but *charged with an anchor sable and encircled by an annulet or*; motto: *'Non sibi sed suis'* (ibid.). The arms of Turbutt as gr. to Revd J.L. Gladwyn-Errington (qv) by RL 1896 were: *azure three fleurs-de-lys in fesse between as many turbots all argent*; crest: *in front of a dexter arm embowed proper grasping a trident in bend sinister or a fountain*; motto: *'Non sibi sed suis'* (FD (1929) II.1972). The Duppa-quartered variant is shown *within a bordure ermine* in Local MS 9555.76.

Turner. Bearwardcote Hall; Derby. *Ermines on a cross quarter-pierced argent four millrinds sable in the centre point a fleur-de-lys of the 2nd*; crest: *a lion passant guardant argent holding in the dexter forepaw a millrind sable* (V. 1634; MI at All Saints' Derby, now lost, Cox & Hope 149; Tilley, II.310, IV.180). Allowed, apparently, to 'Mr Turner' of All Saints' parish, 1634, yet his son, William, was reckoned as a 'person for a grant' in 1687: 'a rich huffing attorney of Clement's Inne'.

Turner. Beeley Hilltop. *Sable a chevron ermine between three millrinds or* (impaling Wright of Osmaston); crest: *a tower proper*; motto: *'Utile quod tacias'*. Displayed by Mr Max Turner and allowed V. 1623 to Turner of Astley, Salop.

Turner. Littleover. *Per pale or and sable a fesse wavy paly of eight gules and ermine between four millrinds three in chief and one in base counterchanged*; crest: *a lion rampant guardant per bend sinister or and ermine holding in the dexter forepaw a millrind sable and* *resting the sinister on a spade proper*; motto: *'Labore et perseverantia'* (FD (1910) 1628). Gr. 1896 to George Henry Turner of Littleover House, general manager of the Midland Railway.

Turner. Swanwick Hall (Alfreton); Wigwell Hall (Wirksworth). *Vairé argent and gules on a pale or three trefoils slipped vert*; crest: *two wings conjoined saltirewise argent charged at the join with a trefoil slipped vert* (Lysons, cl). Used by John Turner of Swanwick Hall (which he built), an owner of coalmines, who was 'a person for a grant' 1687.

Turner. Willington Hall; Stanleigh House (Oakthorpe & Donisthorpe). *Or a chevron between in chief two millrinds and in base a greyhound courant sable*; crest: *in front of a saltire or a bear's head couped sable muzzled of the first*; motto: *'Labor omnia superat'* (FD (1929) II.1973). Gr. 26 Apr. 1920 to Sir John Turner of Donisthorpe (1858–1931), knighted 1920, whose widow was of Willington Hall. The family were from Breedon on the Hill, Leics.

Turner. The Hague and Woodthorpe (Staveley); Troway (Eckington). *Argent on a fesse engrailed between three eagles' heads erased azure as many martlets of the field*; crest: *on a mount vert a unicorn passant reguardant argent semée d'estoiles azure armed maned and unguled or gorged of the 3rd the dexter foot resting on a cross patée of the 4th*; motto: *'Quercus'* (BLG (1937) 2503). John, son of Roger Turnore, was of Woodthorpe *c.* 1460; Robert was of The Hague, 1677; his grandson was Robert, of Troway. In 1863 Samuel Turner assumed by RL the surname and arms (as above) of Wright of Brattleby, Lincs. (gr. 9 Oct 1826).

Turville. Newhall; Swadlincote. *Gules three chevronels vair*; crest: *a dove close proper holding in the beak a branch of olive slipped vert fructed of three or* (as quartered by Rolleston, once in glass at Ashover, Cox, I.33; as quartered by Bradbourne on MI at Ashbourne church and V. 1611; crest: Burke.) Borne by John Turville of Normanton Turville, Leics., C16, who inherited Newhall from Dethick and whose heiress marr. Rolleston of Lea.

Tuschet: see Touchet.

Tutbury, Honour of. *Azure three fleurs-delys or quartering gules three leopards or overall a label of three points ermine and all impaling vairé or and gules* (DAJ VIII (1886) 10). Achievement attached to the famous 'Tut-

bury Horn' (latterly in the possession of the Bagshawes, formerly of Ford). The arms are: John of Gaunt, Duke of Lancaster and Earl of Derby, impaling de Ferrers, Earl of Derby; Gaunt's arms are in their pre-1399 form. The juxtaposition of the coats dates it to after 1268. Most of the honour's lands were in Derbys.

Tutbury Priory. *Azure a saltire vairé or and gules between four crescents argent* (Tilley, II.310). Founded by Ferrers, hence the *vairé*; held large possessions in Derbys.

Tutbury Priory

Twigge. Bonsall; Broadlowash (Thorpe); Derby; Holme Hall (Bakewell). *Azure three bendlets or on a chief argent a fesse dancettée gules*; crest: *an esquire's helm proper* (DAJ LVIII (1937) 57). Used by John Twigge (1751–86), son of Nicholas, of Holme Hall and Broadlowash. Sleigh (*Rel.* VI (1866) 43) attributed to Nicholas Twigge of Holme *argent a fesse gules between three ouzels proper*.

Twigge. Spend Lane (Thorpe). *Azure three bendlets or overall a fesse dancettée gules fimbriated of the 2nd*; crest: *a pelican vulning herself argent beak and legs or* (arms in glass, crest on tombstone, at Thorpe church). Used by John Twigge of Spend Lane (1799–1872) and his son Edward (d. 1911).

Twistleton: see Cockshutt.

Twyford. Horsley; Kirk Langley; Sharrowhall (Thurvaston); Spondon. *Argent two bars and on a canton sable a cinquefoil or* (V. 1611, D369; seal of 1323, PRO, P.810). Sir John de Twyford, who marr. Margaret, sister of Lord Pipard (see Pipard and FitzNicholas), bore the arms as above but the *cinquefoil* on a *quarter* 1322 (Willement Roll); his son Sir Robert, 1343, bore as above but *with a label of three points* (Local MS 6341). The heiress of a cadet branch seems to have marr. a Revell, for this family quartered Twyford V. 1569, although Sayer (*DAJ* XCIV (1974) 26; XCVII (1977) 24) does not mention it. A William Twyford of Spondon – surely close kin – disclaimed V. 1611 but his arms are nevertheless given, with the *cinquefoil of the field* .

Twyford. Belper. *Argent two bars and on a canton sable a cinquefoil or* (MIS at Trotton, Sussex). Sir Harry Twyford of Sunny Bank, Belper (1870–1967), a director of Brettle's, the hosiery manufacturers, and lord mayor of London in 1937, was grandson of Samuel Twyford of Trotton and succ. his uncle, H.R. Twyford, who moved to Belper. The Twyford of Trotton family's title to these arms is questionable (Huxford, p. 410).

Tynmore. Egginton. *Argent a saltire sable in chief a mascle gules* (Burke). Borne by William de Tynmore of Staffs., who marr. a coheiress of Stafford of Egginton, and his son John, 1342.

Tyrell. Bakewell. *Argent a leopard's head jessant-de-lys gules* (Tilley, I.271; cf. Burke). Borne, apparently, by Humphrey Tyrell, who marr. the heiress of Helyon c15.

Tyson. Ashbourne. *Vert three lions rampant argent crowned or*; crest: *a dexter arm embowed in armour bearing a shield* (MI in Bradley church). Borne or used by William Tyson of Ashbourne (1787–1843), marr. to a Meynell of Bradley. The arms belong to a Wilts. family.

Unidentified. Ashover. *Between two bars three fusils* (Cox, I.20). On MI at the church, impaled by Babington.

Unidentified. Belper. *Per pale a bend between three quatrefoils one in chief two in base* (*DAJ* XII (1890) pl. 1). On the old bridge built 1422, demolished 1791.

Unidentified. Brampton. *Argent on a bend azure five bezants each charged with a cross potent sable* (Cox, I.114). Seen by Bassano *c.* 1710 in glass at the church.

Unidentified. Chellaston. *Argent a fesse gules between three doves or a mullet for difference* (Cox, III.411). Seen by Bassano in church there; Cox suggests these arms were used by the Bancrofts.

Unidentified. Chesterfield. *Ermine a fesse between six oak leaves gules* (formerly in the church, Local MS 6341). Perhaps a version of FitzLangley.

Unidentified. Chesterfield. *Gules three lozenges in bend argent on each a fesse dancettée between three billets sable all between two double cotises argent* (in glass at the church *c.* 1611, Local MS 6341). Possibly a garbled variant of an old Hastings coat, with d'Eyncourt overtones.

Unidentified. Derby. *Argent a chevron gules between three elephants' heads erased sable* (hatchment once at St Alkmund's church, Simpson, I.322).

Unidentified. Derby. *Barry nebulée of six argent and azure on a chief quarterly gules and or in the 1st and 4th quarters a lion passant guardant and in the 2nd and 3rd two roses counterchanged* (once painted on wainscot at All Saints', Simpson, I.322). This resembles a form of Basset with an augmentation of some kind.

Unidentified. Eckington. *Argent a fesse gules between three bucks' heads sable* (in church, V. 1569).

Unidentified. Hartshorne. *On a bend between twelve fleur-de-lys six cross crosslets fitchée* (Cox, III.382). Part of a carving on the church tower; Cox suggests that it is an ancient coat of the Hartshornes.

Unidentified. Hazlebarrow (Norton). *Vert three bezants* (quartered by Selioke, D369). Known pedigrees do not suggest a likely family to whom these arms might belong.

Unidentified. Heanor. *Gules a fesse argent between three vans barry of the 2nd and azure* (Local MS 6341; in the church). Somehow allied to the de Greys.

Unidentified. Hope; Haddon Hall. *Per pale sable and gules a talbot statant argent* (Cox, II.262; parlour ceiling at Haddon. At Hope the field is actually *per pale sable and or* and is shown next to Eyre quartering Wells. Possibly a badge of the Talbots. On a C18 pew chart for Hope church (in private hands) this device is recorded as having appeared on a roundel as a crest ensigning the arms of Eyre quartering Padley in stained glass then in the 'centre of the E. window'.

Unidentified. Norbury. *Barry of four argent and gules on a canton of the 2nd a cross of the first* (Cox, III.247). In glass at the church. Perhaps intended for *argent two bars gules* etc ..., thus Broughton, Staffs.

Unidentified. Shardlow Hall. *Gules a chevron or between three beehives argent* (ceramic tile in the hall fireplace).

Unidentified. Walton on Trent. *Barry of six argent and gules on a canton of the last a fleur-de-lys of the first* (this and three following: Cox, II.513, noted by Wyrley 1592). Perhaps a scrambled coat of Muschamp.

A cross patée fleury: probably intended for Gresley Priory.

Or five lozenges in fesse azure: intended for Vavasour or Plumpton?

On a fesse three roses: probably intended for Welbeck Abbey, Notts.

Unwin. Highfield House (Derby). *Azure a crescent or between three fleurs-de-lys argent within a bordure engrailed of the 2nd* (Vv. Staffs. 1583, 1614, 1663). Gr. 18 Nov. 1581 to William Unwin of Chatterley, Staffs., and borne by Revd Edward Unwin of Derby and Wootton Lodge, Staffs., and his sons James and Edward, who owned considerable property in the Dove valley and at Derby *c.* 1833.

Upton. Brailsford; Derby; Holbrook. *Argent on a saltire sable five annulets or* (seal in local collection). Borne or used by Charles Upton of Derby (1752–1814), mayor 1791, high sheriff 1809, who claimed descent from a Leics. family.

D'Uvedale. 'Co. Derby'. *Argent a cross moline gules (Rel.* V (1865) 231; Jenyns' Roll). It is unclear why Sleigh included this coat; moreover, he entered it under 'Dovedale'; possibly he was merely making an unwarranted assumption about the etymology. The cross is blazoned *recercelée* in the Parliament Roll and in Jenyns, but tricked *moline* nevertheless, as on seals of 1339, 1346 (PRO, P.2199, 2178). Borne by Sir John de Uvedale of Sussex and Surrey, *c.* 1318; Note also Henry, son of Agnes de Uvedale of Duckmanton in Henry III's reign (*Darley Cartulary*, H.66).

Vaux. Beeley. *Chequy or and gules on a chevron azure three roses of the first*; supporters: *dexter a griffin sable langued gules beaked and membered or, sinister a buck or*; motto: 'Hodie non cras' (Vv. Northants. 1566, 1618). Borne by Nicholas, cr. by writ of summons Lord Vaux of Harrowden, Northants., 1523, whose father had acquired Beeley. Lord Vaux's son, Hon. Nicholas Vaux, sold to Greaves 1560.

Vavasour. Hazlebadge; Langwith (Scarcliffe); Shipley; Steetley (Whitwell). *Or a fesse dancettée sable*; crest: *a cock gules combed and wattled or* (Parliament Roll). Borne as above by Sir William le Vavasour, summoned to Parliament as Lord Vavasour of Hazlewood Castle, Yorks., 1299 (dormant 1322), and presumably by Sir Robert son of Sir Mauger, sheriff of Nottingham *c.* 1245–55, who inherited Derbys. property from Riboef. The sister and heiress of Robert, son of William, Sir Robert's grandson, carried Shipley etc to Strelley, which family erroneously believed themselves to be heirs general to the barony. However, this is undoubtedly a cadet branch of Vavasour of Hazlewood Castle, although even if the two Roberts, son of William, were

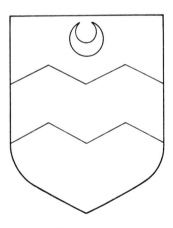

Vavasour

one and the same, the claim has serious doubt cast upon it by both Clay (p. 226 & n.3) and CP (XII (ii), 238f. and n.).

Verdon. Foremark; Hartshorne; Ingleby, Swadlincote. *Or a fret gules* (Willement Roll; as quartered by Talbot, Bess of Hardwick's MI at All Saints', Derby). Borne by John de Verdon, but probably rendered more accurately in Local MS 6341 as *or fretty gules* and attributed to Bertram de Verdon of Foremark and Hartshorne (d. 1192), who had these estates from Ferrers, and who founded Croxden Abbey. Cadets held part of the estates until 1387.

Vermuyden. Middleton Hall (Middleton by Wirksworth); Wirksworth. *Azure a pile between three estoiles or quartering azure a ram salient argent collared or*; crest: *a demi-ram argent collared or* (*DAJ* LXXII (1952) 76 n.4). Gr. and conf. 1629 on the occasion of the knighting of Sir Cornelius Vermuyden (1595–1677), son of Gillis Vermuyden of St Maartensdijk, Netherlands, whose ancestral arms were as above but substituting a *chevron* for the *pile*.

Vermuyden

Vernon. Nether Haddon. *Argent fretty sable*; crest: *a boar rampant gules*; motto: '*Prest à deffendre l'ancient honeur*' (Local MS 6341; various parts of Haddon Hall). William de Vernon of Haddon, very early C13, sealed with *a lion passant*, presumably the origin of the crest. His elder brother, head of the Cheshire branch of the family, bore *or on a fesse azure three garbs of the field*, a derivative of the arms of the Earls of Chester: V. Cheshire 1580. However, the Haddon branch passed to a Francis from Cumberland, who adopted the name of Vernon, and whose descendants bore as above and *a canton* (Sir Richard, seal of c. 1250; Local MS 6341). His son, also Richard, bore *argent a bend fretty sable* (ibid.), whilst John and Richard, a century later, bore *argent a fret sable a quarter gules* (Willement Roll) and *argent fretty sable a quarter gules* (Jenyns' Ordinary) respectively. In 1611 *argent fretty sable* and *argent fretty sable a canton gules* were to be found quartered together (see below, Local MS 6341). In glass at Morley church occurs also *or a cinquefoil gules* ascribed by Cox (IV.325) to Vernon.

Vernon. Sudbury. *Argent a fret sable*; crest: *a boar's head erased sable bristled and ducally gorged or*; motto: '*Ver non semper viret*' (V. 1569 with 20 quarterings). Allowed to John son of Henry Vernon of Sudbury, grandson of Sir John, uncle of George, of Haddon, last of that line. His wife had been the widow of his 2nd cousin, Walter, of Houndhill (Marchington), Staffs., whose son, Sir Edward, marr. John's neice and heiress, uniting both families (hence Vernon quartering Vernon, above). Their son marr. the heiress of the elder (Cheshire) line. The great-grandson of this match, George, was in 1762 cr. Lord Vernon of Kinderton, Cheshire, and was gr. supporters: *dexter a lion gules gorged with a collar and chain reflexed over the back or sinister a boar sable gorged and chained likewise* (BP (1970) 2707). His 3rd wife was the heiress of Earl Harcourt, and their 2nd son assumed by RL 2 Feb. 1831 the additional surname and quarterly arms of Harcourt: *gules two bars or*. Their great-grandson assumed the surname and arms of Harcourt alone by RL 1905 and was in 1917 cr. Viscount Harcourt and Lord Nuneham of Nuneham Courtenay, Oxon. (ext. 1979). In 1728, George son of Henry Vernon of Sudbury had assumed by RL the additional surname of Venables with quarterly arms and crest of Peter, Lord Venables, of Kinderton. The 5th Lord Vernon assumed by RL the surname and arms of Warren only 14 Oct. 1837, although his posterity seem to have reverted to Venables-Vernon only, except those of his yr son who was Borlase-Warren-Venables-Vernon.

Vicar (Vickers). Littleover; Quarndon; Stanley. *Argent on a millrind sable five estoiles of the field* (Burke; Tilley II.310). Richard Vickers of Littleover and Quarndon used these arms and was a usurper V. 1611; they were also used by Thomas Vicars of Loscoe at the same period and by his kinsman, Joseph, son of William Vicar of Stanley, 1697.

Vickers. Bolsover Hill; Park Hall (Barlborough); Tapton House. *Argent on a cross flory gules five mullets of six points of the field on a chief sable three millrinds or*; crest: *two arms embowed vested gules cuffed argent hands proper holding a millrind or*; motto: *'Vigore'* (BLG III (1972) 9207). Gr. to Edward Vickers or Vicars of Millsands, Sheffield, Yorks., 4th son of John, in 1878. He was later of Tapton House and his 2nd son, T.E. Vickers, was of Bolsover Hill 1897–1915.

Voeux: see Des Voeux.

Wagstaffe. Derby; Hasland; N. Wingfield. *Argent two bendlets raguly sable the lower one couped at the top*; crest: *out of a ducal coronet or a staff erect couped and raguly sable* (V. 1611). Gr. Aug. 1611 at Bakewell to Anthony Wagstaff of Hasland, son of Thomas of N. Wingfield. Before the grant they were using as above, but both *bendlets* entire (*Rel.* VI (1866) 43).

Wake. Chesterfield; Hasland; Newbold; Tapton Grove. *Or two bars gules in chief three torteaux*; crest: *a Wake knot proper* (arms: in glass at Chesterfield church 1611, Local MS 6341; Matthew Paris Shields, IV.50; crest: Burke). The Wakes inherited Chesterfield, Hasland and Newbold manors from Briwere 1233, these arms being borne by Hugh, son of Baldwin Wake by the Briwere heiress (ibid.). A descendant, Sir John, was summoned to Parliament by writ 1295 as Lord Wake of Liddel (Longtown), Cumb., and remoter descendants were made bts 5 Dec. 1621. In 1821 Tapton Grove was let to Charles Wake, who left on succeeding as 10th bt in 1846.

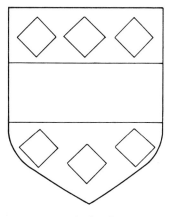

Wakebridge

Wakebridge. Wakebridge (Crich). *Azure a fesse gules between six lozenges sable* (in glass at Crich church 1611, Cox, IV.62; Local MS 6341; seal of 1370, PRO, P.835). The classic example of arms breaching the 'rules' of tincture, although they are also known with the field *argent* (also in glass at Crich, 1569, ibid.). Borne by Sir William de Wakebridge MP, who d. 1370. Curiously, these arms are found on a Chinese armorial plate of *c.* 1740, impaled by Wille (or Selley): Howard, P4).

Waldeschef. Boyleston; Fairfield; Wadshelf (Brampton). *Gules three swords erect argent* (as quartered by Bradbourne, MI at Ashbourne church). Borne by Walter de Waldeschef of Wadshelf, who marr. the heiress of Basings of Boyleston; his co-heiress marr. Ridware early C14. His other dau. and co-heiress marr. Shirley, which family, however, quartered *gules a chevron between three garbs or* for Waldeschef (V. 1569), if identified correctly.

Walkelin. Derby; Radbourne. *Barry of six argent and gules a lion rampant ermine* (as quartered by Pole of Radbourne, V. 1569). Borne by Robert Walkelin of Radbourne (d.

1233). The *barry* is sometimes given as *of eight*; other versions (as recorded by Sleigh, *Rel.* V. (1865) 231) give the field as *gules and azure*. Cadets were the de Mercastons, qv.

Walkelin. Bretby; Hilton; Rosliston. *Argent on a cross sable five lions rampant or*; crest: *a lion rampant or holding in its paw a tulip gules leaved vert* (V. Staffs. 1663). Allowed to Clement Walkelin of Tatenhill, Staffs., but entered without proof for John Walkelin of Wakelin Hall, Hilton, in the D369 MS of V. 1662. The Harl.MS 6104 version gives the arms but no crest, with no reservation, conf. by Dugdale's notes, in which he says 'The crest not proved'. Cf. V. Northants. 1564. On the MI at Repton church the cross is now painted *gules*.

Walker. Aston Hall; Mosborough (Eckington); Stydd Hall (Yeaveley); Sturston. *Argent on a chevron gules between two anvils in chief and in base an anchor sable a bee between two crescents or*; crest: *within a wreathed serpent a dove proper*; motto: *'Juncti Valemus'* (BLG (1875) II.1450.) Gr. to Samuel Walker of Mosborough and Ecclesfield 1778; his 3rd son Joseph was of Aston Hall.

Walker. Osmaston Manor. *Or three pallets gules surmounted by a saltire argent thereon a stag's head erased proper on a chief azure a garb between two mullets of six points of the field*; crest: *a cornucopia proper*; motto: *'Cura et industria'* (FD (1929) II.2020). Gr. (LO) 1886 to Sir Andrew Barclay Walker, cr. a bt 12 Feb. that year. His son, Sir Peter, acquired Osmaston Manor, and his son, Sir Ian, became the ultimate heir of Okeover (qv), which additional surname and arms he took by RL 1956. Sir Peter's brother, W.H. Walker, was in 1919 cr. Lord Wavertree (Lancs.) and was gr. arms as above, but without the *pallets*, and the *saltire ermine*, with supporters: *dexter a horse sinister a stag proper each charged on the shoulder with a garb or* (ibid. 2016). Latter title ext. 1933.

Walker. 'Weston'. *Argent on a chevron patonce and ringed at the point between three crescents sable two plates*; crest: *a greyhound passant argent collared and lined sable.* Conf. 1663 to Humphrey Walker of Salt, Staffs., grandson of George, of 'Weston, Co. Derby', who displayed the arms on a seal of of 1559 (King, 125). 'Weston, Co. Derby' should possibly be Wetton, Staffs. See also Okeover.

Wall. Crich. *Azure a chevron ermine on a chief embattled or three pellets*; crest: *an eagle's head couped argent* (Thompson, IV.214). Gr. before 1536 to Sir Thomas Wall of Crich, Garter from 1534 until his death in 1536, son of Thomas, Norroy 1516–22. Tilley (III.276) adds another crest: *out of a mural crown or a demi-wolf salient proper collared embattled counter-embattled of the first.*

Wall. Cowley (Wensley); Riber Hall; Wensley. *Azure a chevron ermine between three eagles displayed argent on a chief embattled or as many pellets*; crest: *a demi-eagle azure wings addorsed argent* (*Rel.* V (1865) 231). Used by Stephen Wall of Riber Hall (d. 1803) and by John, son of Anthony Wall (1697–1747) of Wensley. George Wall of Cowley, son of John, is credited with the use of a variant of these arms by Tilley (I.105, 271): *azure a chevron ermine on a chief embattled or three hurts*; crest: *an eagle's head couped argent.*

Waller. Chesterfield. *Sable three walnut leaves in bend or between two cotises argent*; crest: *on a mount vert suspended from an oak tree proper an escutcheon azure thereon three fleur-de-lys or*; motto: *'Fructus virtutis'* (Glover, II.290). Used by William Waller of Chesterfield, attorney, living 1772; his brother and nephew were successively town clerks there, 1791–1857 (RBC, p. 238). The arms are those of Waller of Groombridge, Sussex (V. Kent 1619), slightly varied. There is no evidence that William Waller was descended from the Kent family.

Walmesley. Foston Hall. *Gules on a chief ermine a trefoil slipped vert between two hurts*; crest: *a lion statant guardant ermine ducally crowned or charged on the body with a trefoil slipped vert* (*Rel.* V (1865) 231; crest: Burke). Gr. to George Walmesley of Foston Hall *c.* 1829.

Walthall. Alton Manor (Idridgehay); Hackneylane (Darley). *Argent a chevron vert between three ravens proper*; crest: *a dexter arm embowed couped at the shoulder vested gules cuffed ermine hand clenched thereon a falcon close proper beaked or lure of the second stringed of the third*; mottoes: *'Dimidium qui coepit habet'* (above) and *'A bird in the hand is worth two in the bush'* (below) (BLG (1937) 2356). The heiress of Peter Walthall of Hackneylane marr. James Milnes who in 1853 assumed by RL the surname and arms of Walthall. The arms were allowed to Roger

Walthall of Nantwich, Cheshire, V. Cheshire 1580.

Walton. Walton. *Argent a cross flory sable and a bordure engrailed gules* (noted by Wyrley 1592 in glass at Dethick church). Intended for the arms of Robert Brito of Walton who held Little Ogston from Ralph Heriz of Wessington early C13.

Walton(?). Riber Manor (Matlock). *On a pile barry of six a roundel between two like roundels on a chief a rose between two mascles.* Currently displayed, without tinctures, on a wrought iron panel on the gates of Riber Manor.

Walton. Egginton. Arms used not known. Usurper V. 1611.

Wandesford, Butler-Clarke-Southwell-: see Butler.

Ward. Derby; Sutton on the Hill. *Azure a cross fleury between four annulets or* (seal in a local collection, cf. Tilley, IV.161). Used by Samuel Ward of Derby, gent., grand juror at the Busby trial 1681 (*DAJ* XXX (1908) 223), and by his descendant Revd R.R. Ward of Ash and Sutton, early C19.

Ward. Killamarsh. *Azure a cross flory between four lions passant guardant or*; crest: *a wolf's head erased or gorged with a collar sable thereon three bezants and charged on the neck with a trivet of the last*; motto: *'Sub Cruce salus'* (BLG (1937) 2730). Gr. under RL of 1881 whereby Revd Horatio Nelson Ward assumed the additional surname and arms of Nelson, his mother having been Horatia, natural child of Adm. Viscount Nelson. The Wards had been of Killamarsh for many generations.

Ward. Findern; Great Hayfield; Stenson; Willington. *Azure a cross formée or a canton argent*; crest: *out of a mural coronet gules a wolf's head or langued of the first* (hatchment at Willington Church; BLG (1833–5), III.64). Used or borne by Benjamin Ward of Findern and Willington (of a Stenson family), 1712–90. Quartered C18, along with Orme of Burnaston, by Bristowe on MI at Twyford, destroyed 1910.

Warde, De la. Hartshorne. *Vairé argent and sable* (carved on tower of Hartshorne church, Cox, III.382 and n.). Borne by Sir William de la Warde of Roxton, Lincs. (d. 1268; FitzWilliam Roll), whose son, Anketin, marr. the heiress of Hartshorne and whose great-grand-daughter's heiress marr. Meynell (qv),

who adopted these arms in lieu of their own.

Wardewick. Derby. *Vert three lioncels rampant queues fourchés argent* (Jenyns' Ordinary). John de Wardewick bore these arms *temp.* Edward III; the name is extremely rare and, apart from the distinct variant of Walderswick (Sussex), seems to be found as a place-name only in Derby. A fine of 1202 (*DAJ* VII (1885) 201) names Ingram de Wardwick, whose son Peter marr. a co-heiress of de Derby. William son of Peter son of Peter was living *c.* 1300 (*Darley Cartulary*, A xxxvi). The arms are only a proposed attribution here.

Warren. Butterley Hall (Ripley); Derby. *Chequy or and azure on a canton gules a lion rampant argent*, quartering Borlase; crest: *on a chapeau a wyvern argent wings expanded the insides chequy or and azure* (BLG (1937) 2372). Gr. to Rear Admiral Sir John Borlase Warren of Stapleford Park, Notts., who with crest and supplement 2 May 1802; he was b. and educated in Derby and cr. bt 1 June 1775; ext. 1822. His brother inherited Butterley from Horne (qv), which name he adopted. See also Vernon.

Wass. Lea Green. Crest: *out of an Eastern crown and through clouds an arm embowed in armour holding the hilt of a sword point downwards to be enfiled by the crown all gules* (Local MS 9555). Used by Edward, son of Joseph Wass of Lea Green (1839–86).

Waterhouse. Lomberdale Hall (Youlgreave); Middleton Hall (Middleton & Smerrill). *Or three bars wavy azure overall a pile angrailed sable*; crest: *in front of an eagle's gamb erased à-la-quise sable issuant therefrom a wing erect or a millrind of the last*; motto: *'Veritas omnia vincit'* (BLG II (1968) 634). Gr. to Thomas Crompton Waterhouse (1851–1912) C20; his 3rd son, Charles, succ. to the Derbys. estates purchased from Bateman in 1913.

Waterfall. Dore; Totley. *Sable goutée-de-l'eau on a pale between two pallets wavy argent three fountains*; crest: *in front of a demi-eagle wings addorsed sable holding in the beak an escallop or a fountain*; motto: *'Aqua cadit resurgere'* (FD (1929) II.2043). Gr. with remainders to Revd George Howard Waterfall of Dore and Totley, rector of Tollard Royal, Wilts., 10 July 1882.

Watson. Ashford; Bakewell; Heanor. *Barry of six argent and gules three crescents ermine*

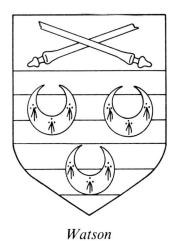

Watson

on a chief of the 2nd two broken spears in saltire or; crest: on a mount vert a demi-dragon
rampant proper (arms: MI at Heanor church;
crest: *Rel.* V (1865) 231). Used by White Watson FLS of Bakewell, who carved the arms
on the MI at Heanor of his great uncle the
sculptor Samuel Watson (1663–1716).

Watts. Upper House, Kinder (Hayfield).
*Ermine on a chief sable a garb between two
bees or*; crest: *a demi-griffin sable wings ex-
tended chequy or and sable the sinister claw
resting on a garb or*; motto: *'Fide sed qui vide'*
(FD (1929) II.2050). Gr. 1852 to Sir James
Watts, mayor of Manchester, of Abney Hall,
Cheshire (whose son purchased Upper
House).

Wayne. Duffield; Quarndon House. *Gules a
chevron ermine between three dexter gauntlets
or*; crest: *a pelican feeding her young or collared gules on the body an ermine spot nest
azure*; motto: *'In Te Domine confido'* (BLG
(1937) 2387). Gr. 1782 to William Wayne of
Duffield, and borne by his son, W.H. Wayne,
also of Quarndon and Warslow. His cousins,
of Sheen, Staffs., used or bore the same arms
but with the motto: *'Tempus et casus accidit
omnibus'* (*Rel.* XII (1872) 96).

Webster. Ashbourne; Brick House (Chesterfield). *Argent a cross between four mullets
sable* impaling Gladwin (Bassano's MS,
Local 3525). Used by Paul Webster of Ashbourne and Chesterfield, who d. 9 Mar. 1715
according to Hunter (FMG I.236), but 26
May 1720 according to Bassano who, after
all, had to paint the hatchment.

Webster. Bolsover; Chesterfield; Tupton.
*Azure on a bend argent (cotised or) betwen
two demi-lions rampant ermine a rose gules between as many boars' heads couped sable*;
crest: *a dragon's head couped reguardant quarterly per fesse embattled vert and or emitting
flames of fire proper*; motto: *'Fides et Justitia'*
(FD (1910) 1655). Used with *cotises* by all
three branches of the families of Webster of
Chesterfield, according to J.P. Yeatman
(*Feudal History of Derbyshire*, II.4), and borrowed from the Websters of Bolsover. Sir
Thomas Webster, grandson of Peter, of Chesterfield, was cr. bt 21 May 1703 (title ext.
1923) and had a grant as above, but without
cotises, 10 Nov. 1720. These arms (with cotises) appear never to have been used with
authority, even by the Bolsover branch,
whoever they were. James Webster of Tupton
of this family disclaimed V. 1662.

Welbeck. Compton. *Argent on a chevron
between three lozenges gules as many martlets
or* (Burke). Borne or used by Richard Welbeck esq. of Compton 1499. The heiress marr.
Salford (qv). Sleigh, who records this version
of the arms, also gives another, with *lozenges
sable* (*Rel.* XII (1872)96).

Welby. Doveridge. *Sable a fesse between
three fleur-de-lys argent*; crest: *a naked arm
embowed issuant from flames proper holding a
sword argent hilt and pommel or*; motto:
'Sorte contentus' (Burke). Arms conf. and
crest gr. 21 Mar. 1563 to Richard Welby of
Halstead (Moulton), Lincs., and borne by
Adlard Welby of Doveridge Manor early
C20.

Weldon: see Burdett.

Wells. Holme Hall (Bakewell). *Ermines on
a canton or a buck's head caboshed sable*;
crest: *a demi-talbot* (V. 1634). Gr. to Bernard
Wells of Holme Hall (son of Thomas of Ashton under Hill, Worcs.) 14 Nov. 1634.

Wendesley. Wensley; Calke; Mapleton.
Ermine on a bend gules three escallops or;
crest: *a man's head in profile bearded couped at
the shoulders proper* (Willement Roll; with

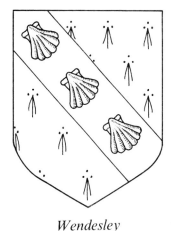

Wendesley

crest, V. 1569). Borne by Thomas de Wendesley *c.* 1390, although on this man's MI at Bakewell the arms appear to be *argent a bend gules.* Allowed with crest to Richard Wendesley of Wensley 1569.

Wentworth. Bakewell; Whitwell. *Sable a chevron between three leopards' faces or;* crest: *a griffin passant argent;* motto: *'En Dieu est tout'* (Tilley, I.272; Vv. North 1530, Yorks. 1575 etc). Sir Roger Wentworth of Wentworth, Yorks., marr. the heiress of Tyrell of Bakewell C15.

West. Darley Abbey; Greenhill (Norton); Newbold. *Argent a fesse dancettée between three leopards' faces sable baronially crowned or a crescent for difference;* crest: *a demigriffin vert collared or holding erect a sword argent hilt and pommel of the 2nd;* (V. 1569). Not all versions of V. 1569 have these arms: the shield is left blank in D369 and there is no entry at all in Local MS 6341. Sleigh attributed to 'West of Newbold' (as Burke; *Rel.* XII (1872) 96): *argent on a fesse dancettée sable a mullet or and a bordure gules bezantée;* but the Lysons make it clear that all the places mentioned above were held together by Sir William West, gr. from the Disso-

lution, 1541. He was also of Amberden Hall (Debden), Essex. Tilley erroneously claims that he was a nephew of the 9th Lord de la Warr.

Westby. Elmton; Whaley (Bolsover). *Argent on a chevron azure three cinquefoils of the field;* crest: *a martlet sable holding its beak a stalk of wheat proper with three ears or;* motto: *'Nec volanti nec volenti'* (*Rel.* XII (1872) 96). Allowed V. Yorks. 1584 and borne by George Westby of Whaley 1610; he was also of Rotherham, Yorks.

Westcott (Westcote). Repton; Willington. *Argent a bend cotised sable a bordure gules bezantée* (Local MS 4556; cf. Burke). William Westcott acquired lands at Repton and Willington at the Dissolution which he sold to Porte 1555.

Whalley. Whitwell. *Argent three whales' heads erased haurient sable;* crest: *a whale's head erased sable* (Vv. Notts. 1614, 1663). Conf. 1614 to Richard Whalley of Kirton, Notts., who d. 1632. He had sold Whitwell (purchased by his homonymous grandfather in 1563) in 1592.

Wheatcroft. Darley; Wirksworth. *Sable a bend raguly argent between two garbs or* (*Rel.* VI (1866) 44). Used (or possibly borne) by John Wheatcroft of Wirksworth 1846. The arms belong to Wheatcroft of Suffolk: see also next entry.

Wheatcroft. Wirksworth. *Azure on a fesse engrailed between three griffins' heads erased or a fleur-de-lys between two roses gules;* motto: *'Orando laborando'* (MI at Wirksworth). Borne or used by George Hanson Wheatcroft of Wirksworth, two of whose six sons were killed in action in the 1st World War and are commemorated in the church under these arms which are not in FD.

Wheeler. Kilburn; Netherlea (Holbrook). *Per pale or and azure three chevronels indented between as many wheels of six spokes in the centre chief point a millrind all counterchanged;* crest: *a griffin's head argent goutée-desang erased gules gorged with a wreath of laurel proper holding in its beak a wheel of six spokes per pale or and azure;* motto: *'Non Omnis moriar'* (FD (1929) II.2071). Gr. C19 to Revd William Cheslin Wheeler, who marr. the Bourne (Denby pottery) heiress and whose son, Joseph Bourne Wheeler, purchased Kilburn Hall 1898.

Wheler. Derby. *Or a chevron between three*

leopards' faces sable; crest: *out of a ducal coronet or an eagle displayed gules*; motto: *'Facie tenus'* (MI at All Saints', Derby, impaling Cole; motto: J. Foster, *Baronetage* (1882), 652). Gr. 1585. Sir William Wheler of Westminster was cr. a bt 11 Aug. 1660 with remainder to his cousin once removed, William Wheler of Martin Hussingtree, Worcs., and d. without issue at Derby 1666.

Whiston. Derby; Idridgehay. Crest: *a unicorn sejant*; motto: *'Fide et amore'* (crest on a livery button in a local collection; motto: Local MS 9555.205). Used by W.H. Whiston of Ecclesbourne Hall, Idridgehay, and Derby, coroner of Derby 1895, of a legal family from Wirksworth.

Whitby. Derby. *Gules three adders coiled and on a chief or as many pheons sable*; crest: *an arrow in pale environed around with a snake all proper; motto: 'Virtus vitium fugere'* (MI at All Saints', Derby, now obscured, impaling Dolphin). Borne by Richard Whitby, attorney of Derby, and of Osbaston, Leics. (1740–1803), son of Thomas, of Oakedge Park (Cannock Chase), Staffs.

White. Duffield. *Gules a chevron between three goats' heads couped argent attired or*; crest: *a goat's head gules attired or in the mouth an oak branch vert fructed of the 2nd* (Vv. 1611, 1634). Conf. to William son of John White 1602 and allowed to the son, William, 1634.

White. Duffield etc. *Argent a fesse chequy gules and or overall on a bend engrailed azure an arrow point downwards of the field*; crest: *a boar's head erased proper pierced through the mouth with an arrow or* (BP (1931) 2471). Gr. 1909 to W.R.D. White, son of Timothy, the famous chemist shop proprietor (1824–1908) who in the 1890s bought the reversion of eleven lordships of manors or supposed manors in the fee of Duffield from the Jodrells. The grantee was cr. a bt 29 June 1922.

Whitehall. Pethills (Kniveton). *Argent a fesse chequy gules and sable between three esquires' helms proper*; crest: *out of a mural coronet chequy gules and sable a demi-lion or collared of the 2nd in the dexter forepaw a falchion proper hilted or* (V. 1662). Gr., apparently, to Whitehall of White Hall (Chinley) 16 July 1634; Joseph the grantee removed to Pethills. Previously he had used arms as above, but field *or, helms azure* (for *proper?*), and, in the crest, the *coronet gules, lion argent*

collared of the first, the falchion broken proper, as borne by Whitehall of Whitehough (Leek), Staffs. (Sleigh, *Leek*, 214; *DAJ* XL (1918) 95).

Whitehall. Yeldersley. *Argent a fesse chequy gules and sable between three helmets proper* (Local MS 4556). Used by John Whitehall of Yeldersley, a 'person for a grant' in 1687. In V. 1611 his ancestor, John son of Robert Whitehall (grandson of Robert, of Sharpcliffe (Leek), Staffs.), was branded a usurper and was then using: *argent a cross crosslet gules* (Local MS 6341.91v).

Whitehead. Hargate Hall (Wormhill). *Azure a fesse between three fleurs-de-lys or*; crest: *a wolf sejant argent*; motto: *'Ad finem fidelis'* (Burke; crest: livery button in a local collection). Borne or used by R. Whitehead of Hargate Hall *c.* 1895, claiming a Gloucs. ancestry. See also Taylor-Whitehead.

Whitehurst. Derby. *Argent a lion's head erased and on a chief gules three bendlets of the field*; crest: *between two palm branches vert a cross crosslet fitchée sable* (Tilley, IV.161; crest: Burke.) Used or borne by John Whitehurst (1761–1834) nephew and heir of John Whitehurst FRS (1713–88), the clockmaker, philosopher and geologist, both of Derby, of a Dilhorne, Staffs., family long settled on an estate there called Whitehurst.

Whittaker. Youlgreave. A Mr Whittaker of Youlgreave disclaimed V. 1662.

Whittington. Derby. *On a bend between two griffins' heads erased three dolphins naiant* (MI at All Saints', Derby, now lost, cf. Simpson, I.355). Used by Luke Whittington of Derby, whose father of the same name (1605–48) was once bailiff and thrice mayor of Derby. The family originated in Belper and the heiress marr. Crompton. The tinctures seems to be lost, and the arms seem not to have been 'borrowed' from any identifiable source.

Whittington. Whittington; Holme (Newbold & Dunston). *Sable a cross engrailed argent between four pomegranates slipped or* (as quartered by Eyre of Holme, V. 1569). Borne by Robert Whittington of Holme C15 whose co-heiresses marr. Eyre and Dethick.

Whitworth. Stancliffe Hall (Darley). *Ermine a bend engrailed sable between a garb in chief and in base a rose gules leaved and slipped proper*; crest: *in front of a mount vert thereon a garb gules three mascles interlaced fessewise or*; motto: *'Fortis qui prudens'* (J. Foster, *Baronetage* (1882), 656). Gr. 1869 to Sir Jos-

Whitehurst

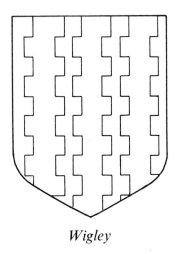

Wigley

eph Whitworth, who was cr. a bt in October that year; title ext. at his death in 1887.

Widmerpool (Widmerpole). Stanton by Dale. *Azure three mullets of six points pierced argent* (V. Notts. 1614) Thought to have been borne by Nicholas Widmerpool of Stanton, 1304, and his posterity to *c.* 1500, unless attributed anachronistically.

Wigfall. Carter Hall (Eckington); Eckington; Renishaw. *Sable a sword erect argent hilted or on a chief indented gules a ducal coronet between two escallops of the third* (V. 1662). Conf. without the escallops, following a seal of 1536–7, between 1612 and 1633 to Zachary son of George Wigfall of Carter Hall, and entered V. 1634; he had been labelled a usurper V. 1611. These arms were allowed to John, son of Henry Wigfall of Renishaw, his nephew, with escallops, V. 1662. The coronet in the arms is given as *ducal* in Harl.MS 6104.

Wigley. Middleton Hall (Middleton by Wirksworth); Wigwell (Wirksworth). *Paly of three embattled argent and gules*; crest: *a boar's head proper maned and tufted sable issuant from flames of fire also proper collared embattled gules* (V. 1611). Arms conf. and

crest gr. 22 June 1611 to Richard son of Henry Wigley. Local MS 6341 gives the arms as *argent three pales embattled gules.* His father used *paly of four embattled argent and gules*; crest: *a leopard's head proper* (DM III.5 (1965) 571–5).

Wigley. Chesterfield; Gatehouse (Wirksworth). *Paly of eight embattled argent and gules*; crest: *a tiger's head proper maned and tufted sable issuant from flames of fire proper collared embattled gules* (Lysons, clii). Allowed, oddly, to Henry, son of John son of Richard (above entry), V. 1662; Dugdale avers that these arms were those granted 22 June 1611 (qv). In fact, the older branch of Wigleys of Gatehouse were by then well established at Scraptoft, Leics., and bore as above but *paly of six* (V. Leics. 1619), as conf. to Sir Edward Wigley of Scraptoft 1689. The heiress of this branch marr. Samuel Hartopp of Little Dalby, Leics., whose grandson, Edward (1758–1808), assumed by RL the additional surname and arms of Wigley 1781.

Wilkins. Measham; Ravenstone Hall. *Gules two swords in saltire argent hilts and pommels or on a chief of the 2nd three mullets pierced sable*; crest: *a demi-griffin reguardant gules* *holding in the dexter claw a sword erected argent hilt and pommel or* (*DAJ* XXXII (1921) 64). When being considered for a grant, the heralds' correspondent wrote of John Wilkins, who purchased Ravenstone in 1680, 'His father dealt in coles as does this gent'. Arms gr. 10 Dec. 1685.

Wilkinson. Chesterfield; Hilcote Hall (Blackwell). *Gules a fesse vair in chief a unicorn passant or all within a bordure sable bezantée*; crest: *a fox's head couped per pale vert and or holding in the mouth a dragon's wing argent* (Glover, II.110). Borne (according to Burke) by John Slater Wilkinson of Hilcote (d. 1869). John, elder son of his ancestor John, assumed by RL 1782 the surname and arms of Lindley of Skegby, Notts. (*Rel.* VI (1866) 44). John Wilkinson, son of John, of Potterton, Yorks. (and 'Blackwell Hall, Derbys.', according to BLG (1848) 1591), assumed the surname and arms of Denison by RL 1785.

Wilkinson. Tapton House. *A chevron vair between three bulls passant* (*Rel.* XII (1872) 96). Borne by George Yeldham Ricketts on assuming the surname (1 Sept. 1831) and arms (1832) of Wilkinson by RL as heir to Isaac Wilkinson of Tapton. His son reverted to Ricketts.

Wilkinson. Belper. *Per fesse gules and argent in chief under clouds proper a meridian sun issuant therefrom six rays or in base four barrulets wavy azure*; crest: *a flowering spray of hibiscus mutabilis proper*; motto: *'Non animum mutant'* (FD (1929) II.2091). Gr. 1913 to Sir William Harry Wilkinson, knighted that year, Consul-General in China 1893–1918, son of Charles Wilmot Wilkinson of Belper.

Williams. Yokecliffe (Wirksworth). *Gyronny of eight ermine and sable a lion rampant or*; crest: *a talbot passant per pale ermine and or* (BLG (1952) 2731). Conf. 15 Mar. 1576 to Roger son of William ap John Thomas of Llangibby Castle, Mon. The family enjoyed a btcy from 14 May 1642 to 1758, when the heiress marr. William Addams of Ancre Hill, Monmouth. Their descendant, Maj.Gen. Sir Godfrey Williams KCIE (1859–1940), settled at Yokecliffe. A coheiress marr. a Wheatcroft (qv).

Willington. Potlock (Findern); Willington. *Gules a saltire vair* (as quartered by Finderne, V. 1569 (Harl.MS 1093) and by Willoughby of Risley, in glass at Wilne church and some

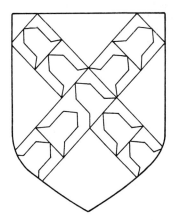

Willington

MSS of V. 1569). The facts seem to indicate that the Findernes quartered these arms retrospectively, for Margery, sister and ultimate heiress of Nicholas de Willington (d. after 1302), was 1st cousin to the first Willington to bear these arms, Sir Ralph son of Ralph de Willington. He bore them *jure uxoris* Joan, dau. and heiress of Champerknowne of Umberleigh, Devon (Dering Roll). One suspects that the family previously bore other arms, now lost, probably resembling those of Toke or Finderne. John de Willington, grandson of Ralph and Joan, was summoned to Parliament by writ as Lord Willington 1331 (arms: Dunstable Roll). His brother Henry (arms: Boroughbridge Roll 1322) was ancestor of Willington of Tamworth, Staffs., and Hurley, Warwicks., Thomas Willington of Hurley being allowed a crest: *a pine tree vert fructed or* (V. Warw. 1619).

Willoughby. Brackenfield; Normanton by Derby; Risley. *Or two bars gules charged with three water bougets argent two and one*; crest: *an owl argent ducally crowned and legged or*; motto: *'Quassata firmiora manent'* (Vv. 1569, 1611). Canting arms as from Bugge, the original surname, and at first borne with *six* *waterbougets* by Hugh son of Hugh of Risley 1431. Allowed to Sir John, of Risley, as above, 1569, his son, Sir Henry being cr. a bt 29 June 1611 (ext. 1653). Hugh, of Risley (d. 1491) bore: *ermine two bars humettée gules* for d'Abridgecourt, *jure matris* (MI at Wilne, Cox, IV.402); his son, also Hugh, bore the crest of Clifton (qv) in the right of *his* mother. These arms (as above) were also borne by Sir Edmund Willoughby, son by his 2nd marriage of Sir Richard, of Risley and Brackenfield (Military Roll) and was ancestor of William, of Normanton (C16). His descendant, William, was made a bt 4 Aug. 1660 (ext. 1670).

Willoughby. Derby. *Or fretty azure a bordure and a mullet for difference* (MI at St Peter's, Derby, Simpson, II.409). Exhibited V. 1662 by gynaecological pioneer Dr Percival Willoughby (1586–1685) of Derby, 3rd son of Sir Percival, *jure uxoris* of Wollaton, Notts., but without the *bordure*.

Willoughby. Pleasley. *Sable a cross engrailed or* (Planché Roll). Borne by Sir Robert Willoughby; actually the arms of Ufford, the heiress of which family had marr. John, 5th Lord Willoughby d'Eresby, of Spilsby, Lincs. (the Bec barony), and quartering *gules a cross moline argent* for Bec: (seal, 1437, PRO, P.877). The original arms of this branch of Willoughby were *or fretty azure* as borne by Robert, 1300 (Caerlaverock Roll). The crest borne by the later Lords Willoughby d'Eresby was: *a man's head affrontée couped at the shoulders proper ducally crowned or*; motto: *'Verite sans peur'* (Burke), gr. 1711. The supporters on the 1437 seal were, however, *on either side a wild man with a ragged staff*. See also Bec; Heathcote.

Wilmot. Chaddesden etc. *Sable on a fesse or between three eagles' heads erased argent as many escallops gules a canton vairé ermine and of the fourth*; crest: *an eagle's head argent murally gorged sable in the beak an escallop gules.* (BP (1970) 2841). Gr. with the addition of the canton of Gresley and the mural collar of the crest under a remainder to that made to Nicholas Wilmot of Osmaston by Derby (qv) 3 Feb. 1663, those in remainder being his cousins Robert and Edward of Chaddesden. Sir Edward Wilmot of Chaddesden was made a bt 15 Feb. 1759. A nephew of the 1st bt testamentarily assumed by RL the additional surname and arms of Sitwell (qv) in 1791.

John Wilmot assumed the additional surname and arms of Grimston by RL 1860; he was son of Sir Robert, 3rd bt.

Wilmot. Catton; Osmaston by Derby. *Sable on a fesse or between three eagles' heads erased argent as many escallops gules*; crest: *an eagle's head argent in the beak an escallop gules* (V. 1662). Gr. to Nicholas Wilmot of Osmaston 3 Feb. 1662. His descendant, Robert, was cr. a bt 10 Oct. 1772 (title ext. 1931). This title was remaindered to his natural son, who was gr. arms as above differenced with *a bordure engrailed of the 2nd*; the crest: *gorged with a collar engrailed azure* (Burke). The 3rd bt assumed the additional surname and arms of Horton (qv) by RL 1823, and his successor, likewise, in 1871. John, brother of the 1st bt, was Chief Justice of the Common Pleas; his son assumed the additional surname of Eardley (1812) and *his* son was also cr. a bt 23 Aug. 1821.

Wilne. King's Newton; Melbourne; Wilne. *Argent a chevron between three wolves' heads erased sable* (MI at Weston on Trent, impaled by Sale, Cox, IV.429). Borne or used by William Wilne of Melbourne *c.* 1579. Bassano read the *wolves' heads* as *gules* in 1710 (ibid.).

Wilson. Derby. *Sable a wolf rampant and in chief three estoiles or*; crest: *a demi-wolf rampant or*; motto: *'Virtus ad sidera tollit'* (Burke). Conf. 1784 and borne by Revd Thomas Wilson of Derby, son of Thomas, Bishop of Sodor and Man. His heirs were the Macklins (qv) and the Pattens (qv). Also borne by his kinsman, Thomas Wilson, high sheriff of Derbys., 1790, and by David Wilson, until 1989 of Hilton, a member of the Cumbrian family to whom the arms were originally granted.

Wilson. Stenson; Twyford. *Sable a wolf salient and on a chief or a pale of the field charged with a fleur-de-lys argent between two pellets*; crest: *a demi-wolf or the sinister paw resting on a pellet charged with a fleur-de-lys or*; motto: *'Wil son Wil'*. (FD (1929) II.2105). Gr. 1836 to Joseph Wilson of Highbury Hill, Middlesex, 2nd son of Thomas Wilson (d. 1794), 3rd son of John, farmer, of Stenson and Twyford, who d. 1747. Joseph was ancestor of the Wilsons of Stowlangtoft Hall, Suffolk. See also Patten.

Wingfield (Winfield). Ashleyhay; Glossop; Hazlebarrow and Norton House (Norton). *Argent on a bend gules cotised sable three pairs of wings conjoined in lure of the field*; crest: *a* cap per pale sable and argent banded gules between two wings displayed all goutée counterchanged (*Rel.* VI (1866) 44). Borne (assuming the various accounts of the genealogy of Wingfield of this family are sound) by Anthony Wingfield of Glossop, and his descendants of Ashleyhay c15–16, a root of Letheringham, Suffolk, and likewise by John son of Ferdinando Wingfield of Norton late c17 and early c18.

Wingfield (Winfield). Eddlestow Hall (Ashover). *Vert on a bend argent three crosses flory sable* (as quartered by Rolleston on MI at Ashover, Cox, I.33, and V. Notts. 1619). Crosses shown as *patée* as quartered by Rolleston V. 1569 and *patonce* V. Notts. Borne by Ralph Wingfield of Eddlestow c. 1350. His ancestor Ralph sealed with *on a shakefork a crescent in chief a mullet* (c. 1200, *DAJ* XVI (1894) 41).

Winnington. Derby. *Argent an inescutcheon sable voided of the field within an orle of martlets of the second*; crest: *a retort azure* (Ballard's Book). Borne by Thomas Winnington, *jure uxoris* of Offerton, Cheshire, c. 1460–83, and painted on a hatchment by Bassano 6 Feb. 1713 for Robert Winnington of Derby, All Saints'. Heiress marr. Wright (see Street).

Winterbottom. Aston Hall (Aston on Trent). *Argent a pale gules piercing a fesse azure and in chief two mullets of the 2nd*; crest: *out of a mural coronet sable a spear issuant between two palm branches in saltire all proper*; motto: '*Summa peto*' (BP (1970) 2862). Arms conf. to William Winterbottom (1777–1844) of Stockport, Cheshire, and Saddleworth, Yorks., in 1825 and borne by Col. William Dickson Winterbottom of Aston Hall early c20. One of his grandsons, Ian, was cr. 1965 Lord Winterbottom of Clopton, Northants, for life.

Wirksworth, Town of. *Per pale dexter a crown ensigning a rose sinister a group of lead miners' tools* (Scott-Giles, 100). Said to have been taken from an ancient seal of arms in use since early c17. No authority.

Wise. Walton Hall (Walton on Trent). *Sable three chevronels ermine between as many adders erect or*; crest: *a demi-lion rampant argent holding a damask rose stalked leaved and seeded proper in the mouth a snake vulnerating him in the shoulder and entwined about the body vert*; motto: '*Conserva me Domine*' (FD

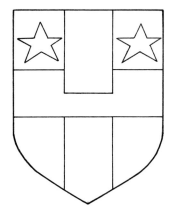

Winterbottom

(1905) 1485). Gr. 1720 and borne by Maj. H.C. Wise, who marr. the heiress of Sir Edward Cromwell Disbrowe of Walton. Their yr son, Henry Disbrowe Wise, was of Walton Hall late c19, early c20. Heiress marr. D.H. Dolben Paul.

Withington: see Hathersage.

Withipole. Mickleover; Newton Grange. *Per pale or and gules three lions passant guardant and a bordure all counterchanged*; crest: *a demi-cat-à-mountain rampant guardant per pale or and gules goutée counterchanged* (Tilley, IV.161; V. Suffolk 1561). Borne by Sir William Withipole of Suffolk, who inherited Mickleover from Reade via Stanhope, and who was gr. Newton Grange 1586.

Wolferstan: see Pipe.

Wollaston. Measham. *Argent three mullets pierced sable*; crest: *out of a mural coronet or a demi-griffin segreant argent holding a mullet pierced sable*; motto: '*Ne quid falsi*' (Vv. 1662; Staffs. 1663; Salop 1663). Arms conf. and crest gr. 10 July 1616 to Henry Wollaston of London, draper, son of Henry, of Perton, Staffs., and borne by William Wollaston of Shenton, Staffs., who purchased the Measham estate 1662 and d. 1688, his heiress marrying Wilkins, qv.

Wolley (Wooley, Woolley). Allenhill (Matlock); Bonsall; Charlesworth; Darley Hall (Darley Abbey); Marston on Dove. *Sable a chevron vairé or and gules between three maidens' heads affrontée couped at the shoulders proper crined or*; crest: *a man's head facing dexter in chain mail couped at the shoulders proper*; motto: *'Honeste et audax'* (V. 1662 (Riber); MI at St Alkmund, Derby 1716, Simpson, II.325). Conf. to Anthony Wolley of Riber 1662. The heiress of Adam Wolley of Allen Hill marr. Revd John Hurt who assumed the surname and arms of Wolley by RL 1827, adding *a canton erminois*. His son marr. the ultimate heiress of Dod of Edge Hall, Cheshire, and assumed those arms (quartering Wolley) and the additional surname by RL 1868, when the *canton* was omitted. Also displayed on the MI (at Southwell Minster, Notts.) of John Wolley MA FZS of Breaston (1823–59). Fairburn (I.604) gives the crests of Joseph Henry Woolley of Kilburn (b. 1828) as at the head of this article and *three arrows two in saltire one in pale points downwards*, with motto: *'Honor Virtutis Praemium'*. He claimed descent from Woolley of Marston. See also Hurt; Wooley.

Wolseley. Ravenstone. *Argent a talbot passant gules*; crest: *out of a ducal coronet or a wolf's head erased proper*; motto: *'Homo homini lupus'* (Vv. Staffs. 1583 1614). Borne by John Wolseley, who purchased Ravenstone 1619 and installed his half-brother Devereux, the heiress of whose brother Walter sold on the latter's death in 1661. A cousin, Sir Robert, was cr. a bt 24 Nov. 1628 and his son, the 2nd bt, was summoned as a peer by Cromwell 10 Dec. 1657. A brother of the 5th bt was created a bt of Ireland 19 Jan. 1745.

Wolstenholme. Cartledge Hall (Holmesfield); Dronfield. *Azure a lion passant between three pheons or*; crest: *an eagle displayed or treading on a snake nowed in fret proper*; motto: *'In ardua virtus'* (*Encyclopaedia Genealogica et Heraldica*, 2nd ser. II (1888) 118). Arms conf. and crest gr. 10 Aug. 1604 to Sir John Wolstenholme, son of John, of Dronfield. His son, also John, was cr. a bt 10 Jan. 1665 (title ext. 1762). Lysons (xcix) blazon the *lion* as *guardant* and the *snake azure*.

Wood. Derby; Chesterfield. *Sable on a chevron between three trees or as many martlets of the field* (V. Kent 1619). Allowed to a grandson of Henry Wood of Derby (himself brother of Charles, vicar of All Saints' there, 1576–92), then of Sandwich, Kent. Borne by his apparent descendant, Ald. Thomas Philpott Wood of Brambling House, Chesterfield, C19.

Wood. Howardtown, Moorfield (Glossop); Whitfield. *Sable on a bend engrailed between two roses argent barbed and seeded proper three fleurs-de-lys gules*; crest: *out of a vallary crown or an oak tree proper fructed of the first*; motto: *'Omne bonum Dei donum'* (BP (1956) 2351). Gr. 1878 to Samuel son of John Wood of Moorfield and Whitfield, Glossop, with remainder to the descendants of his father. His son, Sir Samuel, was cr. a bt 25 Jan. 1921, having 30 Mar. 1912 assumed the additional surname and arms of Hill of Liverpool: *per chevron or and vert in chief two acorns leaved and slipped and in base a crossbow bent all counterchanged*; crest (borne additionally): *on a mount vert a buglehorn stringed gules*. John Wood (1857–1951), son of the grantee's elder brother, John, was on 14 Feb. 1918 also cr. a bt, title ext. 1974.

Wood. Swanwick (Alfreton); Dogpole House (S. Normanton); Pinxton. *Azure three naked savages in fesse proper each holding in the dexter hand a shield argent thereon a cross gules and in the sinister a club resting on the shoulder also proper*; crest: *an oak tree proper acorned or*; motto: *'Pro Patria'* (Burke, FR (1897) 635). Allowed V. Yorks. 1612 to Wood of Copmanthorpe, Yorks., to which family Hunter (FMG I.341) attributed Hugh Wood of Pinxton, who purchased an estate at Swanwick 1555 (d. 1569), and used or borne by his descendants, now in Canada. If Hunter is correct (and some doubt must be expressed) they are collaterals of the present Lord Halifax.

Wood. Wirksworth Hall. *Or a lion rampant between three boars' heads erased sable*; crest: *a demi-man wreathed about the temples and waist with oak fructed the dexter hand grasping a club in bend the sinister arm extended hand proper grasping a wolf's head erased sable*; motto: *'Deus robur meum'* (BLG (1937) 2486). Gr. 1833 to John Wood of Brownhills, Staffs., and borne by a yr son, Nicholas Price Wood (d. 1868) of Wirksworth, and by his cousin John, son of Edmund Wood, who marr. N.P. Wood's heiress. See also Meynell.

Woodiwiss. Derby; The Pastures (Mickleover); Tamworth House (Duffield). *Argent on a chevron vert between three boars' heads eared sable langued gules a buglehorn between two crescents or all within a bordure azure bezantée*; crest: *a boar's head erased sable langued gules* (on a civic invitation of 1882 in Derby Museum, DBYMU 1966-12/3). Used by Sir Abraham Woodiwiss (1828–84), mayor of Derby 1880 and 1881, who was of The Pastures, Littleover, and his five sons, the second of whom, George, used as crest: *an arm embowed in armour grasping a sword piercing a chaplet* (MI at Uttoxeter New Road cemetery, Derby).

Woodroffe. Bakewell; Hope; Great Hucklow Hall. *Argent a chevron between three crosses formée fitchée gules*; crest: *a woodpecker proper*; motto: '*Quod transtuli retuli*' (Bakewell: brass in church; Hope: panel on N. wall of church). Possibly allowed to Ellis Woodroffe of Hope V. 1611, but only one non-local MS (Harl. 1537) includes him; the remainder leave the shield blank. His son, however, was allowed them, V. 1634. The Lysons (p. cliii) blazon the crest as *russet*. The arms were previously allowed to William, son of Robert Woodrove of Bolton upon Dearne (V. Yorks. 1584), with the difference that the crest is blazoned as *a woodcock russet*. He was 5th in descent from a C15 Woodroffe of Hope, the inference being either that it was the Hope branch which in 1611 usurped the arms from the Bolton one or that the arms have a longer pedigree than in fact seems apparent.

Woodyeare. Walton Hall. *Sable semée-de-lys or three leopards' faces argent*; crest: *a demi-griffin segreant reguardant wings inverted sable beaked membered and semée-de-lys or* (V. Kent 1619). Borne by John son of William Woodyeare of Crookhill Hall (Conisbrough Parks), Yorks., who inherited Walton from his mother, the heiress of Jenkinson, 1739, One of John's coheiresses marr. Fountain John Elwin, who assumed the surname and arms of Woodyeare in lieu of his own by RSM 1812, wherein the field was varied by being *per pale gules and sable*. They were conf. 1847. Walton sold 1813.

Wooley: see Wolley.

Woolhouse. Glapwell. *Per pale azure and sable a chevron engrailed erminois between three plates*; crest: *an eagle's head erased erminois beaked gules ducally gorged argent*

(V. 1662). Robert Woolhouse of Glapwell was a usurper V. 1611 and 'promised to come to London', which he did, for he had these arms conf. to him 17 Aug. 1611. Some MSS, however, date this grant 9 Feb. 1612, which seems perhaps more likely.

Woolley. Derby. *Or on a fesse three fleurs-de-lys quartering per fesse indented gules and vert three swans rising argent* (livery button in local collection). Used by William Woolley of Derby, solicitor, 1895.

Worsley: see Tindal-Carill-Worsley.

Worthington. Caldwell Hall; Coton Park (Rosliston); Derwent Bank (Derby); Hartshorne; Netherseal; Newton Park (Newton Solney). *Per fesse dancettée argent and sable on a pale counterchanged between two tridents erect in chief a like trident in base of the 2nd*; crest: *on the trunk of a tree fesswise eradicated and sprouting proper a goat passant argent gorged with a collar gemel sable holding in the mouth an oak sprig fructed also proper*; motto: '*Virtute dignus avorum*' (FD (1905) 1499). Gr. to Albert Octavius Worthington, son of William, of Staffs. and Netherseal, 1879, although with what remainders is unclear, for the arms were borne or used by his brother, W.H. Worthington of Derwent Bank (livery button in a local collection) and by cousins once removed of the grantee: Thomas of Hartshorne, and Henry of Coton Park (1792–1841). The grantee's father was of Newton Park (1836–71).

Wortley. 'Co. Derby'. *Argent on a bend between six martlets gules three bezants*; crest: *an eagle's gamb plumed on the thigh with feathers argent* (Vv. Yorks. 1584, 1612). Sir Francis Wortley of Wortley, Yorks., is usually included in Derbys. lists on the strength of his closeness to Lord Shrewsbury C16; he was sheriff of Derbys. 1577, and marr. the coheiress of Swifte (qv). His grandson was cr. a bt 29 June 1611 (ext. 1665) and was a deputy lieutenant of Derbys. 1623.

Wortley. Norton. *Argent a chevron sable between three Cornish choughs proper* (Papworth 394). Labelled by Papworth 'Co. Derby 1716'. These arms may refer to a Norton family of this name there *c.* 1695.

Wragg. Bamford; Bretby Hall; Eureka Lodge (Swadlincote). *Per bend raguly or and azure two billets on each a fleur-de-lys all counterchanged*; crest: *an estoile or between two sprigs of ragwort fructed proper*; motto:

'De auspice et cum sidere fausto' (BLG III (1972) 979). Gr. C20 to Ald. John Downing Wragg of Derby, Bretby and Swadlincote (1846–1917), son of Thomas of Bamford.

Wray. Churchtown (Darley). *Azure on a chief or three martlets gules*; crest: *an ostrich or*; motto: *'Juste et vray'* (V. Lincs. 1592). Allowed to Sir Christopher Wray of Glentworth, Lincs., 1592, having been gr. to him Feb. 1587 and exemplified to his elder brother Leonard 21 May 1587. The crest appears to have been gr. to William (the former's son, 13 Feb. 1593; he was cr. a bt 25 Nov. 1611 (ext. 1809). Another descendant was similarly honoured 27 June 1660 (of Ashby cum Fenby, Lincs., ext. 1690). Revd Sir William Ulithorne Wray, 11th bt, succ. to the title in the last year of his life (1805); he was rector of Darley and his surviving son d. a year after him. What little surviving property they had was in Derbys.

Wright. Aldercar Park (Codnor Park); Butterley Hall (Ripley); Osmaston Manor (Osmaston by Ashbourne); Yeldersley Hall etc. *Sable on a chevron between in chief two unicorns' heads erased argent crined and armed or and in base on a pile of the last issuant from the chevron a unicorn's head erased of the field armed and crined gules three spear heads of the last*; crest: *a unicorn's head argent erased gules armed and crined or charged on the neck with three spear heads one and two of the 2nd*; motto: *'Ad rem'* (BLG I (1965) 732). Gr. to Samuel, son of John Wright of Gunthorpe, Notts., and Nottingham 1825, with remainder to the descendants of his father. His nephew Francis, of Osmaston, was the progenitor of numerous Derbys. branches of this family; Francis also sought and was gr. a variation of the crest 1845, described above. Previously, it had been: *out of a crescent or a unicorn's head argent erased sable armed and maned or* (Burke). John, son of Francis of Osmaston, assumed by deed poll the surname of Osmaston in lieu of Wright.

Wright. Derby. *Gules on a chevron engrailed argent between three unicorns' heads erased or as many spearheads azure*; crest: *a pascal lamb passant argent holding a banner or thereon a cross gules* (MI once at St Alkmund's, Derby, Simpson, II.325). Used by Dr Richard Wright of Derby, elder brother of the painter, Joseph (1734–97), who d. 1804. The family came from Cheshire, but claimed descent from the Wrights of Unthank (qv) and the arms are an adaptation thereof.

Wright. Eyam Hall; Great Longstone Hall; Unthank Hall (Holmesfield). *Sable on a chevron engrailed between three unicorns' heads erased or as many spearheads azure*; crest: *a cubit arm vested sable doubled argent holding in the hand proper a broken spear or headed azure* (Vv. 1634, 1662). Allowed to William Wright of Great Longstone and Thomas Wright of Unthank and Eyam Hall 1662, the latter with a crescent for difference. These arms appear in panelling of earlier date at Great Longstone Hall, with the motto: *'Toujours droit'*. A seal on a charter of 1310 seems to show a yet more archaic version of the arms, with obvious Ferrers motifs: *on a chevron between three spearheads as many horseshoes* (G.T. Wright, *Longstone Records* (Bakewell, 1906), 56). These must be the arms of Robert son of Peter, the first to take the name Wright, for the family is in reality a *stirps* of Longsdon – cf. seal of John son of Nicholas le Clerk, nephew of Robert: *a griffin* (ibid., 61).

Wright. Ripley. Mr Wright of Ripley. A usurper V. 1611. Arms not known; quite probably as Longstone.

Wright. Snelston. *Sable on a chevron engrailed between three hinds' heads erased or as many spear heads azure* (Local MS 6341). Used by Mr Wright of Snelston, V. 1611, who 'promised to come to London'. See also Street; Turner.

Wychard. Chaddesden. *Azure a chevron argent between three martlets or* (V. Herts. 1572). A member of this family, Henry, was of Chaddesden; his heiress, Agnes, marr. Robert Tickhill of Stanley Grange mid-C15 (Thoroton, *Notts.* (1793), II.40–1).

Wykersley. North Lees (Outseats). *Azure a fesse between three cinquefoils argent* (Burke). Borne by John Wykersley of Broomhall and North Lees (d. 1506), whose grand-dau. and heiress marr. Robert Swyfte.

Wyne, Le. Holme (Bakewell); Wynnelands (Over Haddon); S. Normanton; Wirksworth; Wynn's Castle (Pinxton). *Vert a bend lozengy argent* (as quartered by Okeover, V. Staffs. 1563). Borne, probably by Adam le Wyne of Wirksworth, the heiress of whose son Robert may have carried the quartering to Okeover (possibly via Atlow). A more likely bearer of these arms, living 1356 rather than a century earlier, is Sir William le Wyne of Wynn's Castle, Pinxton, and South Normanton, which he held in succession to Sir John, 1348. Tilley (III.152) gives the arms of Wendesley for these Le Wynes. The Pinxton branch marr. the heiress of Poë (qv), of which family Sir Robert, of London, held Wynnelands early C17.

Wythens (Wyther). Longford Woodhouse; Thorpe. *Gules a chevron counter-embattled ermine between three martlets or* (Tilley, II.314). Borne by Nicholas Wyther or Wythens of Thorpe. The heiress marr. Cokayne, although the quartering one might expect does not emerge. A family of this name was of Woodhouse late C13–C14.

Yates. Church Broughton; Derby; Newton Solney; Sapperton Manor (Church Broughton). *Per chevron gules and or three gates counter-changed* (Tilley). Borne or, more likely, used by Thomas Yates of London, who marr. the heiress of Adam Wolley of Church Broughton, and by his posterity there into the C19.

Yeaveley. Derbys. Arms not known. Mr Yeaveley promised to come to London V. 1611.

Ziani di Ferranti. Baslow Hall. *Per fesse argent and sable a lion rampant counterchanged on a chief of the 2nd three fleurs-de-lys of the* first; crest: *issuant out of clouds proper a demi-lion argent holding in the paws a branch of oak fructed proper* (R. Gayre, *Armorial Who is Who*, 5th Edn. 1976–8, 361). Gr. 15 Jan. 1929 to Dr Sebastian Ziani di Ferranti of Baslow Hall, which he purchased 1913, and based on the family's Italian coat. Conf. 16 Oct. 1961 to his son Sir Vincent Z. di Ferranti MC of Alderley Edge, Cheshire (1893–1980).

Zouche. Alfreton; Codnor Castle; Derby. *Gules twelve bezants on a canton ermine a crescent azure*; crest: *an ass's head argent bridled azure charged on the neck with a crescent azure* (V. 1569). Allowed to Sir John Zouche of Codnor (1559–97) V. 1569, although his grandson, another Sir John, 'promised to come to London' V. 1611; instead, he went to Virginia, 1634. The 1st Sir John's brother and nephew, Sydney and Lindley Zouch 'of the towne of Derby' V. 1611, bore the same.

Zouche. Morley. *Gules twelve bezants a canton ermine*; crest: *a hawk rising argent legged and beaked or standing on a staff raguly and sprouting at the end of the last* (Local MS 6341.66). Borne by William son of Sir John Zouche who marr. the widow of John Sacheverell, née Statham of Morley, C15. His father was 1st of Codnor and bore likewise, being yr brother of William, 5th Lord Zouche of Harringworth, Northants., cr. by writ of summons 1308. The 1st baron appears to have borne *gules bezantée a quarter ermine* (Caerlaverock Roll). The supporters of Lord Zouche C16 were: *on either side an eagle wings addorsed argent* (Burke).

INDEX OF PLACES

Places in Derbyshire are grouped under civil parishes as given in K. Cameron, *The place-names of Derbyshire* (English Place-Name Society, 1959) and the spellings there are used, although not all the minor places in this index will be found in that work. For places outside Derbyshire, the pre-1974 county is indicated, with a cross-reference from the county name in England and from 'Ireland', 'Scotland', and 'Wales'; names unidentified from available O.S. maps, from the ninth edition (1950) of Bartholomew's *Survey Gazetteer of the British Isles*, or from the English Place-Name Society volumes are entered in quotation marks. For foreign places, only countries are entered. The alphabetical arrangement is letter-by-letter.

low & Great Wilne
Wilsthorpe, *see* Sawley & Wilsthorpe
Wilton Castle, Herefs., 74
Wiltshire, 57, 59, 71; *see* also Tollard Royal
Windlehill, *see* Osleston & Thurvaston
Windley, 24, 64; W. Hall in, 89
Champeyne Park (Champion) in, 35, 64
Farnah Hall in, 41, 92
Flower Lilies in, 47
Windsor, Berks., St George's Chapel in, 159
Wingerworth, 24, 88, 144
Stubbing in, 157; S. Court in, 1, 70–1, 88
Wingfield, *see* North Wingfield, South Wingfield
Wingham, Kent, 46
Winshill (now Staffs.), 100
Winster, 57, 79, 110, 113; W. Hall in, 92, 162
Wirksworth, 5, 13–4, 16, 22, 24, 27, 33, 41, 69, 82, 85, 87–90, 97, 103, 106, 125, 148, 152, 162–3, 168, 173, 178, 181; W. Hall in, 179
Cottage Hospital in, 163
Gatehouse in, 175
Manor of, 27
The Old Manse in, 90
Richmond Manor in, 84
Steeple Grange in, 18, 73
Wigwell Grange in, 106; W. (Hall) in, 75, 165, 175
Yokecliffe in, 176
Withcote, Leics., 82
Withington, Lancs., 80
Witton, Lancs., 60
Wolfscote, *see* Hartington
Wollaton, Notts., 177
Wolseley, Staffs., 35
Woodborough, Notts., 129, 157
Wood House, *see* Cheadle (Staffs.)
Woodseats, *see* Castleton
Woodthorpe, Egstow Hall in (formerly), 88
Woodthorpe, *see* Staveley
'Woodthorpe', nr Ashbourne, 67
Woodthorpe Hall, *see* Holmesfield
Woodwall, *see* Parwich
Woolley, *see* Brackenfield
Woolmer Lodge, *see* Bramshott
Wootton Lodge, ?nr Eccleshall, Staffs., 167
Worcester, 150
Worcestershire, 29, 69; *see* also Ashton under Hill, Dudley Priory, Hall Green, Hindlip, Ipsley, Martin Hussingtree, Salwarpe, Upton Warren, Westwood Park
Wormegay, Norfolk, 11

Wormhill, 8, 9, 65
Great Rocks in, 72
Hargate Hall in, 174
Tunstead in, 164
Worsop Wood, *see* Pleasley
Wortley, Yorks. W.R., 180
Wyaston, *see* Edlaston & Wyaston
Wychnor Park, Staffs., 130
'Wycroft Castle', Devon, 58
Wynn's Castle, *see* Pinxton

Yarmouth, Norfolk, 109
Yarnton, Oxon., 56
Yeardsley Hall, *see* Whaley Bridge
Yeaveley, 7, 66, 110, 155
Stydd Hall in, 44, 88, 170
Yeldersley, 90, 113, 126, 174; Y. Hall in, 155, 181
Lady Hole Hall in, 99
Yeovil, Somerset, 126
Yokecliffe, *see* Wirksworth
York, 50, 164
Yorkshire (undifferentiated), 65, 89, 91, 111, 119, 125, 148; *see* also 'Freshmarsh'
Yorkshire, East Riding, *see* Catfoss, Hull
Yorkshire, North Riding, *see* Cundall, Eryholme, Guisborough, Hackness, Hornby Castle, Ingleby Arncliffe, Kirklevington, Newbiggin, Richmond, Thirsk, Whitby, Whorlton
Yorkshire, West Rising, *see* Arncliffe Cote, Attercliffe, Bolton upon Dearne, Bradfield, Burton Grange, Carbrook, Chevet, Conisbrough Parks, Copmanthorpe, Doncaster, Ecclesall, Ecclesfield, Farnley, Finningley, Fixby, Giggleswick, Halifax, Hallamshire, Harrogate, Hazlewood Castle, Heptonstall, Hooton Pagnell, Howgill, Howley, Huddersfield, Kimberworth, Kinsley, Knaresborough, Laughton en le Morthen, Leeds, Methley, Nostell, Owlerton, Plumpton, Potterton, Rastrick, Rotherham, Saddleworth, Sheffield, Shibden, Sowerby, Temple Newsam, Thornhill, Thorpe Salvin, Thrybergh, Tickhill, Wakefield, Wales, Wentworth, Whiston, Wortley
Youlgreave, 11, 23, 31, 42, 66, 95, 109, 138–9, 174
Alport in, 57, 136, 139
Lomberdale Hall in, 13, 171
Yoxall Lodge, Staffs., 70